Liu Xiaoming

NO QUESTION UNANSWERED

No Question Unanswered

Author Liu Xiaoming

Editor Yang Sheng　Li Bin
Designer Dorgel Chung
Typesetter Yang Lu

Published by Joint Publishing (H.K.) Co., Ltd.
20/F., North Point Industrial Building, 499 King's Road, North Point, Hong Kong

Distributed by SUP Publishing Logistics (H.K.) Ltd.
16/F., Tsuen Wan Industrial Centre, 220-248 Texaco Road, Tsuen Wan, N.T., Hong Kong

Printed by Elegance Printing & Book Binding Co., Ltd.
Block A, 4/F., 6 Wing Yip Street, Kwun Tong, Kowloon, Hong Kong

First Published in May 2025
ISBN 978-962-04-5655-8

有問必答

著　　者　劉曉明
責任編輯　楊　昇　李　斌
書籍設計　道　轍
書籍排版　楊　錄
出　　版　三聯書店（香港）有限公司
　　　　　香港北角英皇道 499 號北角工業大廈 20 樓
香港發行　香港聯合書刊物流有限公司
　　　　　香港新界荃灣德士古道 220-248 號 16 樓
印　　刷　美雅印刷製本有限公司
　　　　　香港九龍觀塘榮業街 6 號 4 樓 A 室
版　　次　2025 年 5 月香港第 1 版第 1 次印刷
規　　格　16 開（170 mm × 240 mm）504 面
國際書號　ISBN 978-962-04-5655-8

Contents

Chapter 4 COVID-19

Chapter 5 Q&A with UK Parliament

Chapter 6 Q&A with Scholars and Officials

Chapter 7 Interview with TASS

Chapter 1

China-UK Relations

A Force of Peace and A Force of Friendship

——A Press Conference on the Visit of the 18th Chinese Naval Escort Taskforce to the UK

CCTV: We understand that the Chinese naval escort taskforce has had good communication with the Royal Navy of the UK in the field of anti-piracy. What is the significance of this visit of the Chinese fleet to the Royal Navy's homeport of Portsmouth?

Liu Xiaoming: This visit by the Chinese naval escort taskforce to the UK will involve a series of exchanges and cooperation, including anti-piracy. The schedule has a rich content, multiple objectives, and has proved to be of great significance.

Firstly, the visit fully demonstrates the rich connotation of the comprehensive strategic partnership between China and the UK. The China-UK strategic partnership covers many areas of exchange such as the political, economic, financial, cultural, educational, and in science and technology. Military-to-military exchange is an important component of this relationship. Strengthening this exchange helps enhance mutual strategic trust. This is the third visit of the Chinese fleet to the UK and it comes at the beginning of 2015, marking a promising start for the bilateral relations between the two countries and their militaries for the new year.

Secondly, this visit provides an opportunity for people from all walks of life in the UK to understand China, the Chinese military, and China's national defence policy. The British public can see that China's military is playing an active role on the international stage as the country's economic strength rises and its economy develops rapidly. China is now the world's second-largest economy, contributing around one-third of the world's economic growth every year. In addition to the economic field, China has also made significant contributions to the world in the political and security fields. In terms of maintaining world peace, the Chinese military is a force for peace, actively participating in international escort missions in the Gulf of Aden and the waters off Somalia. Among the five permanent members of the UN Security Council, China provides the highest number of peacekeeping personnel. I hope that the British public will board the ships on the open day and visit the Chinese military at close quarters.

BBC: The Chinese fleet is visiting the port of Portsmouth, which is a symbol of the Royal Navy of the UK. The flagship "HMS Victory" that once docked here brought more than a century of naval dominance to the UK. Currently, some neighboring countries of China are concerned about the growth of China's naval power and its impact on the regional situation. How does the Chinese Navy balance between being a force for peace to enhance strategic mutual trust between countries and being an international blue-water navy to protect China's interests at an international level? How can this balance be achieved?

Liu Xiaoming: In order to understand this issue, the most important point is to understand China's national strategy and national defence policy. China adheres to the path of peaceful development and is an important force in maintaining world peace. China not only strives for world peace in order to achieve its own development, but also makes contributions to world peace and prosperity through its own peaceful development. The development of the Chinese Navy serves this purpose. Some people are concerned about China's military development because they do not understand China's concept of peaceful development and its defensive national defence policy. China is a peace-loving country and has never colonized or invaded other countries in its history. On the contrary, China has suffered invasions and humiliations from foreign powers in modern times. Besides participating in UN peacekeeping operations, China has not sent a single soldier abroad. China is the country that provides the largest number of peacekeeping personnel among the five permanent members of the UN Security Council, with 27,000 military peacekeeping personnel dispatched as of September 2014. As China develops, we will make greater contributions to world peace and stability. The visit of the Chinese naval fleet to the UK is also an important measure for strengthening mutual trust between China and the UK, marking the beginning of high-level exchanges between the two countries' militaries in the new year. After this visit, the UK's First Sea Lord will visit China, and during the visit, the two sides will conduct extensive exchanges on military strategy, navy development, and other issues. There is nothing to worry about vis-à-vis the Chinese Navy becoming a blue-water navy. It is in the blue waters that the Chinese Navy carries out escort missions in the Gulf of Aden and the waters off Somalia. Since 2008, the Chinese Navy has successfully completed nearly 6,000 escort missions for Chinese and foreign vessels, undertaking the international responsibility of protecting the safety of passing ships, maintaining the freedom of navigation at sea, and combating piracy.

BBC (follow-up question): What message would you like to convey to the British public when they see these Chinese warships docked in the British military port? Currently, the Chinese Navy is the second-largest in the world, and some people are concerned about the development of China's naval power. How does China eliminate their doubts?

Liu Xiaoming: I want to tell the British public that the Chinese Navy is a force for peace and friendship. Their visit to the UK aims to promote friendly relations and enhance understanding and friendship.

Just now you called the Chinese Navy the second largest in the world. I don't agree. It is China's economic size that ranks second in the world, not the Chinese Navy. While China has a considerable number of naval vessels, there is still a gap in quality compared to the navies of major maritime powers in the world. The Chinese Navy was the last major navy to possess its own aircraft carrier, even later than countries like India and Thailand.

China has a vast territory and a coastline of over 32,000 Kilometres, with 14 neighboring countries with land borders and 8 with maritime borders. The Chinese Navy has the responsibility to defend its territorial waters and is also willing to work with other navies to maintain regional security and ensure the security of international navigation. There is no need to worry about the development of the Chinese Navy.

Sing Tao Daily: In addition to participating in international anti-piracy operations, if the Chinese Navy encounters disputes or friction with neighboring countries, what role will it play? How does China balance the development of its military strength and the prevention of disputes and conflicts?

Liu Xiaoming: I have already expounded China's position on this issue in response to the question from the BBC reporter. Regarding maritime disputes between China and some neighboring countries, we have always advocated resolving them through peaceful means. But if our interests are infringed upon, we must respond. We cannot lose an inch of the land left by our ancestors, and we do not want an inch of land that does not belong to us. The primary duty of the Chinese military is to defend the country's sovereignty and territorial integrity, safeguard national security and development interests, including maritime rights and interests. At the same time, China's Navy actively engages in cooperation with other navies to jointly maintain regional security, participates in international escort cooperation to ensure the security of international shipping routes, and contributes its own strength to the maintenance and promotion of world peace.

As for the development of the Chinese Navy and its "move into the blue waters", it should not be judged solely by the number of warships and aircraft China possesses, but rather by China's peaceful development strategy and its defensive national defence policy. China's path of peaceful development is written into its constitution, and China does not seek hegemony. We do not seek hegemony today, and we will never seek hegemony in the future. We will not fall into the "Thucydides Trap" that the big powers in the West have historically fallen into, and we will not follow their path of pursuing hegemony. We must chart our own course of peaceful development, which is definitely the path to success. In this regard, we need the understanding of the international media. I hope that your newspaper and other media outlets will provide comprehensive and objective coverage, and avoid following some Western media and hyping up the so-called "China threat".

CRI: 2014 marked the 60th anniversary of the establishment of Chargé d'Affaires-level diplomatic relations between China and the UK and the 10th anniversary of the establishment of a comprehensive strategic partnership. Can you please comment on the recent development of mil-to-mil relations between China and the UK?

Liu Xiaoming: In recent years, the mil-to-mil exchanges between China and the UK have maintained a good momentum of development. There have been frequent exchanges between the top military leaders of the two countries, and the ties have grown deeper.

Firstly, the two militaries have maintained the vice-ministerial-level defence and security dialogue mechanism, continuously enhancing mutual trust and expanding consensus.

Secondly, exchanges and cooperation in professional technical fields and personnel training between the two militaries have gradually deepened. British experts and scholars have come to China for exchanges, and China sends military students to British military academies every year.

Thirdly, the two militaries have conducted productive exchanges and cooperation in fields such as counter-terrorism, anti-piracy and disaster relief.

Fourthly, naval ship visits have taken place. This year, the visit of the Chinese naval fleet lays a good foundation for mil-to-mil exchanges between China and the UK, and the two sides will have a series of high-level visits. These exchanges and cooperation at various levels and in various fields will promote the further development of the mil-to-mil exchanges between the two countries.

China Daily: The Chinese naval fleet has successfully completed its escort mission in the Gulf of Aden. Will the Chinese Navy participate in more international maritime operations in the future and take on more responsibilities and obligations?

Liu Xiaoming: In recent years, the Chinese Navy has actively participated in international maritime operations, dispatching naval escort taskforces to the Gulf of Aden and the waters off Somalia being one of them. The Chinese Navy has also actively participated in international humanitarian rescue missions, such as participating in the search for Malaysia Airlines Flight MH370 and participating in humanitarian relief operations in the Philippines and Indonesia. In the future, the Chinese Navy will continue to actively participate in counter-terrorism, anti-piracy and international humanitarian rescue operations.

Portsmouth News: You mentioned earlier that this is the third visit of the Chinese naval fleet to the UK. What are the differences compared with the previous two visits?

Liu Xiaoming: The Chinese navy fleet had previously visited the UK in 2001 and 2007. This visit comes more than seven years after the last visit, during which time there have been many changes in the international situation, in China-UK relations, in China and in the Chinese Navy itself. In 2007, only two vessels came, while this time, the three visiting ships are all the latest models and well-equipped, representing the best of the Chinese Navy. In the past seven years, the comprehensive strategic partnership between China and the UK has deepened, and cooperation between the two countries has expanded in both quantity and quality. I believe that the visit of the Chinese naval escort taskforce will promote the further development of the relations between the two countries and their militaries.

UK Chinese Journalist: Can you please comment on the work that the Chinese Embassy in the UK and the local Chinese community have done to welcome the Chinese naval fleet?

Liu Xiaoming: The Chinese Embassy in the UK sees the visit of the Chinese naval escort taskforce as a major event in the relations between China and the UK and their militaries and attaches great importance to it. Fully mobilized, we have actively coordinated with the Royal Navy and relevant departments of the British government, and made every effort to ensure a good visit. For example, to ensure a smooth start of the visit of the taskforce, we worked with the British military to adjust the docking time of the ships according to changes in the weather. The Chinese community in the UK, Chinese enterprises and Chinese students are all very happy to welcome the naval ships. Those who are here today to greet the fleet are representatives of the more than 600,000 Chinese in the UK and the 130,000 Chinese students. The visit of the Chinese naval fleet is such a joyous event and major occasion for the Chinese community in the UK.

European Times: In recent times, there have been terrorist attacks in France, and the terrorist threat in the UK is also increasing. What role can the Chinese Navy play in the field of counter-terrorism?

Liu Xiaoming: The Chinese government strongly condemns the terrorist attacks in France. We oppose all forms of terrorism. After the attack, President Xi Jinping made a phone call to President Hollande, strongly condemning the attacks and expressing deep condolences on the loss of life and sincere sympathy to the injured and the families of the victims. China's position on issues of international counter-terrorism is clear and consistent. We advocate strengthening international counter-terrorism through international cooperation. The Chinese Navy has played its due role in international counter-terrorism. They have conducted joint counter-terrorism exercises with the navies of relevant countries and carried out exchanges and cooperation in areas such as personnel training and intelligence. These are concrete manifestations of their active role.

Thank you for your attendance.

Step up Exchanges and Learn From Each Other

——Q&A at Cambridge University

On 13th November 2015, I answered questions from the faculty and students of Cambridge University after delivering a speech entitled "Let the Golden Era Shine Brighter".

Cambridge student: Although China-UK relations have entered a Golden Era, there are still some negative opinions of China in the UK. Some people see China's rise as a threat. Some think China's slowdown poses serious challenges. As the Chinese Ambassador, what would you say to those people? How can such suspicions be minimised?

Liu Xiaoming: My job of course is to reach out to every sector of the UK in order to present a positive Chinese narrative, to drive home the importance of the China-UK relationship and to promote exchanges and cooperation between the two countries. I don't know how closely you followed the State Visit. Before this State Visit, I gave interviews to all the major networks. I call it "full coverage". I appeared on all channels, BBC, Channel 4, Sky News and ITV. I tried to answer various questions such as those on security issues, why China invests in the UK's nuclear power stations, and also human rights in China and cyber security. I think it is natural for people to have some misunderstandings, because the media coverage on China here is not comprehensive. Sometimes it is one-sided. The media pursues sensational reporting. If you compare how China is portrayed in this country and how the UK is portrayed in China, there is quite a contrast.

My job is also to reach out to the major newspapers, *The Times*, *Financial Times* and *The Daily Telegraph*, etc, to have China's voice heard. I have also taken initiative to visit the various media outlets and held discussions with them. I know that even though I give many interviews, they each have 5-10 minutes airtime. The British public will mainly learn about China through the numerous reports written by British journalists. That's why I try to reach out. I visited BBC and went behind the scenes. I had a 2-hour discussion with over 30 senior editors and journalists including the BBC's News Director, the royal and international journalists, and tried to answer their questions. I also invited some editors and reporters from *Financial Times* and *The Daily Telegraph* to the Embassy to brief them on the significance of the State Visit and answered their questions. It is also my job as Ambassador to make myself available and come to talk to you here in Cambridge.

Cambridge student: I wonder if you could elaborate a little bit on what you said about China and the UK working together on counter-terrorism?

Liu Xiaoming: Terrorism is a common scourge for humanity. It is a global issue that calls for the joint efforts of all countries. China and the UK are permanent members of the UN Security Council. We shoulder important responsibility for maintaining world peace and stability. The two governments have maintained a close dialogue on security and counter-terrorism issues, including sharing information. We are both supporters of the relevant important counter-terrorism resolutions at the United Nations.

Cambridge student: Recently, there was the historic meeting between the Chinese President Xi Jinping and the Taiwanese "President" Ma Ying-jeou. What impact will it have on the upcoming election in Taiwan and cross-Strait relations? What's China's view on self-determination?

Liu Xiaoming: First, I need to correct you for referring to Ma Ying-jeou by the wrong title. There is no president in Taiwan. Taiwan is not a country. It is part of China. There is only one President of China, that is, President Xi Jinping. Because of outstanding political differences, the meeting was conducted in a practical manner, with both sides attending as leaders of the two sides of the Strait and both sides addressing each other as "Mr". It was a historic meeting and it will take some time for people to fully grasp its significance.

As to the election in Taiwan, we will certainly follow it closely. But what we care about more is peace and stability across the Taiwan Strait. In order to maintain peace and stability in the Strait, we must adhere to the one-China principle, known as the 1992 Consensus. During the meeting, both sides reaffirmed that relations should continue to be based on this core principle of one-China and opposition to Taiwan independence. The 1992 Consensus has been the prerequisite and foundation for political trust and positive interactions in cross-Strait relations. Abandoning or straying from the 1992 Consensus will plunge cross-Strait relations back into instability. The two sides are yet to be reunified, but China's sovereignty and territorial integrity has never been destroyed. Taiwan's separation from the motherland is temporary, and a legacy of history. Japan illegally occupied Taiwan through the China-Japan War of 1894. In the Cairo Declaration of 1943, it was explicitly stated that Japan should return to China all the Chinese islands it illegally seized, including Taiwan and the surrounding islands such as Diaoyudao. When I was the Chinese Ambassador to Egypt, I visited the Hotel Mena House, the site where the Cairo Declaration was signed by Chinese, American and British leaders. Owing to various reasons, Taiwan has yet to return to the motherland. But that does not change the basic fact that Taiwan has been and will always be part of China.

I believe that the Chinese people on both sides of the Strait have the wisdom and patience to find a peaceful solution and achieve reunification of the motherland. We have waited for over 60 years. The meeting between Xi and Ma shows that our patience has paid off. I have full confidence that more and more people, especially people on the island, will understand that it is in the best interests of the people across the Strait to adhere to the 1992 Consensus, to promote peaceful development of cross Strait relations, to maintain peace and stability in the Taiwan Strait for mutual benefit and to realise the great renewal of the Chinese nation. Taiwan independence has no way out.

Cambridge student: You said that the British media is one-sided when reporting on China. I am just wondering what Britain can learn from China?

Liu Xiaoming: The two countries can learn quite a lot from each other. There are a number of commonalities between China and Britain, including a long history and rich culture. And there are also some differences.

First, the Chinese nation is a peace-loving nation that has no tradition of invading other countries. Even when China was at its strongest, in the centuries spanning from the Tang Dynasty to the Ming Dynasty when China's GDP accounted for 2/3 of the world's total, which is bigger than the United States today, it never invaded other countries. The Chinese navigator Admiral Zheng He of the Ming Dynasty led a 200-strong fleet of ships on voyages to the Indian Ocean and as far as Kenya in East Africa. He was there for trade and friendship, occupying not a single inch of land. Zheng He's voyages long predated Christopher Columbus's discovery of America. All these things would have been unimaginable in Western history. Even today, when it comes to international conflicts, the first thing that comes to our mind is seeking a political solution—how can we address problems through diplomatic means—whereas some Western countries think military force is more effective. Our love of peace and non-militaristic approach is deeply-rooted in China's traditional philosophy and several thousand years of history.

Second, in Chinese culture, we take a holistic and comprehensive approach when looking at situations. There is a Chinese saying that "the water level rises in small streams when the big rivers are full". We place more emphasis on the larger picture and the greater interests of the society and the country, while Western countries, including Britain, focus more on details and individuals.

Third, we stress the importance of planning ahead and have the patience to execute our plans. China has been making plans every five years since 1953. As I said, we are currently drawing up the 13th Five Year Plan. It will be a blueprint for China's economic and social development over the next five years. China also has two centenary goals, which show its ability to fulfill long-term plans. As the former US Secretary of State Henry Kissinger said, a single dynasty in China lasts longer than the entire history of the United States. We are good at thinking for the long-term.

Fourth, the Chinese are a hard-working people. The Secretary of Health Jeremy Hunt once praised the Chinese for being a hard-working people. His remarks drew criticism. I was asked about this in an interview and replied that the Chinese people are hard-working while the British people are creative. China and the UK should step up exchanges and learn from each other.

Cambridge student: Will the disputes between the UK and Argentina over Malvinas Islands affect China-UK relations? Should the UK choose to leave the European Union, would that do any harm to China-UK relations?

Liu Xiaoming: The issue of Malvinas Islands is between the UK and Argentina. We hope it will be resolved peacefully.

With regard to the UK referendum on EU membership, it is certainly up to the British people to decide how they want to vote. We would certainly like to enjoy a good relationship with the EU as an institution and individual EU member states. The UK is an important member of the European Union. The British leaders have said on many occasions that the UK wants to be China's best partner in the West and in the EU. The UK wants to take the lead in the early conclusion of the negotiations on a China-EU bilateral investment agreement and the early launch of the negotiations on a China-EU free trade agreement. If the UK leaves the EU, what kind of leading role can it play? We hope the UK will play an important role in the European Union and continue to contribute to China-EU relations.

Cambridge student: What would you say to the Western allegation that democracy with Chinese characteristics is not real democracy?

Liu Xiaoming: First, we have to share stories about China's democracy. I hope as a Chinese student, you will explain to your teachers and fellow students about China's democracy and how democracy functions in China. All countries are different. Even the UK and the United States, though they speak the same language and share the same cultural tradition, differ in their forms of democracy and legal systems. China has a democratic system with Chinese characteristics, that is to say, the system of People's Congresses with the hallmark of electoral democracy. The Chinese people form people's congresses at various levels through elections. People's congresses then democratically elect the state organs, executive agencies and judiciary authorities. Deputies at and below the county level are directly elected based on universal suffrage. Deputies above county level are indirectly elected. That is to say, county deputies elect municipal deputies, municipal deputies elect provincial deputies, and provincial deputies elect deputies to the National People's Congress, which will then elect the national leaders. There are nearly 3,000 deputies to the National People's Congress. Every year they meet and every five years there is a general election.

As far as we know, the UK has indirect election. The Prime Minister is not directly elected through a nationwide election, but by constituency. The leader of the party that gains the majority seats in parliament will become the Prime

Minister. The President of the United States is elected by nationwide election. Again, that is different from the UK. So you cannot judge whether the system in another country is democratic or not based upon your own system. Number one, there is no perfect democracy. Number two, there is no perfect model of a political system. Number three, all countries are different. We can learn from each other. That's why we have various mechanisms for dialogue, For example, on governance, the rule of law and human rights. The more we carry out such exchanges, the fewer misunderstandings or misconceptions there will be.

Cambridge student: How, do you think, Western businesses might understand the potential of and opportunities for the AIIB and the One Belt One Road? Will the Golden Era of China-UK relations bring any more opportunities for young Chinese in the UK?

Liu Xiaoming: Both Chinese and British leaders attach great importance to the AIIB and the One Belt One Road and have extensive exchanges and active interactions about these initiatives. As Ambassador, I shall do my best to reach out and share my perceptions of these initiatives. Various circles in the UK have gained a deeper understanding about the AIIB and the One Belt One Road.

We certainly encourage young people to go back to China and contribute their talent to the motherland. Every year, we host many delegations from different Chinese provinces. They came here to recruit the bright talents. I hope you can be one of the recruits. Of course, if you choose to stay in the UK, there will also be many opportunities. More and more British companies want to grow their businesses with China and require your help. The Golden Era in China-UK relations will surely bring more opportunities to all of you. I sincerely hope you will contribute to building bridges for China-UK exchanges and cooperation.

Cambridge professor: China is well on its way to become a superpower. How will China balance its relations with the EU and Russia given the tensions in EU-Russia relations?

Liu Xiaoming: China has cooperative and win-win relations with both the EU and Russia. Russia is the largest neighbour and comprehensive strategic partner of coordination of China. The two countries have close economic and trade ties and good political relations. China-EU relations are also very good. Russia is not an obstacle between China and the EU. I do not feel China will face any difficulties in developing relations with Russia and the EU at the same time.

I don't expect China to be a superpower in the near future. We know our place as the biggest developing country. Although the Chinese economy is the second largest in the world, China's per capita GDP lags behind even Romania and Bulgaria, with 80 countries ranking ahead of it. We very much wish to concentrate on our own development. We must take development as a top priority in our national effort.

Cambridge professor: You quoted Charles Dickens in saying that it's the "best of times". But he continues to say it's also the "worst of times". Just two years ago, the *Global Times* which is owned by the Chinese Communist Party said Britain is just an old declining empire only good for travel and study. What has happened in just two years to enable you to talk about this "Golden Era" of China-UK relationship?

Liu Xiaoming: The *Global Times* is one of the media outlets in China and does not represent the Party or the Government. It is just like I can't say the comments in British media represent the British Government. As the Chinese Ambassador, I am here to represent the Chinese Government. I have always believed that the UK is an important country. It is a major country with global influence. As the Chinese Ambassador, in addition to telling China's story in the UK, I have also become a good spokesman for the UK in China. When I conduct speaking tours, I tell people how important the UK is. As an independent media outlet, the *Global Times* publishes different viewpoints. Next time, I shall show you very positive comments they made about the UK.

Cambridge professor: The US Republican candidate Donald Trump has made some negative comments about China. If he is elected US President, how will that affect China-US relations?

Liu Xiaoming: I worked for many years in the United States. I lived there through three elections. I know what American election culture is about. We have to be patient. We follow the comments of the candidates. We pay even more attention to the actions once they take office. To quote an English proverb, "Do not count your chickens before they are hatched".

Cambridge student: How can China and the UK work together in high-end manufacturing?

Liu Xiaoming: There are many areas of great potential and opportunity for China-UK cooperation, High-end manufacturing is one of them, the latest example being the jumbo jet. Rolls-Royce is one of the two biggest engine producers in the world that is expanding cooperation with Chinese companies. The manufacturing of aircraft is very complicated. It involves over one thousand businesses. This can massively increase employment and drive the economy. The UK has realized the shortcomings of over-reliance on financial services. It has adopted strategies to reinvigorate the manufacturing sector, which holds great potential for China-UK cooperation. The UK is also a leader in the automobile industry. The Shanghai Automobile Industry Corporation bought MG. They set up a research centre in Longbridge. They retained all 300 technicians and scientists. SAIC CEO told me that they have benefited from both MG's design and manufacturing capabilities. Geely bought a London Taxi. They are working with British scientists and technicians to produce environmentally-friendly electric taxis. During the State Visit, President Xi and the First Lady were accompanied by the Duke and Duchess of Cambridge on a view of the prototype of the new taxi. I believe it won't be long before all London taxis will be environmentally-friendly and energy-conserving models. Besides, China and the UK have carried out positive cooperation in green energy, telecommunications, robot, aviation and aerospace. I believe as China-UK relations enter this Golden Era, China-UK cooperation in high-end manufacturing will embrace an even brighter future.

What is Happening to China–UK Relationship?

——An On-line Press Conference on China–UK Relations

On 30th July 2020, I held an on-line press conference on China-UK relationship at the Chinese Embassy. Around 30 journalists from 27 media agencies joined the conference, including BBC, Sky News, ITV, *Financial Times*, *The Daily Telegraph*, *The Times*, Times Radio, *The Guardian*, Reuters, the Xinhua News Agency, *People's Daily*, CCTV, CGTN, the China News Service, *China Daily*, *Science and Technology Daily*, *Global Times*, Guancha. cn, AP, Bloomberg, NBC, Russia Today, Quartz, Phoenix Infonews, *European Times*, *The Scotsman*, and *The Manchester Evening News*. Guests from UK's political and business sectors also attended the conference, including Sir Geoffrey Clifton-Brown, the Deputy-Chairman of the All-Party Parliamentary Group on China (APPCG), Mark Logan, the Vice Chair of APPCG, Lord Davidson, Stephen Perry, the Chairman of the 48 Group Club, Lord Sassoon, the President of the China-Britain Business Council, Lord Palumbo of Walbrook Club, St. John Moore, the Chairman of British Chamber of Commerce in China, Meia Nouwens, Research Fellow for Chinese Defence Policy at the International Institute for Strategic Studies, and Veerle Nouwens, Research Fellow at the International Security Studies Department of the Royal United Services Institute on geopolitical relations in the Asia-Pacific region and China. Foreign diplomats in the UK from the ROK, Laos, the EU, Russia, Kyrgyzstan, Mexico, Argentina, Myanmar, Brazil, and Saudi Arabia also attended the event. The press conference was broadcast live via my Twitter account. CGTN, Reuters and the AP also broadcast the conference live. The event was covered by BBC and Sky News in their programs and on their websites.

The following is the transcript of the press conference.

Liu Xiaoming: Good morning! Welcome to today's press conference.

This year marks the fifth anniversary of the China-UK "Golden Era". Since early this year, President Xi Jinping and Prime Minister Boris Johnson have had two telephone conversations, during which they reached important agreements on advancing China-UK relations and enhancing our joint response to COVID-19. The relevant departments of the two governments have been working hard to implement these agreements and carry out cooperation in various areas.

This shows a positive momentum in China-UK relationship that should be cherished so that further progress can be achieved. To our regret, however, this relationship recently ran into a series of difficulties and faced a grave situation.

People are asking: What is happening to China-UK relationship? The British media are also asking: What is causing the current difficulties in China-UK relationship? Has China changed or has the UK changed?

Today, I am going to give you my answer to these questions. My answer is loud and clear: China has not changed. It is the UK that has changed. The UK side should take full responsibility for the current difficulties in China-UK relationship.

First, China's determination to follow the basic norms governing international relations has not changed.

These basic norms include:

• mutual respect for each other's sovereignty and territorial integrity,

• non-interference in each other's internal affairs,

• equality,

• and mutual benefit.

These are the fundamental principles that are enshrined in the UN Charter. They are the basic norms of the international law and state-to-state relations. They are also the basic guidelines that have been written into the Joint Communiqué of China and the UK on exchange of ambassadors and hence form the bedrock for China-UK relationship.

China has never interfered in the internal affairs of other countries, including the UK, and we ask the same from other countries.

Recently, however, the above-mentioned important principles have been violated time and again.

On Hong Kong:

There has been blatant interference from the UK in Hong Kong affairs, which are the internal affairs of China, including:

• groundless accusations against the National Security Law for Hong Kong SAR,

• changes to the policy involving BNO passport holders,

• and suspension of the agreement for the surrender of fugitive offenders with Hong Kong.

These moves have severely disrupted the stability and prosperity of Hong Kong.

On Xinjiang the UK has:

• disregarded the facts,

• confused right and wrong,

• flung slander recklessly at China's Xinjiang-related policies,

• and interfered in China's internal affairs by raising the so-called "human rights issue" in Xinjiang, bilaterally and multilaterally.

These actions have seriously poisoned the atmosphere of China-UK relationship.

Second, China's commitment to the path of peaceful development has not changed.

Pursuing peaceful development is China's unwavering strategic choice and solemn pledge. China has never invaded other countries or sought expansion. China has never and will not export its system or model. China strives for development because we want a better life for our people. We do not want to threaten, challenge or replace anyone.

History has proved and will continue to prove that China is always a defender of world peace, a contributor to global development and an upholder of international order. A stronger China will make the world a more peaceful, stable and prosperous place.

However, some British politicians cling to the "Cold War" mentality and echo the remarks of anti-China forces in and outside the UK. They:

• play up the so-called "China threat",

• see China as a "hostile state",

• threaten a "complete decoupling" from China,

• and even clamour for a "new Cold War" against China.

Third, China's resolve to fulfill its international obligations has not changed.

This year marks the 75th anniversary of the founding of the United Nations. China was the first country to place its signature on the UN Charter. It is now a member of more than 100 inter-governmental international organisations and has signed over 500 multilateral treaties.

- It has faithfully fulfilled its international responsibilities and obligations.
- It has never withdrawn from international organisations or treaties.
- Nor does it believe in "us first" at the expense of others.

It is completely wrong to see the National Security Law for Hong Kong SAR as a violation of the Sino-British Joint Declaration or a failure to honour international obligations.

The core content of the Joint Declaration concerns China's resumption of its exercise of sovereignty over Hong Kong. The National Security Law for Hong Kong SAR fully embodies the comprehensive jurisdiction of the Central Government of China over Hong Kong.

The policies regarding Hong Kong laid out in the Joint Declaration were proposed by China on our own initiative. Thus, they neither represent China's commitments to the UK nor international obligations. The label of "failure to fulfill international obligations" should not be branded on China.

It is the UK side that has failed to fulfill its international obligations and gone against its own pledges by changing the policy on BNO passport holders and suspending the agreement for the surrender of fugitive offenders with Hong Kong. This has created public confusion in Hong Kong, disrupted the implementation of the National Security Law and caused interference in China's internal affairs.

Fourth, China's willingness to develop partnership with the UK has not changed.

During President Xi Jinping's state visit to the UK in 2015, China and the UK issued a joint declaration on building a global comprehensive strategic partnership for the 21st century.

China has always seen the UK as a partner and is committed to developing a sound and stable relationship with the UK. As State Councillor and Foreign Minister Wang Yi said two days ago in his telephone conversation with the UK Foreign Secretary Dominic Raab, China represents an opportunity rather than a threat to the UK. It embodies growth rather than a cause for decline and a solution rather than a challenge or a risk. However, there have been major changes and serious deviation in the UK's perception and definition of China. This is particularly evidenced by the recent ban on Huawei.

The issue of Huawei is not about how the UK sees and deals with a Chinese company. It is about how the UK sees and deals with China. Does it see China as an opportunity and a partner, or a threat and a rival? Does it see China as a friendly country, or a "hostile" or "potentially hostile" state?

The UK leaders have said on many occasions that they want to build a balanced, positive and constructive China-UK relationship. We hope their words will be consistent with their actions.

The world is experiencing increasingly profound changes which have not been seen in a century. COVID-19 is still raging, dealing a heavy blow to economic globalization and resulting in a deep recession in the world economy. What kind of China-UK relationship do we need in face of such a situation?

China and the UK are both permanent members of the UN Security Council and important members of the G20 and other international organizations. Both are countries with global influence. Both shoulder the important mission of safeguarding world peace and of promoting development.

A sound and stable China-UK relationship is not only in the fundamental interests of the people of the two countries but also conducive to world peace and prosperity. We have a thousand reasons to make this relationship successful, and not one reason to let it fail.

How can we make it successful? I think it is critically important to follow three principles:

First, to respect each other.

History tells us that when international law and the basic norms governing international relations are observed, the China-UK relationship will advance forward; otherwise, it will suffer setbacks or even backslide.

China respects the UK's sovereignty and has never interfered in the UK's internal affairs. It is important that the UK does the same, namely, respecting China's sovereignty and ending interference in Hong Kong affairs, which are China's internal affairs, so as to prevent further harm to China-UK relationship.

The second principle is: to engage in mutually-beneficial cooperation.

China and the UK have highly complementary economies and deeply integrated interests. The two sides have both benefited tremendously from cooperation. Such mutual benefit should not be gauged by an over-simplified comparison of who is more dependent on the other or who has been "taken advantage of".

It is our hope that the UK will resist the pressure and coercion of a certain country, and provide an open, fair and non-discriminatory environment for Chinese investment, so as to restore the confidence of Chinese businesses in the

UK.

China and the UK already share broad consensus on safeguarding multilateralism, promoting free trade and addressing global challenges such as climate change. When Brexit is completed and COVID-19 has come to an end, there will be unlimited prospects for China-UK cooperation in the areas of trade, financial services, science and technology, education and healthcare.

It is hard to imagine a "global Britain" that bypasses or excludes China. "Decoupling" from China means decoupling from opportunities, decoupling from growth, and decoupling from the future.

The third principle is: to seek common ground despite differences.

China and the UK differ in terms of history, culture, social system and the stage of their development. It is only natural that we do not always see eye to eye.

Seventy years ago, the UK was the first major Western country to recognize the New China. For the past 70 years, China and the UK have found common ground despite their differences and gone beyond ideological differences to achieve continuous progress in their bilateral relationship.

Today, after 70 years, this relationship has become more substantial and profound. It is not a relationship between rivals, where one side's gain is the other's loss. Still less is a relationship of "either-or" that exists between hostile states. The China-UK relationship is one of partnership, which is defined by equal treatment and mutual benefit.

China and the UK should have enough wisdom and ability to manage and deal with differences, rather than allowing anti-China forces and "Cold-War" warriors to "kidnap" the China-UK relationship.

I often say the "Great Britain" cannot be "Great" without an independent foreign policy. The UK has withstood pressure from others and made the right strategic choices at many critical historical junctures,

• from becoming the first major Western country to recognize the People's Republic of China in 1950, to establish diplomatic relationship with China at the chargé d'affaires level in 1954;

• from taking part in the Asian Infrastructure Investment Bank to building a comprehensive global strategic partnership for the 21st century with China.

Now, the China-UK relationship once again stands at a critical historical juncture. It is my hope that political leaders and visionary people from all sectors in the UK will keep in mind the bigger picture of the international trend, avert various disruptions and make strategic choices that serve the fundamental interests of the people of our two countries.

Thank you.

Now I would like to take your questions.

BBC: Ambassador, good morning. As you said, relations between the United Kingdom and China have deteriorated significantly in recent weeks over Hong Kong, Huawei and Xinjiang. Throughout that process, you and various other government representatives have threatened consequences, counter-measures, even counter-attacks, to use the language of last week. And yet it's still not entirely clear to me what those counter-measures are. So could you elaborate a little bit more? Is China retaliating in secret, or is its bark worse than its bite?

Liu Xiaoming: I want to set the record straight. We made no threats. We threaten nobody, as I said. We just let you know the consequences. People regard some of my remarks as threatening words. I think they quote my remarks out of context. As I said, China wants to be a friend of the UK. China wants to be the UK's partner. But if you do not want to be our friend, and if you want to treat China as a hostile country, you will pay the price. That's simple. It's very clear. That means you will lose the benefits of treating China as a source of opportunities and as a friend. And you will bear the consequences of treating China as a hostile country. So that's very clear.

And you talk about the counter-measures. I think you have already seen that after the UK announced that they are going to change the policy on the BNO, we have responded by saying, we are considering refusing to recognize the BNO passports as legal travel documents. That is because the UK will have introduced a measure that signals a departure from their commitments under the MOU of 1984. At that time, they said they were not going to give right of abode to the BNO holders. And we also agreed to regard the BNO passport as a legal travel document. Now since they have violated their commitments, we have to make a response.

Again, with regard to the agreement for the surrender of fugitive offenders, the UK has suspended this indefinitely. I think this will undermine the basis for legal collaboration between the UK and Hong Kong. China has to make a response to that and we announced that the Hong Kong government also suspends the agreement for the surrender of fugitive offenders with the UK. And they also suspend the mutual legal assistance agreement with the UK because the basis and foundations of the legal collaboration between the two sides have been undermined.

Sky News: Thank you, Ambassador. On Hong Kong, in the last couple of days, we've seen a small number of people being arrested under these new security laws, seemingly just for posting comments on the internet, and also a number of pro-democracy activists today being disqualified from running in the elections. Doesn't this really prove the concerns that the UK has about the national security law undermining Hong Kong's freedoms? If I may, as you mentioned Xinjiang, have you had any more clarity about those images that you were shown a couple of weeks ago on the BBC? European security sources say they believe those men who are shackled and shaven, and in those suits, were members of the Uighur minority. Why were they being transported and treated in such a way?

Liu Xiaoming: First, on Hong Kong, the National Security Law is about plugging the legal loopholes and safeguarding national security. You know, for the past 23 years since the handover, there has been no law to take care of national security. We've seen what happened last year. People talk about "One Country, Two Systems". But we all witnessed how the concept of "One Country" has been eroded, how "One Country" has been put at risk. It's timely for the Central Government and the National People's Congress to enact this law to plug the loopholes.

It has nothing to do with freedom of speech or freedom of expression. It is clearly stipulated in the National Security Law that the basic human rights will be fully respected. This law is only targeted at these very few criminals who intend to endanger the national security. The law is very clear with respect to four categories of crimes it covers. If you do not commit crimes which fall into these categories, you will have no problem with regard to freedom of expression, freedom to march and freedom to demonstrate. So the capitalist system will not change, and Hong Kong will continue to enjoy its independent judicial system, including the power of final adjudication. So I think this law will only make "One Country, Two Systems" more sustainable. And so that's why it's overwhelmingly supported by the people of Hong Kong. About three million Hong Kong residents have signed a petition to show their support for this law because they want to have a peaceful, prosperous and stable environment in Hong Kong.

With regard to Xinjiang, I will respond a little later but I will certainly answer your question.

CGTN: Good morning, Ambassador. So you just mentioned that China might stop recognizing BNO passports as valid travel documents. What would that mean in practice for Hong Kong residents who want to travel to the UK? And also, how do you see a path forward for restoring trust and goodwill between China and the UK which has diminished so much on both sides?

Liu Xiaoming: China has done nothing to weaken the mutual trust between the two countries. As I said, we see the UK as a partner, as a friendly country. We want to develop this relationship and the "golden era" between our two countries. As I have said on many occasions, we are about to celebrate the fifth anniversary of the "golden era". It's a time for celebration. But unfortunately, it's the UK side that has done things to undermine that mutual trust by making unwarranted accusations against the National Security Law, interrupting the implementation of this law and interfering in Hong Kong's internal affairs.

So I think, as I have already said in my presentation, the solution for China-UK relations lies in the three basic principles: mutual respect, non interference in each other's internal affairs, and treating each other as equals and partners. And we do recognize that we have differences. But we need to address these differences on an equal basis and recognize differences. China has no intention to change the UK. I think the UK should have no intention to change China. I think we have more common ground and common interests to unite our two countries than differences that divide us. China and the UK, as countries with global influence, have enormous duties to live up to. We have our responsibility to promote world peace and world prosperity. There are so many items in the common agenda in front of us.

With regard to the specific question you raised. Since the UK violated its commitment with regard to BNO, we have to let them know that we must take our measures by refusing to recognize the BNO passport as a valid travel document.

Reuters: Thank you very much, Ambassador. I just wanted to sort of look at a slightly bigger picture. My apology if this is a stupid question, but it seems clear that US President Donald Trump sees China as the major geopolitical foe of the

21st century. So, do you see a new cold war between the West and China? How do you react to the view that President Xi has been too assertive over recent years, and this has upset the Americans?

Liu Xiaoming: I think you have already answered your own questions. It's not China that has become assertive. It's those on the other side of the Pacific Ocean who want to launch a new Cold War on China. So we have to make a response to that. We have no interest in any Cold War. We have no interest in any wars. When the United States started this trade war against China, we said there would be no winner in a trade war and we wanted to engage with them. Then we had a phase one agreement. We still keep on engaging with them. But I think the coronavirus really worsened the situation, because we have all seen what is happening in United States. They tried to find a scapegoat in China. They want to blame China for their problems.

We all know this is the election year. I've been posted twice to Washington, D.C.. I witnessed five elections, on the ground, in person, not from a distance. People say, US politicians will say anything in order to get elected in an election year. It seems to me this year, it is likely that they are not only to say anything but also to do anything, including treating China as an enemy. Probably they think they need an enemy. They think they need a cold war. But we have no interest in that. We keep on telling the Americans: China is not your enemy. China is your friend and your partner. Your enemy is the virus. I hope that US politicians will focus on fighting the virus and saving lives instead of blaming China.

CCTV: Good morning, Ambassador. My question is: the Director-General of the Confederation of British Industry shared her opinions in *Financial Times* a few days ago. She said that the UK cannot afford to self-isolate from China because of the huge benefits from the collaboration between the two countries. But I think as you just mentioned, some British politicians hold the opposite opinion. So what's your comment on that? And also, if it's allowed, can I ask another question: I think you have watched many videos and pictures in the previous interview with the local media. And also you have stated and clarified many times the Chinese policy on the Xinjiang issue. But I think probably my Western colleagues are still keen on discussing similar topics. Personally I think they probably like to blame China for this issue a lot. So what's your comment on this kind of communication? Thank you.

Liu Xiaoming: As I said in my opening remarks, I think China-UK relations really are mutually beneficial. I quite agree with the Director-General of the CBI.

Let me give you a few figures. Some people say that China gains more from this relationship. I don't think this is true. In the past 20 years, from 1999 to 2020, UK exports to China increased twenty times. Since I became Chinese Ambassador, trade between our two countries has doubled. In the past 10 years Chinese investment increased twenty times. So these two "twenty times" are really self evident.

It has created enormous jobs. And each year Chinese tourism to this country supported 11,000 jobs. Also the UK is the largest recipient of Chinese students in Europe. Of course, Chinese students benefit from studying here. But they make a contribution to this country too. The students' expenditure alone, according to a Cambridge study, supported 17,000 jobs in 2018, not to mention the contribution made by Huawei. They have helped build the telecommunications industry in this country. And also, some "Cold War warriors" as Chinese people call them are trying to find another target in the nuclear project on which Chinese companies are working together with their French and British partners. I think this project will serve the interests of the UK, and also help the UK to achieve its goal of realising zero emissions by 2050. I really hope that the politicians will look at this from an objective perspective. This is a win-win relationship.

Since two journalists asked questions about Xinjiang, I want to make a response.

On issues relating to Xinjiang, there are so many fallacies and lies that permeate the Western media. They can well be called "the lies of the century". Moreover, some Western countries have been using Xinjiang-related issues to discredit China and interfere in China's internal affairs. Regrettably, the UK is one of them. I would like to take this opportunity to debunk the lies and let the facts be known, so as to show you the real Xinjiang.

First, Xinjiang-related issues have nothing to do with human rights, ethnic groups or religions, but everything to do with combatting violent terrorism, separatism and extremism.

Since the 1990s, especially after the 9/11 terrorist attacks, terrorist, separatist and religious extremist forces have launched thousands of violent attacks in Xinjiang, resulting in devastating casualties among innocent people and a huge loss of property. During the riots on 5th July 2009, which shocked Xinjiang and the whole world, 197 lives were lost and more than 1, 700 people were injured.

In face of such grave situations, the Government of the Xinjiang Autonomous Region has cracked down upon violent terrorist activities in accordance with the law and adopted de-radicalisation measures to address the root causes. These measures have been very effective: there has not been a single terrorist attack for more than three consecutive years in Xinjiang, and the basic rights of all ethnic groups, especially the rights to life, health and development, are fully safeguarded. Therefore, these measures have won extensive and heartfelt support from people of all ethnic groups in Xinjiang.

These measures have also marked an important contribution to the global fight against terrorism, and thus won positive responses from the international community. Since the end of 2018, more than 1,000 people in over 70 groups, including officials from the United Nations, members of foreign diplomatic corps in China, permanent representatives to the UN and other international organisations in Geneva, journalists and representatives of faith groups, have visited Xinjiang. They represent over 90 countries. They spoke highly of the counter-terrorism and de-radicalisation measures in Xinjiang, saying that these are in line with the purposes and principles of the United Nations in cracking down upon terrorism and safeguarding basic human rights, and should be fully recognized and shared with other countries.

In October 2019, representatives from more than 60 countries spoke at the 74th session of the Third Committee of the UN General Assembly in recognition of the human rights progress made in Xinjiang. In July this year, representatives from 46 countries delivered a joint statement at the 44th session of the Human Rights Council in support of China's position and the counter-terrorism measures in Xinjiang.

Now I would like to play a video to help you see the harm caused by terrorist, separatist and extremist attacks in Xinjiang, so that you will understand why the measures taken in Xinjiang against terrorism, separatism and extremism are necessary and important. (Video clip is played.)

Second, there are many rumours and lies about the vocational education and training centres in Xinjiang, calling them "concentration camps" or "re-education camps". The truth is they are none of these. They are useful and positive explorations of preventative and de-radicalisation measures.

The centres were established to address the root causes of extremism and prevent further escalation of violent terrorist activities. They operate in line with the principles and spirit embodied in a number of international documents on counter-terrorism, such as the UN Global Counter-Terrorism Strategy. In nature, they are no different from the Desistance and Disengagement Programme (DDP) of the UK, the community corrections in the United States, or the de-radicalisation centres in France.

At the vocational education and training centres, those who have been led astray by extremist ideas or who have committed minor crimes can learn the common language, legal knowledge and vocational skills. Such education and training will strengthen their ability to break away and stay away from extremist ideas and master vocational skills, helping them to not only become law-abiding citizens but also find stable jobs, earn their own living and lead a better life.

At the centres:

• The Constitutional and legal principles on respecting and safeguarding human rights are being strictly followed, the dignity of the trainees is fully respected, and insults and abuse of all forms are strictly prohibited.

• The freedom of trainees is guaranteed. The centres are managed as boarding schools. Trainees can go on home visits or ask for leave to attend to private affairs.

• Meanwhile, the right of the trainees to use languages of ethnic groups is also fully guaranteed. All rules and regulations, school timetables and menus are written in both the common language and languages of ethnic groups.

• The customs and habits of different ethnic groups are fully respected and protected. A variety of Halal food is provided for free.

• The freedom of religious belief is also fully respected and protected. Religious believers have the freedom to attend lawful religious activities while on home leave.

Now I would like to show you a video in which the trainees at the vocational education and training centres tell the stories of their lives then. (Video clip is played.)

Third, let me turn to the four lies and slanders that are widespread in the Western media about Xinjiang. I think it is wrong to allow the lies and slanders to run amok, or to let arrogance and prejudice prevent people from seeing the facts and truth. So it is important to get the facts and truth out there, so that people can make up their own minds from an objective and reasonable perspective.

The first lie is that "nearly a million Uygurs in Xinjiang are detained".

This is a lie cooked up by an anti-China organization and an individual who is anti-China.

The organization is the so-called "Chinese Human Rights Defenders" (CHRD) backed by the government of the United States. Armed with interviews from only eight people who are ethnic Uygurs and based on an extremely rough estimate, the CHRD reached an absurd conclusion that 10% of the more than 20 million people in Xinjiang are being detained at so-called "re-education camps".

The anti-China individual is a man called Adrian Zenz, a far-right fundamentalist funded by the government of the United States. He published an article in the journal *Central Asian Survey*, claiming that "Xinjiang's total re-education internment figure may be estimated at just over one million". According to The Grayzone, an independent news website, Zenz's conclusion is based on a single report by Istiqlal TV. This so-called "Uygur exile media organization" based in Turkey is far from being a media organization. Istiqlal TV is a group that advocates separatism and extremism. And Zenz himself believes that he is "led by God" on a "mission" against China.

A few days ago when I gave an interview on *The Andrew Marr Show* on BBC, Mr. Marr showed me a footage which he said has "been authenticated by Western intelligence agencies and by Australian experts" to prove that a large number of Uygurs are being detained. Now let's see what is really happening.

The video shows transfer of a group of prisoners from the Kashgar Detention House. It has nothing to do with the so-called "detainment of a large number of Uygurs". China's criminal law does not target members of a specific ethnic group or religion. Everyone is equal before the law. The transfer of prisoners by judicial authorities is a normal judicial practice and brooks no distortion or defamation.

The second lie is that "Xinjiang has demolished a large number of mosques".

The fact is, there are 24,400 mosques in Xinjiang, which means there is on average one mosque for every 530 Muslims. This ratio is higher than that in some Muslim countries and also higher than the number of churches per Christian in England.

The Jiami Mosque of Yecheng County and the Id Kah Mosque in Hotan prefecture, which were claimed to have been "dismantled", were in fact renovated and put to use again. Those who cooked up the lies used the photo of the old, dilapidated mosques to support their untruths. But I will refute their lies with photos of the new, renovated mosques.

The third lie is that "forced sterilization is being carried out in Xinjiang".

The fact is, Xinjiang Uygur Autonomous Region is one of the five ethnic autonomous regions in China. It is home to many ethnic groups, including 13 ethnic groups who have been living there for generations. It is a place where 25 million people of all ethnic groups call home and live together in harmony.

The Chinese Government protects the lawful rights and interests of people of all ethnic groups, whether big or small in population. Over the years, the Uygur people and other ethnic minorities have enjoyed a favourable demographic policy. Between 1978 and 2018, the Uygur population in Xinjiang doubled, from 5.55 million to 11.68 million.

The true identities or stories of the so-called "victims" in the on-line videos about Uygurs being "prosecuted" are not what they claim. These self-claimed "victims" are either the so-called "East Turkistan" elements engaged in anti-China and separatist activities, or "actors" trained by anti-China forces in the US and other Western countries to spread rumours about China. Their claims have no factual ground. The relatives and friends of some of these people in Xinjiang have stood up to refute these rumours and lies.

On *The Andrew Marr Show* that I mentioned earlier, Mr. Marr showed me another video of a so-called "victim". This woman in the video, whose name is Zumrat Dawut, claimed that she went through "forced sterilization". However, her sister and brother publicly refuted her lies last November. It turns out that she has never been to any vocational education and training centre. She had an operation because she was diagnosed with a myoma of the uterus when she had her third child, and she has never been "forced to get sterilized". Now let's watch a video interview given by her sister and brother. (Video clip is played.)

The fourth lie is that "mass forced labour is taking place in Xinjiang".

In fact, this is yet another story fabricated by a hidden hand. This hidden hand is called the Australian Strategic Policy Institute (ASPI), which is funded by the US government and arms dealers. This institute made up the so-called "Uyghurs for sale" report last March, which is a distorted description of people from southern Xinjiang seeking job opportunities in central and eastern China and trying to make a living and throw off poverty. The report refers to stories of these people being used as "forced labour".

After that, this absurd report was taken as "evidence" by the US

Congressional-Executive Commission on China to make up the so-called "Global Supply Chains, Forced Labor, and the Xinjiang Uyghur Autonomous Region" report to fling slanders at China.

Now I would like to show you another video to lay bare their lies. (Video clip is played.)

The Chinese people often say, "One does not know how vast and beautiful China is until one visits Xinjiang". This vast and beautiful region is now witnessing sustained economic growth, social harmony and stability, improved wellbeing, and unprecedented cultural prosperity. People of all ethnic groups in Xinjiang are leading a secure life, getting along with each other in harmony, and enjoying the full right to life and development. Their freedom of religious belief and regular religious activities are protected by law. Now is the most opportune time in history for Xinjiang to realize development.

Rumours will not write off China's progress in safeguarding human rights in Xinjiang. Attempts to disrupt the development and prosperity of Xinjiang will never succeed. It is my hope that you will not believe the rumours or the deceptive words of anti-China elements and politicians.

We urge the UK Government to view the progress and achievements in Xinjiang from a comprehensive and objective perspective, to stop making irresponsible remarks on Xinjiang, and to stop using Xinjiang to interfere in China's internal affairs. We also hope that the British media will cast aside their arrogance and prejudice, and report and cover Xinjiang in an objective and fair manner so as to help the British public see the real Xinjiang.

ITV: Thank you, Ambassador. Will China agree to allow a team from the United Nations Human Rights Council to visit Xinjiang and the facilities that you have just shown us in order to carry out an independent investigation, unfettered, without any interference of the Chinese Communist Party to see for themselves what is going on there?

Liu Xiaoming: As I told you, since 2018 about 1,000 diplomats, journalists and representatives from various countries, and international organisations have been to Xinjiang. We also welcome the UN High Commissioner for Human Rights to visit Xinjiang.

What we are opposed to is the so-called "independent investigation" that has ulterior motives. It is trying to use the Xinjiang issue to interfere into China's internal affairs. Xinjiang's door is always open. Each year hundreds of thousands of tourists visit Xinjiang. People who go there with good intentions, who are objective and unbiased, will be welcomed.

Associated Press: Ambassador, thank you for taking my question. I would like to draw upon your long history in the United States to ask you whether or not you believe relations with the US are at "a point of no return", given the statements from the Trump Administration and the continuing threats that they could make against China?

Liu Xiaoming: I certainly hope not. China still believes that good relations based on mutual respect, non-confrontation, cooperation and coordination are in the best interests of the two countries. We have no intention to undermine this relationship. And we'll try our best to engage the US side.

But as I have said on many occasions, you need two to tango. You need two hands to clap.

I also believe that there is broad-based public support for the relations. Since Nixon's visit to China in 1972, both countries have worked to build a relationship based on common interests. I think the common interests of the two countries are still there. The foundations, especially among the American people, are still there. American people still support engagement with China. When we heard the US Secretary of State make these anti-Chinese Communist Party remarks, I called that a declaration of cold war and we've seen many criticisms of his statement by American people. People are concerned about where this administration will take this relationship.

So I don't think we have passed the "point of no return". I think the fundamental interests that tie the two countries together should remain. And I think the people with vision, with farsightedness, are still working to maintain the fundamentals of this relationship. I hope that common sense will prevail at the end of the day.

Xinhua News Agency: On Huawei, Huawei has been saying that it is an independent and privately-held company, not affiliated with the Chinese government. So why has the Chinese government spared no effort to defend Huawei in the ongoing row? And also if the China-UK relations continue to sour, is there any possibility that the two countries will find themselves in a relationship that is characterized by "hot economically" and "cold politically" (*zheng leng jing re*), which once happened between China and Japan? Thank you.

Liu Xiaoming: On the subject of Huawei, I've just published an article in the *South China Morning Post*. I'm not trying to advertise my article, but I really hope that you can spend some time to read this article.

As a matter of fact, I have tried my very best to have my article printed in major British newspapers, because it's really relevant. I think the British public needs to hear the other side of the story immediately after the UK government's decision to ban Huawei. Unfortunately, no major newspaper would like to carry my article.

I've been here for 10 years. Now I really have a taste of what "freedom of the press" is about in the UK. One of your colleagues told me earlier that they only want to carry articles which they believe will sell better. So they do not carry my article on Hong Kong. They do not carry my article on Huawei. So I really have to let my article fly thousands of miles to Hong Kong, to the *South China Morning Post*. They told me they still have some readers in the UK. So I decided, okay, that's good. I encourage you to read my article in which I say, to refuse Huawei is to refuse opportunities, to refuse growth and to refuse the future. I do not need to elaborate on my main points.

I just want to answer your question about China-UK relationship. As I said in my opening remarks, this issue of Huawei is not about one Chinese company. It's about how the UK treats and deals with China. It is about the big picture. Do you treat China as an opportunity or do you treat China as a threat? Do you treat China as a partner or a rival? That is a fundamental issue. You have to make a choice.

Secondly, governments have to provide protection for the legitimate rights and interests of the business people. It's not only true for the Chinese government but also true for the UK government. I've been here for 10 years. I remember vividly how British leaders and politicians worked very hard on behalf of your businesses. I still remember how even your Prime Minister tried to promote the sale of Diageo while our Premier was here, in a hope that there should be a signing ceremony for the Diageo project in China. I still remember that your Chancellor of Exchequer pushed very hard for the Chinese side to buy Rolls-Royce engines. They told us that Rolls-Royce produces much better engines than any other countries, including GE from the United States. I still remember how your Business Secretary even went to China to promote the sale of British Steel, asked Chinese companies to buy British Steel. And they ended up with a buyer called Jingye who agreed to invest in the next 10 years 1.2 billion pounds.

I think there's no question about the government working for the business interests of its country. So I think you can't regard China's efforts to raise the Huawei issue as an example of what some "Cold War warriors" claim—that this shows that Huawei is close to the Chinese government. We treat Chinese businesses as equals. We hope Huawei is succeeding in this country. It's a win-win situation. So that's why I said on the day the British government made its decision that this was a dark day for Huawei, a dark day for China-UK relations, and an even darker day for the United Kingdom because it will miss the opportunity to become a leading country in 5G infrastructure.

You also mentioned the relationship being "cold politically and warm economically". I think the two are related. You need to have a good atmosphere to engage with each other. When I said it was a dark day for China-UK relations, it's because the decision really undermines the trust between the two countries and the credibility of the UK government. So that's why there are a number of concerns from Chinese businesses. I held a webinar with Chinese businesses right after the UK's ban on Huawei. All parties expressed their concerns because there was a perceived security risk, there was an investment risk. So I think you can't separate the two. We have no intention to politicize economic affairs. But you have to realize that trust and credibility are important factors for countries to be able to engage with each other.

Thank you for your questions.

A New Growth Pattern of "Dual Circulation"

——Q&A with Chinese and British Business Communities

(on the 5th Plenary Session of the 19th CPC Central Committee)

After delivering a speech on the Fifth Plenary Session of the 19th CPC Central Committee, I took questions from the Chinese and British Business Communities.

Stephen Perry, Chairman of the 48 Group Club: Thank you, Ambassador, for your comprehensive introduction to the 5th Plenary Session of the 19th CPC Central Committee. I have been interested in the development of the regions. It looks to me like that China will create four major metropolises of maybe over 100 million people each. How could the UK approach these new emerging regions in order to offer their services and goods?

Liu Xiaoming: China is a large country and certain provinces, municipalities and regions are distinctive. Some of the problems China faces are its development which includes imbalance and inadequacy. So how do you achieve a balanced development to ensure that people share the benefits of the reform and opening up? The Party and government have formulated different strategies for different regions.

First, more than 20 years ago, the government initiated the strategy of large-scale development in the western region. After serving as Ambassador to Egypt, I was seconded for two years as an assistant governor of Gansu Province, one of the provinces in the western part of China. The strategy of large-scale development in the western region has been going on for more than 20 years and substantial progress has been achieved. The landscape has changed completely. If you look at the landscape of Lanzhou, the capital city of Gansu Province, you will be very impressed.

Second, the central part of China is relatively developed, but still underdeveloped compared with the eastern part of China. We are following a strategy known as "the rise of the central region". This strategy aims to unlock the potential of the six provinces within this region. This region has very strong advantages, but they're different from the Western part of China and, also, different from the Eastern part of China.

Third, we have the trailblazing development of the eastern region. Most of the region lies in the coastal area and there are more developed cities here like Shanghai, Guangzhou, Shenzhen and many others.

Fourth, the full revitalization of the northeast. It used to be and is still an industrial base within China. In the 1950s, it was home to many projects. It contributed a great deal to China's modernization. Even today, it is still an industrial base and agriculturally very important. It has very fertile land and produces the best quality rice, wheat and so on.

So these are the four big major areas. We have adopted a balanced approach to regional development aiming at better promoting the development of both developed and underdeveloped regions, and achieving common development for the eastern, central, western and northeastern part of China.

And we also have different development strategies for metropolises. There is the coordinated development of the Beijing-Tianjin-Hebei region, the development of the Guangdong-Hong Kong-Macao Greater Bay Area, and the integrated development of the Yangtze River Delta. Each area and each region has its own strength.

Here in the UK, you have schemes such as the Northern Powerhouse and the Midland Engine. So I think there is great potential for China and the UK to dovetail regional strategies. We need to uncover the strengths of each region and find opportunities to work together and develop together to enjoy the benefits of regional cooperation.

Sir Sherard Cowper-Coles, Chair of the China-Britain Business Council: The CBBC sees the fact of China's growth as a great economic power. So we're delighted that the latest figures show in the first eight months of this year, British exports to China rose by nearly 10%. We're delighted that the number of Chinese students in Britain remains stable, that the pipeline of Chinese investments remains extremely promising. And the research which the CBBC has commissioned shows more than 100,000 jobs across the United Kingdom are attributable to our trade with China. So we welcome this opening up. It's important for China, of course. It's vital for China, but also as part of Britain's future prosperity. So with that in mind, a lot of the sinologists around me have been intrigued by the concept of dual circulation. Could you please explain to all of us a bit more of your understanding of the concept of "dual circulation" and how that will help those of us who want to benefit from it.

Liu Xiaoming: I think I gave a brief introduction to "dual circulation" in my speech. To set up a new growth pattern of "dual circulation" is a strategic choice. China is coping positively with changes in the domestic and international situation. It is a long-term strategy rather than an expedient measure.

First, as to domestic circulation. I think you are familiar with the challenges in the international arena. The world economy is experiencing grave recession because of the rising headwinds of protectionism, unilateralism, and also the broad and deep impact of the COVID-19 pandemic. All these have resulted in an obvious weakening in the traditional international patterns of circulation. So we need to make some adjustments to strengthen our domestic circulation in order to consolidate the resilience of economic growth and to enhance the international economic circulation.

Number two, the energy of domestic circulation is strengthened. You know when a country develops to a certain stage, for instance, China has now become the second largest economy, it also opens up a huge domestic market for itself. Like other great economic powers, domestic supply and demand play a more important supporting role in Chinese economic circulation.

Thirdly, the new growth pattern emphasizes that "dual circulation" is by no means a closed domestic circulation. On the contrary, it means that China will be more open both in the domestic and international markets. It allows you greater space to develop and to maneuver. So, we need to make the best use of the domestic market, to unlock the potential of our domestic market. The domestic circulation means the whole country is regarded as a unified market. How should we tap the potential of the huge market in China? China will take full advantage of this huge market and participate extensively in international circulation. Moreover, China will also expand market access for foreign enterprises to build a market-oriented, law-based international business environment. And we will rely on a strong domestic market to attract high-quality global production factors in order to become a fertile soil for foreign investment.

So what we're saying is that the domestic market will play a leading role, but the international market and domestic market will have their role to play in reinforcing each other. Now China will make more efforts to integrate international and domestic market. How should we achieve a win-win situation in both markets? How should we take advantage of both markets? That means there will be more opportunities rather than fewer opportunities for UK business. So, I do hope that UK businesses will take advantage of this concept of "dual circulation", and China-UK cooperation and partnership will contribute to its development. And so, you have nothing to worry about. I do hope my speech will give you the confidence to become involved and to participate in this "dual circulation" and development.

Merethe MacLeod, Executive Director of the Great Britain China Centre: Thank you, Mr. Ambassador, for outlining the Five Year Plan so succinctly for us. You know I represent the Great Britain China Centre and we've worked very closely with institutions in China on the rule of law. I've been very keen to hear your views on how you see rule of law, or what the top priorities for legal reform are to support China's development in the next few years.

Liu Xiaoming: This Five Year Plan, and the goals for 2035, are not only about economic development. It's a multi-dimensional development strategy for China. Take the 14th Five Year Plan for example. It sets the targets for China in the next five years in six new areas. First, to strive to make new strides in economic development. Second, to take new steps in reform and opening up. Third, to make a new development in the social etiquette and civility. Fourth, to make new progress in building on ecological civilization. Fifth, to boost the well-being of the people. Sixth, to enhance the capacity for governance. The third and the sixth points are closely related to the construction of the socialist rule of law.

This is what the plenary session has adopted. The proposals establish the guidelines and directions. In the next Two Sessions, the central government will introduce specific policies, as well as the framework and measures on how to translate these guidelines into specific policies. I advise you to follow the Two Sessions closely. In short, we are building a country that enforces the rule of law.

There will also be comprehensive reforms in legal areas and law enforcement. There will be a great many expectations.

Fang Wenjian, Chairman of the China Chamber of Commerce in the UK: Recently, China signed the Regional Comprehensive Economic Partnership (RCEP) agreement (with 14 other participating countries). With the ratification of the RCEP agreement, will China pay more attention to cooperation with the signatories of the agreement? Will this affect China-UK trade and investment cooperation in the future? With Brexit, China and UK are going to sign free trade agreement. What is the relationship here with the RECP?

Liu Xiaoming: I think that the RCEP is a great achievement. I call it "a victory for free trade". It will provide a big boost to development in the Asia-Pacific region, but that does not mean China will focus only on this region. As I said in my presentation, China has a global vision. We want to build partnerships around the world. The UK and Europe are important partners for China. I would like to call your attention to the important speech made by President Xi Jinping at the opening ceremony of the Third China International Import Expo. President Xi said we would like to sign high-standard free trade agreements with more countries. So, when it comes to the UK, we are open, positive and forthcoming in terms of engaging with our UK partners over here in order to reach a high-standard free trade agreement. We're ready for that.

I think that the UK business community has nothing to worry about. Chinese businesses, like the Bank of China, still feel positive about the UK market. That is why I always quote the figure that over the past 10 years, since I became Chinese Ambassador to the UK, Chinese investment in the UK has increased 20 times. That has never happened before in the history of China-UK relations. The UK still remains attractive to foreign businesses, including Chinese businesses.

Having said that, we have our own concerns as well. First of all, there are the uncertainties created by Brexit. We don't know whether there will be a Brexit with a deal or without a deal, so we are following these negotiations between the UK and the EU very closely.

Secondly, we also have concerns that there are some diehard "Cold War warriors" who regard China as a threat, even a "hostile country", rather than a source of opportunities. They are pushing in the House of Commons to launch a security review with regard to foreign investment. We have been told by the

British government that it is not targeting Chinese businesses.

What we are asking for is that the UK should continue to provide fair, just, transparent and non-discriminatory treatment for Chinese businesses. If the UK continues to provide a business-friendly environment for Chinese businesses, I'm sure there will be further Chinese investments over in the years to come.

Fang Wenjian (on behalf of other participants) : The UK's Foreign, Commonwealth and Development Office (FCDO) has in the last few days made allegations against China to the effect that it has violated the Sino-British Joint Declaration (in response to the Decision of the Standing Committee of the National People's Congress of China on the Qualification of Members of the Legislative Council of the Hong Kong Special Administrative Region). There are reports that possible sanctions have been considered against Chinese and Hong Kong officials on the UK side. In the event of such unfriendly acts by the UK authorities, including the UK government and parliament, what concrete actions would China take to retaliate?

Liu Xiaoming: It has been reported that I was summoned by Sir Philip Barton, the Permanent Under-Secretary and the top civil servant in the FCDO of the UK, to talk about Hong Kong. I made our position very clear that we are strongly opposed to the UK's interference in Hong Kong affairs, which are China's internal affairs. As for the accusation that China is "failing to fulfill its international obligations", I said, this year marks the 75th anniversary of the United Nations. Not many people know that China was the first country to add its signature to the UN Charter 75 years ago. And since then China has continually abided by the UN Charter and has been fulfilled its international obligations. China has joined almost all inter-governmental organizations and has signed more than 500 international conventions. There are no records of China having violated international obligations. I argued in the meeting that it is the UK side that has failed to implement and live up to its international obligations. The key principle of the UN Charter is that every sovereign state should be respected on an equal basis and should not interfere in other countries' internal affairs. So the UK has violated its international obligations by interfering in Hong Kong affairs and China's internal affairs. So I told them that the decision made by the Standing Committee of the National People's Congress of China is reasonable, constitutional, and consistent with the Constitution of

China and the Basic Law.

As I have said on many occasions, now we are encountering some problems in China-UK relations. The major problem is that the basic norms governing international relations, that is to say, respect for sovereignty and non-interference in each other's internal affairs, have been violated. This year is the 70th anniversary of the UK first recognizing the New China. The UK was the first Western power to recognize the People's Republic of China. We always acknowledge that. Over the past 70 years, we have made tremendous progress in China-UK relations. But sometimes we run into difficulties. I always say, if these basic principles are abided by, China-UK relationship will move forward; otherwise, it will suffer setbacks or even backslide. So that's the key reason for the current problems in China-UK relations.

Having said that, we still attach great importance to this relationship because we believe that a good relationship between our two countries not only benefits our two peoples but also contributes to world peace and development. China and the UK are two countries with global influence. We are two permanent members of the UN Security Council. We are important members of the G20. And we have a lot of common agendas globally and bilaterally. So we have every reason to make this relationship succeed. We have no reason at all to let it fail. But, as I said on many occasions, "you need two to tango". We hope the UK side will cherish the hard-won relationship and work together with us.

I always say, the business relationship is the bedrock of the overall relationship. So I always encourage Chinese businesses in the UK to play the role of stabilizer and promoter in this relationship. But, if the political relationship is damaged and if mutual trust is damaged, there will be consequences for the overall relationship. In China we have a saying, "friendship goes ahead of business". I think friendship comes from mutual trust. I do hope, by working together, we can overcome the current difficulties, set the relationship back on the right track and elevate our partnership to a new level in the new year.

Aftab Siddiqui, Adviser to the All Party Parliamentary Group on the BRI and the CPEC: The Belt and Road Initiative is bringing foreign and Chinese domestic markets together. How do we see the Belt and Road Initiative and the "dual circulation" model coming together and what is their relationship?

Liu Xiaoming: "Dual circulation" is a new development pattern that China is promoting under the new situation. BRI has become the largest international cooperation platform. These two are very closely related. As a matter of fact, the BRI is a channel of dual circulation. Via the Silk Road Economic Belt, China is connected with Central Asia and Europe. Via the 21st Century Maritime Silk Road, we're connecting the ASEAN countries. So "dual circulation" provides great impetus for the joint construction of the BRI. I think the BRI and "dual circulation" will strengthen and reinforce each other. Dual circulation will make the BRI more efficient and more productive.

Chapter 2

Hong Kong

The Bottom Line of "One Country, Two Systems" Cannot Be Challenged

——A Press Conference on the Violent Attack against the Legislative Council Complex in the Hong Kong Special Administrative Region

On 3rd July 2019, I held a press conference at the Chinese Embassy on the violent attack against the Legislative Council complex in the Hong Kong Special Administrative Region. More than 40 journalists from 25 media agencies attended the press conference, including *Financial Times*, *The Daily Telegraph*, *The Times*, the *Economist*, *The Guardian*, Reuters, BBC, Radio 4, ITV, Sky News and Channel 4, China's Xinhua News Agency, CCTV, China News Service, CGTN, China Radio International, *China Daily*, *Economic Daily*, *Science and Technology Daily*, *Guangming Daily*, and *Global Times*, as well as CNN, Phoenix Infonews, *European Times*, and *UK Chinese Times*. The following is the transcript of the press conference.

Liu Xiaoming: 1st July is a day for celebration and festivity among the people of Hong Kong. Those from all walks of life commemorate the return of Hong Kong and the establishment of the Hong Kong Special Administrative Region (Hong Kong SAR). However, on this very day, some ultra-radicals stormed the Hong Kong Legislative Council complex in an extremely violent manner and wantonly damaged the facilities inside. Such actions have overstepped the boundaries of freedom of speech and peaceful demonstration, trampled on the rule of law in Hong Kong, undermined public order, compromised the fundamental interests of Hong Kong and challenged the bottom line of "One Country, Two Systems". We strongly condemn such actions. The Hong Kong SAR government will press criminal charges against the violent offenders in accordance with the law, and the Chinese Central Government firmly supports the Hong Kong SAR government in pursuing this serious case and in handling the incident in accordance with the law. We support the SAR government in restoring public order, protecting the safety of Hong Kong citizens in their persons and property and maintaining the prosperity and stability of Hong Kong.

It has to be pointed out that on this major issue of principle, the UK government chose to stand on the wrong side. It has made inappropriate remarks not only to interfere in the internal affairs of Hong Kong but also to back up the violent law breakers. It even attempted to obstruct the Hong Kong SAR government in bringing the criminals to justice, which is outright interference in Hong Kong's rule of law. China has repeatedly lodged stern representations with the British side.

Here, I would like to reiterate that Hong Kong is a Special Administrative Region of China. It is not how it used to be under the British colonial rule. Hong Kong affairs are purely China's internal affairs which brook no interference from any country, organization or individual. We strongly condemn and oppose this gross interference in Hong Kong affairs and in China's internal affairs by the British side.

China's resolution to safeguard sovereignty, national security and development interests is unwavering. Our resolve to uphold the prosperity and stability of Hong Kong is unwavering. Our rejection of foreign interference is unwavering. We urge the British side to seriously reflect on the consequences of its words and deeds and immediately stop interfering in Hong Kong affairs and China's internal affairs in whatever form.

The world media, especially those here in the UK, have been covering extensively what happened in Hong Kong. But to be frank, some reports are severely prejudiced and others are even ill-willed slander. I have received quite a number of requests for interview from different media institutions. So, today, I am holding this press conference in order to allow more media to hear China's stance on the basis of truth and facts with regard to Hong Kong.

Now, I would like to take your questions.

BBC: First of all, if I may, can you give us a guarantee here today this afternoon that China remains committed to the Joint Declaration, an international treaty that China signed up to and which remains in force until 2047?

And second, if I may, can you tell us what Beijing is going to do now? Are you going to use the disruption on Monday to crack down on larger, more peaceful demonstrations that may happen in the future?

Liu Xiaoming: What gives you the idea that China is going to crack down on peaceful demonstrations?

First of all, I think your perception of China's position is completely wrong. China's commitment to "One Country, Two Systems" is unwavering. But I have to make it clear that this is a promise made by the Chinese government to the world. It is a unilateral declaration by the Chinese government, not a commitment to the British government. And it is incorporated in the Basic Law. It is China's unbending position that the basic system in Hong Kong will remain unchanged for fifty years after 1997. With regard to the Joint Declaration between China and Britain, it has fulfilled its mission. According to this document, the British government should restore Hong Kong to China, and China will resume its sovereignty over Hong Kong. The British government will be responsible for its administration during the transition period from 1984 to 1997. That is what is stipulated in the Joint Declaration. Once Hong Kong was returned to China, the British government has no right to cite claims from the Joint Declaration. So I encourage you to read the Joint Declaration.

BBC: I have it in front of me. It outlines very specifically in Point 12 that the basic policies of the People's Republic of China regarding Hong Kong ... they will remain unchanged for fifty years. It is specifically said—it is not just talking about the Basic Law, but also about the Joint Declaration itself.

Liu Xiaoming: No, it talks about "One Country, Two Systems". That will remain unchanged for 50 years, not the Joint Declaration. I hope you will be careful with your choice of words. In the Joint Declaration, we cannot find any clause or articles which give the British government any right to interfere in the internal affairs of Hong Kong, or give them any right whatsoever to what you might term "supervise" the implementation of "One Country, Two Systems".

There is no indication that the central government will, as you described, "crack down" on demonstrations. We have full trust in the Hong Kong SAR government to handle these cases, even this very serious violent case. We have full trust in the Hong Kong SAR government to bring the criminals and law breakers to justice in accordance with the law.

ITV: Because of the British government's interference, as you put it, are you now calling for an apology from the British government?

Liu Xiaoming: We made a strong representation with the British side. We call on them to stop interfering in the internal affairs of Hong Kong and in China's internal affairs. I hope the British side will refrain from inflicting further damage upon the relationship.

Reuters: Reuters spoke to Boris Johnson today and he told us that the people in Hong Kong were perfectly within their rights to be very skeptical, very anxious about the extradition bill, and he will back them every inch of the way. And he would stress to Beijing that the "One Country, Two Systems" approach worked. What do you have to say to him with his line there? Given that it is he or Jeremy Hunt running to be the next Prime Minister, do you think relations between China and Britain will get worse rather than better under the next prime minister?

Liu Xiaoming: We certainly hope that whoever the next British Prime Minister may be will follow what has been agreed by the two governments with regard to the relationship. The fundamentals are that we respect sovereignty and territorial integrity and non-interference in each other's internal affairs. So long as the British government, so long as the new prime minister follows these principles, I don't see that there will be any problem in the relationship. If these principles are violated, there will be problems between our two countries.

Channel 4: When do you think the extradition bill will pass?

Liu Xiaoming: I think that the Hong Kong SAR government has already said it has suspended the extradition bill. I think the Chief Executive made it very clear that they have no timetable for the current legislative council. The current legislative council's term will expire by July 2020. In that case, she already indicated there would be no further actions on the extradition bill before July 2020. So we show respect and understanding, and support her decision. We are behind the Hong Kong SAR government.

Channel 4: Would you expect the bill to be suspended or do you expect it to never return?

Liu Xiaoming: It's up to Hong Kong SAR government to decide. It's also up to the Hong Kong SAR government as to how it will communicate with Hong Kong public and engage with the public, to let them know the rationale: Why this bill serves the interests of Hong Kong, why Hong Kong will be a better place by having this bill, why Hong Kong should not continue to be a haven for fugitive offenders, and Hong Kong should be a place for justice. I hope they will be successful in communicating with the Hong Kong people.

Sky News: You call the people who raided the Legislative Chamber "ultra radicals". Do you see their act as an act of terrorism? Also, you said that you hoped that the British government would refrain from further interference which could further damage the relationship. Have the British government's actions so far with regard to the incidents in Hong Kong already damaged relations between China and Britain? And finally, if I may, what do you say to the people, the conspiracy theorists, that there are agents provocateurs amongst these radicals, that are actually pro-China, whipping up the violent action because it gives you justification for crackdowns?

Liu Xiaoming: First, I do not want to try to characterize the "ultra radicals". It is up to Hong Kong court to decide what they are. They certainly vandalized the facilities in the legislative council. They should be responsible for what they did in breaking the law in Hong Kong. And also I think the relationship in a way has been damaged by the interference of the British government. As I said, the fundamental principles guiding our two countries are mutual respect and non-interference in each other's internal affairs. If the British government goes further, it will cause further damage. That is why I am calling on the British government to reflect on the consequences of its words and deeds with regard to Hong Kong. I do hope that the British government will realize the consequences and refrain from further interference, from further damaging the relationship.

Sky News: What about the agents provocateurs? It is just a rumour among some of the people out there saying that there are pro-China activists at play in the crowds. They are actually behind the violent side of the protest. Is that true?

Liu Xiaoming: First of all, I will not comment on rumours. Secondly, according to what has been explained by the Hong Kong police commissioner, they are actual radicals with the aim of disrupting the public order of Hong Kong. They are law-breakers.

CGTN: The Foreign Secretary Jeremy Hunt has stressed the UK's support for Hong Kong's freedom. As we all know, when Hong Kong was under British rule, they didn't have any form of democracy, including general elections. So why do you think that the UK is so concerned about Hong Kong's democracy now? My second question is about G20. We know that many people believe that the achievements of the Osaka G20 Summit are lackluster except for the China-US leader's meeting on trade talks. So what's your comment on that?

Liu Xiaoming: I think it's totally wrong for Jeremy Hunt to talk about freedom. This is not a matter of freedom. It's a matter of breaking laws in Hong Kong. It was very disappointing for a senior official of his caliber to show support for these law-breaking people. We all remember what Hong Kong was 22 years ago under British rule. There was no freedom, no democracy whatsoever. We all know that all the governors were appointed by the British government; people had no right to elect officials, no right to demonstrate certainly, and they did not even have the right to independent judicial power. The final power of adjudication rested with the Privy Council here in London. But now, everyone without bias would realize how much democracy and freedom the Hong Kong people have compared with 22 years ago before the handover. Now Hong Kong has its own Chief Executive, elected by the Election Committee of the Hong Kong people. And they have enormous enthusiasm for political participation. And the National People's Congress agreed to universal suffrage, one person one vote, to elect their Chief Executive, but unfortunately, it was not passed by the Legislative Council in 2015. And the Hong Kong people enjoy a high degree of autonomy. They run their own affairs. And now they not only have legislative, executive and independent judicial power, they even have the final right to adjudication in Hong Kong. So it's quite a contrast when we compare Hong Kong today with what Hong Kong was 22 years ago. Therefore, I think it's very hypocritical for British politicians to talk about freedom in Hong Kong. When the rule of law was damaged by the law breakers in Hong Kong, instead of condemning this, they showed support and sympathy to these law breakers. I feel very disappointed at their statement.

Phoenix TV: What's your expectation for the new prime minister of UK and his stance on Hong Kong issue, because Boris Johnson made some comments on this today? Do you think (there will be) any consequences arising out of that? Will that affect Sino-British cooperation in the future?

Liu Xiaoming: As I said earlier, we hope that the British government will carry out its commitment to the basic principles enshrined in the joint agreement for the establishment of the diplomatic relations—the basic norms governing the relationship between China and the UK—and refrain from interfering in Hong Kong's internal affairs and in China's internal affairs, and work with us for common good. I think China and the UK have enormous potential and opportunities to work together for the common good and for the prosperity and stability of Hong Kong. Hong Kong, before 1984, was a problem, a stumbling block between China and the UK. Since we reached the Joint Declaration, and especially since Hong Kong returned to China, Hong Kong is no longer a problem between China and the UK. Instead, it is playing the role of a bridge between China and the UK, and has become a positive factor in the relationship. I hope Hong Kong will continue to play this role, rather than become, again, a problem in China-UK relations.

China Daily: Some people say Western media reports on the Hong Kong protests are quite prejudiced. What do you think of media's role on this issue of Hong Kong?

Liu Xiaoming: I shall comment on your question about Hong Kong and come back to your question with regard to the G20. I think we all watched the media reporting here. It is not balanced. They focused on the demonstrations. They even showed some sympathy to these ultra radicals. I made appearances on BBC and Sky News. I presented the other side of the story of what I call the "silent majority" that has been totally ignored by the media here. About 800,000 people signed up to support the amendment of the ordnance. When the Hong Kong SAR government sent out 4,500 letters to solicit opinion, they received 3,000 back in support of the amendment. Only 1,500 showed opposition. But we do not get a single glimpse of that on any media here. So it is very unbalanced. It is not convincing. I do hope that the British media here will do justice to British readers, and present a balanced picture. After what happened on 1st of July, the media here kept on interviewing those in support of the demonstrators. They ignored the strong resentment and opposition from the other side. And we saw the legislators voicing their strong opposition and their strong resentment against these violent actions which hurt the interests of Hong Kong. Yet here we cannot see any report of this at all.

Channel 4: The Joint Declaration, as you know, is an international treaty and legally binding, promises to protect rights and freedoms of the person, of speech, of the press, of assembly, of association, of travel, of movement, of correspondence, of strike, of choice of occupation, of academic research and of religious belief. Can you promise that all those rights and freedoms are one hundred percent intact now as they were at the handover?

Liu Xiaoming: One hundred percent protected and even better if you compare the rights enjoyed today with what they previously were.

Channel 4: What about the imprisonment of Joshua Wong or the closure of the Causeway Bay bookshop, just to cite two examples?

Liu Xiaoming: In a society governed by the rule of law, people are prosecuted in accordance with the law. Freedom of expression does not mean that you can do whatever you like. If you break the law, you have to pay the price. Hong Kong is run by the rule of law. When you look into the specific cases, you should read carefully which law they have broken.

Reuters: We spoke a bit about the two candidates who seek to replace Theresa May. Both look like they might move towards a tougher line on Huawei and its involvement in 5G networks in Britain. What is your response if the next British government moves towards an outright ban on Huawei?

Liu Xiaoming: I think it is still too early to say what kind of position they are going to take. What you are saying is a kind of guesswork. But we have to prepare for all the consequences. I have to say, Huawei is here not only for their own interests. It is here to create win-win situation. Should you lose Huawei, you will miss a lot of opportunities. I think they are here for win-win results. They here made an enormous contribution not only to the telecom industries here in this country, but also in terms of corporate responsibilities. They have created more than 10,000 jobs. They have invested a great deal, with a procurement of more than £2 billion. They have set up a joint research centre. They believe they can grow alongside their British colleagues and they can contribute to the development of Britain's economy and science and technology. What is more significant is that they are open and transparent. They set up their own Cyber Security Evaluation Centre Oversight Board manned completely by British people. They let the British people check their products. There aren't any secrets. No so-called "backdoor". They are very open. I doubt you can find a better company than Huawei in terms of 5G development. I usually caution my British friends that you should treasure these opportunities. If you lose Huawei, you will lose a lot of opportunities. And you will send out very bad and negative signals, not only to Huawei but also to Chinese businesses, or maybe even to the world.

Xinhua News Agency: Ambassador, I am from Xinhua. My question is about the China-US trade tension. Some would say that the meeting during the G20 Summit between President Xi Jinping and President Trump was quite limited, and the suspension of tension is temporary. And some say the tension in China-US trade relationship is still there and will escalate again. What is you view on that? And what are the prospects for the China-US trade negotiation?

Liu Xiaoming: I think the meeting between President Xi and President Trump was of great importance. I think the G20 Summit in Osaka will be remembered for this very important meeting. What is more important is the direction set by President Xi. President Xi summed up the lessons of the 40 years of China-US relations. He pointed out that China and the US stand to gain from cooperation, and will lose out in confrontation. So cooperation and dialogue are better than confrontation and friction. And President Trump also agreed with this. So the fundamental direction set by President Xi is very important in guiding the long term relationship in the future. And secondly, the two sides announced the resumption of trade talks on the basis of equality and mutual benefit. That is very significant. The US side agrees that it will not add new tariffs on Chinese goods. So this important agreement sent out a very positive signal to the international community and the global market. We do hope that the teams from both countries will continue and implement the agreement reached by the two Heads of State. I feel optimistic about the future of the relationship and I feel optimistic about the trade talks between China and the US!

CCTV: I'm from China's CCTV. We all noticed that some of the British officials expressed their deep concern and even made comments on Hong Kong. Why do they still hold strong opinions about China's affairs 22 years after Hong Kong returned to China in 1997? And also some interviewees who spoke to Channel 4 last night wanted Mr. Hunt to be more vocal. What is your comment?

Liu Xiaoming: I think I already covered this. The Foreign Secretary's statement on Hong Kong is totally wrong. The British side should place itself in the proper position with regard to Hong Kong. In the minds of some of the people, they still regard Hong Kong as being under British rule and they forget the fundamentals. We talked about the Joint Declaration. Hong Kong has now returned to the embrace of the motherland. It is a special administrative region of China. It's not part of the UK. I would call on them to keep your hands off Hong Kong. Show respect for what has been achieved in Hong Kong under "One Country, Two Systems". I think if they kept to their proper position and approach the Hong Kong issue with objective perspectives, things will be easier for the two countries to talk about Hong Kong. Fundamentally, this colonial mindset is still haunting some officials or politicians. So I do hope they regard Hong Kong as part of China and regard Hong Kong's business as not being Britain's business. We would like to talk with them. According to the agreement between our two countries, we have no problem with the British side maintaining economic, cultural and trade relations with Hong Kong. As I said, I do hope that Hong Kong will continue to play the role of a bridge and to be a positive factor in the relationship rather than a negative factor.

The Daily Telegraph: You said that the UK government should be mindful of the consequences of their words and deeds. What exactly are the consequences you are talking about? Is China considering some sort of retaliatory actions if the UK continues down this path? And secondly, does the withdrawal of the bill mean that they recognize those people demonstrating in Hong Kong do have a point that this bill does undermine the commitments of the "One Country, Two Systems" settlement?

Liu Xiaoming: There already are consequences. The mutual trust has been weakened. We made several representations with the British side. It hurts the amicable atmosphere of the relationship. You know, we just had a very senior, high level visit by the Chinese Vice Premier who was here to co-chair with Chancellor Hammond the 10th Economic Financial Dialogue. The outcomes have been great, including London Shanghai stock connect. I happened to be the one who signed an agreement on behalf of the Chinese government which lifted the ban on British beef. That means it won't be long before Angus beef and Welsh black beef can be served on the tables of Chinese consumers. But to have good relationship, you need to build mutual trust and you need to follow basic principles. I think this inappropriate comment by British politicians really hurt the relationship. I do hope that the British side will treasure the hard-won relationship and we can move together in the common interests of the people of our two countries. The extradition bill, as I said, has a good point. There is a necessity and it has been done through normal and legal process. But there are some pitfalls which call for improvement, and I think that the Hong Kong SAR government has realized that. They need to communicate more with the public. It doesn't mean that the rationale is wrong. It doesn't mean that the bill is not a good bill. So I do hope that the Hong Kong SAR government will conduct more communications and dialogues, will engage more actively with the public and will listen to their opinions in order to improve the process.

ITV: President Xi strongly believes in the need to maintain the order and keep the country together. If the security deteriorates in Hong Kong, will the Chinese military be brought in as the last resort?

Liu Xiaoming: The Chinese military in Hong Kong is for the defence of the country. According to the basic law, the central government is responsible for foreign affairs and defence affairs. Its duty is to protect Hong Kong from outside enemies, foreign enemies. As I said, we have full trust in the Hong Kong SAR government. We believe and we have confidence that they will handle this case according to law. The Hong Kong police are very professional, and we also have full trust in them.

ITV: If they don't?

Liu Xiaoming: We have full trust. Why don't they? I have confidence that they can handle this properly.

Sky News: You criticize the British media over what you say is their imbalanced reporting of the Hong Kong issue. But in China, in the mainland, do they have full access to all the images of the demonstrations from the very beginning? And secondly, with regards to British comments, it seems that China is very angry with the way that the British government has responded to the protest, but in the UK there has been criticism that the British government is too weak in their response, they are too restrained, and there hasn't been specific support for the violent action. There's only been support for the right to peacefully protest. So why exactly do you have a problem with regard to British comments?

Liu Xiaoming: First, about the media reporting of the incident in China. I think there might be some big difference between the Chinese media—we do have some of the Chinese media here—and the British media. I think the Chinese media believe they have the social responsibility to serve the interests of the people. When the people saw what is happening in Hong Kong, they didn't want to provide a platform for those anti-China elements, or to spread so-called "propaganda" against China. They don't spread rumours to help those anti-China elements.

And about the British media criticism of the British government, that is the problem of the British media. You really have to reflect on what you are calling for. So that is what I am saying: your social responsibility—what serves the best interests of the UK. I know you have 300,000 British citizens in Hong Kong. You certainly would like to see Hong Kong remain prosperous and stable. But what's happening in Hong Kong now just does the opposite. You should take a deep breath and reflect on what will be the consequences. If those law breakers have their way, Hong Kong will be plunged into a lawless society. Will that serve the interests of Britain? Will that serve the interests of stability and prosperity? Will that serve the interests of the 300,000 British citizens in Hong Kong? The answer is definitely NO. So I do hope British media can reflect on what is in the best interests of Hong Kong and the best interests, the national interests, of

Britain.

BBC: Just thinking about your last comment. You seem to be making no distinction between the hundreds of thousands of people who marched and demonstrated peacefully, and a much smaller group who engaged in violence. Do you not draw distinctions between these two?

Liu Xiaoming: I do draw a distinction. I think we could go back to my interview with BBC and Sky News. I said, to start with it was peaceful demonstration, but later on it became ugly. There was attack on the police with toxic powder. Nobody knows what it was. That was why the police evacuated the legislative council in order to avoid further injuries to police officers. There are also concerns about people being trampled. That's what happened later on. So I do draw a distinction.

But the problem was that the British politicians make no distinctions. From the very start they supported the demonstrators, and to the very end they supported and even called the violent elements "very brave". I hate to quote their comments. They even urged the Hong Kong SAR government not to use the violent incident as a "pretext for repression"—basically they are trying to obstruct the legal process in Hong Kong. The Central Government in China has said it will leave the Hong Kong SAR government to handle this case in accordance with the law in Hong Kong. I do hope that those British politicians will make no further comment on the legal process of how the Hong Kong SAR government will pursue this case, with regard to how the government will bring those lawbreakers to justice. I hope they will respect the independent judicial power of Hong Kong, and that was what the British government has been calling for all along. I hope they will not adopt double standards in this case.

China Daily: Some people say that the G20 is not as strong as 10 years ago during the global (financial) crisis. What do you think of the future of the G20?

Liu Xiaoming: President Xi made a very important statement on the summit, and he pointed out the direction the world should take in response to unilateralism and protectionism. President Xi proposed that we need to persist in reform and innovation in order to find more impetus for high quality growth. He also proposed that we need to progress with the times in order to improve global governance and promote the reform of the international financial system. And all these have been welcomed by the international community. So I think the G20 Summit sent out a very positive message to the world. I regard the G20 Summit as a success.

With regard to the future of the G20, I think President Xi also made his contribution to further strengthening the mechanism of the G20. The G20 was born as a result of the 2008 financial crisis. It functioned to coordinate and to strengthen the cooperation between countries. President Xi also made his contribution to further strengthen the G20. We believe the G20 still has a bright future. President Xi insists on placing development at the core of the G20 agenda. There is no doubt that this outcome sent out a positive message to the outside world. We believe the G20 still has vitality and will serve the interests of countries around the world.

Thank you.

The Central Government Has Enough Solutions to Quell Any Unrest

——A Press Conference on the Situation in Hong Kong

On 15th August 2019, I held a press conference at the Chinese Embassy on the radical violence in Hong Kong which has escalated and caused severe damage. More than 50 journalists from 27 media agencies attended the press conference, including BBC, Radio 4, ITV, Sky News, Channel 4, *Financial Times*, *The Daily Telegraph*, *The Times*, *The Guardian*, Reuters from the UK, China's Xinhua News Agency, CCTV, China News Service, CGTN, *China Daily*, *Economic Daily*, *Science and Technology Daily*, *Guangming Daily*, and *Global Times* of China, and Bloomberg, CNN, Canadian Broadcasting Corporation, Phoenix Infonews, *European Times*, and *UK Chinese Times*. The following is the transcript of the press conference.

Liu Xiaoming: On 3rd July, I held a press conference here to answer questions about the amendments to Hong Kong's extradition laws and to explain China's position. For more than a month since then, the opposition in Hong Kong and some radical forces have continued to use their opposition to the amendments as an excuse for various types of radical street protests. The violence involved has escalated and the damage to society has grown. The movement has gone way beyond free assembly and peaceful protests. It is posing a severe challenge to law and order in Hong Kong, threatening the safety of the lives and property of the Hong Kong people, undermining prosperity and stability in Hong Kong and challenging the principled bottom line of "One Country, Two Systems". As a result, Hong Kong now faces the gravest situation since its handover.

A handful of extreme radicals have been undermining the rule of law, social order and "One Country, Two Systems" in Hong Kong. But they have taken cover under the so-called "pro-democracy movement" to hide their real intention and to whitewash their disruptive actions. This "neo-extremism" is both highly deceptive and destructive. The "neo-extremists" stormed the Legislative Council Complex, attacked the Liaison Office of the Central People's Government in Hong Kong, assaulted police officers and brought Hong Kong airport to a standstill by illegal assembly. Their moves constitute severe and violent offences, and already show signs of terrorism. The Central Government of China will never allow a few violent offenders to drag Hong Kong down into a dangerous abyss. We will never allow anyone to harm the rule of law and sound development in Hong Kong. We will never allow anyone to undermine "One Country, Two Systems" for any reason. Should the situation in Hong Kong deteriorate further in that the unrest becoming uncontrollable for the Government of the Hong Kong Special Administrative Region (SAR), the Central Government will not sit on its hands and watch. We have enough solutions and enough power within the limits of the Basic Law to quell any unrest swiftly.

This is a critical moment for Hong Kong. How will this end? This question is on the minds of all those who care about the future of Hong Kong. It is also hitting headlines and making "cover stories" in the British media. Our answer to this question is firm and clear: We hope this will end in an orderly way. In the meantime, we are fully prepared for the worst. So how will this end in an orderly way? I think the following four points are extremely important.

First, the priority now is to support the SAR Government in ending violence and restoring order. I hope that the people of Hong Kong, especially the young people who have been led astray, will have a clear understanding of the current situation in Hong Kong and cherish the sound development of Hong Kong after the handover, which does not come about easily. I hope they will keep the big picture in mind, rally behind the Chief Executive and the SAR Government, uphold the rule of law and justice in Hong Kong, and safeguard national unification as well as Hong Kong's prosperity and stability. The people of Hong Kong from all walks of life must refuse to be used or coerced by radical forces. They should say "no" to all violence and lawlessness. They should support the SAR Government in governing Hong Kong in accordance with law, and support the Hong Kong police in their strict and rigorous enforcement.

Second, the violent offenders must be brought to justice in accordance with the law. It is the basic requirement of the rule of law that all laws must be observed and all offenders must be held accountable. The violent and lawless perpetrators must be brought to justice no matter who they are or however hard they try to whitewash their actions. If anyone in this country questions this point, let me ask them this: Would the UK allow extremists to storm the Palace of Westminster or damage its facilities, and get away with it? Would the UK grant permission to attack police officers with lethal weapons or set fire to the police station without any punishment? Would the UK allow so-called "pro-democracy" rioters to occupy on airport, obstruct traffic, disturb public order or threaten the safety of people's lives and property? Aren't all these regarded as crimes in the UK?

Indulging lawlessness is tantamount to blaspheming against justice. Conniving in violence is tantamount to trampling on the rule of law. No country under the rule of law, no responsible government, would sit by and watch as such violence rages on. The Central Government of China firmly supports the SAR Government and the Hong Kong police in their strict, rigorous and decisive enforcement, so as to bring the offenders to justice as soon as possible and uphold the rule of law and public order in Hong Kong.

Third, foreign forces must stop interfering in Hong Kong's affairs. Evidence shows that the situation in Hong Kong would not have deteriorated so much had it not been for the interference and incitement of foreign forces. Some Western politicians and organizations have publicly or covertly given various types of support to the violent radicals, and tried to interfere in the judicial independence of Hong Kong and obstruct the Hong Kong police from bringing the violent offenders to justice.

I want to reiterate here that Hong Kong is a part of China; no foreign country should interfere in Hong Kong affairs. We urge those foreign forces to respect China's sovereignty and security, to immediately stop interfering in Hong Kong affairs, to stop interfering in China's internal affairs, and to stop conniving with violent offences. They should not misjudge the situation and head down the wrong path. Otherwise, they will "lift the stone only to drop it on their own feet".

Fourth, the media must shoulder due social responsibilities. Since these events in Hong Kong, I have to say, the Western media has failed to play a credible role. Instead of reporting the situation in a just and objective manner, they have confused right and wrong, given unbalanced accounts and misled the public. There has been extensive coverage of the so-called "right to peaceful protest" but few reports on the violent offences committed by the extreme radicals. For instance, the disruption to public order, attacks on police officers and injuries to bystanders. There has not been a word about the extensive public support for the SAR Government and for restoring law and order in Hong Kong. The lawless and violent offenders who undermine the rule of law are whitewashed and named "pro-democracy activists" in media reports. But the legitimate law enforcement measures of the SAR Government and the police aimed at upholding law and order and protecting the lives and property of the people are labeled "repression".

Such selective reporting and distortion have resulted in the prevalence of misinformation and have misled the public, especially young people in Hong Kong. It is fair to say that the Western media has an inescapable responsibility for the current situation in Hong Kong!

I sincerely hope that the Western media will reflect on the social impact of their reporting, shoulder due social responsibility, and report the situation in Hong Kong in a just and objective manner. I hope they will stop speaking up for the extreme violent offenders, refrain from pouring oil over the flame in Hong Kong, and foster a sound environment of public opinion so that law and order can be restored in Hong Kong.

To help you understand the fourth point that I have just made, I would like to show a short video clip, so that you can see some scenes and hear some voices that are absent in the Western media.

(Video clip is played.)

"Order fosters prosperity while unrest brews regression." Given what is happening in Hong Kong, this ancient Chinese teaching could not be more relevant.

It is in the interests of both China and the international community, including the UK, to have a prosperous and stable Hong Kong, where over three hundred thousand British citizens live and work, and where three hundred British companies are doing business.

I sincerely hope that people from all walks of life in the UK will have a clear understanding of the big picture, act in the interests of Hong Kong's prosperity and stability, and refrain from saying or doing anything that interferes in Hong Kong's affairs or undermines the rule of law in Hong Kong. I am confident that with the support of the Central Government of China and under the leadership of the SAR Government and Chief Executive Carrie Lam, Hong Kong will bring violence to an end and restore law and order at an early date. Hong Kong, the "oriental pearl", will once again shine brightly.

Now I would like to take your questions.

Bloomberg: I noticed that there was one moment in the clip when one of the speakers pointed out that the Hong Kong police were not using live ammunition. There have been armed personnel carriers and troops, shown on social media and TV, just outside Hong Kong. If they were to be deployed at some point as you suggest is possible, would they use live ammunition? Would they be entitled to use it?

Liu Xiaoming: I will answer your question in this way. I think the Hong Kong situation has reached a very critical moment. But we have full trust and confidence in the Chief Executive and the Government of the Hong Kong Special Administration Region in handling the situation and bringing it to an end in an orderly way. As I said in my opening remarks, if the situation deteriorates further into unrest that is uncontrollable for the SAR Government, the Central Government will not sit by and watch. We have enough solutions and enough power to put it to an end and to quell the unrest swiftly.

CNN: We have a message from President Trump saying that he is willing to discuss this situation with President Xi Jinping. Has there been any response yet to this suggestion? If it is being considered, will it help to resolve the situation?

Liu Xiaoming: I don't think President Trump proposed formally to have a meeting with President Xi Jinping. I think he tweeted to express his views on Hong Kong. Hong Kong is a ongoing subject between China and Western governments, including the UK and the United States. We are open to discussion. But the important thing to remember is that we do not accept any interference in Hong Kong's internal affairs. We believe it is purely China's internal affairs. We strongly oppose any foreign intervention, including foreign organizations giving financial support and some Congressmen proposing a so-called "Hong Kong Human Rights and Democracy Act". In particular, we are opposed to foreign officials making telephone calls to the SAR Government and exerting pressure by publicly showing their support for the rioters. We strongly oppose this.

Reuters: I noticed that you said in your opening remarks that the behaviour of some of the protesters shows some signs of terrorism. I wonder whether you'd mind explaining to us what would be the red line or turning point over which this would constitute terrorism? Would that then provide, under Chinese Law, a legal justification for the deployment of Chinese forces in Hong Kong?

Liu Xiaoming: From both the video clip and also what is happening in Hong Kong, especially what is happening at the airport, the atrocities have already drawn worldwide condemnation. Many media outlets regarded them as terrorist acts. They are no different from terrorism. They are attacking the police, attacking travelers, even attacking journalists, including one of your colleagues from China. We heard strong condemnation from the Chinese Association of Journalists on this kind of attack. These are signs of terrorism. I would call it neo-extremism. If this goes any further, it might become a terrorist action.

Even if it becomes a terrorist action, I still hope that the Hong Kong SAR Government and the Hong Kong police can handle the situation. What I am saying is that if the situation deteriorates into unrest that is uncontrollable for Hong Kong SAR Government, the Central Government will certainly not sit by and watch.

Russia Today: According to reports, the National Endowment for Democracy in the US has been funding some of Hong Kong protesters. Has Beijing concluded that the Hong Kong protests are entirely a US plot to destabilize China?

Liu Xiaoming: I think you've already partly answered the question. We believe there is a "dark hand" behind this radical movement. As I mentioned in my opening statement, some foreign forces including foreign organizations provided financial support and moral support to the radical movement. In particular, some foreign officials met the leaders of the Hong Kong independence group. This clearly showed that their intention is to make Hong Kong a problem for China, to use Hong Kong to contain China, to prevent China from developing smoothly and to prevent China from becoming a prosperous country. That's for sure! That's why I am saying, in order to end the chaotic situation in Hong Kong in an orderly way, it is very important for the foreign forces to stop interfering further in Hong Kong's affairs, including the activities you have mentioned.

The Times: I wonder if you could respond to the suggestion of the Chairman of the Foreign Affairs Committee that full British citizenship be extended to all Hong Kong citizens. Would China regard that as a provocation?

Liu Xiaoming: I think where some politicians in this country are concerned, although their bodies live in the 21st century, their heads are still in the colonial days. I think some of them still regard Hong Kong as a part of the British Empire. They treat Hong Kong as a part of UK. That's the problem. I think they really have to change their mindsets, place them in the proper position, and regard Hong Kong as a part of China, not a part of the UK.

ITV: You said earlier that Beijing is fully prepared for the worst. Can you clarify exactly what that means? And also people see some satellite images of troops and tanks assembled in Shenzhen. Is this a means of intimidation or is Chinese military action a very real possibility, or even imminent?

Liu Xiaoming: I have already answered this question in my opening statement. The first part concerns the kind of situation where resolute solutions should be needed. I said, if the situation deteriorates further into unrest that is controllable for the Hong Kong SAR Government, then the Central Government will not sit by and watch. And we have enough solutions and enough power to quell the unrest swiftly. If you listen to my remarks word for word, you would get the answer to your question.

ITV: What exactly does "quell" mean though? How would you quell the protests?

Liu Xiaoming: To put them to an end. Thank you.

Sky News: You talked about how Beijing has the power to deal with this problem. Could you give us a sense of the scale of forces you have available to deploy into Hong Kong if necessary? Are they properly trained to deal with what is a civilian uprising, civilian unrest, as opposed to the military problem? And then secondly if I may, this is your second press conference. Last time, we had a different prime minister. Now we've got Prime Minister Boris Johnson. Last time, you said the relations between Beijing and London had been damaged by, for example, our then Foreign Secretary's comments on Hong Kong. What are the relations like now? Are the relations better or maybe healed between the UK and China? Or are they still being damaged? What is your message for the Prime Minister?

Liu Xiaoming: To answer your first question, I think I have already answered your question. First of all, this is a hypothetical question. Currently, we still believe that the Hong Kong SAR Government is capable of doing their job. The Chief Executive is a very capable leader, who enjoys broad respect and support in Hong Kong. So, at this moment, I think they are still handling it very well. We have full trust. We are confident and we have enough solutions and enough power to put this to an end swiftly.

With regard to your second question, we certainly would like to see relations develop further because we believe it's in the interests of China and the UK to have a sound relationship. Of course I didn't expect you to have a new prime minister so soon. So I need to be careful with my press conference. I do not hope that at the next press conference we will be talking about yet another prime minister.

This is the fourth prime minister I'm going to work with. We have expectations. We do hope our relationship will move along the lines of the direction of Golden Era set by President Xi during his state visit. But a good relationship has to be based on the basic principles of mutual respect for sovereignty and territorial integrity, and non-interference in each other's internal affairs. This much was enshrined in the Joint Communiqué on establishing diplomatic relations between our two countries. As long as these principles are followed, the relationship will move forward. When these principles are violated, the relationship will suffer setbacks. So we do hope that the new administration will handle with great caution the Hong Kong issue, which concerns China's sovereignty, which concerns China's territorial integrity, which concerns China's internal affairs. Thank you.

The Guardian: What is your definition of "uncontrollable"? What would you be looking for to define when the situation has become uncontrollable?

Liu Xiaoming: Do you think we have to consult the Oxford English Dictionary for what "uncontrollable" means? Uncontrollable means out of control. We do hope that the situation will remain under control of the SAR Government and the Chief Executive. I believe the current situation is still under control.

BBC Radio 4: Ambassador, you painted the protesters as violent and as extremists. Can I ask you whether you would acknowledge that for every violent or extremist protester, there are many ordinary citizens in Hong Kong—lawyers and civil servants—who are deeply disappointed by what is happening on the Chinese government side, and support the idea that people should have more say in their own administration, and support the fifth demand of the protesters—universal suffrage? Would you acknowledge that there are many people who are not violent or extremist protesters? Can you remind us and the people of Hong Kong why China finds it so objectionable to give them universal suffrage? If I may ask a second question, does China still regard the Joint Declaration signed with Britain in 1984 as applying to and constraining its behavior in Hong Kong?

Liu Xiaoming: Evan, I haven't seen you for quite a while since I last went on your programme. Your first question is about the demonstrators. We certainly have acknowledged the difference between the young people and the radical violent offenders. A few radicals do not represent the majority of the demonstrators. The majority of them have been misled. I think the Hong Kong media has some responsibility here and Western media has some responsibility too.

In any society you have all kinds of complaints. Since Hong Kong's handover, enormous achievements and progress have been made under "One Country, Two Systems". But there is still a lot of room for improvement, such as how young people can advance in their careers. There are many problems in the Hong Kong economy. The Hong Kong economy has depended too much on financial services and real estate, which offers few opportunities to young people. So they have complaints. We understand. The Central Government and the SAR Government have tried very hard to address these problems. We have launched the Guangdong-Hong Kong-Macao Greater Bay Area Development Project. That will give the young people of Hong Kong more opportunities.

If you compare Hong Kong with Shenzhen across the river, it's quite a contrast. In the space of 30 years, Shenzhen has been transformed into a dynamic city full of vigor with many young people, a lot of high-tech and new technology companies like Huawei, Tencent and Dajiang, and many top world-class companies. What world-class high-tech companies can you find in Hong Kong? To address these problems, we have to focus on development. Demonstrations offer no solution. Chaotic situations will only cause young people to suffer more. We will certainly address the concerns of the young people. We certainly understand the difference between the young people who have been misled, who have been led astray as I said, and those radical violent offenders.

Your second question is about the Joint Declaration. I think some people often confuse "One Country, Two Systems" with the Joint Declaration. The Joint Declaration has completed its mission. Its main mission was to ensure the smooth handover of Hong Kong from the UK to China. And it was also its mission to ensure a 13-year smooth transition period between 1984, when China and the UK agreed on the handover and 1997. And that was its main mission. Yes, the Joint Declaration mentioned "One Country, Two Systems". But that is a national policy announced by the Chinese Government. It is incorporated in the Basic Law of Hong Kong. So when we say China is committed to the Basic Law and "One Country, Two Systems" for 50 years, we are not saying we are committed to the Joint Declaration for 50 years.

About universal suffrage, the Central Government is committed to universal suffrage. We believe this is the final aim of political reform in Hong Kong. But it has to proceed in an orderly way and it has to suit the conditions of Hong Kong. If it had not been for the opposition in Hong Kong in 2015, the Legislative Council would have passed a law on universal suffrage. They killed this law and held up the process. There are so many things that are not known by the Western public.

BBC: You talked about there being no place for foreign interference in China's internal affairs. Does that mean the present British government is interfering in internal affairs when it calls for dialogue to end the crisis in Hong Kong? Is one of the solutions that you would examine carefully to find a way through this to move beyond mere suspension of the extradition law? Would you be prepared to move to full withdrawal, one of the basic points raised by the protesters? My second question is about the potential use of force. You said China will use whatever means necessary to quell the protests.

Liu Xiaoming: Not the protest. To quell the unrest.

BBC: If you were to employ the Chinese army in Hong Kong, do you accept that it would have the effect of destroying the "Two Systems" and Hong Kong's autonomy, and do great damage to China because it will suffer economically and in trade as a result?

Liu Xiaoming: I think you have asked three questions and I am trying to remember them all. Maybe the last question first. As I said, we have enough solutions and enough power to put this to an end swiftly. By doing this, we are to be exact defending "One Country, Two Systems". Some of the radical forces call for the independence of Hong Kong. They want to use Hong Kong to infiltrate the Mainland, to disrupt the socialist system in the Mainland. So in both ways, they undermine "One Country, Two Systems". When we talk about "One Country, Two Systems", people have to be aware that it's a complete whole. "One Country" means that Hong Kong is part of China and China has sovereignty over Hong Kong. "One Country" is the precondition for "Two Systems". Without "One Country", there will be no "Two Systems". So, the two are one complete whole. We can't emphasize one at the expense of the other. I think what China is going to do—to put the situation under control—is exactly for the purpose of maintaining "One Country, Two Systems".

About the telephone conversation, as I said, we are open to discussions on Hong Kong. But the important thing is that you can't use telephone conversation to exert pressure on the SAR Government. For instance, you are saying that you are concerned about the police's excessive use of force and you condemn the violence on both sides. That is not fair. You can't give a 50-50. You confuse right and wrong. If you condemn things that are right, you certainly support things that are wrong. The important thing is the nature of the conversation, whether it constitutes an intervention or not. British politicians are visiting Hong Kong all the time. We show no objection to them. But if you make a comment that is interfering in the judicial independence of Hong Kong, you are trying to obstruct it. Just like some politicians have said before, one cannot punish those radicals and violent offenders. It just obstructs the legal system in Hong Kong. That cannot be accepted at all.

We have expressed our concerns about some of the comments by British politicians. I really hope that they change their mindset and keep the big picture in mind. A prosperous and stable Hong Kong is really in the interest of the UK, not only in the interests of Hong Kong and China.

About the withdrawal of the bill. You know the bill has been suspended by the SAR Government. Whether it will be withdrawn is up to the Hong Kong SAR Government to decide. The Chief Executive promised to have further communication and discussions with the public and various sectors in Hong Kong. From the very beginning in my first press conference, I said this is a good bill. I think the intension is to improve the legal system of Hong Kong It serves the interest of Hong Kong. It will make Hong Kong a safe haven of justice rather than a safe haven for fugitives, but it was not well understood. So it might take time for the SAR Government to explain their position, to convince the public that it is in Hong Kong's interest to pass this bill.

BBC Newsnight: In the video, you showed a journalist at the airport surrounded by protesters. You didn't show the other guy surrounded by protesters who turned out to be a law enforcement official from Shenzhen not wearing uniform. How many other such Mainland law enforcement officials are currently operating in Hong Kong?

Liu Xiaoming: Your information is not what I know. Yesterday, an ordinary traveller was rounded up by the rioters at the airport. He was from Shenzhen and he came to the airport to see off a friend. The other one was a journalist from China, who was tied up. Some people regarded him as a police officer, but he turned out to be a journalist who has now been named, a registered journalist.

CGTN: My first question is that, as the violence escalates, the Hong Kong police response will inevitably escalate. We all know what the Hong Kong police are experiencing these days. In other countries, it equates to aggravated assault which will be dealt with seriously. But why are they still the target of blames in some of the media, in most of the Western media, even when they are being so restrained? My second question is that yesterday, some British companies were warned to evaluate the risks to investment in Hong Kong. More than 28 countries have been notified to issue different levels of warnings to travelers to Hong Kong. Analysts say that currently this is a kind of a turning point for Hong Kong's economy. So what is your view?

Liu Xiaoming: I think you are absolutely right in talking about the behavior of the Hong Kong police. I think they exercise their duty with great restraint, more so than in many other countries. They are very professional and have won the praise of their counterparts from many countries, including the US, Canada, and France. You know, if things like this happen in the Western countries, the police will deal with them with much more force.

That reminds me of something just a few months ago, in June. When the Extinction Rebellion applied to put up a demonstration in Heathrow Airport, they were warned by the British police that those involved would face a life sentence and were urged to reconsider. We've all watched how the British police handled the riot in London. And I don't need to remind you of what kind of force they used.

On the Hong Kong economy. Yes, it suffered. What is happening in Hong Kong really damaged the international image and reputation of Hong Kong. It's very sad. Hong Kong is a very safe place. Its rule of law rating is very high. In terms of the Project of Justice index, it places three positions higher than the United States last year. It ranked 16th while the United States ranked 19th. I'm talking about law and order, not safety. On safety matters, Hong Kong is much safer than the other Western cities.

Of course, we all read that the Hang Seng stock has fallen 9% and the Hong Kong dollar has fallen. It's very sad. I think people, as I said in my opening remarks, should treasure the hard-won development of Hong Kong. I do hope common sense will prevail in Hong Kong. I just heard many statements yesterday from business leaders. They've kept quiet for some time, but now they are speaking out. They realized what kind of damage this chaos in Hong Kong may do to the city, to the prosperity and stability of Hong Kong.

Reuters: Thank you for taking a second question. Earlier when my colleague from the BBC asked about the extradition bill, you said it's up to the Hong Kong SAR Government to decide whether it will be withdrawn or not. Just to be completely clear, if Carrie Lam and the Hong Kong SAR Government decided to withdraw the bill fully, would the Central Government of China allow them to do so?

Liu Xiaoming: At the very beginning, many people thought that this move came under the orders or instruction of the Central Government. That was not true. This initiative is completely the decision of the Hong Kong administration.

Chief Executive Carrie Lam has said on many occasions that she received no order or instruction from the Central Government to launch this process. She decided to suspend it and we showed respect, understanding and support. So I hope you will keep in mind the three words I gave you: respect, understanding and support. And I think that we will continue to do this further down the road.

Russia Today: As you know the trade war with the US is continuing and the US government has included Huawei in the list of entities. Do you think there is a chance that the US would do the same to Hong Kong, in terms of getting a fair world trade deal? How would Beijing respond?

Liu Xiaoming: The talks are still ongoing, and I personally feel cautiously optimistic about the future of China-US trade relations. A member of the Political Bureau of the CPC Central Committee and Director of the Office of the Foreign Affairs Commission of the CPC Central Committee Yang Jiechi is in New York and has had a talk with Secretary Pompeo. They had a very candid discussion on bilateral relations, including trade issues.

On Hong Kong, China will never compromise its principles for a trade deal. We will not barter away our principles. It's purely China's internal affairs which brook no foreign intervention, no matter which country it comes from.

Bloomberg: The entire Hong Kong business community would agree with you when you said that the unrest has been very bad for the economy, bad for Hong Kong's position as a global financial centre. And yet many would also argue that if the Chinese Central Government were to intervene directly, that could be even worse. Do you not think that the position you laid out here, should allow more space for engagement with the protesters, in the interest of, as you said, maintaining stability, economic well being and the international image of Hong Kong?

Liu Xiaoming: Let me ask you this. If Hong Kong's situation becomes uncontrollable and unrest goes on and on, will it serve the interests of the business community in Hong Kong? Or if the Central Government intervenes with a resolute solution and puts an end to the unrest as quickly as possible, will that serve their interests? I think the answer would be the latter.

But that's an extreme situation. That is not a real situation. And we hope to see the situation end in an orderly way, which includes that the people should rally behind the Hong Kong SAR Government and rally behind the Chief Executive to support the Hong Kong SAR Government to put this to an end, to bring the violent and lawbreakers to justice, and to restore order. That is the top priority of Hong Kong today.

BBC Radio 4: Thank you for taking a second question. You draw a distinction between the violent protesters and nonviolent protesters. Can you unequivocally tell the people of Hong Kong that if the violence stops but peaceful protest continues, there is no way that the central Chinese authorities will intervene in the internal affairs of Hong Kong? It is only the violence that China will quell or stop.

Liu Xiaoming: I hope you will go back to my opening statement. I said that if the situation in Hong Kong deteriorates into unrest that is uncontrollable for the Hong Kong SAR Government, the Central Government will not sit by and watch. And we have enough solutions and power to quell the unrest swiftly in accordance with the Basic Law of Hong Kong. What you are talking about is a situation that is not happening. It is still under the control of the Hong Kong SAR Government.

BBC Radio 4: It may go beyond control?

Liu Xiaoming: That shows your lack of understanding of the situation. You have underestimated the capability of the Hong Kong SAR Government and the Hong Kong police. They are fully prepared and equipped to handle peaceful demonstration—but it has to be peaceful.

CNN: Thank you for taking a second question. You talked about how patient you've been right now, and you were suggesting that you have the resources and solutions to quell it swiftly. What sort of timeline we are looking at? Let's suppose by this time next week, do you think the Hong Kong SAR Government will be able to resolve the crisis by itself? Or we will still be having this conversation next week?

Liu Xiaoming: As I said, we have full trust in the Hong Kong SAR

Government and its Chief Executive, with the strong support of the Central Government. I hope they will put an end to the unrest at an early date, as soon as possible and restore order. Maybe we do not need another press conference. We'll see.

Thank you.

What Would Be the Way out for Hong Kong?

——The Third Press Conference on the Situation in Hong Kong

On 18th November 2019, I held a press conference at the Chinese Embassy expounding China's principles and position on the escalating violence in Hong Kong. About 50 journalists from 22 media agencies attended the press conference, including BBC, ITV, Sky News, Channel 4, *Financial Times*, *The Daily Telegraph*, *The Guardian*, Reuters, Xinhua News Agency, CCTV, China News Service, CGTN, *China Daily*, *Science and Technology Daily*, *Global Times*, AFP, RT, Phoenix Infonews, the *South China Morning Post*, *European Times*, *UK Chinese Times*, and the *UK Chinese Journal*. The following is the transcript of the press conference.

Liu Xiaoming: Good morning! Welcome to the Chinese Embassy.

This is the third press conference that I have held on the Hong Kong question. In the past five months, the incident arising from the relevant amendments has evolved into incessant violence. The recent escalation of illegal, violent activities has pushed Hong Kong into an extremely dangerous situation.

Those who truly care about Hong Kong would ask these questions:

- What is happening in Hong Kong?
- How shall we see the current chaos?
- What would be the way out?

Four days ago, during the 11th BRICS Summit in Brazil, President Xi Jinping made clear the solemn position of the Chinese Government on the situation in Hong Kong. He said,

"The incessant extreme violent offences in Hong Kong trampled on the rule of law, disrupted public order, severely undermined the prosperity and stability in Hong Kong, and gravely challenged the bottom line of 'One Country, Two

Systems'."

He pointed out: "The top priority for Hong Kong is to end violence and restore order. We will continue to firmly support the SAR Government under the leadership of the Chief Executive in governing Hong Kong in accordance with the law. We firmly support the Hong Kong police in their strict and rigorous enforcement of the law. We firmly support the judicial institutions of Hong Kong in bringing violent offenders to justice in accordance with the law."

He further emphasized: "The Chinese Government remains unwavering in its determination to safeguard China's national sovereignty, security and development interests, implement 'One Country, Two Systems', and oppose any interference from external forces in Hong Kong affairs."

This important statement represents the most authoritative voice from the Central Government of China on the current situation and future of Hong Kong. Every word carries weight.

First, President Xi Jinping's speech reveals the nature and severe consequences of the extreme violent offences.

The current situation in Hong Kong has nothing to do with the so-called "democracy"or "freedom". The nature of the issue is that extreme violent offenders have disrupted law and order in Hong Kong, have attempted to destabilize Hong Kong and undermine "One Country, Two Systems". Their activities are extreme, violent and illegal.

These extreme violent offences have trampled on the rule of law and disrupted public order in Hong Kong.

For the past five months, the self-labeled "peaceful protesters" have resorted to senseless beating, smashing and arson; they have carried out premeditated attacks against police officers and made a failed assassination attempt on a member of the Legislative Council; and they have turned many universities into their strongholds and besieged and attacked students from the Chinese Mainland.

While claiming they stand with the weak, the rioters have indiscriminately hurt ordinary citizens and even doused a citizen who opposed their vandalism with flammable liquid and set fire to him.

While claiming they safeguard democracy and freedom, the rioters have restricted or even deprived others of personal freedom and freedom of speech.

Such inhuman, murderous violence in broad daylight tramples on the bottom lines of law, morality and civilization and must not be tolerated!

The anti-China extremists have also taken such violence abroad and into the UK. Some of them, wearing black masks, created trouble in front of the Chinese Embassy in the UK. They defaced the Embassy gate and painted "Hong Kong independence" slogans on both sides of the gate. Some besieged the Secretary for Justice of the Hong Kong SAR, who was invited to an event in London. She was pushed to the ground and sustained arm injury.

We express the strongest indignation and condemnation over these violent acts!

The extreme violent offences have severely undermined prosperity and stability in Hong Kong.

Hong Kong is known for its free and open economy, inclusive and diverse culture, professional and efficient management, and law-abiding and safe society.

But today,

• Hong Kong citizens live under the "black terror" created by violent extremists, with their life and property being under severe threat.

• Hong Kong's GDP, after contracting for two quarters in a row, shrank by 2.9% year-on-year in the third quarter. It is now in a technical recession. The Office of the Government Economist of the Hong Kong SAR revised down its growth forecast for the full-year to minus 1.3%.

• Hong Kong's international rating has been downgraded. Its international image and business environment are being severely impacted.

In media reports, Hong Kong is now associated with incessant violence and disorder. The success and achievements of the past 22 years since the handover are being eroded. The one time "oriental pearl" is turning into an "oriental scar". Hong Kong the "fragrant harbour" is sliding into "an abyss of chaos". The future of Hong Kong, if such a situation continues, will be unimaginably dreadful.

The extreme violent offences have challenged the principled bottom line of "One Country, Two Systems".

The opposition and the violent extremists in Hong Kong have advocated "Hong Kong independence" and publicly clamoured for the "liberation of Hong Kong".

This reveals their true, sinister political agenda behind the so-called public petition. They are actually aiming to undermine "One Country", which is the basis of "One Country, Two Systems". They attempt to destabilize Hong Kong and paralyze the SAR Government, so that they could seize administrative power and separate Hong Kong from the motherland.

"One Country, Two Systems" is one complete concept. "One Country" is the precondition and basis of "Two Systems". Without "One Country", "Two Systems" will no longer exist. Violent offences that undermine "One Country, Two Systems" will never be tolerated.

Second, President Xi Jinping's speech points to a way out for ending the chaos in Hong Kong, namely, the top priority for Hong Kong is to end the violence and restore order.

The basic requirement of the rule of law is that laws must be observed and offenders must be brought to justice. No society would in any way tolerate or indulge extreme violence.

To restore law and order, violence must end and violent perpetrators must be brought to justice. This is the only way to safeguard the interests of the public, ensure a better future for Hong Kong, and cement the foundation of "One Country, Two Systems".

The SAR Government, the police and the judicial institutions of Hong Kong should be given strong support in upholding the rule of law, and in taking forceful measures to curb and combat all types of violent offences and terrorist activities. We firmly support them in bringing the offenders to justice as soon as possible, and in safeguarding the rule of law and public order, so as to bring stability to Hong Kong and tranquillity to the people.

Third, President Xi Jinping's speech demonstrates the strong determination of the Chinese Government to safeguard national sovereignty, security and development interests and implement "One Country, Two Systems".

At the fourth plenary session of the 19th Central Committee of the Communist Party of China concluded last month, it was reiterated that "One Country, Two Systems" is an important policy of the Communist Party of China in leading the Chinese people to realise the peaceful reunification of the motherland.

The Chinese Government will continue to implement fully and faithfully "One Country, Two Systems", "the Hong Kong people administering Hong Kong", and a high degree of autonomy. For this formula to work in Hong Kong, there are three bottom lines, namely, no tolerance for any activity that,

One, undermines national sovereignty and security;

Two, challenges the authority of the Central Government or the Basic Law;

and, three, uses Hong Kong for infiltration or sabotage against the Chinese

Mainland.

At the same time,

• The Chinese Government will improve the system of overall jurisdiction over Hong Kong in accordance with the Constitution and the Basic Law.

• We will also improve the arrangements for Hong Kong to integrate into the overall development of the country, match complementary strengths with the Mainland and achieve coordinated development.

• And we will work to address deep-seated problems hampering social stability and long-term development.

Fourth, President Xi Jinping's speech shows the firm resolve of the Chinese government to oppose external interference in Hong Kong affairs.

External forces that have indulged and fanned violence in Hong Kong cannot absolve themselves of the responsibility for the recent escalation of violence in Hong Kong. They confuse right and wrong, and refer to the extreme violent offenders as "peaceful demonstrators" and "pro-democracy protesters". At the same time, they are piling blame on the Hong Kong police who are performing their duty, safeguarding the rule of law and protecting the safety of life and property of Hong Kong citizens.

Some Western countries have publicly supported the extreme violent offenders.

• The US House of Representatives adopted the so-called "Hong Kong Human Rights and Democracy Act" to blatantly interfere in Hong Kong affairs, which are China's internal affairs.

• The British Government and the Foreign Affairs Committee of the House of Commons published China-related reports, making irresponsible remarks on Hong Kong.

• What is worse, certain British politicians even planned to present an award to a chief propagandist for "Hong Kong independence" who has instigated extreme violence.

• To those who question external interference in Hong Kong affairs, aren't these facts enough to address their doubt?

We would like to tell these external forces solemnly that the Chinese Government remains unwavering in its resolve to oppose any external interference in Hong Kong affairs! We urge these forces to immediately stop any form of interference in Hong Kong affairs and in China's internal affairs, and immediately stop condoning violent offences. Otherwise, they will lift the stone only to drop it on their own feet!

Just as we did at my last press conference, we have made a short video clip to help you see the extreme violent offences in Hong Kong. This will show you the true face of the so-called "peaceful demonstrators" and "pro-democracy protesters", and how dangerous the situation in Hong Kong has become.

(Play video clip.)

After watching this clip, I hope you will agree with me that the facts and truth will prevail.

I have said to the British people from all walks of life on many occasions that a prosperous and stable Hong Kong under "One Country, Two Systems" is in the interests of both China and the world including the UK. There are 300,000 British citizens and more than 700 British companies in Hong Kong. Continued chaos in Hong Kong will bring nothing but harm to the UK.

I sincerely hope that the British people will keep the larger picture in mind and have a clear understanding of the current situation. I hope they will support the SAR Government in ending violence, restoring order and upholding the rule of law, resist and oppose any words or deeds that interfere in Hong Kong affairs, and do more things that are conducive to the prosperity and stability in Hong Kong, so that chaos will end as soon as possible and the "oriental pearl" will shine brightly once again.

Now I would like to take your questions.

BBC: I wrote an email to you this week, actually, about the labour camps in Xinjiang. Why won't you tell me the truth about those camps?

Liu Xiaoming: You jump to Xinjiang. Please sit down. I'll answer your question. First of all, I would say there are no so-called labour camps, as you described. There are what we call the vocational education and training centres. They are there for the prevention of terrorism.

BBC: I have seen the orders sent to camps. They changed the way people behave, and the language they speak. So they are brainwashing camps.

Liu Xiaoming: That's disinformation. Xinjiang is a very beautiful, very peaceful and prosperous region in China. But it had become a battleground. You know, thousands of terrorist incidents happened in Xinjiang between 1990s and

2016. Thousands of innocent people were killed. So there's been an enormous uproar among the people of Xinjiang for the government to take resolute measures to tackle this issue. So since the measures have been taken, there's not been a single terrorist incident in the past three years. Xinjiang has again turned back into a prosperous, beautiful and peaceful region. If the same thing happened in the United Kingdom, would you—let me ask you this: if a certain region had rampant terrorist extremist activities, and people suffered severely and called for actions from the UK government, what would you do?

And remember what we're doing, what we here called "preventative measures", have nothing to do with the eradication of religious groups. You know, religious freedom is fully respected. I hope that in the future you'll have an opportunity to visit Xinjiang. You will see with your own eyes what is happening in Xinjiang, and see that the people enjoy freedom, enjoy a prosperous life. You know, in Xinjiang there are about 28,000 religious sites and 30,000 clergymen. There is one mosque for every 530 Muslims in Xinjiang, many more than a lot of Muslim countries in terms of ratio, many more than here in Britain. So there's no such thing as the repression of freedom of religion. People enjoy full religious freedom. The purpose of setting up these training centres is because some young people have committed minor crimes that are not serious enough to be tried or for them to be sent to prison. The government gave them the opportunity to learn Mandarin. Uygur people have their own language, but if they want development, if they want to prosper, if they want to communicate with the other parts of the country, they need to have Mandarin language skills and also they need to learn some professional skills. Because you know, the lack of basic legal knowledge makes them vulnerable to extremist forces.

Mandarin is widely used. Language is just one of the courses. They also learn professional skills; they also learn legal knowledge, so that they can live off their own profession. That's the purpose. This measure has been successful. First, Xinjiang as I said is much safer. Last year, the number of tourists increased by 40%, and GDP increased more than 6%.

BBC: The documents that I've seen make it quite clear that people are held there without sentence, without even charge, and they will be there for at least a year before they are released.

Liu Xiaoming: I'm telling you the documents, the so-called documents you are talking about, are pure fabrication. If you want to see documents about this vocational education and training centre, we have many. We have her seven white papers published. So before you leave the Embassy, I hope you will take some documents, the official documents. Don't listen to fake news. Don't listen to fabrications.

Channel 4: Thank you Sir. If it's for young people, why are there so many elderly women and elderly men in the camps in Xinjiang that has been documented? I have talked to people who were in the camps. And, on Hong Kong, you talked about integration into the Mainland's development. With all that's happening in Hong Kong, is it your aim to integrate Hong Kong more into Mainland China to make it more "One Country, One System"?

Liu Xiaoming: I already said those students who are taking courses in the centre are those who have committed some minor crimes, not serious ones, not to be tried. So that's what I'm saying. So we want to give them better opportunities. We hope that they will not commit a serious crime that will put them in prison. That's the purpose. And it turned out this has been very successful. I think most of them are young people, and also some elderly people. Age is not a big issue. The issue is about their behaviour. Do they constitute a potential threat and risk to the society?

On Hong Kong, I think I said earlier in very clear-cut terms that the Chinese government is committed to "One Country, Two Systems".This policy has been reaffirmed by the Party during the Fourth Plenary Session of the 19th Central Committee and reiterated by the President on so many occasions including when we celebrated the 70th anniversary of the founding of the People's Republic of China. When we say "integration", we mean that the Mainland will provide more opportunities to Hong Kong. You know, especially in terms of economic development. You know this Greater Bay Area project that includes Guangdong, Hong Kong and Macau. It offers enormous opportunities. The opportunities will bring more development in Hong Kong that will address some deep-seated problems. You know, we all heard voices in the recent incidents in Hong Kong to address this disparity of the income, to address the problem of opportunities for young people, to make Hong Kong more prosperous. That's the basic idea. We will certainly continue with "One Country, Two Systems", which has been very successful. But what is happening now is "One Country, Two Systems" is being eroded by these violent extremist offenders. As I said in my opening statement, "One Country, Two Systems" is a complete concept. You can't separate the two. And "One Country" means Hong Kong is now part of China. Hong Kong has returned to China, it is part of China. Period. So we can't agree to external interference in Hong Kong affairs. So "One Country" is the precondition. It is the basis for "Two Systems". If "One Country" is undermined, there will be no "Two Systems".

South China Morning Post: Mr. Ambassador, just now you mentioned you urge the international community to support the SAR government in ending violence. What we've seen so far is the SAR government has not been successful in ending violence, and to the contrary, violence is escalating. May I ask if the deployment of PLA troops would be part of the Chinese government's consideration?

Liu Xiaoming: I would say the SAR government including Chief Executive herself has tried very hard to communicate with the local community and reached out to other citizens in Hong Kong. I think according to my count, they have held more than 100 events, engaging, communicating with local people, and I think they have tried very hard. You need to give them an opportunity. You need to give them time. But in order to have a civilized dialogue, you need to have a conducive environment. The current violent situation in Hong Kong is not conducive, is not favourable for the SAR government to have a serious, productive communication with local people. You can't put the cart before the horse.

With regard to the deployment of PLA, they are there, in the Hong Kong Garrison. They are there to safeguard China's sovereignty, security and territorial integrity and they are responsible for the security of Hong Kong. As I said in my previous press conference, we have full trust in the Hong Kong SAR government and the Chief Executive. When President Xi met the Chief Executive two weeks ago, he spoke highly of the performance of the SAR government, the Chief Executive and her team. We make full acknowledgement of their performance and express a high degree of trust in her and her team. So I think now the Hong Kong government is trying very hard to bring the situation under control. But if the situation becomes uncontrollable, the Central Government certainly will not sit on its hands and watch. We have enough solutions and enough power to end the violence.

South China Morning Post: And I have a second question if I may. Just a few days ago, Mr. Jasper Tsang, who used to be the Chairman of the Legislative Council of Hong Kong and a former Chairman of the DAB, the biggest pro-China party in Hong Kong, gave an interview and he supported the idea of pardoning those who committed a minor crime and launching an independent inquiry into the police. He is one of the most respected pro-China figures in Hong Kong. What do you think of his opinion?

Liu Xiaoming: I will leave this to the Hong Kong SAR government to handle and respect the independence of the judicial institutions in Hong Kong. I will not comment on the judicial procedures in Hong Kong. Thank you!

Sky News: You have kind of repeated what you said in your previous press conference in terms of that question about whether there will be PLA involvement, But what does "uncontrollable" chaos look like? It seems that we've had five months now, and it's not getting any better. Isn't the policy of allowing the Hong Kong authorities to deal with this actually failing and either there's going to have to be some serious compromises made and demands met of the protesters, or the Chinese government's going to have to actually get involved and send troops on the ground? And a second question. About Xinjiang, do you have a comment on *The New York Times*' reports over the weekend? It's released hundreds of documents. Thank you.

Liu Xiaoming: First question first. I think the Hong Kong government is still effective in dealing with the situation. But the important thing is, while the Hong Kong government is handling the situation, I would call on external forces to stop interfering in Hong Kong affairs. Stop inciting further violence. Stop adding fuel to the violence. We should respect the Hong Kong SAR government in governing Hong Kong in accordance with the law. Your second question is about *The New York Times*' so-called "report". I can categorically deny that there are such documents. Such a story is sheer, pure fabrication. And this is not the first time *The New York Times* has made up stories. I think the story was made up with ulterior motives, and it's not worth making any substantial comment on it. Thank you.

The Daily Telegraph: You've spoken about external forces fueling violence. You spoke about the true agenda being independence for Hong Kong among the protesters and then you talked about the British government, specifically the Foreign Affairs Select Committee. You keep talking about external forces inciting violence. Are you accusing the British government of inciting violence and promoting Hong Kong independence?

Liu Xiaoming: I will say that we have made our position known to the British side when they made irresponsible remarks on Hong Kong. I think that when the British government criticizes the Hong Kong police and criticizes the Hong Kong SAR government over their handling of the situation, they are interfering In China's internal affairs. And it looks like they are balanced, but as a matter of fact, they are taking sides. With regard to "independence", we appreciate the British government's position that they oppose Hong Kong independence. I think the senior officials said on several occasions that independence is not an option. Of course, I would like to see more strong condemnation of this so-called independence. That's number one. Number two, I hope the British side will live up to their words. So I said we do not want to see them merely pay lip service. I want to see them take actions against so-called Hong Kong "independence".

ITV News: We've just seen a sharp deterioration in the last 24 hours regarding the situation in Hong Kong. Are your words now some kind of warning that a crackdown may be imminent?

Liu Xiaoming: I'm not talking about crackdown. I think the Hong Kong police is carrying out their duties. Many people have complained about the Hong Kong police. But in my view, they are the most professional police force in the world. And they exercised great restraint. If similar things happened on a British campus, if similar things happened in the Palace of Westminster or its surrounding areas, what would you expect the British police to do? I'll leave you to answer that. But it is exactly because the Hong Kong police tried very hard to avoid casualties of the students who have been, I would say, "brainwashed" by some extremists that they have tried very hard. If it were not for this, we would probably have a different picture, a different situation.

The Guardian: Could I just ask you, given what's going on in Hong Kong at present, do you think it's feasible that the local elections can go ahead next week? And secondly, can you tell me why the Chinese government opposes the idea of British National Overseas passport holders being given a right of abode and a right to work permanently in the UK?

Liu Xiaoming: I will start with the last question. According to China's nationality law, all Hong Kong compatriots, born in Hong Kong, are regarded as Chinese nationals. And also in China, we do not recognize dual citizenship. So I think that's my answer to your last question. What is your first one? The election. We certainly would like to see the election go ahead. I think it's up to the Hong Kong SAR government. I do hope that the situation will improve and people will be able to go to the polls, without fear. I do hope that the order will be restored and people can have the freedom to select their council members. So that is certainly our hope.

BBC: Two questions, Mr. Ambassador. First of all, you showed us a very emotive edit of violence on the streets of Hong Kong, violent scenes that we've all seen on our TVs, on social media for months. What you didn't show us was any violence being committed against the protesters, violence which has been going on for months and started a long time before.

Liu Xiaoming: You are talking about the police?

BBC: I'm not actually just talking about the police. I'm talking about police, but I'm also talking about unknown groups of people, the famous "white shirts" who attacked people on the Hong Kong Metro back in the summer. In other words, the violence is occurring on both sides. And I just wondered whether you would acknowledge that there has been violence used on both sides, and that what we're seeing in some ways is a response to that process. And my second question is, back in 2008, slightly more people in Hong Kong saw themselves as "Chinese" than "Hongkonger". It was at the time of the Beijing Olympics. People expressed enormous pride. That number has gone down ever since to the point now where very, very few people describe themselves as "Chinese" and more and more people describe themselves as "Hongkonger". Are you worried that you are losing the faith, the trust, the citizenship if you like, of 7 million

Hongkongers?

Liu Xiaoming: First, I would say we are opposed to violence of all kinds. That's number one. Number two, you have to understand the cause of this violence. So if you do not understand the cause, you do not know how to handle it, so you do not know how to address this problem. I think these extreme forces, they are the starters of all violence. They should be brought to justice. And all the law breakers should be brought to justice. There can be no doubt that if you want to have rule of law in a city, in a society. With regard to the Hongkongers versus Mainlanders, I think people would reflect. I can't say we are going to lose a generation. You know these rioters do not represent the young generation, even the students. As I said, some of them do not understand the full picture. I think we have a responsibility to communicate with them to tell them about their motherland and what has changed since the handover. We should compare Hong Kong today with Hong Kong 22 years ago. When Hong Kong was under British colonial rule, it had no liberty, no freedom, and no rights. The governor of Hong Kong was appointed by the British government. But now Hong Kong has their fifth Chief Executive elected by the Hong Kong people. Even though the system is not perfect, as I said on many occasions, the largest room in the world is the room for improvement. We are open. We are committed to doing a better job to make Hong Kong a more beautiful, safe, and democratic place. Thank you.

It seems to me that time's up, and I have taken all the questions. Thank you for your attention.

Law is Beginning of Order

——An On-line Press Conference on the Law on Safeguarding National Security in the HKSAR

On 6th July 2020, I held an on-line press conference at the Chinese Embassy on the Law on Safeguarding National Security in the HKSAR.

Some 50 journalists from 33 media agencies attended, including BBC, BBC Radio 4, Sky News, Channel 4, ITV, *Financial Times*, *The Daily Telegraph*, *The Times*, *The Guardian*, *The Economist*, Reuters, Xinhua News Agency, *People's Daily*, CCTV, CGTN, CRI, China News Service, *China Daily*, AP, Bloomberg, NBC, CBS, AFP, RT, CBC, Phoenix Infonews, the *South China Morning Post*, *European Times*, *UK Chinese Times* and *UK Chinese Journal*. BBC, Sky News, and CGTN broadcast the press conference live.

The following is the transcript of the press conference.

Liu Xiaoming: Good morning! Welcome to today's press conference.

On June 30th, one day before the 23rd anniversary of Hong Kong's return to China, the Standing Committee of the National People's Congress adopted the Law of the People's Republic of China on Safeguarding National Security in the Hong Kong SAR. This law is now added to the list of laws in Annex III of the Basic Law. It will be applied by promulgation in Hong Kong SAR.

This law is an important milestone in the implementation of "One Country, Two Systems", because it provides powerful support for the steady and sustained implementation of "One Country, Two Systems" and it is a strong safeguard for the rights and freedoms of Hong Kong residents. It is of both practical and historic significance.

After the law was adopted, the British media carried massive reports and comments, which, to be frank, were full of misinterpretation, misunderstanding and even distortion.

Today, I want to use this press conference to help the British public understand this law comprehensively, objectively and accurately. I would like to begin by answering the five questions frequently asked by the British media.

Question one: Why is the National Security Law for the Hong Kong SAR necessary?

National security is the basis and precondition for prosperity and stability in Hong Kong. Article 23 of the Basic Law authorizes the Hong Kong SAR to enact laws on safeguarding national security. However, 23 years after Hong Kong's return, nothing has been done and there is no legal framework or enforcement mechanism in terms of national security in the Hong Kong SAR. As a result, the city is left "defenceless" against the anti-China forces seeking chaos and disruption.

Since the turbulence over the proposed amendment bill in June last year, these forces have openly clamoured for "Hong Kong independence" and "self-determination". They have taken actions such as beating, smashing, looting, arson, confronting police enforcement with violence, and storming the Legislative Council of the Hong Kong SAR. They have even called for "waging armed revolution to gain independence". Such activities trampled on rule of law, undermined social stability, hit the economy hard and put national security at serious risk.

The situation has been distressing for the people of Hong Kong. They cried out for the chaos to end quickly, for order to be restored and for Hong Kong to walk out of this desperation. In light of such a situation, establishing at the national level a sound legal framework and enforcement mechanism for safeguarding national security in the Hong Kong SAR meets people's aspiration. The National Security Law must be enforced without delay.

Question two: Does the National Security Law for Hong Kong SAR contravene "One Country, Two Systems"?

The answer is a definite "No". This law is not only in line with "One Country, Two Systems". It also ensures the sustained implementation of this policy.

The National Security Law for the Hong Kong SAR declares at the outset that:

It is enacted for the purpose of "ensuring the resolute, full and faithful implementation of the policy of 'One Country, Two Systems' under which the people of Hong Kong administer Hong Kong with a high degree of autonomy".

"One Country, Two Systems" is a complete concept. "One Country" is the precondition for "Two Systems". "Two Systems" is subordinate to and derived from "One Country". Only when "One Country" is safe and secure can "Two Systems" be safeguarded. What is the meaning of "One Country"? "One Country" not only embodies China's resumption of the exercise of sovereignty over Hong Kong. It also means that the Central Government has comprehensive jurisdiction over Hong Kong.

As is true in all countries, the Central Government is responsible for upholding national security. Through Article 23 of the Basic Law, the Central Government of China authorizes the Hong Kong SAR to enact laws on safeguarding national security. This authorization, however, does not change the fact that by it nature legislative power belongs ultimately to the Central Government. Nor does it prevent the Central Government from establishing a legal framework and enforcement mechanism for safeguarding national security in Hong Kong SAR.

In response to the activities that challenge and harm "One Country, Two Systems", the National Security Law for the Hong Kong SAR was enacted to safeguard the authority of "One Country" for the purpose of upholding and improving, rather than changing, "One Country, Two Systems".

Question three: Will the National Security Law for the Hong Kong SAR impair the high degree of autonomy in the SAR or the rights and freedom of the Hong Kong people?

The answer is again a definite "No".

The National Security Law fully integrates the comprehensive jurisdiction of the Central Government and the high degree of autonomy enjoyed by Hong Kong SAR:

• It does not alter the current capitalist system in Hong Kong.

• It does not change the high degree of autonomy or the legal system in the SAR.

• And it does not affect Hong Kong's administrative, legislative or independent judicial power, including that of final adjudication.

This Law clearly stipulates:

"Human rights shall be respected and protected in safeguarding national security in the Hong Kong Special Administrative Region. The rights and freedoms, including the freedoms of speech, of the press, of publication, of association, of assembly, of procession and of demonstration, which the residents of the Region enjoy under the Basic Law of the Hong Kong Special

Administrative Region and the provisions of the International Covenant on Civil and Political Rights and the International Covenant on Economic, Social and Cultural Rights as applied to Hong Kong, shall be protected in accordance with the law."

This Law outlined four types of criminal activities that jeopardize national security. They are: secession, subversion, terrorist activities and collusion with a foreign country or with external elements to endanger national security. The Law targets a very few criminals but protects the great majority of the Hong Kong people.

That is why, in only eight days, nearly three million Hong Kong people signed the petition in support of the Law. This bears full witness to the overwhelming aspiration of the Hong Kong people for stability and security.

Question four: Has China failed to fulfill its international obligations by enacting the National Security Law for the Hong Kong SAR?

My answer again is a definite "No".

This year marks the 75th anniversary of the founding of the United Nations. China was the first country to put its signature on the UN Charter. China is now a member of more than 100 inter-governmental international organisations and signed over 500 multilateral treaties.

- China has been committed to upholding international law and the basic norms governing international relations.
- It has faithfully fulfilled its international responsibilities and obligations.
- It has never withdrawn from international organisations or treaties. Nor does it believe in "us first" at the expense of others. This label is more suited to some other countries.

It is completely wrong to confuse the Sino-British Joint Declaration with "One Country, Two Systems" and accuse China of failing to honour its international obligations.

The "copyright" for "One Country, Two Systems" belongs to Deng Xiaoping. The Chinese Government governs the Hong Kong SAR in accordance with the Constitution of China and the Basic Law, not the Joint Declaration.

The policies for "One Country, Two Systems" of the Chinese Government are fully embodied in the Basic law and faithfully implemented. There is no question of China having failed to fulfill its international obligation!

Now let me turn to the fifth question: Who has failed to fulfill their international obligations and who has trampled on the norms governing international relations?

Sovereign equality and non-interference in other countries internal affairs are fundamental principles of international law and basic norms governing international relations. China has never interfered in the internal affairs of other countries, including the UK, and we hope the UK will also abide by this principle.

The UK side well knows that Hong Kong is no longer under its colonial rule, and that Hong Kong has returned to China and is now part of China. The UK has no sovereignty, jurisdiction or right of "supervision" over Hong Kong after the handover.

However, the UK Government keeps making irresponsible remarks on Hong Kong affairs through its so-called "six-monthly report on Hong Kong". It makes unwarranted accusations against the National Security Law for the Hong Kong SAR, and even talks about changing the arrangements for "British National (Overseas) "(BNO) passport holders in Hong Kong.

These moves constitute a gross interference in China's internal affairs and openly trample on the basic norms governing international relations. The Chinese side has lodged solemn representation to the UK side to express its grave concern and strong opposition.

I want to emphasize that Hong Kong is part of China. Hong Kong affairs are China's internal affairs and brook no external interference. One important task of the National Security Law for the Hong Kong SAR is to prevent, suppress and punish collusion with a foreign country or with external elements which endanger national security.

No one should underestimate the firm determination of China to safeguard its sovereignty, security and development interests. Attempts to disrupt or obstruct the implementation of the National Security Law for the Hong Kong SAR will be met with the strong opposition of 1.4 billion Chinese people. All these attempts are doomed to failure!

Law is the beginning of order. The National Security Law for the Hong Kong SAR is the fundamental solution that will end the chaos and restore order in Hong Kong.

I am confident that, under the strong leadership of the Central Government of China, with the concerted efforts of all the Chinese people, including Hong Kong compatriots, and with the strong safeguards of the National Security Law for the Hong Kong SAR, Hong Kong will become a safer, better and more prosperous place.

Thank you!

Now I would like to take your questions.

CGTN: China has said it reserves the right to take corresponding measures to the UK's decision to offer citizenship to 3 million Hong Kong residents. Can you give us more details about what those measures would be and when they will be announced? Secondly, if I may, Boris Johnson says that he is still a sinophile but the National Security Law for HK is a clear and serious breach of the Sino-British Joint Declaration. How do you think the relations between China and the UK could be saved from deteriorating any further?

Liu Xiaoming: I think I already answered your question in my opening remarks. With regard to BNO, with regard to specific moves, you have to ask the British government what they are going to do next. I also said that the relationship between China and the UK, or between any countries, has to be based on international law and the norms governing international relations. The fundamental principles of international law are sovereign equality and non-interference in each other's internal affairs. This was incorporated into the UN charter. It was also included in the Joint Communiqué on the Agreement on an Exchange of Ambassadors between the UK and China about 40 years ago. These are the basic norms of the relationship.

This year is the 70th year since UK recognized the New China. In the past 70 years, we've seen ups and downs in the relationship, but on the whole, the relationship has moved forward. The reason why we have seen downs is because these principles were violated. When we have had ups in the relationship, it means these principles were abided by. So when the principles are abided by, we will witness the leaps and bounds in the relationship. But when these principles are violated, the relationship will suffer setbacks and even backslide. Thank you.

BBC: Article 38 in this new law says that it applies even where the individual is neither a Hong Kong resident nor physically in the territory. How does this use of universal jurisdiction fit alongside international law where it's kept normally for the most serious crimes? And how can journalists, activists, and others be sure that they're able to continue exercising their freedom of speech without being prosecuted if they set foot in Hong Kong?

Liu Xiaoming: You mentioned Article 38. That is a common practice. Even by British law, those who commit a crime, who work against the interest of the UK, should be accountable no matter where they are. If they conduct activities that endanger national security either inside the UK or outside the UK, they will be held responsible. I don't think there's anything new to the National Security Law when it comes to safeguarding Hong Kong security.

With regard to journalists, I think the law is very clear. It outlines the four categories of crime against the national security of China. As long as a journalist abides by the law, you should have nothing to worry about. You can conduct your work. Also, as mentioned, human rights are fully respected. That applies not only to Hong Kong residents but also to every resident and every person working and living in Hong Kong. And those human rights include freedom of the press and freedom of speech. So there's nothing to be worried about as long as you abide by the law.

Sky News: The UK government is looking again at the decision of allowing Huawei into the UK network. They are actually going to make a U-turn on the decision on Huawei and not allow Huawei anymore into the 5G network. What impact would that have on UK-China relations? If I may, you said that China does not interfere with UK affairs, and yet some people would disagree with that and say that China is actually conducting subversive activity, trying to influence elements of UK politicians, academia and even business to further its influence and interests. How do you respond to that?

Liu Xiaoming: I would totally reject any accusation of China interfering in the UK's internal affairs. I've been ambassador here for more than 10 years, and I never came across any incident in which we've been accused by the UK government or any institutions with hard evidence of China's interference in the UK's internal affairs. If you have evidence, please show me. But do not spread disinformation and make false accusation against China. As I said in my opening remarks, China is fully committed to the basic norms governing international relations and that has been our consistent policy.

With regard to Huawei, I have written many articles and made many speeches on Huawei. I don't think we have enough time to talk about that. So I want to be brief on Huawei. Huawei is a win-win example of China-UK collaboration. We believe that to embrace Huawei, to include Huawei, is not only in the interest of China. I think it's also in the fundamental interests of the UK. The British government has its ambitious plan for full 5G coverage for the UK by 2025. I think Huawei can do the job. But if the UK chooses to pay a higher price for less advanced products, it's up to you. I always say that we have to work for the best and prepare for the worst. Huawei has operations in 170 countries and no country has found evidence that they are operating by the back door. They have been very transparent. They set up the center for analyzing their products that is completely managed by British people, not people from Huawei. They have built confidence. Throughout the world, can you give me the name of another company that sets up a center for itself to be examined by the host country? No. So they have nothing to fear. If you do not want Huawei, it's up to you. I always say when one door shuts, another door opens. In China, we have a saying when the West turns dark, the East will be brighter. I heard a lot of fuss and noises about Huawei, but we have nothing to fear. I told our business community here, you have to be more confident; once you have good products, you should not worry that they don't have the market. I think the world is big enough to accommodate Huawei. I really believe that having Huawei is a real win-win situation, not only for Huawei but also for the UK. But of course, at the end of the day, it's up to the British government. We have tried our best to tell the story of Huawei, but we cannot control the British government's decision. I heard there is a lot of speculation. We are ready for any scenario and consequences. I think Huawei will survive and prosper. The more pressure from the so-called "superpower" and its allies, the stronger Huawei will grow. That is my belief.

Bloomberg: Thank you, Ambassador. Just a very brief follow-up on the Huawei question. The decision taken by the UK government is quite clear that it will be based on security concerns, rather than on the commercial relations you bear in mind. And it is also quite clear that the United States is concerned about Huawei's security. What you are saying is that China doesn't see it as a security issue at all, and that it wouldn't be concerned at the political level that the UK will make such a decision.

Liu Xiaoming: I think it's up to the UK to make the final decision. In terms of security, I think Huawei has done their best to address the concerns about security. When you talk about security, are you talking about security from the political perspective? There are many kinds of security. One is about telecommunications, whether the technology is safe enough and resilient enough to protect you, not only from the so-called states, but also from some individual hackers or other companies. So you cannot generalize security. But Huawei has made every effort to address security concerns and tried to improve their technology. Analysis of intelligence agencies said the risks are manageable and the technology in general is safe. That's why the UK government made the decision to include Huawei, even though they have imposed a 35% cap. If it is decided that Huawei will be rejected, it's up to them. As I said, the world is big enough to accommodate Huawei. They have operations in 170 countries. If the UK gives up, they still have 169 countries. I tried to encourage people from Huawei to look forward. First, you have to work and convince the UK partners and UK people, government and business that you have the best technologies and your price is the most competitive, and you are addressing their concern by keeping improving your technologies. You are the leader. But if they decide not to choose you, it's up to them. You still have to develop. Huawei has been developing despite so many measures. I have full confidence in them.

So you mentioned security, this is also the point I want to make. When some British politicians talk about Huawei, they link Huawei to UK's relations with China. Some of them regard China as a threat, even as a hostile country. I think that is totally wrong. That is inconsistent with the consensus reached by the two leaders of our countries. When President Xi was here, many people talked about the "Golden Era", but they have no idea what the "Golden Era" is about. Actually the "Golden Era" was proposed by the British side, it was proposed by the British leader. We think that it is in the interests of the two countries, then we agreed with terming our relationship a "Golden Era". But if you do not want the "Golden Era", if you treat China as an enemy, that is completely wrong and not in your interest. That reminds me of Brzezinski, the American strategist who helped to normalize the relationship between China and the US. Dr. Brzezinski had a very fine line: If we make China an enemy, China will become an enemy. So we want to be your friend and partner. But if you want to make China a hostile country, you have to bear the consequences. Thank you.

The Times: I want to know whether there will be any attempts to prevent Hong Kong holders of British National (Overseas) status from taking up Britain's offer to come to UK.

Liu Xiaoming: We have heard quite a lot of talk about revoking British position on BNO. When we reached the agreement in 1984, the British government promised, in the exchange of MOU, that they would not give citizenship to BNO holders in Hong Kong. But now they have decided to revoke their position, which we regard as walking away from their international obligations. People talk about China's response. Our first response is that we criticize the British move. We don't think they have honoured their commitment. Secondly, we think it is an interference in China's internal affairs and a political manipulation against the National Security Law. Thirdly, we will have to wait and see, and have to decide our counter measures in accordance with the actual actions to be taken by the British side.

The Economist: Ambassador, can I ask you please to elaborate on the consequences for the UK in response to its position on Hong Kong? For example, do you foresee consequences for British companies operating in the Chinese market, for bilateral trade and in what sectors in particular? Do you see risks for British banks or for companies serving consumer industries to operate in China? Thank you.

Liu Xiaoming: As I said in my opening remarks, the relationship between states has to be based on basic principles, including respect for each other, respect for sovereignty and territorial integrity, non-interference in each other's internal affairs and respect for the core interests and major concerns of each other. That has been reaffirmed by our top leaders. During the pandemic, President Xi and Prime Minister Johnson had two telephone conversations. They both reaffirmed their commitment to these basic principles. But once these principles are violated, there will certainly be consequences for the relationship. Mutual trust will be weakened. Confidence will be weakened. But with regard to specific consequences in specific areas, we have to wait and see. We do hope that the UK side will stand by the fundamental interests between China and the UK. We should bear in mind the big picture of the fundamental interests of the relationship. Thank you.

Xinhua News Agency: A recent survey found that the number of the Chinese students who would choose the UK as the first country to study abroad has for the first time overtaken that of the US. Will China's attitude and policy regarding

Chinese students studying in the UK change if the Sino-UK relations are further dented by political differences?

Liu Xiaoming: We would certainly like to say that normal relations between China and the UK will move forward, including the exchanges of the students. I have also read some reports. Because of what is going on in the US, there is more demand from Chinese students to study in the UK. We welcome this and encourage more students to come here. The education section of the Embassy has been very busy, providing information and answering questions and enquiries from Chinese students. We are helping them to get in touch with various universities. Right now, I have not seen any negative consequences from educational cooperation. We have 200,000 Chinese students studying in the UK. During the pandemic, I wrote letters to the presidents or vice chancellors of 154 universities which host Chinese students. In addition to asking them to take good care of Chinese students, I also expressed my commitment to a stronger relationship between China and their respective universities.

Reuters: We've got some Brits looking again into Huawei. The British government is talking about introducing new laws about foreign takeover and acquisition, which is believed to be specifically aimed at Chinese firms. You spoke earlier about the "Golden Era". From China's point of view, is the "Golden Era" over between the two countries? If it isn't, what does Britain need to do to keep it going?

Liu Xiaoming: The "Golden Era" was an idea proposed by the UK side and endorsed by both sides. Whether it's over or not—I certainly hope not—but whether it's over or not is not up to Chinese side. I think, during the pandemic, we still heard the British leaders express their commitment to the "Golden Era". You know, I always say, for any kind of relationship, you need two to tango, you need two hands to clap. So I do hope that our relationship will develop further and will enjoy steady growth in the best interests of the two countries. But, as I said, it's up to both sides. We have every reason to share a good relationship with the UK, and we regard the UK as a partner. We never use the words that "the UK is potentially a hostile country". You've never heard this word from any Chinese leader nor any Chinese official. So I really want to remind the British leaders, the British officials, they have to be careful with regard to how to characterize the nature of the relationship.

The Guardian: Ambassador, you mentioned that the Security Law is very popular in Hong Kong. You said that three million people have signed the petition. But you know, in the district elections last year, we've seen pro-democracy movements doing very well. Can you guarantee the election this autumn will be held on the same basis as the ones that were held, and will increase the freedom to stand and freedom to campaign?

Liu Xiaoming: We have a different interpretation of what was going on in Hong Kong. You regard it as a pro-democracy movement. But we think they are violent, rioting and law-breaking activities, even terrorism. If people were to storm the UK parliament, I don't think you would regard them as a "pro-democracy movement". We've seen so many things happening on the streets of London in the past few weeks. I never read the British media describe them as a "pro-democracy movement". You regard them as law-breakers and rioters. But why, when it comes to Hong Kong, do you have a different standard? So I think this approach absolutely exposes a double standard. And with regard to the election in September, I think the election will be conducted in accordance with the law in Hong Kong. And, you know, when we talk about the National Security Law, it will be implemented according to the law. As I said, this Law has incorporated fully both the comprehensive jurisdiction of the Central Government and the high degree of autonomy of Hong Kong. So Hong Kong people will administer their affairs. Nothing has changed as long as you do not violate the National Security Law. Hong Kong's social system, legislative system and legal system will all remain unchanged. Nothing has been altered. You should have confidence in Hong Kong.

The Daily Telegraph: Morning, Mr. Ambassador. I am reporting on retaliatory measures if the UK pressed ahead with a plan on passports and residents back to the UK, but we are short of detail. Can you offer any detail on what measures might be taken? Can I also ask you another issue? Ofcom today will severely criticize CGTN over its broadcast involving a Briton, Peter Humphrey, saying he was forced to confess on air while under duress, can you offer a comment on that please?

Liu Xiaoming: On the BNO, I think I answered previous questions. My answer will be the same. We have made our position clear to the British side. We hope that they will reconsider their position. With regard to what the response China is going to make, we have to wait and see what will be the specific actions from the British side.

With regard to CGTN, I think they already made a rebuttal to the accusation of Mr. Humphrey. The accusation is totally not based on fact. And I think they have made their position very clear. Thank you.

NBC: Thank you very much, Mr. Ambassador. You talked about how this new National Security Law doesn't violate the decades-old policy of "One Country, Two Systems" but the spirit of that agreement on "One Country, Two Systems" allows a great deal of political freedom and freedom of expression in Hong Kong. There are reports this morning that books are being removed from public libraries written by activists. There have been activists—you've described them as "rioters" and "terrorists"—who have been detained. So my question is, is this the end of freedom of expression as people have known it in Hong Kong for the last several decades?

Liu Xiaoming: Not at all. Hong Kong people will be protected in their freedom of speech and freedom of press. You mentioned some of the books. It really depends on what the book is about. If a book is aimed at inciting secession and subversion, that will be tantamount to a kind of crime. You'll have to read the National Security Law carefully. In the UK, there are many laws governing national security. If you voice opinion in support of terrorism and hatred, that can be regarded as a criminal act. Why can the UK have this law but China cannot have a National Security Law to punish those who incite secession and subversion, who incite actions that endanger the national security? I think this is a common practice. When you talk about freedom of speech and freedom of the press, I think, as I said, this law will protect the majority, the great majority, of Hong Kong people in exercising their rights of freedom of the press, freedom to march, freedom of demonstration. But you can't do things to endanger national security, i.e. only four categories of crime. There is a boundary. Even with regard to the freedom of expression, freedom of speech, protected by the International Covenant, there is also limit. You can't do this at the expense of national security and public order. It's clearly stipulated. I do recommend you to go back to read this Covenant on Civil and Political Rights, an international document. So people have nothing to worry about. As long as they abide by the National Security Law, as long as they do not cross the line prohibited by the National Security Law, they should be one hundred percent free. They should have nothing to fear.

So that's the problem. The British media, and the American media too, exercise what I would call a scaremongering practice. They demonise this law. That's totally wrong. They don't read the law carefully. There are four categories of crime. They have been very carefully stipulated in a very detailed way. As long as you do not cross the boundary, as long as you exercise your rights within the limits protected by the Constitution, by the Basic Law, by the International Covenant, you should have no problem at all. Thank you.

Financial Times: Thanks very much Ambassador. A lot of British businesses in Mainland China and Hong Kong are worried about the law. What will happen if the Hong Kong police request to use their data or system and they refuse?

Liu Xiaoming: The Hong Kong Police will carry out the National Security Law in accordance with the law. The National Security Law has made it very clear that the law enforcement people, including the police, including the people working in the national security office based in Hong Kong, have to abide by the law in China and also the law in Hong Kong. The police enforcement people will carry out the National Security Law in accordance with all laws on the ground. Thank you.

Russia Today: Thank you, Mr. Ambassador. The Boris Johnson government is looking to give millions of Hongkongers citizenship to escape Chinese laws. Why is the UK so ready to give citizenship to Hong Kong as a former British colony but not to other former British colonies, such as Iraq which suffered an illegal war that thousands fled?

Liu Xiaoming: Firstly, some of the politicians in UK still have a very strong colonial mindset. They fail to recognise that Hong Kong is no longer under British colonial rule. Hong Kong was returned to China 23 years ago. That's their problem. That's why they have this passion. They still regard Hong Kong as being under British colonial rule, they try to make irresponsible remarks, and they try to interfere in Hong Kong affairs. But that's totally wrong. They fail to realise that Hong Kong is now part of China.

Secondly, they fail to realise that the stability and prosperity of Hong Kong is not only in the interest of China. It's also in the interest of the UK. The UK has 300,000 citizens living in Hong Kong and more than 700 businesses there. So the prosperity and stability of Hong Kong is in their best interest. That's why, I am talking about how 3 million people in Hong Kong signed a petition to support the National Security Law, including major British business people from HSBC, Swire, Jardine and Standard Chartered. But those politicians try to criticise them. That's wrong because that stability and prosperity in Hong Kong is in their interest. You can't do business or live a normal life without a peaceful environment. Look at what happened last year. People did not even dare to walk in the streets under this so-called "black terror". People cried for chaos to end as quickly as possible. That was what gave birth to the National Security Law.

Channel 4: Thank you, Ambassador. Can I just get back to the issue of Huawei? What are the consequences for Britain if Huawei is removed from 5G (development in the UK)? And would you consider that a hostile act?

Liu Xiaoming: The consequences, there might be many. First, it damages Britain's image as an open, business-friendly, free and transparent environment as it claims to be. So that's why in the past 5 years, the Chinese investment in the UK has been bigger than the Chinese investment in the previous 30 years. Because Chinese business people believe the UK is business-friendly, and they can do business here. But if you get rid of Huawei, it will send out a very wrong message. It will tarnish Britain's image as a free trade country. That's number one.

Number two, it will tarnish your image as a country which follows independent policies. It means you have succumbed to foreign pressure. You can't make your own independent foreign policy. I always say, Britain can only be Great when you have your independent foreign policy. If you do not have an independent foreign policy and you have to dance to the tune of another country, how can you claim to be Great Britain?

Thirdly, I think it will also send out a very bad message to the Chinese business community here. They are all watching how you handle Huawei. If you get rid of Huawei, it will send out a very bad message for other Chinese businesses. It will also send out a very bad message for other foreign businesses.

Fourthly, there is also an element of trust. When you have a sound relationship, it has to be built on mutual respect and mutual trust. In China, we have a saying: You can't make your policy in the morning and then change it in the evening. How would people be able to trust you? So I think it's a matter of trust here. I do hope that the British government will make decisions in the best interest—not only in the interest of China-UK cooperation—but also in the interest of itself. Thank you.

China Daily: Thank you, Ambassador. Some people think the National Security Law in Hong Kong will also help protect British investments and their legal rights in Hong Kong. Mr. Ambassador, what is your opinion?

Liu Xiaoming: Absolutely. I think I have answered your question in my previous remarks. You can only do business in a stable and peaceful environment. So that's why the National Security Law is welcomed, not only by the ordinary people who are very concerned about their security, but also by the business communities; not only British businesses but also many other businesses. There is a report that the American Chamber of Commerce expressed their confidence in Hong Kong. That is because the National Security Law can guarantee a business environment for people including the British. So I do hope the British public, including the British media, approach the National Security Law from an objective, correct and accurate perspective. Do not try to demonize this law. This law will provide a guarantee and protection for safety and prosperity of Hong Kong. As I said in my opening remarks, with the safeguard of the National Security Law, Hong Kong will become a safer, better and more prosperous place. Thank you.

Thank you for your attention and thank you for attending today's press conference.

Chapter 3

South China Sea

China is a Staunch Force for Peace and Stability in the South China Sea

——A Keynote Speech and Q&A at the International Institute for Strategic Studies

(International Institute for Strategic Studies, 20th May 2016)

On 20th May 2016, I delivered a keynote speech entitled "China is a Staunch Force for Peace and Stability in the South China Sea" at the International Institute for Strategic Studies (IISS), after which I took questions from the audience. The transcript of the keynote speech and Q&A is as follows:

Liu Xiaoming: It is truly a delight to be back again at the International Institute for Strategic Studies (IISS) after three years. Back then, I was invited by Dr. John Chipman to deliver a speech about China's Diplomacy in the New Era. Today my speech is also about China's diplomacy, but I shall focus on one issue—the South China Sea.

Recently the South China Sea issue has attracted much attention and media coverage. However, the articles and reports show that the truth and the facts behind the issue remain unclear to most people. Misunderstandings still exist.

So I have chosen to speak about this issue at the IISS, a prestigious institution that focuses on international security. I shall expound on China's position and policy, and then take questions from you. In this way, I hope our interaction today will help you to gain a more comprehensive and accurate understanding of the issue.

In order to be objective, impartial and rational on the issue of the South China Sea, one must get to the root of the issue and put it in perspective. So I would like to begin with the history of China and the South China Sea.

The islands and reefs in the South China Sea have been Chinese territory since ancient times. I emphasize "ancient times" to highlight the historical facts that put the South China Sea firmly on the map of China. To elaborate on this, let me share with you four "Firsts".

China was the first to discover the islands in the South China Sea.

Some countries attempt to claim some of the islands on grounds of "prior possession". They try to get away with their illegal occupation by referring to the Nansha Islands as *Terra Nullius*. In fact, as early as 200 BC, during China's Han Dynasty, the Chinese undertook large-scale and frequent sea-faring and fishing activities in the South China Sea. There is clear evidence that the South China Sea was already used by China as an important shipping route since ancient times. It follows that, because of frequent shipping, the Chinese became the first to discover the islands in the South China Sea.

Marwyn Samuels is known for his studies on the South China Sea. He wrote a book in the 1980s called *Contest for the South China Sea*. In this he wrote:

"Along the way, both literarily and figuratively, the South China Sea and its islands helped shape the geographical cognita of the Chinese world order."

Second, China was the first to name the islands in the South China Sea.

Today, the Nansha of the South China Sea are called the Spratly Islands in the West. This name comes from a British sea captain called Richard Spratly who thought it was he who had "discovered" and "named" the islands in 1843. But actually the Chinese had named the Nansha Islands about 2,000 years before he did.

In various Chinese historical records dating back to over 2,000 years, the South China Sea is known as *Zhang Hai*, or "rising sea", and the islands, reefs, shoals and sands as *Qi Tou*, or "rugged peaks". In historical documents of later dynasties after the Han Dynasty, ancient names referring to today's Xisha Islands, the Nansha Islands and individual islands in the archipelagoes are clearly recorded.

A popular sailing guide called *Geng Lu Bu* was compiled by Chinese fishermen. This was during the Ming and Qing Dynasties between the 14th and 20th century. In this book, the names of dozens of islands of the South China Sea, including those in Nansha, are recorded. Many of these names have been widely adopted and used by international sailors until this day.

Third, China was the first to exercise administrative jurisdiction in the South China Sea.

Ever since China's Tang Dynasty, about 1,200 years ago, successive Chinese governments have exercised jurisdiction over the South China Sea. This included islands and the waters around them. China's sovereignty was established through administrative establishment, naval patrol, resource development and management.

In the 10th century, during China's Song Dynasty, local chronicles explicitly recorded that the islands in the South China Sea were under the administrative jurisdiction of Qiongzhou, which is present-day Hainan province.

In 1279, China's famous astronomer Guo Shoujing was recorded traveling to the South China Sea and building observatorial facilities. The Governments of the Ming and Qing dynasties both placed the South China Sea under the supervision of naval patrols.

Fourth, China was also the first country to develop the islands in the South China Sea.

For centuries, the Chinese have been engaged in fishing, planting and other activities on the islands and in the nearby waters. The traces of this continuous habitation can be seen through archaeological evidence found on many islands. The fact that only Chinese people lived on the Nansha islands is recorded clearly in the book called *The China Sea Pilot* published by the British Navy in 1868.

The aforementioned four "Firsts" are based on substantial and concrete historical evidence. They testify to the fact that the islands of the South China Sea have long been Chinese territory under successive, peaceful and effective administration.

Until the 1970s, it was widely recognised by the international community that islands in the South China Sea belonged to China. Let me give you two examples:

• In 1883, Germany sent military vessels to Xisha and Nansha for surveys. The Government of Guangdong Province protested to the Germans, citing Chinese sovereignty. Germany had to stop the survey and withdrew their team.

• In 1958, the Chinese government issued a declaration on territorial waters applicable to all Chinese territory including the Xisha, the Nansha and other islands in the South China Sea. Vietnam's then prime minister, Phạm Văn Đồng, sent the Chinese Premier Zhou Enlai a diplomatic note which explicitly recognizes that the Xisha and the Nansha belonged to China.

I could give you more examples like these if we had more time.

History speaks for itself as to who owns those islands in the South China Sea. Then how did the disputes arise?

Since the 1970s, some countries have tried to lay claim on the natural resources in the South China Sea. It was then that some nations began to make territorial claims. Vietnam and the Philippines sent troops and illegally occupied some of the islands. That is how the disputes started. Up till today, Vietnam has occupied 29 islands, the Philippines eight and Malaysia five.

In 1982, the United Nations Convention on the Law of the Sea (UNCLOS) was concluded after 9 years of negotiations. With the development of the maritime legal system in the 1980s, countries around the South China Sea gradually made further claims. These include the Exclusive Economic Zone (EEZ), the continental shelf and other maritime rights and interests. The overlapping claims in some cases gave rise to disputes over maritime delimitation. This has caused further complications to the issue of the South China Sea.

It is clear that there are two disputes at the centre of the South China Sea issue:

• One is the territorial dispute caused by illegal occupation of Chinese territory.

• The other is the dispute over maritime delimitation caused by overlapping claims of maritime jurisdiction.

These two disputes are intertwined and have made the issue highly complex. However, one thing is clear: from whichever angle one chooses to look at the issue, China has never been the troublemaker. Quite the opposite, China has been a victim.

Then what is China's position and policy?

For a long time China has exercised a high-level of self-restraint and forbearance when it comes to this issue. We have always approached the disputes in a constructive and responsible manner. If China had not maintained self-restraint, the South China Sea would not have been what it is today.

I would like to summarize China's position through five "commitments":

First, China maintains a strong commitment to peace and stability in the South China Sea.

For years, China has been a staunch force safeguarding and maintaining regional peace and stability. Building friendship and partnership with neighbours has always been a top priority in China's policy towards neighbouring countries.

The Chinese people are a peace-loving nation. Moreover, China's development requires a peaceful environment. In the past three decades it has been peace and stability that have enabled China to industrialise at a speed and scale unprecedented in human history. This advance by China can be largely attributed to the peaceful and stable environment in its neighborhood and beyond. So, China would be the last to wish to see instability in the South China Sea. It means that China would be the first to oppose conflicts in the South China Sea.

Second, China maintains a strong commitment to solving disputes peacefully through friendly consultations and negotiations.

The ultimate resolution of territorial disputes, regardless of their mechanisms or processes, has to be agreed between parties directly involved. The dialogue must be based on negotiations on an equal footing if such a resolution is to be fundamental and lasting. Negotiations and consultations are the most effective way of resolving disputes. This is because they can, to the greatest extent, reflect the principle of sovereign equality and the will and wishes of the parties involved.

Since the People's Republic of China was founded in 1949, we have signed boundary treaties with 12 of our 14 neighbors with land borders. These treaties involved over 20,000 kilometers of boundary. Most of the neighbors are medium-sized or small nations, but none of them has ever complained about the approach of China in the negotiations. These are examples of how China has resolved disputes through face-to-face negotiations with other countries directly involved in the disputes.

The South China Sea disputes do not need to be an exception. Experience shows that only negotiation and consultation could help the parties concerned to constantly build mutual trust, manage problems, narrow differences and advance cooperation. Negotiation and consultation are the most realistic and effective approach to the South China Sea issue.

Third, China maintains a strong commitment to rule-based dispute management.

China and the ASEAN countries signed the "Declaration on the Conduct of Parties in the South China Sea" in 2002 and are now working closely on the drafting of the "Code of Conduct in the South China Sea", or COC for short. Since the start of the COC consultation, there has already been much progress.

China and the ASEAN countries have worked actively to set up the "Senior Officials' Hotline" in response to maritime emergencies, and the "Point-to-Point Hotline Communication" on search-and-rescue. All sides have also agreed to establish "Preventive Measures to Manage Risks at Sea", which will serve as the interim measure prior to the final conclusion of the COC. What has happened over the years testifies to the efficiency of rule-based dispute management.

Fourth, China maintains a strong commitment to the freedom of navigation and over-flight.

China is the biggest littoral state in the South China Sea. The vast majority of China's energy supply and trade pass through the South China Sea. This means China cares more than any other nation about freedom of navigation and over-flight in the South China Sea.

Recently "freedom of navigation" has become a hot subject. Some people talk about "protecting the freedom of navigation".

This creates a dangerous misunderstanding as it implies that the safety and security of ships passing through the region are under immediate threat. The reality is that more than 100,000 vessels pass through the South China Sea every year. None of them has ever run into any problem with freedom of navigation.

If there were a real threat to maritime traffic in the South China Sea then this would immediately result in a leap in shipping insurance rates. This has not happened. The Reuters news agency reported in January that there are no signs of commercial shipping being affected in the South China Sea. The report went on to say that the South China Sea area was not listed as a high risk area by the industry's influential Lloyd's Joint War Committee. This means insurers do not charge additional premiums for vessels operating in the region.

Business people, particularly insurers, are the most responsive to risks. Yet they haven't sensed any threat to freedom of navigation in the South China Sea. This makes me wonder what kind of "freedom of navigation" some people are feeling so eager to protect.

The fact is, "freedom of navigation" has recently been used as an excuse by the United States to flex its military muscles in the South China Sea. The United States sends military jets and warships on close-in reconnaissance missions in the waters and air space adjacent to China's islands and reefs. Such dangerous actions have increased tension and posed a threat to China's sovereignty and security.

For example, just ten days ago, the USS William P. Lawrence, a guided missile destroyer, illegally sailed into the waters near China's Nansha islands. The ship manoeuvered in the sovereign waters of China without the permission of the

Chinese government.

Actions such as this, I am afraid, cannot be regarded as protection of "freedom of navigation". They are a manifestation of superior military power and the assertion of maritime dominance. These actions have posed the biggest threat to the real freedom of navigation and the peace and stability in the South China Sea.

To those who claim that they care about freedom of navigation and over-flight, I hope they will act in strict accordance with the international law and respect the sovereignty and security of coastal state.

The actions of the United States should be judged at all times by its approach to international law. If the United States had a serious commitment to maritime law then it would have signed the UNCLOS. China has signed UNCLOS along with most other member nations.

Respect for international law and peaceful dialogue on disputes is crucial to the stability and peace in the South China Sea.

Military provocation and intimidation in the name of "freedom of navigation" is highly dangerous. Such actions directly undermine regional peace and stability.

Turning to my next point, about China's commitment.

Fifth, China maintains strong commitment to win-win cooperation.

China values friendly and cooperative relationships with its neighbours. We have taken the initiative to call on all parties involved to "shelf differences and engage in joint development" in the South China Sea. This provides a useful approach to the resolution of the issue. And it is an approach that takes into consideration the interests of all parties concerned. To put this into practice, China has engaged in a series of cooperative initiatives with relevant countries.

In 2005, oil companies from China, Vietnam and the Philippines signed the "Agreement for Joint Marine Seismic Undertaking in Certain Areas in the South China Sea". This was an effort for the joint development of oil and gas resources in the South China Sea.

In 2011, China announced the establishment of China-ASEAN Maritime Cooperation Fund with a total of 3 billion RMB yuan, or more than £300 million. This was set up to fund maritime cooperation projects.

Two years ago, China put forward the initiative of the 21st century Maritime Silk Road. This demonstrated the mutual benefits which the ASEAN countries can enjoy by becoming regional hubs of development. These measures and initiatives are evidence of China's efforts and good faith in seeking further and deeper maritime cooperation with its neighbours.

The aforesaid five "Commitments" constitute China's position on the South China Sea. They demonstrate China's sincerity:

- Resolving the issues.
- Securing the regional peace and stability.
- And promoting the common development in neighboring areas.

Recently a number of hot issues have cropped up with regard to the South China Sea. In turn I will share with you my views.

The first one is about the "arbitration".

The reference to the Arbitral Tribunal was unilaterally initiated by the Philippines. Many media reports are creating misunderstanding by not explaining clearly the circumstances of the "arbitration".

A crucial point is that the Tribunal was not a permanent arbitration body nor was it a court of law.

For any arbitration to work it requires the proactive participation and agreement of both sides. Another critical point is that China refused to participate in the arbitration. From the very start of the reference from the Philippines for the arbitration China made it clear this was not an acceptable way to resolve the dispute.

Some media and politicians are now ramping up this topic of arbitration. They are erroneously making the following claims:

- If China does not accept the ruling of the arbitration panel it will be breaking international law.
- It would be seen as "violating the international law" and "undermining the rule-based international system".

These claims are completely wrong.

China's rejection of the arbitration and its non-participation in the arbitral process is an act of exercising its legitimate rights empowered by the international law.

By contrast, it is the Philippines who is challenging the legal and moral bottom line of the international community because the arbitration is totally unreasonable, unfair and illegal.

My second point about the arbitration is that it was unreasonable.

It was not reasonable because the Philippines went against its commitment to China and other ASEAN countries. Let me briefly summarise the logic of this point. China and the Philippines reached a number of bilateral agreements long ago on resolving disputes through bilateral negotiations. In the Declaration of Conduct reached between China and Philippines and other ASEAN countries, it is clearly stipulated that "the parties concerned undertake to resolve their territorial and jurisdictional disputes by peaceful means".

In 2011, the Philippines issued a joint statement with China to reaffirm its commitment to negotiations and consultations. However, a year later, it suddenly went back on its clearly written commitment. Without notifying China, or even asking for consent from China, the Philippines unilaterally initiated the arbitration against China. *Pacta sunt servanda* is a basic rule in international relations. This is the bottom line of morality that every country must strictly observe. To put it simply, the Philippines has reneged on its words and deeds.

Another point is that the arbitration was unfair.

It was unfair because the islands in the arbitration case have been the sovereign property of China since ancient times. What the Philippines is doing is robbing its neighbour and asking the court to rule in its favour over the ownership of the booty. No one in the world should find this reasonable.

Here in Britain, there is always an emphasis on a "rule-based international system". But if rules can be abused, as they are in the Philippine arbitration, what should we expect from such rules and order?

The arbitration is illegal for three apparent reasons:

First, the UNCLOS stipulates that State Parties have the right to settle a dispute by any peaceful means of their own choice. The aforementioned arbitration was unilaterally forced ahead by the Philippines, who did not seek consent from China. This violates China's legitimate right under the international law.

Second the UNCLOS also states:

"If the States Parties have agreed to seek settlement of the dispute by a peaceful means of their own choice, the (arbitration) procedures apply only where no settlement has been reached by recourse to such means and the agreement between the parties does not exclude any further procedure."

China has always been open to bilateral means and clearly bilateral means between China and the Philippines has not been exhausted.

Third, the UNCLOS states:

"When a dispute arises between State Parties concerning the interpretation or application of this Convention, the parties to the dispute shall proceed expeditiously to an exchange of views regarding its settlement by negotiation or other peaceful means."

However, the Philippines has never had any consultations with China. Its unilateral initiation of the arbitration is an overt violation of law.

It should also be noted, for the record, that both China and the Philippines signed and ratified the UNCLOS. Compared with what the Philippines did, China has truly implemented and championed the international law.

The 15 submissions made by the Philippines concern territorial sovereignty and maritime delimitation. The UNCLOS has no jurisdiction over issues related to sovereignty.

As for maritime delimitation, China made a declaration in 2006 in accordance with Article 298 of the UNCLOS. This made it very clear China would exclude disputes on maritime delimitation from compulsory arbitration. So China has exercised its legitimate rights conferred by the UNCLOS. China's action complies with the international law.

It should be noted that over 30 other countries, including the UK, have made similar declarations on the same principle of exclusion. These declarations have constituted an inseparable part of the UNCLOS. The reasonable and legitimate appeals and concerns of these countries should be considered. If the Philippines' arbitration case became a convention to be followed, then any of these 30 countries could be dragged into arbitration without prior notice. This would be a serious damage to state sovereignty, international order and the dignity and authority of international law.

There has been speculation in the media that the Tribunal may soon make public its report on the so-called "arbitration" triggered by the Philippines.

China is not hiding from any outcome. China has been totally consistent in its respect for international law. What China refuses to do is participate, accept, recognize or implement any arbitration that has no legitimacy in upholding international law.

The Tribunal is running a risk of undermining its authority and legitimacy. The Tribunal has created a situation where the arbitration is clearly unreasonable, unfair and illegal. Despite this the Tribunal has still chosen to proceed with the arbitration with only the Philippines participating. This raises grave concern about the Tribunal's impartiality and legitimacy. It also calls into question the political intention behind the arbitration. The arbitration in essence is a political initiative under the cloak of law. China will never accept the result whatever comes from the Tribunal.

Although China rejects the arbitration, the door to bilateral negotiation remains open. China and the Philippines are close neighbors. The Chinese and the Philippine peoples have had a long tradition of friendly ties. The Philippines has just elected a new President. We hope that the new Philippine government will work with China on a proper settlement of differences and bring the situation in the South China Sea back on track following the principles established by the UNCLOS and international law.

Another issue I want to talk about is the developments on China's islands in the South China Sea.

Development on some of the Nansha islands began a few years ago. The building efforts will improve the living conditions on the islands and will serve mainly civilian purposes. This includes providing necessary and emergency public services to China and to other countries in and from outside the region. The facilities built include lighthouses, maritime communication facilities, search-and-rescue facilities and medical centers. They will enable China to better fulfill its international responsibility and obligations, such as maritime search-and-rescue, disaster prevention and relief, scientific maritime research, meteorological observation, eco-environmental protection, navigation safety and fishing services.

There are necessary defence facilities deployed according to Chinese security assessments. Such deployment on China's own islands falls within the right of self-protection that every sovereign state is entitled to under international law.

In January 2016, according to Reuters news agency, "some shipowners believe a greater Chinese presence could actually improve safety".

The Reuters report quoted ship owners saying: "If China is to base search-and-rescue assets on the (disputed) islands then there would potentially be faster response times, improving the chances of rescue and survival."

Earlier I described the crucial importance to international trade of the safe and free of navigation for ships through the South China Sea. Reasonable observers would then applaud China's investment and actions to make this critical international artery safer.

However, some people complain about the scale and speed of the building efforts. I want to remind these people that scale and speed are not the benchmark for right and wrong. The scale and speed of China's building efforts match China's international responsibility in the South China Sea. Why would

China sit on its hands and refrain from doing the right things simply because of its size?

Some others accuse China of "changing the status quo". I would like to ask this question: What is the "status quo"?

China is undertaking construction work on its own islands. China is not changing any "status quo".

And I also like to ask those who are so keen on not "changing the status quo": Why are they silent when some countries illegally occupy China's islands and go in for large-scale construction activities there?

The third issue is the so-called "militarisation" of the South China Sea.

Recently the "militarisation" has been hyped up and the United States shouts the loudest. However, it is not difficult to see who is "militarising" the South China Sea.

More than half of the US military force is deployed in Asia-Pacific. Yet, this is a region that has been largely peaceful and stable for many years.

In addition to this huge military force, the USA, together with its allies in the region, frequently flexes its military muscles. This is shown with the conduct of highly-targeted military drills. Then there are the military jets and warships on in-close reconnaissance missions in the waters and air space adjacent to China's islands and reefs. It is these provocative and hostile actions that have raised the tensions in the South China Sea. These acts have sent wrong signals to the Philippines and others who have recklessly deployed military facilities on their illegally occupied islands.

The answer to the question of who is "militarising" the South China Sea is nothing but self-evident. Going forward it is the hope of China that the United States:

- Will act as a big country with responsibility.
- Be prudent in what it says or does on this complicated issue.
- Commit to and respect widely agreed international law, such as the UNCLOS.
- And work with China to safeguard stability and peace.

Therefore, to solve the "militarisation" issue, the United States needs to:

- First of all, stop its dangerous provocations that challenge China's sovereignty and security.
- Secondly, stop being provocative with its "militarisation".
- And thirdly, take concrete steps to facilitate peace and stability in the

region.

Ladies and Gentlemen:

Complicated and sensitive as the South China Sea issue is, the region has maintained overall stability thanks to the joint efforts of China and its neighbours. China will, as it grows in strength, make greater contribution to the stability and prosperity of the South China Sea region. As President Xi Jinping once said, China pursues maritime capability through peace, development and win-win cooperation.

What China has achieved today can be largely attributed to its path of peaceful development. And China will keep to this path.

Looking into the future:

• China is confident and capable of resolving disputes through negotiations and consultations.

• China has shown a steadfast commitment to upholding international law.

• China has been steadfast in safeguarding peace and stability of the South China Sea through cooperation.

• China is ready to join hands with other countries to create a peaceful resolution.

• And China can always be counted on to build the South China Sea into a sea of peace, a sea of friendship and a sea of cooperation.

Thank you.

Now I am pleased to take your questions.

KPMG: Sir, I just want you to clarify one point. You said that the US warships' transiting near the islands was illegal and is not covered by the right of innocent passage set out in the UNCLOS, which does say warships can go through other people's territorial waters provided certain conditions are maintained.

Liu Xiaoming: I think the US abused the so-called right of "innocent passage". They didn't show respect for China's sovereignty. They did not notify China first of all. And they didn't seek to get permission from China. So that is totally against international law and international practices.

LSE: Thank you for sharing your insights. Towards the end of your presentation, you hinted at the tension between the US and China. It seems to me that the tensions between the Philippines and China, between the Vietnamese and China could be managed. At the systematic level, as you can see, the US is seen as the system manager, which is to maintain the status quo, and China has been described for over a decade in analysis by semi-official documentations as the "near peer rival". It seems that the fundamental thing is managing the tensions between the US and China. What is China doing to make the transition of the relations between China and US peaceful, calm and stable?

Liu Xiaoming: As I said in my presentation, from the very beginning, China has not been a trouble-maker. Instead, China is a victim in all this. I hope I made myself clear. Before the so-called "rebalancing strategy" of the US, the South China Sea and the region had been peaceful. China and the neighboring countries including the Philippines and Vietnam have been talking to each other. We have the "Declaration of Conduct" and we have managed our differences effectively. This dispute has been there for 30 years. The area has been quiet and stable. But when it comes to the so-called US "rebalancing" strategy in 2009, I think some countries became emboldened and they thought they had the US behind them. The Philippines changed their approach and submitted the so-called "baseline". The Vietnamese also changed their approach. The Philippines refused to talk to us and then they unilaterally went in for the so-called "arbitration". There are many ways to resolve disputes. According to the UNCLOS, arbitration is only supplementary, while the main method for resolving disputes is peaceful negotiations and consultations between member states. Yet the Philippines resorted to the so-called supplementary measures which are not the main course. I think they thought they had the support of the US.

China wants to have good relations with the US. There is no doubt about it. Over half of my diplomatic career has been devoted to working for a better relationship between China and the US. I was posted twice in Washington, D.C.. We want to have good relations. We also know that without a good relationship between China and the US, there will be no peace or prosperity in the Asia-Pacific region. So we tried very hard and we tried to engage them in consultations. I'm very pleased to see that currently the Security Consultation is right now taking place in Washington, D.C.. The Deputy Minister of Foreign Affairs of China is talking to US Deputy Secretary of State. We do have these channels. But the important thing is that the Americans should change the stereotypical mindset of regarding China as a threat. I think that is the problem, that they have been haunted by the fear that China would someday take their place as the leader of the world. That is not China's dream. China's dream is to revitalize the Chinese nation. We know what we are doing and we know the tremendous challenges ahead of us. We have 1.3 billion people to take care of. After my tour in Egypt, I was seconded to Gansu, one of the western provinces in China, as an assistant governor. I know how poor that area is. I know there are challenges and tremendous tasks for China to achieve its modernization. China is the last country who wants to have bad relations with the US. We are not interested in becoming a superpower. The UK used to be a superpower. A superpower should take on a lot of responsibilities. Our primary task is to achieve development and to take good care of our people.

IISS: I just want your thoughts on the recent incident that the Pentagon went on record to say yesterday that China made an "unsafe" intercept by sending two aircrafts to make unsafe intercept, to US EP-3 reconnaissance aircraft. In your opinion, is this US antagonism?

Liu Xiaoming: I think it is a dangerous move on the US part. The Americans are trying to challenge China's sovereignty over these reefs. That is a very dangerous move. They do it under the cloak of the so-called "freedom of navigation". We know the ocean is wide enough for the military aircraft and vessels to have freedom of passage. But they made a close reconnaissance. They want to challenge China's defence capabilities. So this is a very dangerous move. The case you mentioned in fact has been refuted by the spokesman of the Chinese Foreign Ministry. China has every reason to defend its sovereignty. Chinese aircraft wanted to find out what the American aircraft wanted to do. But they did it in a very professional way. They moved within safe boundaries. We've tried to avoid anything unexpected happening, especially conflict. But if the Americans keep on doing this, I think they will be walking into very dangerous waters.

BBC: I have two questions. Ambassador, you criticized the Court of Arbitration. I have heard Chinese officials do that before, but I can't remember when, saying that it wouldn't accept the result. Can you confirm that that is what you are saying: you are not going to accept the results of the rulings of this court regardless of what they are? Another related question, you seem to be linking the tribunal's rulings with sovereignty. It's my understanding that it's got nothing to do with sovereignty. They are merely going to rule on the status of reefs, islands, rocks, islets in the South China Sea. You've already said that China has been planting and fishing on these islands for many centuries. Why do you then reject that narrow definition they are looking at? Because that for sure will help your case. If you are certain and you see to it that your claims are right, why don't you accept their results?

Liu Xiaoming: Let me tell you why. As for your first question, the arbitration tribunal you refer to from the very start is illegal. How could you expect an illegal tribunal to result in a good case? We have had no obligation at all, from the very beginning. We think the tribunal itself is a violation of the UNCLOS and international law.

BBC: What are the obligations that you are not going to accept?

Liu Xiaoming: We are not obligated at all by this arbitration. I can say in very clear-cut terms: no matter what decision the arbitration is going to make, it makes no difference to China's sovereignty over these islands, and is not binding at all as it is illegal and unfair as I said clearly in my presentation. With regard to what decision will the arbitration make, I already gave the example. When some people rob you and put their booty from the robbery before a court, asking the judge to make a decision, whether on ownership or status of this booty, as long as the judge handles this case, it has an impact on the ownership and on the sovereignty. The Philippines tried to divert the attention on this case. They tried to wrap up the case under the cloak of law. Of the first 15 submissions, 8 have been rejected because the tribunal is concerned about getting involved in the dispute. That is too obvious for them to be seen to violate the UNCLOS. Despite the change in tactics, it doesn't change the essence of this case. So from the very beginning, this case has been about sovereignty and delimitation. It is beyond the authority and jurisdiction of arbitration, even by the UNCLOS. The establishment of the arbitration tribunal itself is a violation of the UNCLOS. China is fighting this case according to international law. It is fighting this case in order to protect the international law.

LSE: I'd like to ask your view on US economic narrative in the South China

Sea. Where do you think it stands now? On the security side, Ashton Carter and others are quite proactive in escalating their rhetoric. But on the economic side, the American narrative, the TPP, now stands in jeopardy. Whether or not it will be ratified either before or after the change in presidency is very much up in the air. China's successful narrative in Southeast Asia has been primarily economic. Do you see the change in the presidency as working toward China's continuing successful conversation with Southeast Asia?

Liu Xiaoming: Of course we will watch US presidential election very closely and with great interest. No one can predict the outcome of the election. But I would say, we are ready to deal with whoever is elected by the American people, and whoever is the new occupant of the Oval Office. We put more emphasis on what they will do after the election. I hope the new administration will set store by and bear in mind the interest of China-US relations. China stands ready to work with the US to move China-US relations forward.

Director Inkster (Moderator) : Thank you very much. I'm afraid we have run out of time so I have to draw a halt to the proceedings here. Let me make one brief observation, which is, we found in the IISS now that the strategic salience of China is such that it is taking an increasing amount of our time. I think we concluded recently that one in every three of our books has China as a topic, which I think tells you something. I'd like to invite all of you to join me again in thanking Ambassador Liu for the very detailed and comprehensive speech.

China Does Not Accept or Recognize the Award

——A Press Conference on the Award of the South China Sea Arbitration

(19th July 2016, Chinese Embassy in the UK)

Liu Xiaoming: Ladies and Gentlemen:

Good morning. Welcome to the Chinese Embassy. Today's press conference will focus on one subject. That is China's position on the South China Sea arbitration ruling.

On 12th July, the so-called tribunal for the South China Sea arbitration unilaterally initiated by the Philippines announced its award. The Chinese government immediately reaffirmed its solemn position that China does not accept or recognize the award.

Chinese President Xi Jinping stressed the following points:

The relevant islands and reefs in the South China Sea have been the territory of China since ancient times.

China's territorial sovereignty and maritime rights and interests will in no circumstances be affected by the ruling of the Philippines'-initiated arbitration.

China will not accept any proposition or action based on the ruling.

China remains firmly committed to safeguarding the peace and stability of the South China Sea.

China remains committed to settling disputes with the countries directly involved through peaceful negotiations based on the recognition of historical facts and in accordance with international law.

To further elaborate on China's position, the Chinese government issued two statements and a white paper and interpretations of these documents by senior officials have also been released.

The Chinese Government issued the "Statement on China's Territorial Sovereignty and Maritime Rights and Interests in the South China Sea".

The Chinese Foreign Ministry issued the "Statement on the Award of 12th July 2016 of the Arbitral Tribunal in the South China Sea Arbitration Established at the Request of the Republic of the Philippines".

China's State Council Information Office published a white paper entitled "China Adheres to the Position of Settling Through Negotiation the Relevant Disputes Between China and the Philippines in the South China Sea".

The Statements and White Paper provide authoritative, comprehensive and clear-cut elaborations on China's position.

In-depth readings of these documents have been provided by State Councillor Yang Jiechi in an interview, by Foreign Minister Wang Yi in his remarks, and by Vice Foreign Minister Liu Zhengmin in a press briefing on the White Paper.

Here, I would like to talk very briefly about these documents.

The Statement by the Chinese Government reaffirms China's territorial sovereignty and maritime rights and interests in the South China Sea.

The Statement underscores the facts that China is the first to have discovered, named, and explored and exploited the Nanhai Zhudao, or the South China Sea islands, and relevant waters. China is the first to have exercised sovereignty and jurisdiction over them continuously, peacefully and effectively.

The Statement explicitly points out that China's territorial sovereignty and maritime rights and interests in the South China Sea include its sovereignty over the Nanhai Zhudao.

China has internal waters, territorial sea, a contiguous zone, an exclusive economic zone and a continental shelf, based on the Nanhai Zhudao.

China has historic rights in the South China Sea.

The statement also emphasizes that China is always firmly opposed to the invasion and illegal occupation by certain states of some islands and reefs of China's Nansha Qundao, or the Nansha Islands, and firmly opposed to activities infringing upon China's rights and interests in relevant maritime areas under China's jurisdiction.

At the same time, China stands ready to continue to resolve the relevant disputes peacefully through negotiation and consultation with the states directly concerned. China is ready to work with them to jointly maintain peace and stability in the South China Sea and to ensure the safety of and unimpeded access to the international shipping lanes in the South China Sea.

The Statement by the Chinese Foreign Ministry focuses on the arbitration.

It points out that the subject-matter raised by the Philippines for arbitration are beyond the jurisdiction of the UNCLOS.

The arbitration infringes on China's right as an UNCLOS state party, namely the right to choose the procedures and means for dispute settlement by its own will.

The arbitration also violates a series of bilateral agreements between China and the Philippines and the commitment made by China and ASEAN member countries to resolve relevant disputes through negotiation.

The tribunal has in essence expanded its power, exceeded its authority and abused arbitration proceedings. Its ruling is therefore null and void and has no binding force.

China will neither accept nor recognize it.

The White Paper offers an overall elaboration of how China's sovereignty over the Nanhai Zhudao was established in the course of history, and what China has been doing to uphold its territorial sovereignty and maritime rights and interests.

The White Paper sheds light on the origin and development of the disputes between China and the Philippines.

It aims to get to the root of the issue and set the record straight.

At the same time, the White Paper reiterates China's unchanging commitment to negotiation and consultation as the right way to settle disputes.

China believes only a negotiated result can gain understanding and support from the people of the countries concerned.

Only a negotiated result can be effectively implemented.

And only a negotiated result can be enduring.

As State Councilor Yang Jiechi said in his interview, as long as China and the Philippines stay committed to the principles and spirit of the DOC, stay committed to dialogue and consultation to manage differences properly, and stay committed to friendly and win-win cooperation, Sino-Philippine relations will have a bright future.

I have copies of these documents and transcripts of the interview and remarks prepared for your reference, in both Chinese and English. These should help you to gain an indepth and comprehensive understanding of China's position. Please feel free to take the copies with you after the conference.

Now I would like to take your questions.

China Daily: The Chinese President Xi Jinping said that China is committed to peacefully resolving relevant disputes through direct negotiations. But he also said that national sovereignty and maritime interests will not be influenced under any circumstances by the ruling. So my question is, outside these two areas he mentioned, what are the areas that China is willing to negotiate? Thank you.

Liu Xiaoming: The position that President Xi elaborates is the consistent policy of China. When it comes to the issue of The South China Sea, our position is clear and consistent. We have sovereignty over the islands in the South China Sea. And we also realize there are disputes over some of the islands. So we propose to "shelf the differences and seek joint development". This principle consists of twelve words: "Sovereignty belongs to China, differences can be shelved, parties seek joint development." So, China will not negotiate its sovereignty on the islands of the South China Sea, but we realize that there are disputes over some of the islands and we are ready to have negotiations and consultations to ensure that disputes will be resolved by peaceful means and through diplomatic negotiations.

Xinhua News Agency: My question is about a law research paper by former deputy legal advisor to the Foreign and Commonwealth Office, Chris Whomersley. Chris Whomersley argued in a recent research paper that the tribunal's argument is "not convincing" and the way the tribunal handles the arbitration case is "potentially destabilizing" to international relations because it actually allowed the Philippines to resile, abandon its undertakings in a formal document like the DECLARATION ON THE CONDUCT OF PARTIES IN THE SOUTH CHINA SEA (DOC). Could you briefly comment on this argument of Chris Whomersley, and to what extent do you think it is true?

Liu Xiaoming: I agree with him. I always oppose arbitration. I would say, it sets a very bad example. Some people believe it belongs to the dustbin. Some people believe it is useless. I was a student of international law. I believe it should be regarded as a negative example for teaching because it will be remembered in the history books as a failed case. It has violated international law in many aspects. To begin with, I would say it violates the basic purpose of the UN Convention on the Law of the Sea (UNCLOS). The purpose of UNCLOS is to ensure a stable and peaceful environment in the oceans and also stable and peaceful relations between states. Yet this tribunal, instead of serving the purpose of the UNCLOS, caused further tension between countries. It denied the diplomatic channel of negotiations for solution. It even denied the legal status of the DOC which is a very solemn official document reached by China and 10 ASEAN countries. So it did not fulfill the purpose of finding a peaceful solution. Rather it added fuel to the fire in the tension between the countries concerned. Also it added fuel to the fire in the tense situation within the region. So it is a very bad practice. As I said in my opening remarks, China will not recognize it, or accept it. It has no binding force. And we also hope that no country will take the ruling seriously. No country will make further claims based on the so-called ruling. The ruling is illegal. It has no legal status. If new claims were to be made based on the ruling, it would lead to new illegal actions that will further endanger regional peace and stability.

Propeller TV: I am from Propeller TV. Do you think there have been any implications from the Philippine government about a turnaround in China-Philippines relations? Thank you.

Liu Xiaoming: We certainly hope so. Since President Duterte took office, we have heard some encouraging words, positive comments, that he'd like to see China and the Philippines maintain good relations, that he'd like to see China and the Philippines resolve these disputes through bilateral negotiations. In fact, that is what we have been working for over many years. That is why we have strongly opposed this imposed arbitration from the very start. We believe this arbitration will lead nowhere. So we still believe, as I said, that negotiation is the only path that can lead to a solution. So we are open to cooperation with the new government of the Philippines, and we certainly expect further actions from the new Philippine government. As you know, there is a saying in Chinese, "listen to what you say, but watch out for what you are going to do". I do hope that their actions will match their words, and we can start bilateral negotiations and set relations back to its normal track. China and the Philippines are neighbouring countries across the sea. And China and the Philippines have enjoyed very good relations for thousands of years. We always believe that disputes will not prevent the two countries from having good relations. And, we do hope that President Duterte and his government contribute to new prospects in China-Philippine relations.

Financial Times: I would like to just ask you for a bit more explanation on the question of the tribunal itself. From what I've read, China's main objection to the tribunal is, first of all, that an arbitration should be agreed to by both parties, and secondly, that the tribunal has no jurisdiction over the ruling that it had. But I've looked at the UNCLOS and there are two articles which appear to run counter to China's position. The first article is Article 286, and it says that the interpretation of the UNCLOS can be brought by any party to the tribunal. So it doesn't say "both parties" but "any party". The second is 288, which says the question of jurisdiction should be settled by the tribunal itself. So could you explain China's position on that please?

Liu Xiaoming: We have different views with regard to how Articles 288 and 286 should be interpreted. Let me first say that our opposition to this tribunal is not only confined to the points you've made. I advise you to read carefully the Chinese Government statement, the Foreign Ministry statement and the white paper. I have summarized after reading these documents that this tribunal at least violated international law in eight aspects.

Firstly, it violated the UNCLOS. The UNCLOS has no jurisdiction over the matter of territorial sovereignty. This arbitration is about territorial sovereignty, although it has been meticulously packaged by the Philippines as being a technical case. From the way it ruled, everybody must come to the conclusion that it is about China's sovereignty over the islands and the adjacent waters.

Secondly, it violated the UNCLOS in terms of maritime delimitation. China and over 30 countries have already made optional exception statement to exclude from arbitration matters concerning maritime delimitation, historic bays or titles, military nature and law enforcement activities and so on. This declaration of optional exception is regarded as part of the UNCLOS. Everybody, I believe, agrees that this ruling is pertinent to maritime delimitation. So that is why we are saying the result shows that the tribunal has wilfully exceeded its power and violated China's right under this declaration. The reason why the parties belonging to the UNCLOS made such declaration is they realized that disputes might arise from the differences in maritime delimitation. If this declaration is denied, it will set a bad example. Today it's China, but who will be the next one tomorrow?

Thirdly, it denied the bilateral agreements that we have already signed. The Philippines has a series of bilateral agreements with China with regard to how to resolve the disputes through diplomatic negotiation. There are a series of bilateral documents, declarations, agreements signed between our two countries.

Fourthly, it violated the DOC signed by China and ASEAN countries. The DOC is part of international law and this declaration ensures that the parties are committed to maintaining peace and stability in the region through peaceful consultation and negotiation. It plays a very important role and has been respected and adhered to by China and ASEAN countries.

Fifthly, The arbitration denied China's sovereignty over the islands, denied China's historical rights, including the "dotted line", and challenged the basic norms enshrined in the UN Charter, namely safeguarding state sovereignty, independence and territorial integrity. So the arbitration is a serious violation of international law.

Sixthly, the arbitration, based on a distortion of Article 286, accepted the case and denied China's right to choose its own means of settling the dispute.

Seventhly, it set a bad example by misinterpreting the Convention and undermining the integrity and seriousness of the UNCLOS.

Eighthly, this arbitration deviated from the purpose of the UNCLOS to promote peaceful settlement of disputes. Rather, it intensified tensions in the region.

To come back to the articles you mentioned, the arbitration has its own right to interpret whether it has jurisdiction or not, but it should reach its judgments based on the facts. When it comes to the interpretation of an article, in addition to what rights you have, you also have to realize the obligations you have to live up to. So the arbitration only capitalized on the rights but failed to recognize the obligations. The obligation is to respect the UNCLOS provisions on jurisdiction and respect the declaration that China has made to exclude maritime delimitation. So the tribunal itself is not given the absolute right to determine whether it has the jurisdiction or not. Nor is it exempt from its obligations under the UNCLOS.

People's Daily: I have two questions. Firstly, what do you think is the impact of the so-called "arbitration" on Sino-Philippine relations? In your opinion, how will Sino-Philippine relations develop in the future? The second question is, as we all know, over the centuries, even over the recent decades, the South China Sea has been a very peaceful, and very quiet sea. But now it becomes hotter and hotter, and more complicated. What do you think is the reason for that?

Liu Xiaoming: First of all, the ruling of arbitration certainly has no impact, with no binding force, because we regard it as illegal, and not to be taken as the basis for future negotiations. If the Philippines agrees with us, I think we can resume our bilateral negotiations very soon. If the Philippines takes the ruling as the basis for negotiations, I don't think that will lead us anywhere.

I do hope countries in the region will share China's position. We already have some countries which share and support China's position, and some countries have expressed concerns over the consequences of the ruling. I do hope that China and ASEAN countries will reach consensus with regard to what serves the best interests of China and ASEAN, and what serves the best interests of maintaining peace and stability in the region. We've heard positive comments from the new Philippine government, but we do not know yet what their position is regarding the ruling. There is no way that we will implement the ruling. I hope the parties concerned will not take further illegal action, which will further escalate the already tense situation. That's something we do not want to see.

With regards to the second question, before 1970s nobody had challenged China's sovereignty over the South China Sea. The dotted-line was widely respected. It had been printed in many official maps published in the U.S., Britain, France, the former Soviet Union and many other countries. After oil and gas were found in 1970s, some regional countries rushed to invade and illegally seize the islands. We mounted strong opposition to this kind of illegal occupation by the countries concerned. As you know, during that time China was going through the Cultural Revolution, and the internal disruption prevented China from reaffirming and safeguarding its sovereignty over these islands. That was very unfortunate.

What happened in recent years, I think, had something to do with the so-called "rebalancing strategy" of the United States. Even though we had some problems in these years with neighbouring countries, the Philippines, Vietnam, Malaysia, to name a few, we did have bilateral discussions. China and Vietnam had reached agreement on maritime delimitation of the Beibu Bay. We even had a joint development project which includes the Philippines. This was a tripartite agreement on seismic survey and joint exploitation. But the projects failed to be implemented when the so-called U.S. "rebalancing strategy" came into being. Those countries were emboldened to challenge China's sovereignty. Now, instead of working behind the scene, the U.S. jumps to the front to challenge China's sovereignty by sending their warships and airplanes to have those close-in reconnaissance on China's air space, territorial sea and waters. These moves are causing tensions. We do hope these tensions will be reduced. We hope to work together with countries concerned, including the United States, so that we can make the South China Sea a sea of peace, a sea of cooperation and a sea of friendship. That is what has been reiterated by the Chinese leaders when they reaffirmed China's commitment to peace and stability of the region.

China Radio International: The Hague Tribunal is a legal institution set up under the framework of a UN convention. What is China's justification for "not accepting" and "not recognizing" its ruling? And what does it really mean to "not accept" or "not recognize" the arbitration ruling? Does it imply that China will do nothing whatsoever about it?

Liu Xiaoming: First of all, I like to correct this argument by pointing out that this tribunal has no relationship with the United Nations. It's not part of the International Court of Justice. It even does not have much to do with the Permanent Court of Arbitration (PCA). This tribunal was set up on a temporary basis at the request of the Philippine government for this arbitration case. Its only relation to the PCA, to my knowledge, is that they use the PCA's office building, and they borrowed some staff from the PCA secretariat. That's all. Its legal basis was very weak.

What I should further mention is the composition of the tribunal, namely the five arbitrators. Apart from one arbitrator designated by the Philippines, all the other four arbitrators were appointed by the Japanese judge Shunji Yanai, who was the then ITLOS President. He used to be the Japanese ambassador to Washington. I am very suspicious of his political motives. He is a policy advisor to the current Japanese Prime Minister Shinzo Abe, and he has helped Abe to change Japan's peaceful constitution and the status of the Japanese armed forces and assisted in lifting the ban on the collective self-defence strategy. This is a person who wanted to challenge the post World War II order, and I think this case gave him another reason to do so again.

China's sovereignty over the islands of the South China Sea dates back 2,000 years. In recent times, these islands were illegally seized by Japan during the Second World War. Later, after the Second World War, they were returned to China under the authority and articles of the Cairo Declaration and this was reaffirmed by the Potsdam Proclamation. If this tribunal were allowed to deny the DOC, and if this case were established, this would embolden other coastal countries to follow suit and incur a string of similar tribunal cases. In the next ruling, maybe they would say that the Cairo Declaration and the Potsdam Proclamation had no legal status. I do not know where it would lead.

According to the Cairo Declaration, all the territories and islands occupied by Japan must be returned to China, including the South China Sea islands. In fact, the military officers of China used the American ships to recover the islands. That the arbitral tribunal characterized the Taiping Dao of the Nansha Islands as a "rock", not an island, exposed that the purpose of arbitration is to deny China's sovereignty over the Nansha Islands and relevant maritime rights and interests. This violates international law, and is totally unacceptable. It has been strongly condemned by the Chinese people from both sides of the Taiwan Strait.

China did not participate in the arbitration because from day one, we believed this was a political farce. When you look at the composition of the tribunal and the political motives behind the ruling, you will know what the outcome will look like from the very beginning. We know it will lead to nowhere. We naturally showed no interest in it. When China says the ruling has no binding force, it means China will certainly not be bound by this ruling and we also hope that no other country would implement the so-called "ruling". As I said, how do you expect this discredited, illegitimate tribunal to make credible rulings? If the rulings were implemented, it would cause further damage to the situation.

The Daily Telegraph: What would you say when people who are not part of the disputes are saying that China is cherry-picking international law, and yet China is talking about its peaceful rise, it has to follow international law, as China is following in other areas? Secondly, can you give your thoughts on the way you perceive America's role in these disputes, in the sense that America encourages the Philippines to make this claim?

Liu Xiaoming: I can't agree with you when you say China is "cherry-picking". I think we have a legal basis to argue. Like I have said, there are eight areas in which this tribunal violates international laws. China abided by all the regulations of UNCLOS. China stood behind bilateral agreements, including those signed with the Philippines. And China is committed to the DOC with the ASEAN countries. So I would say, China is a country which abides by international law, plays by the rules. A basis of international law is the UN Charter, and China, being a Permanent Member of Security Council, bears the responsibility of safeguarding the UN Charter. There should be no doubt about it.

With regard to the United States, I think there should be a big question mark over U.S. behaviour with regard to the South China Sea. They have not ratified the UNCLOS, and they have kept on breaching the UNCLOS, yet they acted as if they were the guardian of the UNCLOS. If they love the UNCLOS so much, why couldn't they ratify the UNCLOS? I think they are concerned that the UNCLOS might prevent their so-called "freedom of navigation and overflight". They want to go anywhere they want, and they do not want to see any restrictions on them. That's number one.

Number two, I think this arbitration case is politically motived. It is part of their strategy. On the one hand, they sent their warships and airplanes to areas close to China. On the other hand, they seized this legal case launched against China, so as to humiliate China diplomatically, damage China's image, and also give them a legal base to challenge. But I think this intention is doomed to failure, because they do not have a good legal base from the beginning. This has already turned out to be a political farce. So far, we have not heard many countries voice their support for this ruling. By comparison, we have over 70 countries supporting China's approach. We have about 290 political parties and organizations from over 70 countries expressing their support for China's position, the position that we believe the diplomatic negotiation between sovereign states is the only solution, rather than forced arbitration. We do hope that after this ruling, common sense will prevail. All the coastal countries will come to the negotiation table and accept China's proposal to shelve disputes, and to have serious diplomatic discussions and work for the joint development. That serves the interests of the countries concerned. We also hope the United States will respect the concerns and rights of China. We believe the U.S. has its interests in the region. But they cannot protect their interests at the expense of other countries' interests. China and our neighboring countries share a common destiny and common interests. China is the last country that is willing to see instability in this region. A lot of trade and commercial commodities pass through these channels and shipping lanes. China will continue to safeguard peace, stability, and freedom of navigation and overflight in this region.

European Times: Some people say the South China Sea dispute is a case of China's view of historical sovereign rights versus America's idea of rule-based international order. How do you view this? Do you think it will be a protracted dispute? My second question is that you mentioned negotiation is the only solution to the dispute. Are you already in preparation for it?

Liu Xiaoming: First on your first question about the historical rights that we must safeguard. "Historical" means the rights and interests of China have been formed through the course of history. Some people say China discarded its strategy of "keeping a low profile" and China no longer focuses on its economic development. China is seeking more power. I think that is incorrect. In fact, what we are defending is basically what has been ours since ancient times. The dotted line is not a creation of new rights. It was there since 1948 and has been recognized by the international community. It was not until something precious was found under the sea that countries began to seize and invade China's islands. China does not ask, has not asked and will not ask for anything more than what belongs to us. As I said in an interview with the Reuters, we are not interested in an inch of land that belongs to others. We are not jealous of others. But we treasure what we have. China lost so many territories when the country was very poor and when it was invaded by foreign powers and was subjected to foreign occupation as a result of unequal treaties. So it really is in China's DNA. We will defend China's sovereignty, rights and interests. So I would say we hope that the historical rights will be reaffirmed by the international community.

China's historical rights had been respected before the 1970s by the United States in many historical documents, legal documents, and international law. But things have changed. They have new allies and new interests. In an article I contributed to the *World Post*, I said "Superpowers are used to coming and going". Countries should know that your neighbours are more important than superpowers. You cannot choose your neighbours. You have to live with your neighbours.

China does not want to challenge America's position in the world. But we cannot accept an unequal international order. China respects the current international order and China is a beneficiary of this international order. So that is why we have said time and again that China would like to work with the international community to safeguard the post-war order. We have no interest in disrupting this order or in starting a new order. But the world has changed. You need to keep up with the times. You need to make adjustment in order to meet demands, especially from the developing countries. China regards itself as one of the members of the developing countries.

As President Xi said, the Pacific Ocean is big enough to allow China and the United States to work together, rather than have conflicts with each other. We do hope that the United States will realize that China has no interest in challenging U.S. dominance. We acknowledge that although the U.S. is not a regional country, it has economic and security interests in the region. We respect that. We hope the United States will also respect the interests of China, so that the two largest Pacific countries can work together to maintain peace and stability in the region.

Thank you for your presence. I look forward to seeing you again.

Let No Fleeting Clouds Block Our Vision

——A Keynote Speech and Q&A at Chatham House

On 25th July 2016, I delivered a keynote speech entitled "Let No Fleeting Clouds Block Our Vision" at Chatham House, and I expounded China's position on the award of the South China Sea arbitration and China's policy initiatives on the South China Sea issue. Present at the event were over 300 people from the political, business, academic and diplomatic circles of the UK as well as major media organizations. Following the speech, I answered questions from the audience on issues including the impact of the US presidential election on China-US relations, the nature of the South China Sea arbitration, the legal status of the dotted line in the South China Sea, the negotiations on the Code of Conduct in the South China Sea, China's construction on its islands and reefs, resource development in the South China Sea, the impact of the arbitration on China's relationship with neighboring countries, disputes between China and Japan over the Diaoyu Islands, trends in China's diplomacy, etc.

Founded in 1920, Chatham House, the Royal Institute of International Affairs, is one of the largest research institutes on international affairs in the UK, boasting of a high-level research team and enjoying prestigious reputation in international studies both in the UK and worldwide. With more than 3,000 members and close connections with the British government, business, media and academia, it has considerable influence on UK foreign policy. Its research mainly focuses on international strategies, international relations and foreign policies. The full text of the speech and Q&A are as follows:

Liu Xiaoming: It is a great pleasure to be back. This is my fifth visit to Chatham House since I began my term as Chinese Ambassador to the UK.

Recently Brexit has been the hottest topic at the Chatham House. I did not expect such a big turnout for my speech. This shows the importance of the issue of the South China Sea and the necessity for me to share with you where China stands on this issue.

With regard to the South China Sea, one issue has been a headline maker recently. That is the arbitration unilaterally initiated by the Philippines. Right after the arbitral tribunal announced its ruling, China made a series of responses.

The Chinese Government issued the "Statement on China's Territorial Sovereignty and Maritime Rights and Interests in the South China Sea".

The Chinese Foreign Ministry issued the "Statement on the Award of 12th July 2016 of the Arbitral Tribunal in the South China Sea Arbitration Established at the Request of the Republic of the Philippines".

China's State Council Information Office published a white paper entitled "China Adheres to the Position of Settling Through Negotiation the Relevant Disputes Between China and the Philippines in the South China Sea".

Chinese leaders and senior officials also made remarks or gave interviews to highlight and interpret the above two statements and the white paper.

They reaffirmed China's territorial sovereignty and maritime rights and interests in the South China Sea. They disclosed the nature of the arbitral tribunal which expanded and exceeded its power and abused the arbitration proceedings. They expounded on China's solemn position of not accepting or recognizing the illegal ruling.

Today, I want to discuss with you face-to-face about why China believes the ruling is illegal, and why it is null and void.

First, the tribunal has no right of jurisdiction. The subject on which the Philippines unilaterally initiated this arbitration, and the real intention behind it, are in essence related to territorial sovereignty and maritime delimitation. Issues of territorial sovereignty are clearly beyond the scope of the UN Convention on the Law of the Sea (UNCLOS). And issues of maritime delimitation have been excluded by the declaration that China made years ago in accordance with the UNCLOS. From the very beginning, the tribunal enlarged and abused its power recklessly to areas outside of its jurisdiction. How could a tribunal thus established go ahead to ensure procedural and substantive justice?

Second, the arbitral proceedings are against the rules of the UNCLOS. According to the dispute settlement mechanism of the Convention, bilateral channel between state parties comes before arbitration. The third party settlement will be applied only when bilateral means have been exhausted. China and the Philippines have long agreed to resolve relevant disputes through bilateral consultations and negotiations. The two countries have never shared any bilateral communication over the filing of the arbitration. On what basis did the tribunal conclude that bilateral means have been exhausted? However, the tribunal disregarded the fact that none of the pre-conditions for initiating the arbitration had been met and forced ahead with the case. Such a procedure is utterly unreasonable and unusual. It contravenes the general practice of international arbitration under the Convention. Hence, the proceedings of the arbitration were illegal. And as everyone knows, procedural justice is the pre-condition and foundation for substantive justice.

Third, the arbitration ruling is an aberration from the fundamental purposes of the Convention. The Convention is aimed at settling disputes and differences in a reasonable and equitable way. But the tribunal's practice, overtly biased and politically motivated as it was, went the opposite way. The tribunal accepted every illegal claim made by the Philippines while all of China's reasonable concerns were rejected. To save the Philippines from breaching of its own commitment to bilateral negotiations, the tribunal belittled and nullified the Declaration on the Conduct of Parties in the South China Sea (DOC) as well as a series of bilateral agreements reached between China and the Philippines. To maximize its denial of China's legitimate rights, the tribunal even shrank the Taiping Island into a rock.

This indeed reminds me of a Chinese idiom: Calling a stag a horse. This idiom comes from the story of a high-handed prime minister during the Qin Dynasty who exceeded and abused his power. But that was a story from over 2,000 years ago. Today, in the 21st century, it is inconceivable that the arbitral tribunal could relive the same story. Two thousand years ago, by the order of a prime minister, a stag could be deliberately called a "horse". Today, at the hands of the tribunal, an island suddenly becomes a "rock". Time has changed. But the tribunal is playing exactly the same trick and its motive is just as hidden from the broad daylight. The obvious bias of the tribunal has solved no problem or dispute. Rather, it has created problems and intensified disputes. The arbitration thus has no substantive justice.

The arbitration is therefore illegal in jurisdictional, procedural or substantive terms. So, from the very beginning, it has been nothing but an illegal political farce.

It was not surprising when some prestigious jurists concluded that the ruling "will be widely regarded as the fruit of a poisonous tree, and it will fail, therefore, to garner the necessary support".

To those who insist on regarding the ruling as a "treasure", I would say that this ruling created nothing but a costly "hallucination": the excitement may last a while but what follows would be endless suffering.

China is firmly opposed to the arbitration and its ruling, and will stick to its consistent policy. The arbitration has zero possibility of becoming a "watershed" in developments in the South China Sea. Nor will it be allowed to disturb the overall peace and stability the region now enjoys.

First, the arbitration ruling will by no means affect China's territorial sovereignty and maritime rights and interests in the South China Sea. In international law, the principle *ex injuria jus non oritur*, says that illegal acts cannot create legal effect. The illegal ruling is nothing but waste paper, not only to China, but to any party concerned. China will not accept any third-party dispute settlement that does not have China's prior consent. Nor will we let others impose solutions on us.

Second, the arbitration ruling will by no means affect China's commitment to finding a peaceful solution through bilateral negotiations and consultations. I wrote an article on this subject. As its title says, China is not motivated by a desire to rule the South China Sea. China has always been committed to settling disputes through peaceful consultation and negotiation with countries directly concerned based on respecting historical facts and international law. China calls on all parties to exercise self-restraint in the process of resolving disputes, and to refrain from taking actions that will intensify or complicate the disputes. Pending an ultimate settlement of the disputes, China supports the creation of a temporary and transitional arrangement, agreed by all relevant parties based on mutual understanding and the spirit of cooperation. China has all along called for "shelving differences and engaging in joint development". This commitment has not changed and will not change.

China remains committed to negotiation with the Philippines for the sake of dispute resolution and the improvement of bilateral relations. This hasn't been changed by the arbitration. The arbitration unilaterally initiated by the former Philippine government has caused damage to China-Philippines relations. But the Philippines is one of China's close neighbours. We therefore hope the new Philippine government will consider the overall interests of China-Philippine relations and the common interests of both countries. We hope it will come back to the track of dialogue and consultations.

The momentum of cooperation between China and the ASEAN has not been changed by the arbitration, either. This year marks the 25th anniversary of the dialogue partnership between China and the ASEAN countries. The two sides will co-host a special commemorative summit in September. This will be an opportunity to outline the future cooperation strategy for closer unity and greater benefit for the people of both sides. With regard to the South China Sea issue, China is always ready to engage in friendly and candid communications with the ASEAN countries. China will comprehensively and effectively implement the DOC and steadily advance the consultation of the Code of Conduct in the South China Sea. China will follow the "dual track approach". This means the relevant disputes will be settled properly by the countries directly concerned through friendly consultations and negotiations, while peace and stability of the South China Sea shall be jointly maintained by China and the ASEAN countries.

Today, the foreign ministers of the ASEAN member states and China issued a Joint Statement. In the Joint Statement:

• The parties reaffirmed that the "Declaration on the Conduct of Parties in the South China Sea" (DOC) is a milestone document.

• The parties concerned undertake to resolve their territorial and jurisdictional disputes by peaceful means, through friendly consultations and negotiations by sovereign states directly concerned.

• At the same time, the parties encourage other countries to respect the principles contained in the DOC.

Third, the arbitration ruling will by no means affect China's commitment to peaceful development. China has long been working to build, uphold and contribute to international law and the international order. China's sovereignty and maritime rights and interests in the South China Sea are in fact part of the international order established after the Second World War. China's relevant claims have never exceeded the scope of the current international order. In this sense, China's rejection of the arbitration is to uphold the post-war international order. It is to prevent the Convention from being politically hijacked. It is to protect the authoritativeness and the integrity of international law, including the Convention. Since the founding of the People's Republic of China in 1949, we have signed boundary treaties with 12 of our 14 neighbours with land borders through consultation and negotiation. We have completed maritime delimitation with Vietnam, also through consultation and negotiation. These powerful examples demonstrate that China abides by international law, upholds international order and works for regional peace and stability.

The South China Sea is an important shipping lane. It has a bearing on the interests of many countries, including that of China. Therefore we understand the international concerns over the South China Sea issue. We have never rejected the legitimate rights and interests of non-regional countries. We have always been committed to safeguarding the freedom of navigation in the South China Sea. However, we are opposed to the "gunboat diplomacy" of certain countries operated under the pretext of "protecting the freedom of navigation and overflight" and "maintaining regional peace". We are opposed to them taking advantage of the arbitration to hype up or create tensions in the South China Sea. The South China Sea must not become an arena for some big powers from outside the region to flex their muscles. The Chinese people are firmly determined to protect our national sovereignty and maritime rights and interests. Our determination will not be swayed by threats or intimidation.

Let no fleeting clouds block our vision. Let the right way lead us on.

The South China Sea issue is a legacy from history. At the same time it concerns the real interests of today. Geopolitics is also involved. Resolving this issue will take time, patience and mutual understanding and respect between countries concerned.

For a solution to be fundamental and enduring, it has to be peaceful, it has to have gone through an equal-footed consultation and negotiation between the countries directly concerned, and it has to be based on respecting historical facts and international law.

The South China Sea should be a sea of peace, a sea of friendship and a sea of cooperation. This is China's commitment. And it takes the joint efforts of China and its neighbours to turn this into reality.

Thank you. Now, I would like to take your questions.

Question: We know that there is an important election in America. America's role on the South China Sea issue is very significant, even though it has not ratified the UNCLOS. So what kind of opportunity or challenge do you see from a Clinton presidency or a Trump presidency for China-US relations and the issue of the South China Sea?

Liu Xiaoming: I think it's still too early for me to make predictions, but we have to be ready to deal with either of the two. Hillary Clinton was the Secretary of State, and she has visited China many times. We don't know Donald Trump that well. I have read some Western media reports saying that China might be concerned about a Trump administration. I'm not that worried. I had been working on China-US relations for years and had followed many presidential elections. I think I understand American electoral politics. We listen to what they are saying today, but we must pay more attention to what they are going to do after the election. I'm confident that whoever becomes US president will set store by the national interests of the United States, and will attach importance to the relationship with China. I am confident about that. I believe that China and the US have a broad relationship. We may have some differences, there may be up and downs in the relationship, but I believe what unites China and the United States is more important than what divides us.

Question: Ambassador, thank you very much for your statement. You say that China is happy to negotiate on the South China Sea, and I think it will assist the negotiation if China could clarify the meaning of the "dotted line", what is intended by the line? Whether it is a claim for the rights of everything within the line, or it is the basis for China to generate for themselves maritime rights? It will be great for China to clarify it. And if I may ask another thing that the arbitration tribunal report also reviewed several fishing practice by Chinese fishermen, including the use of explosives in the South China Sea, one of the world's richest fishing grounds. So would you tell us what kind of steps China will take to put an end to these actions?

Liu Xiaoming: First I will say that China has long stood on the side of resolving disputes through bilateral negotiations with our neighbouring countries on the basis of respect for historical facts and in accordance with international law. It is not something that we have only put forward recently, and we are still behind the commitment. We do hope that the neighbouring countries and China will engage in diplomatic negotiations to find solutions with which both sides can be content.

Regarding the "dotted line", this is something inherited from history, as are our territorial sovereignty and maritime interests as well as historical rights. It is based on many facts that China was the first to discover, to name, to explore these islands and areas, including development and jurisdiction on these islands, and also including the fishing activities by Chinese fishermen. So the dotted line has been recognized by the international community since it was announced in 1948. No country, I know you are shaking your head, but no country challenged the dotted line until the 1970s, when natural gas was found. Then some countries rushed into this area and illegally seized, invaded, and occupied 42 islands or reefs, 29 by the Vietnamese, 8 by the Philippines, 5 by the Malaysians. China has sovereign rights over all these islands. They are part of the Nansha Islands. So I think the dotted line has been on the map, if you check your record, the maps published officially by a variety of authorities by the US, France and even Britain. They all show the dotted line, which is regarded as showing respect for the Chinese sovereignty over this area.

With regard to the fishing activities, we are of course regulating the fishermen's activities. The government does not support any fishing activities that damage fishing resources. That's one reason why we are also in discussions with neighbouring countries in order to find solutions on how together we can bring good order to fishing activities. With regard to the fishing activities, I want to remind you that fishermen of some neighbouring countries indulge in a lot of illegal damaging activities. So efforts are called for from China and its neighbouring countries to find a solution to this problem together.

Question: Some people might have actually seen you saying there's zero possibility of the ruling of the international law being enforced, given that sovereignty has been ruled out of the UNCLOS. I was very concerned. You know a peaceful resolution of this very tense dangerous situation requires international law to be respected by all. But your side ruled out the possibilities for the peaceful solutions for all the parties. And when you talk about the bilateral negotiation between a big power and a small power, does it mean some kind of might is right in the 19th-century-style? Thank you!

Liu Xiaoming: When I say there is zero effect, I'm talking about the effect they have on China's territorial sovereignty, maritime rights and interests. You would not expect that China's territorial sovereignty and maritime rights would be affected at all by this arbitration. I think I made this point very clear, you could not expect there would be change because of the arbitration. If you expect there to be an impact on China's territorial sovereignty and maritime rights and interests, I think you will be proved wrong. You should never expect anything to happen in this respect.

Arbitration is a very unsatisfactory way to resolve this issue. China will not accept it. It violates the UNCLOS, and it is illegal. The UNCLOS places the bilateral agreements, bilateral discussions ahead of arbitration. Arbitration will only apply when the state parties of the UNCLOS cannot resolve their problems by bilateral negotiations. So, I cannot agree with the argument that the tribunal is resolving disputes in accordance with international law.

China and the Philippines agreed that we were going to have bilateral negotiations. These negotiations never took place because the Philippines thought they received support from the United States. They believe they can get something from the arbitration case and are no longer interested in talking with China. The tribunal violated the basic proceedings of the UNCLOS, but we remain committed to bilateral negotiations. It is endorsed again today by Foreign Ministers from China and the ten ASEAN countries, including the Philippines, in a joint statement pledging to implement the DOC in full. It's very interesting that the Philippines is one party that has agreed to the new joint statement, which is also supportive of the bilateral negotiations between directly concerned parties as a means to solve disputes peacefully through dialogue and consultation. But on the other hand, they (the Philippines) still have illusions about these rulings. I do hope that they can get out of this dilemma, the sooner the better. So that's why I'm saying that these things have no effect on China's rights and China's sovereignty over the South China Sea, and will not have impact on China's commitment to bilateral negotiations with neighbouring countries. We believe the only solution that can be lasting and enduring is that the related countries meet face to face rather than to hold a tribunal arbitration that is imposed on a sovereign state. Just like here in this country, I do not foresee that if Britain wanted to negotiate with the other countries through peaceful means to find solutions to their disputes, you would accept an arbitration imposed on yourselves before these negotiations had even started. I don't think you would accept that. You would believe that a sovereign country has the right to find a solution rather than to be faced with having a tribunal case imposed on it. So that's what I'm saying.

You talked about big country and small country. Although China is big in size, we always stand for the position that countries big or small should be equal. Out of the 14 countries which neighbour China, we have reached boundary agreements with 12. Some of them are small countries, such as Nepal and Myanmar, but we have resolved the difficult border issues through peaceful and friendly methods on an equal footing. I think China is a guardian of international order and international law. We are still hoping that we can find a solution to the disputes with the Philippines, Vietnamese, Malaysians and other countries. We can work together to ensure peace and stability in this region.

Question: I have some strong words about the utility of the troops, and nice words about China's approach. But Mr. Ambassador, don't you think that building air strips on unoccupied reefs and sending ships full of tourists create more tension than unilateral arbitration in the region?

Liu Xiaoming: China has always called for restraint. But some countries even started building military facilities on their illegally-occupied islands. When the Philippines or Vietnam built air strips on the illegally-occupied islands, the Western media kept silent. Some Western politicians turned a blind eye to this. In face of the provocations, China could not help but to build facilities to counter their measures. We are doing this on our own land. I hope you understand my point. Those countries went back on their word, built military facilities and deployed missiles, tanks and artillery on the territory they illegally seized and occupied. And China is forced to make a response to this.

So I don't think China's actions have caused any damage to the region. On the contrary, China is building facilities that will provide public services in terms of meteorological research, oceanic research, and environmental protection. Building lighthouses is very beneficial for the safety of shipping in the South China Sea. Hundreds of thousands of vessels pass through the South China Sea. This has been appreciated by local business people. I read earlier this year that the Reuters conducted a poll. Many ship owners appreciate China's efforts and they believe the public services and public goods provided by China in building these services, like lighthouse and other rescue facilities, really shorten the time of rescue, and have done a great deal to improve the environment for shipping in the area. And I think China is really committed to this.

Having said this, I would encourage you to read the statement published today. Both China and the ASEAN countries agreed that the parties concerned will exercise self-restraint. That shows the commitment China has made to maintain peace and stability in the area. Let me read this line, and I hope this helps you to understand the situation.

"The Parties undertake to exercise self-restraint in the conduct of activities that would complicate or escalate disputes and affect peace and stability including, among others, refraining from action of inhabiting on the presently uninhabited islands, reefs, shoals, cays, and other features and to handle their differences in a constructive manner."

Question: Mr. Ambassador, would you just explain a little bit more about how China plans to use the resources in the South China Sea, those resources under the sea bed, because presumably you do have ambitions for those resources? Could you explain a bit more about your plans?

Liu Xiaoming: As I said, China has legal maritime rights and interests in this area. And of course, there are some Chinese oil companies doing the drilling. You know that all these activities are within the scope of China's sovereignty. We realize the disputes in some areas and we are ready to talk to relevant countries about joint exploration and joint development.

In fact, China and Vietnam reached agreement on some joint development programmes. In fact there is a project between China, Vietnam and the Philippines. When it comes to the natural resource exploration in disputed areas, we are open to discussions with neighbouring countries.

Question: I have been studying China for a number of years, I found, your Excellency, that your speech was an excellent presentation. Now to the question, do you think it is right for countries that do not sign the UNCLOS, or shall we say by proxy, make utilization of international law in a very disguised way. Is that indeed correct?

Liu Xiaoming: Absolutely incorrect.

Question: Thank you very much. Ambassador, I think you have explained China's position extremely well, and I think all of us have got a much better understanding on the arbitration decision that has zero legal effect. You don't accept it for the reasons you explained. On the territorial claims, you explained China's historical territory rights and you also explained China is developing public services in the South China Sea, building lighthouses and other beneficial things. So why are your neighbours Vietnam, the Philippines, not to mention Japan not accepting these issues?

Liu Xiaoming: I noticed when you say China's neighbours are not accepting China's policy, you used plural forms. I would say they are not in the majority.

The truth is, we have a very good neighbourhood. Our largest neighbour, Russia, has good relations with China. The DPRK where I had worked, South Korea, Pakistan, India, Kazakhstan, Nepal, Bangladesh, Vietnam, they all have very good relations with China. Relations between countries sometimes have ups and downs. What binds us together is interest.

Indeed, some countries do not accept China's policy because they have maritime disputes with us. Take Japan for example. We have problem with Japan over the Diaoyu Islands. The islands should be returned to China, according to the Cairo Declaration. We believe the Diaoyu Islands are ours, but when we normalized relations with Japan, we did not want the issue standing in the way. Deng Xiaoping proposed shelving the disputes. He believed future generations would be wiser and would find a solution finally. So the status quo has been there for over 40 years. It was not until recently that the Japanese government wanted to, in their words, "nationalize" the island, and the right wing segment wanted to buy this island to achieve illegal occupation. They rocked the boat, and they forced us to respond to their provocative actions.

The South China Sea is the same thing. China has been the victim, but we still believe countries, big or small, should be placed on an equal footing in bilateral negotiation to find solutions. We have been successful with Vietnam in settling some territorial disputes. We reached agreement on the maritime delimitation of the Beibu Bay. I am not saying we are trying to copy what we have achieved between China and the Vietnam, but we are confident that we can find solutions. But we should be given time on these very complicated issues. Confidence and patience are required.

Now we have the geopolitical factor. Some big countries, much bigger than China, want to use the issue of the South China Sea as an excuse for so-called "rebalancing strategy", to flex their muscles and to show their presence. That makes things more complicated. That is something that we would not like to see.

Question: Ambassador, nobody is bigger than China. You made very strong statement there. It's one of the strongest I've ever heard and China is very angry.

To some extent, I think the Chinese are very right to be angry. You're going to have to be very patient, and try not be angry. Let's talk about the sphere of influence. How does your long-term policy look in the sphere of influence? Where China will be 20 to 30 years from now? Which parts of the Pacific do you feel you will consider as part of the post-war world order and as your sphere of influence because you have concerns about that? China, the US and Russia have huge problems in common and we should be working with one another, not arguing about these islands of South China Sea. Could you talk a little bit on how you foresee China's sphere of influence evolving?

Liu Xiaoming: Sorry for saying this. I think you are still using a Cold War mentality to judge things. I am talking about the post-war order after the Second World War, not the Cold War order. This basic order is part of the international order that is guaranteed by the UN Charter.

And I can't agree with you when you say China's "sphere of influence". China has no interest in having a "sphere of influence". The number one reason is that, you said no country is bigger than China, and you are wrong from the very beginning. China is still a developing country. China is the second largest economy, that's for sure, but in per capita income, China ranks lower than 80th in the world, much poorer than the UK, to say nothing about the U.S. per capita GDP is more important than total GDP, because that concerns the livelihood of the people.

After my tour in Egypt, I was seconded to Gansu, one of the poorest provinces in China, as an assistant governor. You probably have never heard the name of that province. It is so poor that people even have problem getting drinking water. Many local people have to depend on purified rain water collected in a cell. There are still hundreds of thousands of people living under such conditions. I traveled a great deal in that province. One of the purposes is to get to know the reality of the country that I represent. Shanghai, Tianjin, Guangzhou do not represent all of China, just like London is not all of the UK. If you go to the north of England or Scotland, you will find a different country. That's the same with China. So China must face enormous challenges in developing its economy and allowing 1.3 billion people to have a better and happier life.

We are not interested in challenging the so-called American "leadership".

We are not interested in building the so-called "sphere of influence". We are only interested in building our country to make China a more advanced and modernized country. Why do we care about these islands? China had been the victim of foreign aggression for over 100 years before the founding of the PRC. A lot of unequal treaties were imposed on China. China lost a large portion of its land. Now China is an independent country standing on its own feet. People care about their territory. As I said, we are not interested in a single inch of foreign land that does not belong to us. We are not jealous of it. But we will defend every inch of the land that belongs to us by every means available to us. So if you have been to China, you will understand a saying in China, that is, "an inch of land is more precious than an ounce of gold". So it is in the DNA of the Chinese people to defend our sovereignty, territorial integrity, and maritime rights and interests.

Question: I am from the Japanese Embassy. Since you talked about Japan and the Senkaku Islands (the Diaoyu lslands of China), so I have to respond. First of all, on the matter of victimhood, we are not talking about history from 70-80 years ago. So I do suggest we do not talk about victimhood but talk about the rule of law. China is a big country within the UNCLOS. By becoming a party of the UNCLOS, China has to accept articles on dispute settlement and it must comply with them. The UNCLOS has stated that the matter should be decided by the tribunal. So it is very clear that China is bound by the treaty and by acceding to the UNCLOS. You cannot make both deals at the same time. In terms of the Senkaku Islands, in 1951 when the San Francisco Treaty was concluded, China objected, but from 1952 to 1971 China never claimed the Senkaku Islands. So we can sense a kind of manipulating use of history. It's a bit too much.

Kerry Brown (Host): Do you have any questions?

Liu Xiaoming: You could apply for another opportunity to make a speech. I think this time the floor is given to me. What is your question?

Question: I want to ask why don't you declare by which date that COC can be concluded? Please if you can specify the date of COC conclusion?

Liu Xiaoming: I think you have no right to ask me this question, because as I said, Japan is not a party to the negotiations of the COC. So when you ask China to set a deadline, I think that's too much. It's too arrogant, because this matter is up to China and the ASEAN countries to negotiate. China already made a commitment to working actively with the ASEAN countries to reach the COC as soon as possible. Because this matter is very complicated—it not only concerns China but also concerns the ten ASEAN countries—and since China always treats others as equals and always respects others' views, China cannot set a date.

As far as the Diaoyu islands are concerned, we could spend a whole day on this. This topic has been debated many times at the very top level and working level between China and Japan. One thing is certain, that is, you mentioned, the San Francisco Treaty has never been accepted or recognized by China from day one. The Diaoyu Islands is part of China and was illegally stolen by Japan by means of war. This is the term used by the Cairo Declaration signed by the leaders of China, UK and US. Namely, that these islands, i.e., all islands in the Pacific Ocean stolen by Japan should be confiscated and returned to China. After the Second World War, the Cold War followed. Japan became America's ally. So they changed their mind and thought, why should they return the islands to China? I don't need to refer back to history on that.

Question: Thank you very much Ambassador. You made a very strong argument on the issue of the South China Sea. You began by saying that the Tribunal does not have jurisdiction over territorial sovereignty and maritime demarcation and you are right. The tribunal says repeatedly that it does not have. My question is that why do Chinese government representatives keep on talking about how the tribunal has violated the territorial sovereignty and maritime delimitation? Actually it has not.

Liu Xiaoming: Talking about sovereignty, I think it's very clear that this is the whole purpose of the Philippines' arbitration case. They want to use the arbitration to deny China's sovereignty over the islands. That's the basic logic. I don't know how much they have spent. Some say they spent 30 million U.S. dollars on lawyers' fees. They spent that large sum of money just for a ruling on the status of uninhabited islands? I think they are not that stupid and mad. I think the purpose is to use this tribunal's ruling to deny China's sovereignty and maritime rights. That's very clear. Anyone who has no bias, to say nothing about the experts, should realize their real intention behind this.

Secondly, how can you separate the land features from the country who owns it? In appearance, the ruling was not on China's sovereignty, but in the essence, it says you can't claim sovereignty and maritime rights. We regard the South China Sea islands as a whole, but they single out each feature. They want to dismantle China's sovereignty bit by bit. The ruling actually deprives China of our sovereignty over the islands. I think their aim is obvious.

They also deny China's historical rights. The dotted line is one of them. Such denial goes against the basic principles of the UNCLOS. The UNCLOS respects the historical entitlements. China made exceptional declarations to exclude any compulsory arbitration on matters concerning maritime delimitation and historical rights. The exceptional declaration has been made not only by China but by more than 30 countries including the UK. Why does the UNCLOS accept the exceptional declaration? This is because they do not want to create a problem for a sovereign state. The whole purpose of the UNCLOS is for sovereign countries to live in a peaceful environment with regard to maritime delimitation.

Kerry Brown (Host): We are extremely grateful to you for bringing China's perspective on the South China Sea. We hope you will have the sixth and seventh time to speak at Chatham House in the future. Thank you very much.

Liu Xiaoming: My pleasure.

Chapter 4

COVID-19

Facts Speak Louder than Words

——A Press Conference on China's Fight against Novel Coronavirus Epidemic

On 6th February 2020, I held a press conference at the Chinese Embassy on China's fight against the Novel Coronavirus. More than 50 journalists from 27 media agencies attended the press conference, including BBC, ITV, Sky News, Channel 4, 5 News from Channel 5, Reuters, *Financial Times*, *The Daily Telegraph*, *The Times*, *The Guardian*, *The Evening Standard*, *The Daily Mail*, Leading Britain's Conversation of the UK, Xinhua News Agency, CCTV, China News Service, CGTN, *China Daily*, and Bloomberg, AFP, RT, the National of United Arab Emirates, *South China Morning Post*, Phoenix Infonews, *European Times*, *UK Chinese Times* and *UK Chinese Journal*. Also present at the press conference were envoys and diplomats from the diplomatic missions of the Philippines, Cambodia, Canada, Finland, Spain and the ROK to the UK. BBC, Sky News, CGTN and RT broadcast the press conference live.

The following is the transcript of the press conference.

Liu Xiaoming: Good morning! Thank you for joining us at the Chinese Embassy for today's press conference on updates about the novel coronavirus situation and the prevention and control measures in China.

Since the outbreak of the disease, the Chinese Government has taken a series of decisive and rigorous prevention and control measures. The speed, intensity and coverage of China's response have been unprecedented in the world. Let me use three "greats" to expound China's actions.

First, the Chinese Government has attached great importance to epidemic prevention and control.

President Xi Jinping has made important instructions on many occasions, emphasising that the safety of life and the health of the people are the top priority. He also twice called the meetings of the top leadership and set up a taskforce to map out plans for epidemic prevention.

Premier Li Keqiang, entrusted by President Xi, went to Wuhan to lead the counter-virus efforts. The whole nation has been mobilized; prevention and control efforts have been deployed and strengthened across the country. China has gone all out to fight the disease.

• At the national level, the relevant government departments are shouldering their responsibility; the military has been mobilised to help.

• In all the places, the counter-virus taskforces are led by key Party and government officials.

• At the very frontline of treatment and care, medical workers are making selfless sacrifices and showing tremendous courage.

• In communities, the people stand united to wage a "people's war" against an invisible enemy.

The vigorous measures are taking effect gradually. On the whole, the epidemic is preventable, controllable and curable.

Second, the Chinese Government has demonstrated a great sense of responsibility.

Since the outbreak, the Chinese Government has taken the most comprehensive and strict prevention and control measures, many of which go far beyond the requirements of the International Health Regulations. By taking these measures, China is safeguarding the lives and health of not only the Chinese people, but also the people of the whole world. China is doing its best to safeguard global public health.

• Temporary measures for collective quarantine have been implemented in Wuhan and other places to prevent the further spread of the disease.

• More than 6,000 medical professionals from all over the country have arrived in Hubei Province, including Wuhan.

• Medical supplies such as masks, hazmat suits and medicines, and daily necessities such as meat and vegetable have been transported to the affected areas without delay.

• Two specialised hospitals, the Huoshenshan Hospital and the Leishenshan Hospital, were built in ten days and have started to receive and treat the critically ill.

I want to emphasize that, although a large number of people have been infected with this virus, the mortality rate in China, which stands at 2.1%, is very low. This is much lower than Ebola (40.4%), SARS (10%) and MERS (34.4%). In the United States, more than 19 million people have fallen ill with the flu so far this season, with the death toll being ten thousand. This is more serious than the coronavirus infection. Currently in China, the number of cured patients is rising. We are fully confident about beating the virus.

China is also honouring its obligation. Dr. Tedros, the Director General of the World Health Organisation, has expressed full recognition for China's prevention and control efforts, and spoken highly of the tremendous contribution that China has made to the world in fighting the disease. He said that China "is setting a new standard for outbreak response".

China attaches great importance to containing the potential spread of the virus to other countries and regions. It has strengthened management and control on the overseas travel of Chinese citizens, and called on the Chinese people to take up their social responsibilities to help prevent the further spread of the disease.

As of 3rd February, there were 153 confirmed cases outside China, which accounted for less than 1% of all cases. This is a testament to the efficiency of the measures that China has taken its important contribution to preventing the spread of the disease and protecting the health and safety of the people of China and the whole world.

Third, the Chinese Government has attached great importance to enhancing international cooperation.

China is open, transparent and responsible in its cooperation with the world.

First, China has shared with the WHO, the relevant countries, and the regions of Hong Kong, Macao and Taiwan the information about the epidemic, including the genetic sequence of the virus. This has been highly appreciated by the WHO and many countries. China has also kept in close touch with many countries at the bilateral level on the prevention and control of the disease.

Second, China has attached great importance to the safety of foreign nationals in China and tried its best to address the difficulties they face by keeping them informed about the epidemic through various channels, including through foreign representative institutions. As of midday on 6th February, 19 foreign nationals in China have been tested positive for the disease, of which, two have been cured, and 17 are under quarantine and treatment. All are in a stable condition. China has also offered assistance to other countries, including the UK, that decided to evacuate their nationals from Wuhan.

Third, China is enhancing its cooperation with the international community on the research and development of the vaccine. We are working together to safeguard the safety of public health around the world.

In face of the epidemic, people have shown great care towards each other. Government officials and people from all walks of life in many countries have expressed their sympathy, trust and support for China. Many governments and international organisations have donated supplies for epidemic prevention and control.

Here in the UK, in addition to government aid, the business community, the Chinese associations and Chinese students have donated money and supplies through various channels. A few days ago, a ceremony was held here at the Chinese Embassy, where more than 20 Chinese community and student associations in the UK made donations in funds and kind. We have been deeply touched and greatly encouraged. We would like to express our heartfelt thanks to all those in the UK who have shown their care and kindness!

Ladies and Gentlemen:

The Chinese Government has the firm resolve and has taken vigorous measures to prevent the spread of the disease. This will continue to be its most important work.

First, we will try our best to treat the infected.

Every life counts. The right to survival and health is the most basic and important human right. Medical institutions all over China are doing their very best to increase the hospitalization rate and cure rate, and reduce the infection rate and mortality rate.

Second, we will strengthen epidemic prevention and control efforts in key areas.

By key areas, we mean Hubei Province, especially Wuhan City. Prevention and control measures are being improved and strengthened in this Province.

• Patients are being diagnosed, reported, isolated and treated in a most timely manner.

• Monitoring of the epidemic development is strengthened.

• The infected are treated in specialised hospitals.

• People who have had close contact with patients are under close medical observation.

All these are aimed at preventing the further spread of the disease.

Third, we are enhancing international cooperation on epidemic prevention and control, and on scientific research.

China will continue working closely with the WHO and the relevant countries and regions.

A few days ago, China published multi-language versions of the *Guide for General Public to Prevent Pneumonia Caused by the Novel Coronavirus*, which has been shared with all countries in the world through social media and other channels at top speed. This demonstrates China's sincerity in working with the international community to fight the disease. This also shows China's determination to take up its responsibilities as a reliable global player.

As I understand, researchers from China, the UK and other countries are working round the clock to trace the transmission route of the virus, to follow closely its evolution, share the relevant data and case information, to design prevention and control strategies and measures, and develop new drugs and vaccines.

Ladies and Gentlemen:

It is understandable that there are concerns in the UK and the rest of the world about the epidemic. Some people are worried that it might have a negative effect on China's economy or even the world economy. Overreactions have been seen from individual countries. There has been panic among the public, and even insulting and discriminatory remarks and behaviors targeting the overseas Chinese community. With regard to these issues, I want to stress the following four points:

First, the impact on China's economy should be seen against a larger picture.

At the moment, the epidemic is exerting a relatively severe impact on the service sector, including transport, tourism, hospitality, catering, films and entertainment.

But the impact will be short-term and temporary. It will not change the fundamentals of China's economy, which will maintain sound growth in the long run.

China's economy is highly resilient and has enormous potential for growth in the mid-to-long term. China has the capability and confidence to minimise the economic impact of the epidemic.

The World Bank, the IMF and well-respected economists across the world have all agreed that the impact of the epidemic on China's economy is temporary, and they have full confidence in the future of China's economy.

Second, understanding of the epidemic should be objective and reasonable.

The WHO has reiterated that it disapproves of and is even opposed to travel and trade restrictions on China. In recent days, the UK, at the bilateral level, has fully recognised China's tremendous efforts and effective measures in fighting the virus. It also expressed the willingness to enhance cooperation with China and do its best to assist China in these efforts.

It is our hope that governments of all countries, including the UK, will understand and support China's efforts, respect the professional advice of the WHO, avoid overreaction, avoid creating panic, and ensure normal cooperation and exchanges between countries.

Third, media reports of the epidemic should be objective and fair.

The Coronavirus has been hitting the headlines in many countries, including the UK. Many of the reports speak highly of China's counter-virus efforts or offer objective and reasonable advice. We appreciate that. However, some reports are biased, or even contain malicious slander and disinformation.

Rumours and panic are worse than the virus itself. Confidence and determination are of vital importance in overcoming the epidemic. The issue of public health suppresses national borders and requires the joint efforts of all sides, including the media, who should shoulder their due social responsibility in this battle against a common enemy of all mankind.

Fourth, we should join hands to oppose any insulting or discriminatory words and behavior.

I fully agree with Dr. Tedros, the Director General of WHO, who said, "This is the time for facts, not fear. This is the time for science, not rumours. This is the time for solidarity, not stigma."

I believe this is a time for reason and cool-headedness. This is the time for a scientific approach and a rational response. It is my hope that people from all quarters of society will stand up against this challenge and pull together.

Ladies and Gentlemen:

A Chinese saying goes, "When people are of one mind, they can move Mount Tai."

I am confident that under the strong leadership of the Communist Party of China, and given the strengths of socialism with Chinese characteristics, the solidarity and perseverance of the Chinese people, and the broad support from the international community, we will beat the virus!

Every time I hosted a press conference, I played a video clip. Today, I want to share a heartwarming clip showing how our British friends are standing with us to meet the challenges.

(Video is played.)

Now I would like to take your questions.

CGTN: First of all, Ambassador, You mentioned cooperation with the British (on vaccine). Can you just elaborate on that?

Secondly, is it true that you are unhappy that Prime Minister Boris Johnson hasn't sent a personal message showing support for China?

Liu Xiaoming: Yes, we have been collaborating with British scientists. There were already some joint labs between China and the UK, before the outbreak of the disease, on prevention of the epidemics, between Chinese institutions and universities here, such as Oxford University and Imperial College. And now they have begun to work around the clock. Now they have a target to work towards a vaccine and medicines to fight this coronavirus. So we hope that it won't be long before they will have made substantial success in their joint efforts. The governments are very supportive of their efforts, and my Embassy tried our very best to facilitate the communication and the exchanges between the scientists of our two countries.

We are thankful to the British government for their support. Since the outbreak, our two governments have maintained very close contact. Cabinet Secretary Sedwill and Foreign Secretary Raab had telephone conversations with their counterparts, Director Yang Jiechi, and State councilor and Foreign Minister Wang Yi. The British side spoke highly of the prevention and control measures taken by China, and also offered to help, and we appreciate that. There's no such issue with regard to disappointment or discontent about the British government's response.

BBC: You spoke just now about your frustration at what you call the "overreaction" and "panic" that has been generated by some foreign governments including the UK. Can you be more specific? What was it that you felt was an overreaction? Are you referring to the British government's warning to British nationals in China, saying "if you can, leave".

Liu Xiaoming: As I said, the channel of communication between China and the UK at the government level is very open, not only at the top level, but also at the working level. I have had very good communication with my counterparts in the Foreign Office, including the Acting Permanent Under-Secretary and the Director-General. And my deputy and counselors also maintained almost daily contact with their counterparts. In our conversations, we express our position that the measures taken by China are effective. There should be no panic, and there should be no overreaction. We advise the British side to follow the professional advice of the WHO. And the British side agreed with us. Of course they spoke highly of our efforts, and recognized the effectiveness of the measures taken by China. They also told us they would follow the WHO advice.

It seemed to me that the words do not match with the deeds. I noticed, probably you also notice, that the WHO Director-General has spoken publicly about his reservation, or maybe his criticism, of the British government's latest advice to ask all British nationals to leave China. He does not think this is helpful. He does not think this, what he described as, "blanket approach" towards the epidemic in China, is helpful. Because there's quarantine in one city, but not the whole of China. Life is still normal in most parts of China. And so I do say again, in private and in public, that I hope the British government and the British public should take an objective, cool-headed view of what is going on in China. And I do hope that they should regard it first as a threat to the whole world that calls for international effort. We should support each other, rather than weaken the others' efforts. So that is my advice.

5 News: Mr. Ambassador, you say you're very pleased with the British cooperation and there is close contact, and yet you accused overreacting.

Liu Xiaoming: I'm not accusing. I like to see their words meet their actions.

5 News: Given that close contact you spoke about, how surprised were you when that advice was given to British nationals in China?

Liu Xiaoming: We don't think there should be such a panic. We were given notice before they made a formal announcement. So that's why we keep close contact. And we advise them. We don't think it is a good idea. We believe that the epidemic is controllable, preventable and curable. And so we asked the British side to take an objective, cool-headed approach, and also to ensure the normal exchanges and cooperation between the two sides. That should not be interrupted.

ITV News: Are you concerned that, if there are further cases confirmed in the UK, it will discredit everything you just said about China's ability to contain this virus?

Liu Xiaoming: I cannot rule out new cases, because this is really something we do not know well. That's why there are intensive efforts by scientists from all countries, especially in China and the UK, to work together and try to find a cure, medicines and vaccines. I give one example why we said it's curable and controllable. So far twice as many cases have resulted in cure rather than death, and the number of the cure is still increasing. The whole country is mobilised. Just as President Xi said we are racing against time, and we will try our best to keep ahead of the further spread of the disease. So, I think we are confident. Since there are about 1,150, or something like that, cured cases. Of course I know the death toll now is 563. But if you compare the two, we have had more cured cases than cases of death.

Sky News: There has been reports of an increase in hate crimes against Chinese students, Chinese citizens in the UK, including the universities, ever since the outbreak of this virus. What's your reaction to that? What do you think of that?

Liu Xiaoming: I would say, in general, the public is very supportive of and sympathetic towards China. As we see in the video clip, the pupils and teachers in this primary school show their solidarity with China. So I think the general public here is very supportive. We appreciate that. There are some cases of hatred and discrimination against Chinese nationals. We have raised this issue with the British government and the police. We have also issued advice and warning to Chinese citizens, either living here or traveling to this country, about these incidents, so that they will stay alert and keep safe. And also we give contact information. If such cases occur, they should first report to the police and get in contact with the Embassy. We will provide consular protection.

We did receive some reports from universities and even some middle schools and primary schools. I think there are many reasons for it, such as a lack of understanding of the epidemic and also misinformation by some of the media. I think you should take up your responsibility to report the epidemic in a responsible and scientific way, so people will know there is nothing to worry about. Of course, there is also some deep-seated racism, not only in this country, but elsewhere too. I think at the time of crisis like this, countries should stand together. People should realise that we as mankind have a common enemy. We should say no to discriminatory words and behaviour. That's why I am calling for the public, the media and people from all walks of life to stand together, to pull together, in face of the same challenges.

Bloomberg: Several minutes ago, you made a comparison between this Coronavirus and MERS, SARS and the US seasonal flu. And really what you said is that this is not as serious.

Liu Xiaoming: I am talking about the death tolls.

Bloomberg: Are you trying to get across the message that this is not significant? This outbreak is still at a very early stage. Is this not a message to people in China and to people wherever that this is not as serious as these other outbreaks?

Liu Xiaoming: The message I am trying to get across is that there should not be a panic. It's a disease. It's an epidemic. We attach great importance to the seriousness of this epidemic. But we believe that we have the confidence, resources and capability to overcome this virus. Now the whole nation has been mobilized from the top to the very grassroots level. I have shown you there has been an increase in the number of cured cases. That gave us the reason. Just yesterday, President Xi convened another meeting, in which he called the medical personnel to work around the clock, to make sure the death toll is reduced, and the cure rate increased. That will give people more confidence that we can win this battle. I definitely think that we have a strong leadership, we have the strength in our system to mobilise the whole country, our people are united, and also, we have the support of the international community. Of course I can't predict when the inflection point will come. We do hope it will come sooner. But I can't say when we will get there. On the one hand, we have to depend on ourselves. The scientists and researchers are working very hard. And also we are engaging with scientists and researchers from other countries including the UK, who have offered generous support. The UK is a leader in epidemic prevention. I'm pleased that we have this foundation of cooperation. The scientists started to work together long before the outbreak of the disease. I do hope that people would not panic about it.

Channel 4 News: Have you formally or informally approached the Foreign Office at any point over the past few days to ask them to review their request for British nationals to get out of China as soon as they can?

Liu Xiaoming: Yes. We did tell them overreaction is not helpful. We asked them to take the advice of the WHO to make a reasonable response. Do not overreact.

The Guardian: It has been two weeks now of quarantine of Wuhan. Is this quarantine indefinite? Is the Chinese government planning measures to support people who are actually going to run out of money? And the other report we hear from Wuhan is that there are a lot of people who are saying that the hospitals are so overwhelmed that they are just not able to get tested. How are you confident that you are picking up all of the cases or even the majority of the cases?

Liu Xiaoming: Definitely, the quarantine cannot be permanent, but it is currently still necessary. As I said the government has gone all out to take actions. And also, you know, it's a comprehensive approach. So that's why I'm saying that the whole nation has been mobilised, not only the medical staff—the medical staff are on the very frontline, giving treatment to the critically ill and the people who need medical care—but also the logistics and transportation. Do you have a correspondent based in Beijing? It seems to me that he's not doing a very good job. I am not critical of your reporting. You know, the departments concerned give daily briefing these days. I follow what is going on, closely. Of course my focus is to engage with the British government in order to coordinate other efforts.

The Minister of Transportation, the Customs Inspector General and the Minister of Industry gave all the briefings about the supply, as I said, the supply of basic needs, food and vegetables. And I think there shouldn't be a panic. With regard to this, I can't say people enjoy a normal life, but daily necessities are guaranteed. And the President and Premier both emphasised that, as I said, the safety of life and health are top priorities of the government. So this is not only referring to the people who are ill, but also to the people who are not infected, so we have to make sure that they have the daily necessities. Of course, it will take some time. The quarantine efforts really have been effective in preventing the further spread of this disease. It's necessary and these measures have been spoken highly of by the WHO.

You talk about some complaints. And I think it's understandable. You know this outbreak of disease comes so unexpectedly. It's a crisis, I would say. I think the central government has made a very effective response. At the grassroots, at the local level, I would say people have also been mobilised, but it will take time for people to understand the nature and the urgency of this outbreak. I think, they have all come to know now. I can't say that China is prepared for this outbreak. We don't have enough beds, hospitals, that's for sure. So that's why we have built two emergency hospitals within just 10 days. I don't think any other country can do this, but we tried. We tried our best to treat as many patients as possible. And there have also been some efforts at the grassroots level. In communities, clinics have made every effort to take care of the patients as well. We will do our best.

Russia Today: Ambassador, you did say there was economic damage caused by coronavirus. Is it the case that the bias in misinformation, as you alleged, on the part of media, maybe some of the journalists here, is designed to damage China economically?

Liu Xiaoming: I've read some reports in the local media. They, on the whole, still have confidence in China's economy. I just gave you an example. I think *The Daily Telegraph* carried one piece; they believe Chinese economy is still resilient. And I think The *FT* also carried similar reports. So, I'm not saying the media in the UK are talking down China's economy. I'm just stating the fact that China's economy is resilient. I hope you will also adopt an objective, reasonable approach when reporting on China.

Financial Times: Ambassador, how many reports you've had of Chinese citizens in this country being stuck here—people who may have come as tourists, may have come for the Lunar Festival, not able to get home because of transport difficulties, may have come for business trips—is that a significant number? How are you helping them if it is a significant number? Are you looking after them to make sure that they have money and accommodation, etc.

Liu Xiaoming: We are trying our best to help them. Some people from Wuhan and Hubei got stranded. The government tried to get chartered flights to take them home. And here we are also trying to get in touch with the people from Wuhan and Hubei to see if they encounter difficulties and if they have a request to get home, but faced with the difficulties. But many of them told us they would like to stay. They still have business. They haven't finished their work here. So we are very open. We try our best to help them.

The Times: There have been some warnings from the WHO about ensuring that the global reaction to the crisis are driven by medical need and not political need, and I wonder if you had any sense of any countries taking more political approach? I'm thinking in particular of the context of the trade dispute with the US, and the fact that the travel advice issued by the British government came on the heels of similar advice from the US?

Liu Xiaoming: You are absolutely right. There are some people who tried to take advantage of this for political gains. We have expressed our resentment and opposition to some American politicians. We think it's harmful to the interest of the United States, not to say damaging to the collaboration between the two countries. I am confident that the two sides will continue to work together to implement the Phase One economic and trade agreement because, as I have said on several occasions, this is a good agreement. It's beneficial not only to China and the US, but also to the world. Of course, you need two to tango. So, we are committed to implementing this agreement. And I hope the other side will do the same.

LBC: It's been reported that you have some concerns about Boris Johnson's failure to engage with the Chinese government directly on this issue, so I wonder if you could say a little bit more about that. And secondly, what is your take on the advice that was given to British citizens living in China? As you said, that's against the WHO's advice. What's your sense of why that advice was given by the UK government?

I think the channel of communication is good. The Prime Minister held a Chinese New Year Reception at Number 10. Both my wife and I were invited. We had a good conversation. I conveyed greetings from the Chinese President and Premier. As a matter of fact, when he was elected, Premier Li sent him a message of congratulations. And I took this occasion to convey greetings from the top leaders from China face to face, and he also reciprocated his greetings to Chinese leaders. And he told me he was still committed to the "Golden Era" of China-UK relations. So it's a very affirmative commitment. I think the channel of communications between our two governments is very good.

As for your second question, the second question is not that difficult to answer, I think. You'll have to ask the Foreign Office, or maybe the Foreign Secretary himself, what is the reason for him to give this advice? I can't read their minds. I can only say my advice is: do not overreact.

The Daily Telegraph: I just want to clarify something. I was in Beijing for two days. You said that life in China is very much normal, but that was not the case. I have traveled in your cities in the last few weeks since the outbreak occurred. The cities are shut down, the ones outside of the official quarantine zone. All the transport has been closed. People are afraid to go outside. So what you said before isn't really true? And I just want to make that clear.

Liu Xiaoming: What I'm saying that you can't regard the whole country as being in the same situation as Hubei and Wuhan. The whole country is different. In other countries you do not need the whole nation to be mobilised. I'm not saying everything is normal in China. I'm just saying you shouldn't overreact to what is going on in Hubei and Wuhan, as if the whole of China were an epidemic zone. So do not overreact. That is what I'm saying.

The Daily Telegraph: Your people at home are overreacting. They are very worried about what's going on. I've interviewed people whose family members have died within days of the onset of symptoms, who were never tested for the coronavirus and thus are not included in the official count. So how confident are you that these numbers that are coming out from the National Health Commission are indeed capturing all the cases that could be out there?

Liu Xiaoming: My advice to you is to stay with official figures. Do not believe in rumors. Do not spread rumors. Do not spread panic. I think this is the time, as I said in my presentation, the time for cool headedness. Do not panic. And also my advice to you—you are from *The Daily Telegraph*, right?—It's okay that you focus on individual cases, but do not miss the big picture. When you miss the big picture, you will not know what the real situation is in China. That is my piece of advice to you. Thank you.

The Daily Telegraph: I wanted to know what kind of directives the central government is giving to local governments, because a lot of provinces and cities are also implementing basically quarantine situations. Even if the city itself has not announced as such, they're shutting down the transport including roads, there are temperature checkpoints, you know, there are compounds where people cannot get back in if they had traveled anywhere in the country for the last 14 days. So where are these actions coming from, are they coming from the local governments, or is the central government asking the local officials to do this?

Liu Xiaoming: Generally speaking, the government should shoulder their responsibility. As I said, in all places, the key Party and government officials are now leading taskforces to address this crisis. That is their responsibility.

And the instruction from the central government is very clear. I think the President twice called the top leadership meeting, that is the Standing Committee of the Political Bureau. It's very rare in Chinese history to have two top leadership meetings in such a short period of time. And he called another meeting yesterday to issue important directives. I hope you will read them, word for word, sentence by sentence. These are the instructions from the central government. We asked local government to follow the central government instructions. And, of course, if the local government, including officials, failed to do their duties, they will be accountable for their misconduct.

BBC: Somebody said that this crisis has shown both the strength and weakness of the Chinese one-party state. On the one hand, the astonishing mobilisation of resources in a very short space of time—the two emergency hospitals you referred to.

But equally, the Chinese Politburo Standing Committee has referred explicitly to the shortcomings and deficiencies of the initial response—in other words, the lack of transparency, the blame culture, the desire to close it down rather than actually get to grips with this virus—very, very quickly. So how do you respond to that challenge? How much does this crisis challenge the political model of the Chinese state?

Liu Xiaoming: First, I should correct you: China is not a one-party state. China is a country led by the Communist Party, but we have eight democratic parties working together with the Communist Party. So I recommend that you should read about some of the basics of China's political system. And they are also very active. Many of the members of the democratic parties are top scientists and they offer their opinions. They advise the government on what to do in fighting this virus.

No system is perfect. I don't think you can say, in the very affirmative way, that the British system is perfect. It has taken three years to figure out Brexit. I don't want to be critical. But I think every system has room to improve. So, that's why I always say the largest room on earth is the room for improvement.

And I'm pleased that you read very carefully the press release of the top leadership meeting that we recognize there are shortcomings. There is room for improvement so that we can do a better job in the future. And you're right. This is a challenge. Maybe we have a different understanding of the challenges. My understanding of the challenges is that they challenge us to improve our work and our system. But we are very confident in our system. As I said in my opening remarks, if it were not for this system, I do not know what kind of situation we will be facing. If you imagine a similar situation happening in the UK, I would not try to second guess what you are going to do with regard to this situation.

If there is no more question, that's the end of the press conference. Thank you very much for coming to the Embassy. I look forward to seeing you in the future.

A Keynote Speech and Q&A with "Asia House": Confidence and Solidarity Will See Us through to Final Victory

(Chinese Embassy / Asia House, 23rd April 2020)

On 23rd April 2020, I attended an "Asia House" webinar and delivered a keynote speech entitled "Confidence and Solidarity Will See Us through to Final Victory". This was followed by a discussion with Lord Green, the Chairman of "Asia House" and Q&A with online participants. The event was chaired by Michael Lawrence, the Chief Executive of "Asia House", and attracted an audience of nearly 250, including Sir Douglas Flint, the UK's Special Envoy to the BRI, Lord Powell, Lord Sassoon, the Honorary Chairman of the China-Britain Business Council, Caroline Wilson, Ambassador-designate to China, officials from the UK's Cabinet Office, the Foreign and Commonwealth Office, HM Treasury, Department for International Development, and the Department for Business, Energy and Industrial Strategy, ambassadors and diplomats from more than 20 countries, and representatives of the business, media and academic communities from the UK, the US, Europe and Asia. The conference was broadcast live on my Twitter, and covered live and reported by the BBC and Sky News. The full text of the speech and Q&A are as follows:

Liu Xiaoming: Thank you, Lord Green, for your kind invitation and warm introduction. As Lord Green said, having been Chinese Ambassador to the UK for more than 10 years, I am no stranger to Asia House, but this is the first time I have joined you online.

As the world enters the third decade of the 21st century, the outbreak of COVID-19 is posing unparalleled challenges to mankind, striking an unprecedented blow to the world economy and having a profound impact on the international landscape. In this battle, every country in the world is facing a severe test.

How well is China performing in this test? Today I would like to share with you my views by answering the following three questions:

- First, what does China's experience mean to the global response to COVID-19?
- Second, will China continue to be an engine for world economic growth in the context of the pandemic?
- Third, why does China believe international solidarity is the most effective weapon against the virus?

Currently COVID-19 continues to ravage the world, and the global response to this challenge is at a critical moment. China was the first country to report the virus, and also the first to have achieved preliminary but important success in containing the virus. I think, China's efforts bear three-fold significance to the global response to this public health crisis.

First, China has built a strong "line of defence" for global public health.

In the early days of the outbreak, China acted responsibly and quickly by adopting the most comprehensive, strict and thorough measures of prevention and control in the interests of the Chinese people and the rest of the world. Across the nation, 1.4 billion people have rallied behind the government and are waging a "people's war" against the virus.

After strenuous efforts and enormous sacrifices, China became one of the first countries in the world to have brought the epidemic under control. For one whole month, there have been only sporadic cases and the spread of the virus within China has been basically cut off.

Through persistent efforts, wisdom and sacrifice, China has built the first line of defence for the world, offering protection for life and health.

Second, China has accumulated valuable experience for the global response to the pandemic.

In fighting its battle against the virus, China has always focused its efforts on the welfare of the people and relied fully on the support of the people. This has become the most salient Chinese experience in this battle.

In record-short time, China established a multi-dimensional and multi-layered network of prevention and control involving everyone from the Central Government to the local communities. The whole nation was mobilized to support Wuhan, the epicenter of the outbreak.

The measures that China has taken are based on science. The principles of early diagnosis, early report, early quarantine and early treatment have been followed. COVID-19 patients were admitted into designated hospitals with the best experts and sufficient resources for timely and tailored treatment. And both traditional Chinese medicine and Western medicine have been used to treat patients.

China attaches great importance to balancing counter-epidemic measures and ensuring normal economic and social activities. We have kept in mind both domestic and global impacts when taking actions. And we have been working to gradually bring economic activities back to normal.

Leaders of many countries have spoken highly of China's efforts, and recognized that China's experience offers useful lessons to the world.

Third, China has provided assistance to other countries in the spirit of solidarity.

China has engaged actively in international cooperation in an open, transparent and responsible manner to deal with the crisis.

China notified the world about the outbreak without delay, and acted quickly to identify and share the genetic sequence of the virus. At the same time, China has been sharing its experience of prevention, control and treatment with other countries without reservation, and set up an on-line knowledge centre, which is open to all countries.

China has donated $20 million to the WHO. Today, China announced a further donation of $30 million, which will be used to contain COVID-19 and bolster the public health system in developing countries.

China has also sent 17 teams of medical experts to 15 countries. It has provided or is in the process of providing much-needed medical supplies, including masks, protective gowns, testing kits and ventilators, to more than 150 countries and international organizations, including the UK.

Despite the difficulties at home, China has been increasing supply of pharmaceutical ingredients and medical and protective equipment and materials to the international market. From 1st March to 10th April, China exported about 7.2 billion masks, 55.57 million protective gowns, 3.59 million infrared thermometers, 20,000 ventilators and 13 million pairs of goggles.

The assistance from China has injected positive energy into the global response to COVID-19 and shored up international confidence in winning this battle against the virus.

Now I would like to move on to the second part of my speech and talk about China's economy in the context of the outbreak, which I know you have all been following closely.

A few days ago, the IMF downgraded this year's growth expectations by a big margin, warning that the impact of COVID-19 on the world economy might surpass that of the Great Depression.

The outbreak has also taken its toll on China's economy and social conditions. In the first quarter, China's GDP contracted by 6.8% year-on-year.

In face of the unprecedented risks, challenges and uncertainties, it is all the more important that we shore up confidence, keep up our courage, and work hard to turn challenges into opportunities and ensure continued growth. I think we can draw confidence from the following three facts:

First, China's economy will maintain steady growth in the long run. This momentum has not changed and will not change.

China has a solid economic foundation:

• As the world's second largest economy, China's GDP reached $14.4 trillion in 2019, 3.1 times compared with that of 2008 during the international financial crisis, which was $4.6 trillion, and 8.6 times compared with that of 2003 amid the SARS outbreak, which was $1.67 trillion.

• China is the only country in the world that has all the industries under the United Nations classifications.

• With a population of 1.4 billion, including 900 million workforce and more than 400 million middle-income earners, China enjoys broad prospects for economic growth.

• China's economy has enormous potential for further growth. The per capita GDP has just crossed the $10,000 line, which is only one fourth that of the UK and one sixth that of the US. The urbanization rate stands at only 60%.

As I said earlier, China attaches great importance to balancing counter-epidemic measures and economic and social activities. Within the country, life is gradually returning to normal, and economic activities are approaching or have already returned to the normal track.

As of today, 99% of major industrial companies have resumed operation. March manufacturing PMI increased by 16.3 percentage points over February. According to the latest IMF World Economic Outlook, China's economy growth will rebound to 9.2% in 2021.

Second, China's economy will pursue high-quality development. This goal has not changed and will not change.

While COVID-19 will remain on the government agenda for some time to come, China has lost no time in turning our attention to the economy.

- We will continue to follow the new development concept.
- We will press ahead with supply-side structural reform.
- We will improve the market-based allocation of production factors.
- We will pursue high-quality growth through further reforms and by opening up further to the world.

We have stepped up macro-policy regulation to counter-act the impact of COVID-19. Measures have been taken to safeguard employment, the financial market, foreign trade, investment, FDI and expectations stable. On this basis, we have taken further steps to protect basic livelihood, market entities, food and energy security, stable industrial and supply chains, and the normal operation of the grassroots communities. All these efforts are aimed at ensuring overall economic growth and social stability.

We have also taken measures to expand domestic demand and increase effective investment. The battle against this pandemic has created new opportunities for development, such as the "stay-at-home economy" and the "cloud office". China is seizing these opportunities. We will leverage the internet, big data, artificial intelligence and other new technologies to accelerate the development of emerging industries, such as the digital economy, smart manufacturing, and medical and health care. Efforts are also being made to transform and upgrade traditional industries, a expand investment in strategic and emerging industries, and to develop the green economy.

These efforts will ensure that China's economy remains on the track of high-quality growth.

Third, China will continue to be the powerhouse and stabilizer for the world economy. Our commitment has not changed and will not change.

China has been committed to opening its market wider to the world. Measures have been taken to:

- increase market access,
- improve the business environment,
- expand import,
- increase outbound investment,
- facilitate the unimpeded flow of goods around the world,

• and promote high-quality cooperation on the Belt and Road Initiative.

The 127th China Import and Export Fair will take place online in mid-to-late June. This will be the first time that this longest-running trade event in China will be held online. In November, China will hold the third China International Import Expo. Both events will create huge opportunities for the mutually-beneficial trade and cooperation between countries of the world.

China is also calling on the international community to step up macro-policy coordination in order to stabilize the market, secure growth, protect wellbeing, and ensure that the global supply chain is open, stable and safe.

On top of that, China is the "factory of the world". Steady economic growth in China provides a strong support for global recovery.

Now I would like to move to the third part of my speech and talk about how the international community should work together to win the battle against COVID-19.

The question being asked or debated around the world today is this: Has the pandemic united or divided the world?

My answer to this question is this: The on-going battle is living proof that countries of the world belong to one and the same community with a shared future. In the battle against the pandemic, cooperation is the most effective weapon if the international community wants to claim final victory over the virus.

First, we need global, unified action to win the battle against COVID-19.

At the Extraordinary G20 Leaders' Summit last month, President Xi Jinping put forth four important proposals:

• First, we need to fight a global war.

• Second, we need to take international collective action.

• Third, we need to support international organisations in playing their active roles.

• Fourth, we need to enhance macro-economic policy coordination.

He also made a number of specific proposals regarding intergovernmental cooperation, including joint R&D into drugs and vaccines, a G20 COVID-19 assistance initiative and joint efforts to stabilize global industrial and supply chains. These could be the areas where the countries of the world could work together to meet the challenges of the global public health crisis.

China will continue to enhance its cooperation with other countries, shoulder its due responsibilities and contribute to the final victory of this battle.

Second, we should enhance solidarity and shore up confidence.

This virus does not respect borders or discriminate between races. In face of the crisis, playing the blame game is futile; arrogance and insolence will only poison the cooperation between countries.

It is against human conscience to deliberately affix the "virus" label to a specific region, to politicize public health issue and stigmatize a specific country. Such moves will only drive a wedge between countries, undermine international cooperation and harm the interests of all mankind.

It is important that countries of the world reject ideological bias, place human lives above everything else and form the maximum synergy to bring the pandemic under control.

Third, we should uphold multilateralism and support international organisations in playing an active role.

China is committed to multilateralism. We have been working to strengthen and improve the system of global governance with the UN at its core.

Since the outbreak of COVID-19, the WHO has taken an objective, scientific and just position, and played an important role in coordinating and promoting international cooperation. This has won extensive recognition from the international community.

Going forward, China will continue, as always, to support the WHO, including supporting its leadership in the current battle against COVID-19.

China will also work actively to strengthen cooperation on public health matters with countries along the Belt and Road routes and to join hands with them to build a "Silk Road of Public Health".

Fourth, we should promote inclusive cooperation in order to build an open world economy.

There may be difficulties and headwinds, but there is no reason for us to stop cooperating in an open spirit or to seek development through cooperation. Advocates of "decoupling" and a "technology blockade" will only find themselves in self-imposed isolation, restriction and backsliding.

China will remain committed to reform and opening up, and enhance coordination in macro-economic policy with other countries. We will begin to focus on what we should do after the pandemic. This includes taking all necessary measures to ensure the stability of global industrial and supply chains, to promote trade and investment liberalization and facilitation, and to build an open world economy.

Ladies and Gentlemen:

China and the UK are important partners in this battle against the virus. In the matter of one month, President Xi Jinping and Prime Minister Boris Johnson had two telephone conversations. This demonstrates the firm determination of our two countries to work together to meet the challenge of this public health crisis.

At the present moment, our two countries are sharing information and experience and conducting joint scientific research. We are both advocates of multilateralism. We are both supporters of the important role of the WHO in a united global response. We are both proponents of international cooperation under the framework of the G20. And we are both promoters of better global governance on public health.

At this crucial moment, it is important that China and the UK shoulder our responsibilities, stand together with each other, and resist noises and disruptions. We should add positive energy into our joint response to the pandemic and make new contributions to global public health.

I am confident that China and the UK will emerge from this test with a more mature and robust relationship, with broader and deeper cooperation, and with a stronger and enduring friendship between our peoples.

As a Chinese saying goes, "Victory is ensured when people pool their strength; success is secured when people put their heads together."

China stands ready to join hands with the international community, including the UK, to shore up confidence and address the current difficulties.

Together we will win this battle against the virus. Together we will create a better and brighter future for the world!

Thank you.

I am ready to take your questions.

Lord Green: Thank you Ambassador Liu and thank you very much to those who are with us. There will be many people who share the appeal for constructive international cooperation and engagement in this unprecedented situation. Unprecedented is a word that is becoming extremely frequently used, but we think it is unprecedented at least since the Second World War. It poses all sorts of challenges for individual countries. China was the first into it and seems to be the first out of it. I guess caution is always necessary. Britain as you know is still struggling, and all of Europe is struggling with this.

It seems to me that there are some short, medium and longer term challenges, some of which are deeply impacted by COVID-19, and some are not. It seems to me that clearly in the short term, we have the question of how to exit from lockdown strategies. This as you know is a topic that gets a lot of conversation in this country and around Europe more generally, and it's causing a lot of anxiety in the US as well, and maybe in some parts of East Asia. Japan has taken a particular route, which is almost explicitly allowing the possibility of a second wave of the virus. So different strategies are all agonising with the difficulty of getting out of the COVID-19 situation, particularly since we all recognise that it will take some while for an effective vaccination to be available against the virus. There are some short term challenges that have to do with the immediate economic impact of COVID-19, which we all wrestle with. For example, how tourism will reemerge as an important economic force; and about the retail industry, to what extent many small businesses will be shut down and so on.

Then there is the whole macroeconomic picture: country after country have released enormous support packages, fiscal and monetary. What are the medium term consequences of those? Does this mean that we will face, a little further down the track, a period of renewed austerity, as nations try to repair the balance of their finances? Does it mean higher taxes? Does it mean higher inflation? There are all sorts of questions that will be around. They'll be around for the Chinese authorities, I think, as the Chinese economy rebounds. They are clearly going to be around in the British context, and in a broad European context. The US will face it and it comes with a different way because it's in a special position vis-à-vis the dollar. And that's the kind of medium term challenge that's created by COVID-19.

I think there are some medium and longer term challenges that are not affected by COVID-19. I think that the trade order is one question. Even before the virus we were all struggling with the fact that the WTO was losing its ability to effectively arbitrate disputes because of the absence of appellate judges. I noticed that, on the 30th March, right in the thick of the pandemic, the EU and China and a number of other nations agreed on the multi-party interim appeal arbitration arrangement. There is a question in my mind about how the UK can get itself involved in that. But I think we should all recognise this is an important step in shoring up the work of the WTO. You talked about the reasons we all recognise about the WHO. I think the WHO is one important international organization, whereas the WTO is an equally important international institution that is part of a functioning multilateral order, and we all have some concerns about that. Let's face it, in both cases, America has chosen to take a less constructive view at least temporarily. And I think it's the common interest to re-establish a conviction about the importance of that international multilateral order.

And then finally, I think there is the longer-term question which is in no way going away, and that is about bio-diversity, environmental degradation, climate change. In the short term, we have seen how the decline in economic activity has improved levels of pollution in cities around the world, and has led to a reduction in carbon dioxide emissions, but in no way was it anything other than temporary. I believe that the continuing demographic pressure, the continuing pressure of urbanisation, the continuing pressure of economic development means that we are going to continue to have to grapple with this fundamental longer term challenge and COVID-19 in no way affects that. It's made it more difficult in the short term, of course by forcing China to postpone the Kunming COP15 bio-diversity conference, and forcing the UK to postpone the Glasgow COP26 which was due in November. I hope that those postponements are only for a relatively short period of time, because of all the common agendas you, Ambassador, have quite rightly referred to, this one is perhaps the most important of all. It's the most profound and the longest term. We should not allow COVID-19, and the tragedies and difficulties of the present circumstances, to take our eyes off that ball.

So there's a lot going on; We live in extraordinary times. There are plenty of challenges posed by COVID-19.

There are also challenges that inevitably affect international relationships. The big question of China and America, which we Europeans look at with hope and prayer, but this relationship will only develop on a constructive basis. And I think that there's therefore plenty of need for us to continue to have the sort of dialogues with what this occasion represents. One is here at "Asia House", we have an extremely important role in providing a platform for these dialogues, both about shorter term issues from micro to macro economics, and about the medium term issues of the trade order, and about the longer term issues of climate change cooperation and its impact on economic development.

Let me stop there. I wonder if any of what I've just said resonates with you. Ambassador?

Liu Xiaoming: Yes, Lord Green. You've touched upon many areas. I would say that I quite agree with you on many of these areas, and your points.

You talk about the challenges in each country. I think each country is different from the other. The UK is different from Germany, Italy, or France. We follow the situation very closely. But despite the differences, I think there's a commonality between countries in fighting against this virus. I talked, in my presentation, about the China-UK collaboration. I think that also applies to China's collaboration with other countries. When we're faced with these common threats, countries should work together.

First, I think we should support each other. In terms of medical supplies, when China was at its critical moment, the UK government sent two shipments of the most needed medical supplies. But now you are fighting your battle, we reciprocate your support. Just as Minister Gove said, you received much more than what you donated to China. Currently, I think ventilators are badly needed. 750 ventilators have already been shipped to the UK, and there are more to come. There are other medical supplies and equipment that we are ready to supply to the UK and to the world.

The other area is the sharing of experience. China was one of the first countries to have achieved significant progress, and we'd like to share with other countries our experience on how to contain the virus, and how to treat the patients. I'm very pleased that we are maintaining constant communications between the two sides. Secretary Matt Hancock just had a telephone conversation yesterday with his counterpart Ma Xiaowei, the Chinese Health Minister. They had a very productive and in-depth discussion on collaboration between China and the UK in fighting to the virus. They shared their experience and compared notes.

The third area is international cooperation. I touched upon that in my presentation. You used the word in a very polite and very British gentlemanly expression about the "unconstructive" approach by the United States. We are very disappointed by the US decision, but we believe that the WHO plays a very important role, especially at this critical moment. We need to support the WHO in leading the international response to this virus. I'm pleased that the UK government decided to continue to support the WHO. So China and the UK share this common position.

In addition to its 20 million U.S. dollars donation, just a few hours before our event today, the Chinese government announced that we are going to donate another 30 million U.S. dollars to the WHO. Maybe they knew that the "Asia House" and you were going to have this event, so I can share with you firsthand information. (Laughter) We especially hope it will be used to support the public health system in developing countries in Africa and in some other places.

The fourth area where China and the UK can cooperate and also the international community can enhance its collaboration is as you said macro economic policy, that is a way to ensure that the world economy will resume growth.

In China, the major industries have already resumed 99% of their former production, and the government has introduced more policy measures to support small and medium sized businesses—that is also very important. What's more, it is still our goal to support the WTO to ensure trade liberalisation and facilitation. We would also like to work with the UK.

Climate change is very important to our agenda as well. It's a pity that we have to postpone both conferences-the COP15 and the COP26. At the very beginning of this year, I regarded it as a year of China-UK collaboration on climate change. As a matter of fact, our two countries worked very closely and coordinated with each other despite the virus.

Although we have had to postpone the conferences, the preparation work is still ongoing. I keep very close communication with Secretary Sharma. He has been designated as the President for the COP26, and we have a new Minister of Environment, Huang Ruaqiu. So I tried to connect the two of them. The working teams of our two countries are still talking to each other online.

The other important issue is that when we are enhancing international collaboration on fighting against the COVID-19 virus, we should also be on guard against a political virus. Like I said in my speech, some politicians and some forces are trying to find a scapegoat and to play a blame game in order to shirk their responsibility. You know we call on governments of all countries to focus on fighting the virus, on protecting the lives of its people, rather than fighting each other, rather than undermining international collaboration. That is also very important. So we are very disappointed, and we rejcct these so-called "accusations" from some of the American politicians. We don't think this disinformation against China serves the purpose of international response to this virus.

On China-US relations, we have every reason to maintain a sound and good relationship. President Xi had several telephone conversations with President

Trump. We always believe that China and the US will gain from cooperation and lose from confrontation. We also believe it is not only in the interests of China and the US to have a sound and good relationship, but it's also in the interests of the world. We would like to have a good relationship with the US, based on mutual respect, non-confrontation and mutual collaboration, and we are working towards this goal. But you need two to tango, right? You know, the Chinese leaders, or Chinese ambassadors, Chinese diplomats are spreading the words of a community with a shared future for mankind, and are trying very hard to shore up the confidence of the international community. However, at the same time, some politicians, some people are trying to spread disinformation and rumors across the world.

That is not helpful at all! So we really hope that China and the US can work together, and the international community can work together for the common goal that serves the interests of all mankind.

Adam Keswick from Jardine Matheson Holdings: Hello Ambassador. Thank you for your words, and Stephen, yours too. I thought it is very encouraging to hear everything you've said. I hope that the networks of communications that have been put in place to fight this virus can continue to promote the economy after we've tackled this, which I'm sure we will. Ambassador, your views of what China will be doing, all of which I took a lot of comfort from. But more specifically, I feel that the eyes of the world will be watching the upcoming NPC meeting whenever that takes place. But presuming it will be sometime later in May, it would be very interesting to get your views on what specific messages, do you think, are going to come out of that meeting that the rest of the world can take further comfort from in terms of battling the virus, and also a return to some form of economic normality. Just be interested to have your views on that.

Liu Xiaoming: I think this will be very important. We call it the "two sessions". It has been postponed. It will set policies and guidelines, not only for the development of China for this year. I think it will draw up the plan, or what we call the 14th Five-Year Plan. So, the significance of the two sessions will extend beyond this year. Of course, COVID-19 will be high on the agenda. And I wouldn't speculate on what other items will be on the agenda. But as I said in my speech that COVID-19 not only poses challenges to China, but also creates opportunities for development. I think both delegates of the National People's

Congress and deputies of the People's Political Consultative Conference will focus on the new areas, the new points of growth for the future development. So, I would recommend that you follow these two sessions very closely.

Emma Roberts from BHP: Ambassador, it is very good to hear your summary of China's economy as it's moving out of the crisis and BHP obviously has very a strong relationship with its Chinese customers where its commodities are concerned. So far we've seen this demand remain rather stable even during the peak of the crisis within China. BHP has been able to work with its customers to continue that supply. However, I think there's certainly some concerns and there's been some recent press reports about whether that demand from China may ease off towards the later part of the year. Perhaps China is experiencing a dropping off of exports from Western economies as these Western countries try to come out of their lockdown and struggle to get their economies up and running. What's your thought on China's continued emergence from its crisis and the continued risk of China's economy? Do you see a dipping in that as Western economies struggle to get back, or remain rather steady and strong?

Liu Xiaoming: I think that as China gradually resumes production, it will continue to play a role, as a powerhouse of the world economy. As 99% of the major industries have resumed, China will continue to play a role as the factory of the world. China is a huge market. So we will contribute to the restoration of global growth. The outbreak of COVID-19 really brings some opportunities for us to restructure our economy. Some areas might hold great potential, including the stay-home economy, the digital economy, AI and also the medical area. Here's an example. From March 1st to April 10th, China exported about 7.2 billion masks, 55.57 million protective gowns, 20,000 ventilators and 13 million pairs of goggles. So China is really a source of medical supplies. That is also China's contribution, not only to the global response to the virus, but also it will help build the industrial and supply chain in the future.

China is committed to building an open world economy. China has achieved success in the past 40 years because of the policy of reform and opening up. I think China will stick to this policy to continue its success. There's no reason for China to close its door or abandon the reform. So reform will be ongoing and China will be open wider to the world. The 127th China Import and Export Fair will be held online in June. And also the third China International Import Expo will be held in November. These will be very valuable opportunities for China to engage with the outside world. I've been talking to British senior officials from the Department of International Trade, as well as business leaders in the UK, inviting them to participate in these two events. It will provide enormous opportunities for our two countries to work together to resume the momentum of economic growth.

Laura Mann from AstraZeneca: Thank you so much for your excellent remarks. AstraZeneca places very high value on partnership with China before and during COVID-19. We've been able to donate nine million masks around the world, and to the countries most in need, in partnership with the World Health Organization and World Economic Forum. I wondered, in your head, what do you see as the further opportunities to continue to strengthen the bilateral relationship between the UK and China? For example, in health care and life sciences.

Liu Xiaoming: As I said earlier, our two countries continue their dialogue at a very high level. You know, President Xi Jinping had two telephone conversations with Prime Minister Johnson in little more than one month. That was very rare. I've been here as ambassador for more than 10 years, and I've never seen our top leaders have such intensive communications in such a short period of time. On the ministerial level, we are having very intensive communications, as Director Yang Jiechi talked to Sir Mark Sedwill, and State Counsellor and Foreign Minister Wang Yi talked to Secretary Raab. And here in London, I have kept very close contacts with ministers and secretaries. We compare notes and share experiences.

And, China and the UK are working very closely on developing the vaccine. The scientists of our two countries are working very closely. Imperial College, Oxford and Cambridge are working very closely with their counterparts in China. While the Chinese medical team was here, they held online discussions with British experts and doctors. So we have had very intensive interactions with each other. In addition to supplying medical equipment, the vaccine really is the final solution to the battle. Both President Xi and Prime Minister Johnson expressed their support for the scientists of the two countries to work together in this very important area.

What is more in the international arena, China and the UK both work very closely. We're both supporters of multilateralism and full supporters of the WTO. You know, Lord Green cares about it very much. We see the UK as a partner for China on the Belt and Road Initiative. We are now working with the countries along the Road to build a "silk road for public health".

I think there is another area in which China and the UK can share experience and can work together. Climate change, As I said, China and the UK are leaders in environmental protection. We're supposed to host the COP15 and the COP26. They have been postponed, but not cancelled. We're still working on them. You know, when this pandemic is over, the two countries will host these two conferences. They will set the agenda and direction for climate change and for environmental protection. So, there are enormous opportunities between our two countries.

And trade between us. I think there's still a great future for the trade between our two countries. Last year, a new record was set in bilateral trade—an increase of more than 7%, despite the downturn of global growth of the trade. The UK is now China's third largest trading partner within the EU. China is the third largest export market for the UK. Chinese investment in the UK is also increasing. In the past five years, the total Chinese investment has been bigger than the previous 30 years combined. Now, the UK is the number one destination in Europe for Chinese investment. Chinese businesses here are very active. A few days ago, I participated in an online donation event held by the China Chamber of Commerce in the UK. They donated ventilators, face masks, goggles and protective gowns to the NHS. And that shows their global vision and sense of social responsibility. We encourage all these interactions between China and the UK.

David Sayer from KPMG: Thank you. I'm about to say, I enjoy this remarkable technology and for that I want to address a question. You've said to me in the past that every challenge has an opportunity. And I do think, this remarkable technology allows us to have a much more direct and immediate dialogue with Chinese firms. I've been talking to clients in the UK that I can bring my Chinese partners into a virtual meeting, far more easily and far more acceptably than it's been in the past and I think that's one of the changes we'll be seeing. Virtual dialogue is becoming, and has proved it's workable. It's becoming utterly acceptable. And in the past having a dialogue with Chinese firms has always involved 20 hours on planes and the rest. I think one of the things coming out of this is the potential to accelerate dialogue between the UK and China across so many dimensions. And I just wonder the ways in which we can celebrate the facilitation of that, and whether the Embassy can play a role.

Liu Xiaoming: Yes, I'm very pleased that you have been one of the beneficiaries of this new technology. Once you have Huawei participating in your 5G development, the speed and quality of these online meetings will be even better. I know that Prime Minister Johnson has a very ambitious plan to have full 5G coverage in the UK by 2025. I think Huawei will be a big help on this. We do hope that not only will the leaders of our two countries talk to each other, but also business leaders. I held several online meetings. As a matter of fact, this "Asia House" is really one of those webinars I have attended, and soon I will have another one with the CBI. And then another one with the CBBC. I already had one with the British Chamber of Commerce in China. We had this real time discussion. I think we benefit greatly from this technology. We should stay committed to free trade, to building our business friendly environment. The UK is well known for supporting a free and open economy. That's very important. That's why the UK can become No.1 destination for Chinese investment. I held a meeting with many Chinese business leaders. I asked them, "Why are you here, compared with other European countries? Why do you invest your money here?" Take Jingye. I just participated in Jingye's acquisition of British Steel. They told me they found the UK very open and transparent, and the political leaders, business leaders, local leaders and local community welcome Chinese business with open arms. That's the secret of the UK's success. So, I do hope that this trend will continue. It is really not only for the benefit of China-UK collaboration. It is also for the benefit of the people of the UK.

James Landale from BBC: You placed great emphasis on international cooperation. Will China, as a result, cooperate with any independent international investigation into the origins of this pandemic? Will China provide any investigators with full access to all the relevant data, locations and witnesses?

Liu Xiaoming: China has been open, transparent and responsible from the very beginning. We have invited the WHO experts to China. They visited not only Wuhan but also other places and cities. They came up with a very extensive and comprehensive report about their study in China.

I hear quite a lot of speculation and disinformation to the effect that the Chinese are covering up and hiding something. This is not true. I do not know if you have read the WHO report. Some people already leapt to judgement beforehand. Each time they hear American politicians accusing and criticizing China for hiding or covering up, they just turn to them. But when Chinese spokesman spoke about the fact, I read very little coverage here in the Western media. They already have prejudice and bias against China. That's the problem.

I would advise the media including the British media to be balanced and objective. I'm not calling on you to be friendly to China, but just to be balanced. While you are reporting that the US Secretary of State is so-called "criticizing" but actually "stigmatizing" China, you should also report the counter argument given by China. You should also report the WHO's comment. When the media harbours this bias, they only report something they would like to hear. They don't report the other side of the story. That's the problem.

The Chinese government has been transparent and open, and has responded very quickly. When Americans complain that one month after the outbreak China had not shared information and has not reported to the WHO and international organizations, that's not true. The virus was first reported on 27th December by Dr. Zhang Jixian. She reported much earlier than Dr. Li Wenliang. We recognize Dr. Li as a hero and he gave his life fighting this virus. But he did not report to the authorities and he shared the story three days after Dr. Zhang Jixian made a report to the local health authorities. Then the government adopted very strict and swift actions, notified the WHO four days later, and shared information with Americans seven days later. So that's how Americans could have taken action to bring their nationals back and to close the border. If you check the timeline on what China was doing, you will find we have been transparent and straightforward with all the information.

You talk about having an independent investigation. It's up to the WHO. We support the WHO. We believe we should play by international norms and international rules, not by some other countries' rules. Some other countries have even sued China in their local courts. It's absurd. I've twice been posted to Washington, D.C.. This is not the first time that some politicians want to play the world police. This is not the era of "gunboat diplomacy". This is not the era when China was still a semi-colonial and semi-feudal society. This is the third decade of the 21st century. Those people cannot understand it. They think they still live in the old days when they could bully China and the world. If the WHO does not act their way, they cut off their support and criticize the WHO for being "China-centric". That's simply not right. So we are calling for international cooperation. That's the only weapon and the only way out to win this battle against the virus. Not by scape-goating, not by playing games, not by politicizing the virus, not by spreading a political virus. We have to guard against this while fighting this invisible enemy.

China is not an enemy of the United States. China is a friend of the United States, a partner for the United States in fighting against the virus. If they regard China as an enemy, they are choosing the wrong target. Despite these politicians spreading disinformation about China, China has provided 1.8 billion face masks to the U.S.. That means six face masks per person in the United States. We still try to lend a helping hand to the American people when they need us.

Iolo ap Dafydd from CGTN: You mentioned some of China's priorities after this pandemic. Where specifically do you think does China want to prioritize?

Liu Xiaoming: First we need to resume production. We must strike a balance between fighting against the virus and ensuring the gradual resumption of production so that social order and normal life will return to their regular track.

That is a top priority. But we also have to guard against the recurrence of the virus, because the risk now is more about imported cases. The government has adopted some measures to take care of the imported cases and we also need collaboration from other countries to achieve our goal. We have to be careful to ensure that the hard-won progress will not be reversed by suddenly lifting restrictions. In Wuhan, the ban on outbound traffic has been lifted, but there are still some restrictions in certain sectors. Schools have not fully resumed. There are certain requirements. If you meet the requirements, you can gradually resume in those sectors.

And also, we are engaging actively with the rest of the world. On diplomatic engagement, we have important agendas in front of us like climate change. I'm working now with Secretary Sharma and other senior officials on how we can engage with each other to pick up the momentum where we left off before the outbreak. We are also working very hard with the Department of International Trade on the free trade agreement between China and the UK after Brexit. I'm talking to the Ministers and the Secretary of State. So, we have a very busy agenda ahead of us. Most of them are online now. We want to make sure once this is all over, we can pick up the momentum.

Lord Green: Ambassador Liu, it has been a remarkable discussion. I've enjoyed it enormously. Your final remarks are extremely good ones, to end on that powerful reminder that there is a huge range of issues on which we have every opportunity to cooperate effectively, and that we need to keep the momentum up. And remember, there will be a time after COVID-19, lots of lessons to be learned about it, lots of shorter term issues about repairing macro economic damages. There will also be fundamental longer term issues on which we have so much in common and where we have so many opportunities to work together. So I really appreciate, on behalf of "Asia House", your taking the time to be with us. And I look forward to many future engagements. You mentioned that you are in your 11th year here. That means you know this country extremely well. And I have always enjoyed your comments on this country, because you have great insights into it and into the dynamics of the relationship. There are lots of, tremendous, opportunities for us in the midst of this crisis. And we need to never lose sight of that.

So, thank you for joining. And thank you to all of our guests. Thank you to our corporate members and all of our guests for joining us on what I think is an extremely valuable session. Thank you.

Liu Xiaoming: Thank you. See you next time.

Chapter 5

Q&A with UK Parliament

Making Our Planet A Better Home for All

——A Keynote Speech and Q&A at the APPCG Webinar on China-UK Cooperation on Tackling Climate Change

(13rd October 2020, Chinese Embassy / UK Parliament)

Liu Xiaoming: It is a real delight to join you again at the APPCG webinar. Today we will focus on China-UK cooperation on climate change.

The year 2021 will be an important year for joint global response to climate change. China and the UK will host the COP15 and the COP26 respectively. These are not only important events in China-UK relations but are also of great significance to global cooperation and governance on climate change and environmental protection.

Against the background of the raging COVID-19 pandemic, tackling climate change has become an increasingly urgent task. Mankind faces five major challenges where climate change is concerned.

The first challenge is global warming.

The global average temperature is now more than one degree Celsius above pre-industrial levels. The rise in global sea level has averaged 5 millimeters per year in recent years. In the future, some places may no longer be suitable for human habitation.

The second challenge is the deterioration of the eco-environment.

While creating unprecedented wealth, industrialization has caused serious pollution and posed severe challenges to biodiversity.

The third challenge is COVID-19.

This pandemic has drawn attention of many countries away from climate change. The COP15 and the COP26 have to be postponed.

The fourth challenge is the imbalance in response capacity.

Compared with developed countries, the impact of climate change on developing countries is more severe.

It remains a daunting task for the international community to redress the imbalance of development between the North and the South and to get everyone on board in tackling climate change.

The fifth challenge is the withdrawal from international treaties and organisations.

A certain country withdrew from the Paris Agreement. Such a unilateral and bullying move has led to severe setbacks in global cooperation and governance on climate change.

Last month, at a high-level UN meeting in commemoration of the 75th anniversary of the founding of the UN, President Xi Jinping announced that China will:

- scale up its nationally determined contributions,
- adopt even more forceful policies and measures,
- and strive to reach a peak in carbon dioxide emissions by 2030 and achieve carbon neutrality by 2060.

This attests to China's audacity in taking up responsibilities in line with the requirements of sustainable domestic development and the goal of building a community with a shared future for mankind. It is a display of China's firm resolve to make an active response to climate change.

This announcement has been highly commended by the international community. In the words of Prime Minister Boris Johnson, this is "fantastic" and "a powerful signal to the world".

China and the UK are important partners in climate change response and environmental governance. There is enormous potential for closer cooperation between our two countries.

First, China and the UK can join hands and be the champions of global governance on climate change.

China has taken vigorous efforts to implement its National Climate Change Strategy and to fulfill its international obligations under the Paris Agreement.

- From 2005 to 2019, China's carbon emissions per unit GDP dropped by 48.1%.
- The proportion of non-fossil fuels in total energy consumption increased to 15.3%.
- And China has more than half of the world's "new energy" vehicles.

The UK has set the target of net-zero emissions by 2050.

Hosting the COP15 and the COP26 respectively will enable China and the UK to play a leading role in promoting global governance on climate change.

President Xi Jinping and Prime Minister Boris Johnson have reached an important political consensus on stepping up coordination and mutual support in hosting the COP15 and the COP26 respectively.

There have been close communications between the Minister of Ecology and Environment of China Huang Runqiu and Secretary Alok Sharma.

I myself have remained in touch with Secretary Sharma and Sir Laurie Bristow, the UK Government's COP26 Regional Ambassador.

On an operational level, a China-UK joint working group has been set up.

Going forward, our two sides should enhance communication and coordination, and fully engage the governments, legislatures, business community, media and academia, so as to make these two conferences successful.

Second, China and the UK can join hands and be the promoters of green development.

Against the ravaging epidemic, the Chinese Government has adopted a coordinated approach to economic and social development. We have lost no time in promoting green production and a green way of life, and improving the system of climate finance and investment.

The UK has unique strengths in clean energy and low-carbon technology.

It is important that China and the UK enhance cooperation in "new energy" and low-carbon cities. These will enable us to achieve win-win results in both ecological conservation and high-quality economic growth.

China has mature technology and rich experience in the operation and management of clean energy, such as nuclear energy. The Hinkley Point C nuclear power station is a flagship project of China-UK cooperation on clean energy. Upon completion, it will meet 7% of the UK's total demand for electricity and help to eliminate 9 million tons of CO_2 emissions every year. This project is completely in the common interests of both sides. We should work together to make it a success.

Our two countries should also encourage closer cooperation between our industries in renewable energy, green finance and the green Belt and Road. This will help to boost green recovery in both our two countries and the rest of the world.

Third, China and the UK can join hands and be the pioneers in green innovation.

Both China and the UK are pursuing innovative development in green technology, energy and financial services.

In clean energy, our two countries have signed the Clean Energy Partnership Work Plan for 2019-2020 to step up cooperation on the relevant technologies.

In green finance, China and the UK have signed up to the Green Investment Principles for the Belt and Road Development. There will be huge potential for cooperation in this aspect.

In green transport, the Chinese companies Geely and BYD have actively invested in the UK, becoming shining examples of China-UK cooperation on green transport.

Fourth, China and the UK can join hands and be the defenders of multilateralism.

It is important that China and the UK stand up for multilateralism. Under the principle of equity and common but differentiated responsibilities and respective capabilities, China and the UK should make the utmost efforts to:

• implement nationally determined contributions,

• contribute to the comprehensive, balanced and effective implementation of the Paris Agreement,

• help developing countries to scale up capacity building,

• deepen international cooperation,

• improve the system of governance,

• and chart the course for global governance on climate change.

Ladies and Gentlemen:

Tackling climate change and protecting biodiversity are important areas of China-UK cooperation. They are also our mission as major global players.

As President Xi Jinping said at the UN high-level meeting,

"We need to take up our lofty responsibility for the entire human civilization, and we need to respect Nature, follow its laws and protect it. We need to find a way for man and Nature to live in harmony, balance and coordinate economic development and ecological protection, and work together to build a prosperous, clean and beautiful world."

The UK Parliament plays an important part in the UK's response to climate change. It is my sincere hope that you will continue to play a positive role and support green cooperation between our governments and businesses. I also look forward to your thoughts and ideas on hosting a successful COP15 and COP26.

Let's work together to make greater contribution to building a community with a shared future for mankind and making our planet a better home for all!

Thank you!

Now I am ready to take your questions.

Richard Graham: One of our speakers raised the question about whether the COP15 conference in Kunming will be able to go ahead on the currently planned timing given the current situation of COVID-19. How confident are you that it will be able to go ahead as planned?

Ambassador Liu: I'm very confident about that. We are still seven months away from the conference, and in China, life has returned to normal and production and social work also have resumed. Of course, we are following the pandemic very closely, both at home and around the world. As President Xi Jinping said at the UN Summit on Biodiversity, "I want to welcome you to Kunming, the beautiful 'City of Eternal Spring', next year, to discuss and draw up plans together for protecting global biodiversity, and work in concert to build a beautiful world of harmony among all beings on the planet."

Lord Lucas: What are your suggestions on further China-UK cooperation in "new energy", in particular "new energy" vehicles?

Liu Xiaoming: On the electric vehicle we'll be more than happy to carry out mutually-beneficial cooperation with the UK. By the end of 2019, China owned 3.81 million "new energy" vehicles, which accounted for more than half of the world's total. The annual increment has been over one million units for two years in a row, making China a world leader in this aspect. Both the electric buses produced by BYD and the all-electric cabs produced by Geely after investing in the London Taxi Company have contributed to carbon emission reduction here in this country. China is also the largest investor in renewable energy. We have made vigorous efforts to develop solar and wind power. I believe there are enormous opportunities and huge potential for China and the UK to work together in the relevant areas.

Lord Lucas: How do you see the prospects of China-UK cooperation in nuclear power?

Liu Xiaoming: China has mature technologies, rich operation and management experience in nuclear power. China stands ready to enhance cooperation with the UK in this area. As of the end of 2019, China had the world's third largest installed capacity, trailing only the United States and France. We had 47 nuclear power units with a total capacity of 48.75 million kilowatts. The Hinkley Point C project is an important flagship project in nuclear power involving China, France and the UK. It will help the UK to realize its net-zero emission target by 2050. Though there are some contrary noises, it is my hope that our two sides will resist these disruptions and work together to promote this important project.

Sir Geoffrey Clifton-Brown: The UK has phased out all its coal-fired power stations. In order to meet the 2060 target, when will China phase out all of its coal-fired power stations?

Liu Xiaoming: In China, we are phasing out coal-fired power stations gradually. But we can't give you a date on that because China is still a developing country. We have enormous challenges facing us in terms of development. China is a large country and its development is imbalanced and inadequate. After my ambassadorship in Egypt, I was seconded as an assistant governor of Gansu province, one of the western provinces in China, which is very much dependent on coal energy. So, we have to address the imbalance of economic growth. On the other side, we also have to gradually scale down the consumption of coal to meet our targets on CO_2 emission. So it will take time, but the commitment to achieving carbon neutrality by 2060 is still there. Once we set a target, the policies will follow through. There will be a gradual scale-down of fossil fuel consumption through the green energy technologies. We have built the world's largest clean coal supply system. We have more than 800 million kilowatts of coal-fired ultra-low emission units. We lead the world in emission standards. China has set an example for the world in the clean application of coal. We encourage green consumption, green innovation and green development. When we have all these factors combined, we are confident that the fossil fuel consumption will be reduced gradually so as to promote green and high-quality development.

Lord McConnell: I have one question on Belt and Road Initiative projects. Do you think the BRI projects could reduce or indeed eliminate financing projects on coal energy in various BRI countries, like Pakistan and so on?

Liu Xiaoming: The Belt and Road Initiative is not only a road to economic prosperity but also a road to green development. China has always adhered to the green concept in the BRI development, promoting green and low-carbon infrastructure and operation management, emphasizing ecological conservation in investment and trade, and strengthening cooperation in the fields of ecological and environmental governance, biodiversity protection and climate change.

In 2019, China jointly initiated the BRI International Green Development Coalition with more than 140 partners in 42 countries. We have implemented the Belt and Road South-South Cooperation Initiative on Climate Change. Since 2012, the annual expenditure on South-South climate cooperation has reached 72 million U.S. dollars.

We attach great importance to green development and biodiversity with regard to the BRI, both in terms of the project design and the project implementation. For instance, you mentioned Pakistan. When Chinese companies built the Karachi-Lahore Highway in Pakistan, they planted nearly 300,000 trees and more than 5 million square meters of grassland along the road. Along with new road infrastructure, they also contributed to the local environment.

China will adhere to the concept of open, green and sustainable development, and work with its BRI partners to build a green "Silk Road". We have actively carried out third-party market cooperation with developed countries including the United Kingdom on a green development, pooling more efforts in international cooperation on climate change.

Lord McConnell: I wonder, in relation to both of the summits planned for next year, if there are concrete plans in place to engage with global multinationals, more than just a sponsorship level? And what are the preparations for that?

Liu Xiaoming: We believe the private sector is an important force in environmental protection and green development. We encourage the private sector and businesses, academia, and the media to participate in both the COP15 and the COP26. In the COP15, there will be a series of fringe events involving businesses and local governments from all over the world. I had a very good conversation with the Lord Mayor of London, discussing how the businesses of our two countries can work together on green finance to support the two conferences. For the COP26, in addition to sending the Chinese government delegation, we're going to set up the China Pavilion, which would involve Chinese local governments, NGOs and other institutions. I told our business people that I hope they will shoulder their responsibilities, seize the opportunities and strengthen cooperation with their British partners. I hope there will be more collaboration between our businesses on existing projects and on finding new projects for green development so as to promote global sustainable development.

A Keynote Speech and Q&A with the APPG on International Conservation of the UK Parliament

(28th October, 2020, Chinese Embassy / UK Parliament)

Liu Xiaoming: It is a real delight to join you at the "International Legislators' Summit—Protecting Nature: The Road to Kunming" hosted by the APPG on International Conservation.

In 2021, China and the UK will host the COP15 and the COP26 respectively. These are two big events not only for China and the UK but also for global governance of the environment. Therefore, 2021 can well be called "a big year" for global governance on the environment.

Exactly 200 days from now, the COP15 will be held in Kunming, known in China as the "City of Eternal Spring". It is highly significant and meaningful that we gather online today to "warm up" for this conference.

As we speak, COVID-19 is still ravaging the world, dealing a severe blow to economic growth and the social progress of mankind. Against this backdrop, protecting biodiversity becomes an increasingly prominent and important task. This is reflected in the following three aspects:

First, protecting biodiversity is the top priority of mankind.

As the mass extinction of wildlife accelerates, the loss of biodiversity and the degradation of the ecosystem pose major risks to the survival and development of mankind.

Second, protecting biodiversity is the inherent requirement of ecological conservation.

A sound ecosystem is essential to the prosperity of civilization. Biodiversity reflects the harmonious coexistence of man and nature. Protecting biodiversity will help strike a balance between economic growth and ecological conservation.

This will in turn form a virtuous cycle between the conservation of nature and a better life for mankind.

Third, protecting biodiversity requires countries of the world to uphold multilateralism.

Only in the spirit of multilateralism and only when every country does its best and works for mutual benefit can countries of the world enhance cooperation on protecting biodiversity and promote sustainable development.

At the UN Summit on Biodiversity last month, President Xi Jinping said,

"We need to take up our lofty responsibility for the entire human civilization, and we need to respect nature, follow its laws and protect it. We need to find a way for man and nature to live in harmony, balance and coordinate economic development and ecological protection, and work together to build a prosperous, clean and beautiful world."

At the COP15, the parties will focus on the theme of "Ecological Civilization—Building a Shared Future for All Life on Earth" and strive to reach agreement on the Post-2020 Global Biodiversity Framework. This conference provides a platform for the parties to take a historic step towards reversing the loss of biodiversity and write a splendid chapter of joint global efforts to protect biodiversity.

By hosting the COP15, China will display three determinations:

First, the determination to promote ecological conservation.

China has made vigorous efforts to advocate and practice the concept of ecological conservation. We believe that clear water and green mountains are worth more than mountains of gold and silver, and that a sound ecosystem is in the interests of everyone. And we have championed international cooperation on ecological conservation in the world.

• China has written ecological conservation into its Constitution.

• It follows the concept of innovative, coordinated, green, open and shared development.

• It has made biodiversity protection part of its plans for economic and social development and ecological protection and rehabilitation.

• And it has worked vigorously to achieve a modernization that ensures harmony between man and nature.

These efforts of China are in line with the three objectives of the Convention on Biological Diversity, namely:

• The conservation of biodiversity;

• The sustainable use of the components of biodiversity;

• and the fair and equitable sharing of the benefits arising from the use of genetic resources.

They are also in line with the vision for 2050, namely "Living in Harmony with Nature", which was outlined in the Strategic Plan for Biodiversity.

The COP15 will be the first global conference of the United Nations that focuses on "ecological conservation". It will send a powerful message about building a shared future for all life on Earth and bringing global ecological conservation one step forward.

Second, the determination to protect biodiversity.

China has adopted vigorous and effective policies and measures in this aspect.

China is taking a holistic approach to the conservation of mountains, rivers, forests, farmlands, lakes and grasslands and making coordinated efforts to advance biodiversity governance.

We have stepped up national legislation for preserving biodiversity, and we are drawing red lines for protecting ecosystems. We have set up a network of national parks, carried out major biodiversity conservation projects and increased public participation and awareness.

Over the past 10 years, China has increased forest coverage by more than 70 million hectares—more than anywhere else in the world.

We have also made long-term, large-scale efforts to combat soil erosion and desertification, and we have taken effective action in wetland protection and restoration.

As a result of these efforts, China now has one of the world's largest banks of genetic resources.

In China, 90 percent of terrestrial ecosystem types and 85 percent of key wild animal populations are under effective protection.

The COP15 will serve as an important platform for China to share its practice and experience in biodiversity protection with the rest of the world and for the parties to pull together in biodiversity protection.

Third, the determination to take part and assume the lead in global biodiversity governance.

China is an important contracting party to and defender of the Convention on Biological Diversity (CBD).

• It was one of the first to sign and ratify the CBD.

• It has fulfilled its obligations under the CBD and helped to create synergy between the CBD and other international conventions on the environment.

• It has attained the goal of setting up nature reserves ahead of schedule.

Together with its partners, China has initiated the Belt and Road Initiative International Green Development Coalition to step up protection of biodiversity and the ecosystem.

Under the framework of South-South cooperation, China has also made vigorous efforts to help other developing countries build up their capacity in managing the environment.

At the COP15, the Post-2020 Global Biodiversity Framework will be formulated, which will chart the course for global governance on biodiversity in the coming ten years and beyond.

China stands ready to work with all the parties at the COP15 to promote the cause of post-2020 global governance on biodiversity.

Ladies and Gentlemen:

The year 2021 will be critical for global governance on biodiversity. China and the UK are important partners in global governance on environment. There is enormous potential for China and the UK to cooperate and take action on protecting biodiversity and climate change. It is important that we support and coordinate with each other to make the COP15 and the COP26 a great success.

First, China and the UK should follow the strategic guidance of our leaders and step up coordination and cooperation on hosting the COP15 and the COP26.

Last month, at a high-level UN meeting in commemoration of the 75th anniversary of the founding of the UN, President Xi Jinping announced that China will:

• scale up its nationally determined contributions,

• adopt even more forceful policies and measures,

• and strive to reach a peak in carbon dioxide emissions by 2030 and achieve carbon neutrality by 2060.

President Xi Jinping and Prime Minister Boris Johnson have reached important agreements on enhancing coordination and mutual support on the COP15 and the COP26.

In the video message just now, the Chinese Minister of Ecology and Environment Huang Runqiu emphasized the importance of China-UK cooperation.

Going forward, China and the UK should step up coordination and cooperation with regard to the policies and agenda of the two conferences. We should promote Nature-Based Solutions and derive from them a coordinated settlement for problems of climate change and biodiversity. And we should encourage the two conferences to support each other and succeed together.

Second, China and the UK should deepen green cooperation and take the lead in global sustainable development.

China has issued and vigorously implemented its National Biodiversity Conservation Strategy and Action Plan (2011-2030). It has been exploring ways to coordinate biodiversity protection with green development and a better life for the people. And it has been championing low-carbon, circular and sustainable ways of life and production.

The UK has issued the 25-Year Environment Plan to advocate sustainable development and restore biodiversity on land and in the ocean.

China and the UK can enhance dialogue, exchanges and business cooperation. We can tap the potential for green cooperation in areas such as climate change, biodiversity protection, low-carbon economy, green finance, green technology and energy transition. We can also step up tripartite cooperation in building the green Belt and Road.

Together, we can advance the implementation of the UN 2030 Agenda for Sustainable Development and provide new impetus for global sustainable growth.

Third, China and the UK should uphold multilateralism and help to build synergy among the parties for better governance of biodiversity.

Both China and the UK should uphold the principle of common but differentiated responsibilities, ensure the fair and equitable sharing of benefits, and accommodate developing countries' concerns over funding, technology and capacity building. We need to build a fair and reasonable multilateral system of environmental governance where the parties shoulder their due responsibilities.

China stands ready to work with all participating parties, including the UK, to conclude an ambitious and pragmatic Post-2020 Global Biodiversity Framework at the COP15 through an open, transparent and parties-driven process. Together we can draw up a blueprint that is both grand and feasible, and we can open up broader prospects for global biodiversity protection in the future.

The city of Kunming is known for its long history, splendid culture, pleasant weather and beautiful landscape.

At the UN Summit on Biodiversity, President Xi Jinping said, "I want to welcome you to Kunming, the beautiful 'City of Eternal Spring', next year, to discuss and draw up plans together for protecting global biodiversity and work in concert to build a beautiful world of harmony among all beings on the planet."

As the host and incoming president of the COP15, China will exert every effort to get everything ready for the conference and make it a milestone in global governance on the environment.

I appreciate the enthusiasm and support of Chairman Gardiner and the APPG on International Conservation. I look forward to more ideas and suggestions from British parliamentarians and the people of the world who support environmental actions on how to make the COP15 and the COP26 successful. I also want to listen to your thoughts on deepening China-UK cooperation on global governance of the environment.

Let's join hands to write a new chapter on ecological conservation and build a shared future for all life on Earth!

Thank you!

Now, I would like to take your questions.

Canadian Former MP Stetsky: Could Ambassador Liu shed further light on China's ecological protection red line system?

Liu Xiaoming: Regarding China's ecological protection red line system, I would like to elaborate on three points:

Firstly, the ecological protection red line is regarded as the "lifeline" at the national level. This is an important institutional innovation in the planning and management of China's territorial space. It plays a crucial role in maintaining the ecological security pattern, safeguarding the functions of ecosystems, and ensuring sustainable economic and social development. China has planned that by the end of 2020 the ecological protection red line should cover approximately 25% of its territorial land area.

Secondly, the red line is defined according to the different level of protection needed. It is drawn around ecologically vital and fragile areas. This covers various types of nature reserves primarily composed of national parks. Strict management reduces the human impact upon the ecological environment. By the end of 2018, the total number of various types of nature reserves in China had reached 11,800 and the total area exceeded 1.728 million square kilometers, accounting for over 18% of the territorial land area, surpassing the goal of 17% set by COP10 for 2020 ahead of schedule.

Thirdly, ecological resources within the red line are utilized rationally. The red line in China serves as a boundary that cannot be crossed in protecting biodiversity, adjusting economic structures, planning industrial development, and promoting new urbanization. However, it does not mean absolute preservation and the non-utilization of every space within the line. The red line is not creating a "no-go zone" nor a "developmental vacuum". The Chinese government encourages the rational utilization of high-quality ecological resources within the red line and explores mechanisms to realize the value of ecological products, transforming green mountains and clear waters into "mountains of gold and silver", achieving the conversion of ecological advantages into economic advantages.

In addition, China has formulated and implemented the "China Biodiversity Conservation Strategy and Action Plan" (2011-2030) in 2010 in accordance with the spirit of the relevant convention. This action plan outlines China's overall goals, strategic tasks and priority actions for biodiversity conservation in the next 20 years. Since 2015, through the implementation of major biodiversity conservation projects, a nation-wide investigation and observation of wild animals and plants has been conducted, with records exceeding 2.1 million, continuously tracking and evaluating the progress of the implementation of the "China Biodiversity Conservation Strategy and Action Plan" (2011-2030). We are willing to enhance communication with all parties on the ecological protection red line system and promote the implementation of respective national action plans.

Kenyan MP Chepkovoni: How will China's Belt and Road Initiative help countries along the route achieve clean, green, and sustainable development?

Liu Xiaoming: The Belt and Road is not only a road to economic prosperity but also a road to green development. In practice, China has always adhered to the concept of green development, emphasized alignment with the UN 2030 Agenda for Sustainable Development, promoted the green and low-carbon construction and operation management of infrastructure, highlighted ecological civilization concepts in investment and trade, and strengthened cooperation in ecological environment governance, biodiversity conservation, and climate change response. In the future, the Belt and Road Initiative will focus on strengthening green cooperation in three aspects:

Firstly, establishing green mechanisms. In 2019, the BRI Green Development International Alliance was established, with ten thematic partnerships including "Biodiversity and Ecosystems" and more than 150 Chinese and foreign cooperative partners from over 40 countries. China has implemented the Green Silk Road Ambassador Program, jointly enhancing environmental protection capacity-building with developing countries, and training over 2,000 environmental officials, experts, and technicians from more than 120 countries. The Chinese government has also established the Belt and Road Environmental Technology Exchange and Transfer Center to promote joint research and development and the application of advanced ecological environmental protection technologies.

Secondly, promoting green development. Chinese companies consider environmental factors fully when undertaking and designing Belt and Road projects. For example, while building the Karachi-Lahore Motorway in Pakistan, Chinese companies planted nearly 300,000 trees and grassed over 5 million square meters of area along the highway, contributing to local environmental greening as well as infrastructure. Similarly, in Pakistan, when constructing the Hub coal-fired power station, advanced clean coal-fired technology was used, with approximately 10% of the total project budget allocated for pollution control, and the emissions were fully compliant with standards.

Thirdly, strengthening cooperation on green finance. Over 30 large financial institutions globally have signed the "Green Investment Principles of the Belt and Road Initiative" (GIP). The GIP includes fully understanding environmental, social, and governance risks; fully disclosing environmental information; fully utilizing green financial instruments; and adopting green supply chain management. China encourages financial institutions to support the green development of BRI. In 2019, Industrial and Commercial Bank of China issued the first BRI inter-bank cooperation mechanism green bond, further promoting cooperation on green finance under the BRI. China will adhere to open, green, and sustainable concepts, actively carry out third-party market cooperation on green development with developed countries including the UK. Through platforms such as the BRI Green Development International Alliance, China will help partner countries achieve green, clean, and sustainable development.

South African MP Frolick: How does China see the role of the United Nations Convention on the Law of the Sea in marine ecological environment protection?

Liu Xiaoming: The ocean is an indispensable part of the Earth's ecosystem, and protecting marine biodiversity is crucial for China's sustainable development. As a signatory to the United Nations Convention on the Law of the Sea, China has always been committed to complying with international law. This includes the United Nations Convention on the Law of the Sea. The "Sino-French Beijing Initiative on Biodiversity Conservation and Climate Change" reached between China and France in 2019 explicitly calls for mobilizing all countries to establish a legally binding international instrument under the United Nations Convention on the Law of the Sea so as to conserve and sustainably utilize biodiversity beyond national jurisdiction. Currently, China has approved the establishment of over 40 national-level marine parks, and established over 270 marine natural/special protected areas (marine parks) at all levels, with the number and area of marine protected areas continuously expanding and the types of protected objects becoming increasingly diverse. China will work together with all countries to carry out marine biodiversity protection and jointly build a protective barrier for marine biodiversity in order to make more contributions to protecting these vibrant blue resources.

British Lord Randall: How can public awareness and enthusiasm for biodiversity protection be increased in the context of the pandemic?

Liu Xiaoming: Biodiversity protection is not solely the responsibility of the government; all sectors of society should participate extensively. Enhancing public participation awareness is one of the eight strategic tasks outlined in the "China Biodiversity Conservation Strategy and Action Plan" (2011-2030). We have established mechanisms for public participation in biodiversity conservation, conducted various forms of biodiversity conservation publicity and education activities, guided the public to actively participate in biodiversity conservation, and strengthened biodiversity popular science education in schools. At next year's COP15, there will be parallel meetings and numerous side events and exhibitions to fully encourage and promote social participation in the conference. At the COP26 venue, China will, following customary practice, set up a "China Pavilion"—a platform for Chinese local governments, research institutions, non-governmental organizations, and others to participate in the multilateral climate process and contribute to green and low-carbon development. China is willing to work with the UK to encourage more enterprises, non-governmental organizations, and other sectors of society to participate in the COP15 and the COP26, contributing to the success of the conferences and promoting global biodiversity protection.

Mexican MP García: How do you see the relationship between the COP15 and the COP26 next year? How can "Nature-Based Solutions" be more widely adopted?

Liu Xiaoming: President Xi Jinping pointed out at the UN Biodiversity Summit that humanity and nature are a community of shared future. Both biodiversity protection and climate change response are important aspects of global environmental governance. Biodiversity protection can help mankind to better mitigate and adapt to climate change, and mitigating and adapting to climate change can also reduce the threat to biodiversity. The two are mutually reinforcing. The COP15 and the COP26 can synergize in three aspects:

Firstly, jointly building an ecological civilization. Both climate change and biodiversity are related to human survival and development. We should take the two conferences as an opportunity, stand at the height of responsibility for human civilization, respect nature, follow its laws and protect resources, explore the road to harmonious coexistence between man and nature, and promote coordination between economic development and ecological protection.

Secondly, jointly promoting green development. Both climate change and biodiversity are closely related to post-pandemic economic recovery. We should adhere to the directions indicated by the UN "2030 Agenda for Sustainable Development", and persist in green, inclusive, and sustainable development. By holding the two conferences, we can find green development opportunities from nature protection, realize win-win results in ecological environmental protection and high-quality economic development, and foster vitality for the post-pandemic economic recovery.

Thirdly, jointly upholding multilateralism. International treaties such as the Convention on Biological Diversity, and the United Nations Framework Convention on Climate Change and its Paris Agreement are the legal basis for global environmental governance and important achievements of multilateral cooperation. These enjoy extensive support and participation from all parties. We should take the two conferences as an opportunity to firmly uphold the international system centered on the United Nations, safeguard the dignity and authority of international rules, and unite global environmental governance efforts.

Both China and the UK attach importance to "Nature-Based Solutions" (NBS), which is also one of the important areas for the UK to host COP26. China and the UK should actively promote NBS, take it as a synergistic solution to climate change and biodiversity loss, promote efficiency through synergy, and promote global green, low-carbon, and sustainable development.

China and New Zealand jointly led the work on NBS at the 2019 UN Climate Action Summit, and released documents such as the "Policy Advocacy for Nature-Based Climate Solutions", and established a follow-up cooperation platform, the "NBS Friends Group". We have also proposed the NBS action initiative of "Delineating Ecological Protection Red Lines, Mitigating and Adapting to Climate Change". These contribute Chinese wisdom to NBS enrichment.

Going forward, we are willing to strengthen exchanges and cooperation with the UK on the NBS, jointly promote various parties' understanding of the value of nature, encourage governments, financial institutions, enterprises, and all other stakeholders to prioritize the NBS in the process of biodiversity protection and climate change response, formulate ambitious plans, and take practical actions, allowing the NBS to play a greater role in supporting ecosystem protection and climate change response.

Chapter 6

Q&A with Scholars and Officials

China Is A Builder of World Peace

——A Dialogue with "Asia House" in the UK

On 24th June 2019, I attended the "Asia House" dialogue in the UK and held discussions with Lord Green, Chairman of the "Asian House", on Xi Jinping's diplomatic thoughts, China's domestic and foreign policies, and related hot topics, answering questions from the audience.

Lord Green: Today, "Asia House" is honored to invite Chinese Ambassador to the UK, Liu Xiaoming, as a heavyweight guest to discuss this extremely important topic, China. China's rapid development in the past few decades has changed the global landscape. The world economic center has shifted from the West to the East. Currently, the UK is at a crucial period of Brexit and is reshaping its relationship with the world, with a focus on expanding partnerships in Asia. How to keep a balance between China and the US is a topic of great concern to all sectors here in the UK. We look forward to hearing Ambassador Liu's views on the current international situation and how China interacts with the world on major issues.

Liu Xiaoming: I am delighted to be here at "Asia House" once again for a dialogue with Lord Green, Chairman of "Asia House", and other members on topics such as China-UK relations and Chinese foreign policy. The timing of every invitation from the "Asian House" has been excellent. Last May, I delivered a speech here on China-US economic and trade issues, coinciding with the agreement reached between China and the US. Since then, the situation has been full of uncertainties and fast changing. Today, the tension in China-US economic and trade relations is showing signs of improvement, and President Xi Jinping and President Trump are about to hold a meeting at the G20 summit. This is attracting widespread attention.

Looking at the world today, we are living in a rapidly changing era, and the world is undergoing a great transformation unseen in a century. In this context, China's development has become a topic of global discussion. Some people see it as an opportunity, some as a challenge, and others as a threat. So what does China's development mean to the world? Let me refer to Xi Jinping Thought on Diplomacy. This is the fundamental principle and guideline for our actions, and building a community of shared future for mankind is its core tenet.

China adheres to the path of peaceful development and promotes the building of a new type of international relations and a community with a shared future for mankind; China adheres to opening up and cooperation, promotes the Belt and Road Initiative, and shares China's development opportunities with countries around the world; China does not seek to challenge or replace anyone, and will not go down the old path that "a strong country must be a hegemon". China will always be a builder of world peace, a contributor to global development, and a defender of the international order.

Currently, unilateralism is on the rise, and protectionism is rampant. In such a situation, China and the UK, as influential countries in the international community, should strengthen their cooperation and make a strong statement in support of multilateralism, advocating free trade, and jointly addressing global challenges such as climate change, making contributions to the development and progress of human society. Last week, the 10th China-UK Economic and Financial Dialogue was successfully held in the UK, achieving 69 fruitful outcomes. I believe that an important message conveyed through this dialogue is that China-UK cooperation is mutually beneficial; it not only benefits both countries but also the world. Looking ahead, China is willing to continue to regard the UK as a partner in promoting the building of a new type of international relations and a community with a shared future. China will contribute to creating a better world.

Lord Green: I have visited China several times and witnessed the tremendous achievements of China's reform and development. However, China's future development faces challenges such as the imbalances between the eastern and the western regions, an aging population, and water shortages. Ambassador Liu, what are your views on these issues? How will China address these problems?

Liu Xiaoming: 2018 marked the 40th anniversary of China's reform and opening up. In over 40 years, China's economy has risen from the tenth in the world to the second, successfully lifting 700 million people out of poverty. People's living standards in China have greatly improved, with significant increases in life expectancy and a continuous improvement in people's sense of gain, happiness, and security. However, China is still a developing country. Our per capita GDP is still far behind that of developed Western countries. When observing China, one should see its "multifaceted" nature. There are metropolises like Beijing, Shanghai, and Shenzhen, which can rival European cities, as well as relatively underdeveloped western provinces. You mentioned the water resource issue earlier, and I can personally relate to it. Over ten years ago, I served as assistant governor of Gansu Province, one of the poorest provinces in China, where many people had difficulty accessing clean drinking water and had to rely on purified rainwater for themselves and their livestock.

Regarding the main contradictions in Chinese society today, the 19th National Congress of the Communist Party of China accurately identified the contradiction between the growing demand for a better life and imbalanced and inadequate development. Looking ahead, we still have a lot of work to do, and the burden on our shoulders is heavy. China's rise and development are not about challenging other countries internationally, but about solving the many challenges it faces in its own development, continuously improving people's livelihoods, and achieving the goal of lifting everyone out of poverty by 2020, making development more balanced and comprehensive.

Lord Green: I am deeply concerned about the current global trade situation, with US President Trump frequently taking unilateral and protectionist measures such as imposing tariffs, which has had a huge impact on the World Trade Organization (WTO) and the global trade order. Ambassador Liu, how do you see the global trade situation, and how will China respond?

Liu Xiaoming: I share your concerns about trade issues, as I am also concerned about the wave of unilateralism and protectionism. China believes that the WTO is still at the core of the multilateral trading system. Of course, this system is not perfect and needs necessary reforms to make global trade more standardized, convenient, and open. We live in an interconnected "global village", and if all countries base their trade rules purely on their own interests, or prioritize their own interests over others in a so-called "me-first" approach, this will inevitably lead to a "trade war" and have a negative impact on global economic growth.

Therefore, China supports the WTO in playing its due role, as well as supporting necessary reforms to the WTO. However, WTO reforms should be based on consensus among all parties. Although this will take more time, the costs will be much smaller for all parties. China opposes the "winner takes all" or "zero-sum game" approach and believes that only mutually beneficial cooperation can lead to win-win development.

Lord Green: Does the concept of "win-win development" that you mentioned refer to China's proposal to build a community with a shared future for mankind? I understand the original intention of China's proposal, but against the current backdrop of the China-US competition, can the community with a shared future for mankind become a reality?

Liu Xiaoming: I am optimistic about this because cooperation based on mutual benefit between countries is fundamentally possible. President Xi Jinping's proposal to build a community with a shared future for mankind has received positive responses from the international community and has been incorporated into United Nations and G20 documents.

There are no "winners" in a trade war, and both China and the US will suffer losses. I have seen a survey that suggests that if the trade war continues, the US will be the biggest "loser". Recently, I have also noticed that many American entrepreneurs are dissatisfied with the government's imposition of tariffs. China does not want to see a "lose-lose" situation and hopes that people will eventually return to "rationality" and recognize the negative impact of a trade war without having to pay a price for it.

Lord Green: As you just mentioned, the world is undergoing a major transformation. The balance of power is changing significantly, especially with the rise of developing countries. In such a situation, what role do you think Europe will play on the world stage? Currently, there is no result on Brexit, and many European countries are facing challenges from populism. How does China see the role of Europe?

Liu Xiaoming: China advocates for the development of a multipolar world, believing that this is beneficial to achieving lasting peace and stability in the world. China attaches importance to the role of Europe, considering it to be an important pole in the world strategically. In terms of trade, Europe is China's largest trading partner. China is committed to developing relations and conducting pragmatic cooperation with the European Union and individual European countries, maintaining good relations with major countries such as the UK, France, Germany, Italy, as well as actively cooperating with the "16+1" cooperation involving Central and Eastern European countries. This year, President Xi Jinping and Premier Li Keqiang paid successful visits to Europe where the two sides jointly reaffirmed the importance of China-Europe relations. This demonstrates the importance China attaches to Europe.

Regarding the issue of Brexit, we are following closely the progress here and believe that it is a matter between the UK and the EU. We believe that both sides have the wisdom and capability to handle related issues properly. China hopes that the UK and the EU can reach an agreement that satisfies both parties and is willing to promote the parallel development of China-Europe and China-UK relations.

Lord Green: I have noticed that there are different opinions within the UK on dealing with relations with China. In addition, the Europeans have been sceptical about the "16+1" cooperation. How do you view these issues?

Liu Xiaoming: I have heard the view that the UK must choose sides between China and the US, hence the different opinions on developing relations with China. I want to point out that mainstream opinion in the UK sees China's development as an opportunity rather than a challenge or a threat, and most people support the advancement of the "Golden Era" of China-UK relations.

There are indeed some misunderstandings in Europe about the "16+1" cooperation between China and Central and Eastern European countries. In fact, the "16+1" cooperation has achieved positive results and is mutually beneficial for both China and the EU. In terms of the level of development, many countries in Central and Eastern Europe fall below the EU average and face common problems that hinder their further growth. Therefore, they have a strong desire to enhance cooperation with China. China has maintained close communication and exchanges with Europe, hoping to address any doubts or misunderstandings through increased trust and clarification. We want everyone to understand that

China is committed to taking a different path from that followed by previous big powers in their rise. China's development will bring more opportunities to Europe and the world.

Lord Green: India and Japan are important countries in Asia, but both countries have delicate relations with China. For example, India has reservations about the Belt and Road Initiative, and there are significant unresolved historical legacies between China and Japan. How do you view China's relations with India and Japan?

Liu Xiaoming: China attaches great importance to its relations with India and Japan, which are important neighboring countries. Without good relations between China and India and between China and Japan, there will be no lasting peace, stability, and prosperity in Asia. Regarding China-India relations, some Western media outlets are keen on playing down the significance of the positive aspects to this and continue to hype up the differences between the two countries. However, our common interests are much greater than the differences. Both countries are members of the BRICS and have extensive common interests on various issues. In recent years, President Xi Jinping and Prime Minister Modi have met several times on different occasions, establishing a good personal friendship and working relationship, which reflects the high importance China's leaders attach to the development of China-India relations.

Regarding China-Japan relations, there are indeed "bitter memories". The Chinese people have every reason to be concerned about Japan's attitude towards history because we do not want history to "repeat itself". China is willing to improve relations with Japan, and President Xi Jinping will soon visit Japan to attend the G20 summit. We hope that this will inject strong impetus into the improvement and development of China-Japan relations.

Michael Lawrence, CEO of "Asia House": The Huawei issue is currently a focus of attention in the UK. What is your view on Huawei's development prospects in the UK?

Liu Xiaoming: First of all, I would like to point out that Huawei is an excellent company, not only leading the world in the field of 5G communications but also making significant contributions to economic and social development in the UK. Last month, during my return to China, I visited Huawei in Shenzhen and interacted with company executives and employees at Huawei University. I found that Huawei is looking forward to pragmatic cooperation with the UK.

Over the past 5 years, Huawei has created more than 7,500 jobs in the UK, with purchases and investments amounting to 2 billion pounds, and plans to invest a further 3 billion pounds in the future. More importantly, Huawei attaches great importance to cybersecurity issues, proactively investing in establishing a cybersecurity certification center in the UK, employing an all-British supervision team, regularly assessing risks, and continuously improving technology. There is no equipment without any risk in the world, but Huawei is willing to cooperate with the UK government, business, and academic circles to improve the security and reliability of their equipment. In fact, the UK side assesses that the security risks of Huawei equipment are "manageable".

I have heard it commented that if Huawei equipment is banned, the UK's 5G construction will be delayed by one to two years. What worries me more is that the UK is known for its open and inclusive market environment. If Huawei is banned, it may send a very negative signal, especially impacting Chinese companies' investment and operations in the UK. That is what I least want to see. The name of this country is "Great Britain", and its "greatness" lies in its independence. We hope that the UK government will make decisions in its own long-term interests and conducive to the overall China-UK cooperation, rather than following the instructions or succumbing to the pressure of others.

Professor Morrison, Coventry University: I attended Ambassador Liu's speech a few years ago and heard at that time that in the global supply chain, China only earned 5 cents in profit for every $1 worth of goods it produced. Hence there is a great potential for growth. How much has China's profit in the global supply chain increased now? How do you see such progress?

Liu Xiaoming: As you know, China cannot stay at the "low end" of the global supply chain forever. In recent years, the Chinese people have worked diligently and actively developed medium and high-end industries. We have indeed made some progress. However, China attaches more importance to enlarging the "cake of common interests", allowing all parties to benefit more rather than just taking a larger share of the "cake" for itself and leaving everyone competing for limited resources. This is the philosophy that China adopts when conducting cooperation with other countries.

As a career diplomat, I have been superintending China-US ties for a long time. The current China-US economic and trade relationship reminds me of a statement made by a US leader over 30 years ago when I was posted to Washington, D.C.. He said that the US was concerned about the trade deficit with China, but the solution was not to reduce China's exports to the US, but to increase US exports to China. I agree with this view, and I hope that today's US leaders will follow the same logic. The imposition of tariffs by the US on China not only disrupts the global supply chain but will ultimately lead to losses for US companies and ordinary American consumers.

James Richards, Chairman of Asiability: The recent Hong Kong issue has aroused widespread concern in British society. Ambassador Liu, in an interview with the BBC, stated that the "Sino-British Joint Declaration" is "no longer meaningful". Does the Chinese government still adhere to the "One Country, Two Systems" policy in Hong Kong?

Liu Xiaoming: Thank you for watching my interview, but your quote is not accurate. The mission of the "Sino-British Joint Declaration" was to ensure the smooth transfer of government in Hong Kong. After Hong Kong's return to China in 1997, the "Sino-British Joint Declaration" completed its historical mission. I have noticed that some British media question the Chinese central government's commitment to "One Country, Two Systems". I want to emphasize that "One Country, Two Systems" is not a promise to the UK. It is a commitment by the Chinese central government to all Chinese people, including Hong Kong residents, and this is fully reflected in the "Basic Law". Currently, the Hong Kong SAR government's handling of the "amendment"-related work is precisely a vivid embodiment of the practice of "One Country, Two Systems". Some foreign media and forces describe the Hong Kong "amendment" as undermining "One Country, Two Systems". To use a British expression, this is completely "barking up the wrong tree". Some senior British government officials have also made some irresponsible remarks recently, which is interference in Hong Kong affairs and in China's internal affairs. If the British side sincerely hopes that Hong kong will enjoy long-term prosperity and stability, it should not interfere with the lawful governance of the Hong Kong SAR government.

Lord Sassoon, Chairman of the China-Britain Business Council: Ambassador Liu mentioned the 69 important outcomes achieved in last week's UK-China Economic and Financial Dialogue. This will strongly promote practical cooperation between the UK and China and greatly inspire the UK business community. Regarding WTO reform, what is the possibility of achieving it in the end? How can China and the UK cooperate on this issue?

Liu Xiaoming: WTO reform is a complex systematic project aimed at reflecting the new realities of the world economy, particularly taking into account the major concerns of developing countries, promoting global trade liberalization and facilitation, improving the dispute settlement mechanism, and promoting the construction of an inclusive and open world economy.

Not long ago, China released a "Proposal on WTO Reform", which detailed the "China Solution". I suggest that everyone take a closer look at it. China and the UK have shared interests in WTO reform, and we are willing to work with the UK to improve the WTO and the multilateral trading system.

Lord Green: Thank you, Ambassador Liu, for your wonderful speech. China's relations with the world have become one of the most significant strategic issues of our time. Ambassador Liu has provided an in-depth interpretation of the spirit and essence of Xi Jinping's diplomatic thoughts and vividly expounded on the key aspects of China's foreign policy. Ambassador Liu is a frequent guest at "Asia House", but this is the first time that "Asia House" has invited the ambassador to a dialogue. We look forward to continuing our dialogue with Ambassador Liu and creating a better platform for the UK to get closer to Asia, understand China, and comprehend China.

Thank you, everyone!

Pulling Together in Four Aspects

——A Keynote Speech and Q&A at the Webinar with UK Think Tanks On Post-Pandemic China-Europe Relations

On 15th July 2020, I held a webinar with the Official Monetary and Financial Institutions Forum (OMFIF) and the Centre for European Reform (CER) on China-Europe relations after the pandemic. I delivered a keynote speech entitled "Join Hands to Contribute Positive Energy and Create a Better Future for China-Europe Relationship". Around 100 people attended the event, including David Marsh, the Chairman of the OMFIF, Meghnad Desai, the Chairman of the OMFIF Advisory Board, Charles Grant, the Director of the CER, Sir Sherard Cowper-Coles, the Chairman of the China-Britain Business Council, members from the two think tanks, and representatives from the economic, financial and academic sectors of the UK, Europe, North America, Australia and South America, and journalists from 14 media agencies took part in the conference, including BBC, Sky News, Reuters, *The Daily Telegraph*, *Financial Times*, *The Guardian*, *The Independent*, CGTN, The Associated Press, Bloomberg, NBC, Agence France-Presse and Bulgarska Televizija. BBC and Sky News broadcast my keynote speech and part of the Q&A session live and run the coverage in their prime time programs. The transcript of the webinar is as follows:

Liu Xiaoming: It is a real delight to join you on-line to talk about China-Europe relations after the pandemic.

This year marks the 45th anniversary of China-EU diplomatic relations. In the past 45 years, China's relationship with Europe has become increasingly comprehensive, mature and steady. This relationship has delivered tangible benefits to the people of both sides and contributed a positive impetus to world peace and prosperity.

Last month, the 22nd China-EU Summit was held on-line. President Xi

Jinping held a meeting with President of the European Council Charles Michel and President of the European Commission Ursula von der Leyen, and Premier Li Keqiang co-chaired the summit with the two presidents. These meetings charted the course for the relationship between China and Europe after the pandemic.

As COVID-19 continues to ravage the world, the international landscape and the system of global governance face profound changes. This most serious pandemic in a century has revealed four global deficits.

First, the health deficit.

COVID-19 has spread to more than 210 countries and regions, affecting more than 7 billion people, infecting over 13 million people and claiming over 560,000 lives. It has been the gravest global public health emergency after the Second World War. It poses severe challenge to the safety and health of mankind, and requires the joint response of the international community, including China and Europe.

Second, the development deficit.

This pandemic has resulted in a severe recession in the world economy. According to the OECD forecast, the European economy would be the hardest hit this year.

International travel and trade has been disrupted by restrictions and the global industrial chain is under severe strain. The IMF and the World Bank predicted respectively a 4.9% and a 5.2% contraction in the world economy this year. How we should achieve economic recovery and continued growth is a daunting task for all countries.

Third, the peace deficit.

The pandemic has aggravated the severe challenges arising from incessant regional conflicts and wars, raging terrorism, and grave humanitarian crisis. People in many countries, especially children, are still suffering. World peace, security and stability are under grave threat.

Fourth, the governance deficit.

The pandemic has revealed the weak links in the global public health governance system which is in urgent need of improvement. Surging protectionism, unilateralism and anti-globalisation, and the politically motivated blame game are eroding international solidarity and undercutting the joint response to the pandemic. They also pose grave challenges to the global governance system and multilateral mechanisms.

COVID-19 reminds the world that mankind belongs to a community with a shared future. Scapegoating and shirking responsibilities are unhelpful for solving problems or saving lives. Solidarity and cooperation are the only right way forward in this fight against the virus.

Both China and Europe are major global players, with big markets and great civilisations. It is important that the two sides join hands to contribute:

- to the global response to COVID-19,
- to world economic recovery,
- to improving global governance,
- and to overturning deficits.

First, China and Europe should work together to safeguard the health and safety of mankind.

China attaches great importance to cooperation with the international community, including Europe, on fighting the pandemic.

At the 73rd World Health Assembly last May, President Xi Jinping called for the building of a global community of health for all. He also announced that in the coming two years, China will provide 2 billion U.S. dollars in international aid; when China is successful in developing a vaccine and has put it to use, the country will share it for the global public good.

China also took an active part in the Coronavirus Global Response Pledging Conference initiated by the EU and the Global Vaccine Summit hosted by the UK.

Going forward, China and the EU should:

- continue to share experience in epidemic-containment,
- enhance cooperation on the R&D of vaccine and medicines,
- strengthen support to regions with weak public health systems,
- and actively explore tripartite cooperation between China, the EU and Africa on epidemic response.

Together China and the EU could help to strengthen global defence against threats to public health, and contribute to building a global community of health for all.

Second, China and Europe should work together to uphold world peace and stability.

China and the EU have, between them, one tenth of the world's land area, one quarter of the world's population and two permanent members of the UN Security Council. There is every reason that China and the EU should play a key role in safeguarding world peace and stability.

China and Europe should enhance strategic dialogue to step up coordination and communication on major international and regional issues. This includes:

• supporting the settlement of all hotspot issues and regional conflicts through peaceful dialogue and consultation;

• upholding a global non-proliferation regime so as to safeguard global strategic stability;

• supporting measures aimed at cracking down upon terrorism of all forms and addressing both the symptoms and root causes of terrorism, with a view to containing the spread of extremist ideas.

Third, China and Europe should work together to promote development and prosperity in the world.

In face of the challenges from COVID-19, it is all the more important to stay committed to open cooperation.

As two major economies, China and the EU should be the "dual engines" of the world economy that:

• drive economic recovery,

• bring economic activities back on track in an orderly manner,

• and safeguard the open, stable and secure global industrial and supply chains.

To achieve these goals, China and the EU should enhance coordination on macro-economic policies and uphold an open world economy.

In the first half of this year, the China Railway Express offered an important passage for unimpeded trade between China and Europe, with 5,122 trains shuttling between China and Europe, increasing by 36% year-on-year.

New areas such as connectivity, green development, ecological conservation, environmental protection, the digital economy and artificial intelligence will create fresh opportunities for the mutually-beneficial cooperation between China and Europe.

The two sides should stay open to each other and strive to complete negotiations on the China-EU Investment Agreement with a view to reaching a comprehensive, balanced and high-standard agreement.

Fourth, China and Europe should work together to improve the system of global governance.

China and the EU are both committed to multilateralism:

• Both support greater democracy in international relations.

• Both safeguard the international system with the UN at its core, the international order based on international law, and the multilateral trade system with the WTO as its cornerstone.

• Both support the WHO in playing a leadership role in global response to COVID-19.

The two sides share common interests in:

• safeguarding global public health,

• tackling climate change,

• developing clean energy, clean transport and green technology,

• and preserving bio-diversity.

The two sides share broad consensus on advancing reforms in the WTO and upholding free trade.

In this year that marks the 75th anniversary of the founding of the United Nations, China and Europe should work together to enhance communication and coordination, safeguard multilateralism and improve global governance.

Ladies and Gentlemen:

In the 45 years of China-EU diplomatic relations, win-win cooperation has been the main theme. In face of the new challenges brought by the pandemic, this relationship has some new problems to solve.

By this I mean the misgivings and doubts of some politicians in Europe who:

• see China as a "systemic rival",

• regard China as a "potentially hostile state",

• and believe there will be no going back to "business as usual" with China.

So now, China and Europe have the same questions before them:

• What kind of relationship do they want post-pandemic?

• What should they do to preserve the overall interests of China-Europe relations?

In my opinion, China and Europe should pull together in the following four aspects:

First, respect each other and reject interference in other countries' internal affairs.

Mutual respect for sovereignty and territorial integrity, non-interference in other countries' internal affairs, equality and mutual benefit are the basic principles enshrined in the UN Charter and the basic norms governing international relations.

The experience of the past 45 years since China and the EU established diplomatic relations has told us that when these principles have been upheld, the China-Europe relationship will make progress; otherwise, this relationship will suffer setbacks or even retrogression.

China has never interfered in other countries' internal affairs, and we strongly oppose interference in China's internal affairs by other countries.

Last month, the Standing Committee of China's National People's Congress adopted the National Security Law for the Hong Kong SAR to deal with the enormous risk Hong Kong faces in safeguarding national security.

This Law is aimed at preventing, suppressing and punishing four types of criminal activities. They are secession, subversion, terrorist activities and collusion with a foreign country or with external elements to endanger national security:

• The Law plugs the legal loophole in terms of national security in Hong Kong.

• It targets very few actions and activities that gravely jeopardize national security.

• It will not affect the high degree of autonomy of Hong Kong.

• It will not alter Hong Kong's independent judicial power, including the power of final adjudication.

• It will provide better safeguards for the rights and freedoms of Hong Kong residents.

• And it will ensure better protection of the legitimate rights and interests of foreign investors in the city.

It is not surprising that the National Security Law for Hong Kong SAR has been warmly welcomed by Hong Kong residents. Nearly three million Hong Kong citizens have signed the petition in support of the Law. More than 70 countries in the world, including some European countries, have voiced their support.

However, some European politicians have made irresponsible remarks regarding this Law. They are interfering in Hong Kong affairs, which are internal affairs of China.

I want to emphasize that Hong Kong is part of China; Hong Kong affairs are China's internal affairs and brook no external interference.

It is my hope that the EU side will:

• view the National Security Law for the Hong Kong SAR from an objective, reasonable and fair perspective,

• take concrete steps to observe international law and the basic norms governing international relations,

• and stop interfering in Hong Kong affairs, which are the internal affairs of China.

Second, China and Europe should see each other as partners and abandon the "Cold War" mentality.

China and the EU have established a comprehensive strategic partnership. The two sides are building a partnership for peace, growth, reform and civilization.

China will always pursue peaceful development. It is committed to peaceful co-existence, mutually-beneficial cooperation and common development with all countries, including European countries. It has always seen Europe as an equal partner rather than a rival.

Between China and Europe, there is no geopolitical discord or conflict in fundamental interests; there is more cooperation than rivalry, more consensus than differences.

Those who see China as a "systemic rival" or a "potentially hostile state" have got it all wrong: they have chosen the wrong target and they are heading in the wrong direction.

What China cares most about is improving the well-being of the Chinese people. China's priority is to realize national rejuvenation. And in the pursuit of this purpose, China aspires for a peaceful and stable world.

China and Europe should:

• deepen mutual trust through an equal-footed dialogue,

• achieve win-win results through cooperation,

• and deal with differences appropriately through constructive communication.

It is important that China and Europe facilitate each other's success in a positive cycle, rather than engaging in a knockout match where one side's gain is built on the other's loss.

Third, China and Europe should seize the opportunities to be found in each other's development and reject zero-sum game.

China's development creates opportunities rather than challenges, much less threats, to Europe.

China and the EU, as two major markets of the world, account for one third of the world's total economy. The two sides are each other's second largest trading partner. And the two economies are highly complementary.

During the outbreak of COVID-19, enormous vitality and growth potential emerged from the "stay-home economy", "cloud office", intelligent manufacturing, life and health industries, and public health. These areas have created new opportunities and new space for China-Europe cooperation.

As China deepens reform and opens its market wider to the world, China-Europe cooperation will face more promising prospects.

I am confident that the mutually-beneficial cooperation between China and Europe will not only deliver more benefits to the peoples of the two sides but also provide greater stability and certainty for a world that is full of uncertainty.

Fourth, China and Europe should learn from each other and promote the progress of different civilizations side-by-side.

Both China and Europe, as important birthplaces of Oriental and Western cultures respectively, have splendid and time-honoured cultures.

The two sides differ in their history, social system and developmental stages. However, these differences should not become obstacles for exchanges between the two. Instead, they can provide driving forces for mutual learning.

The Chinese people believe that there is harmony without uniformity. We also believe that you should not do unto others what you do not want others to do unto you. China does not copy the developmental model of other countries. And China does not export its model to other countries.

The EU regards "united in diversity" as its motto. It values equality, inclusivity and diversity.

It is important that China and Europe respect, appreciate, learn from and support each other. As two major civilizations that have contributed greatly to human progress, China and Europe should work together to translate the diversity and differences in our world into vitality and impetus for further progress. This will enable different flowers of diverse human civilizations to come into full blossom.

Ladies and Gentlemen:

As an old Chinese saying goes,

"All living creatures grow together without harming each other;

"All roads run parallel without interfering with one another."

This should form the guideline for developing relations between not only individuals but also countries.

History tells us that openness brings progress, inclusivity leads to integration, and cooperation delivers win-win outcomes.

I hope we can join hands to contribute more positive energy to China-Europe cooperation so that after the pandemic, the relationship between China and Europe will make further progress at a higher level and embrace a better, brighter and more promising future.

Thank you!

Now I would like to take your questions.

David Marsh from the OMFIF: Thank you, Mr. Ambassador. It seems that you've missed an opportunity to bring Europe together on China's side, and to promote a kind of distance with the United States. Why haven't you taken that opportunity?

Liu Xiaoming: I think there's a lot of misunderstanding of China's position. We are not trying to drive a wedge between the United States and Europe. I know they are allies, and we simply want to be friends with everybody. We want to have good relations with the United States. I've been posted twice in Washington, D.C.. Half of the 45 years of my diplomatic career was dedicated to China-US relations. We want to have good relations with the United States. We always believe that there will be no world peace or prosperity without a sound, stable relationship between China and the United States, but this relationship has to be based on mutual trust and equality. You need two to tango and you need two hands to clap. So we want to have a good relationship devoid of conflict, devoid of confrontation, but instead with mutual respect and win-win cooperation based on coordination, cooperation and stability. That is what we are working for.

On China-Europe relations, as I said in my presentation, which I don't need to repeat, we want to see Europe and EU as partners of China, not rivals. We see each other as opportunities, and I am very pleased that we are one another's second largest trading partners. And there is enormous common ground, common interests to tie our two sides together.

David Marsh: Could I just ask one simple question please, which relates to the UK but may also have some bearing on the European countries, which is the question of telecommunications. We've had the decision yesterday by the British government that we won't go ahead with Huawei in the UK, even though we know what that company has done on the 5G network within a few years, and it will be bringing costs to the UK. What do you think will be the concrete results in terms of China-UK collaboration from that decision, which was announced yesterday?

Liu Xiaoming: I think it first of all undermined the trust between the two countries. You know, mutual trust and mutual respect are really the basis for a relationship, not only between individuals but also between two countries. Yesterday I tweeted, "Disappointing and wrong decision by the UK on Huawei." I would even say it's not only disappointing, it's disheartening. You know, it's a good company. They've been here for 20 years. They not only invested £3 billion in this country but also created 26,000 jobs, paid their taxes and contributed greatly to the telecom industry of this country and to the local community. What they have done for this country is described by British media and some politicians as "hurting the country". It's very disheartening. The way you treat Huawei will be observed very closely by other Chinese businesses. When mutual trust is undermined, it'll be difficult for the businesses to make more investments here.

So you don't need the government to say anything. I think that businesses can reach their own conclusions. So I think the trust is seriously damaged between the countries and between the governments and the businesses.

David Marsh: Will the Golden Era between Britain and China be upheld or become somewhat more tarnished?

Liu Xiaoming: The Golden Era really needs the both sides to make efforts. The Golden Era was proposed by the UK side. When President Xi Jinping was here in 2015, the UK leader proposed that we should build the Golden Era. We think this Golden Era is a reflection of the level of China-UK relationship. It is in the interests of the two countries. So we embraced this idea, we endorsed it and we agreed to this idea. So we work together to build this Golden Era. This is the fifth year of the Golden Era. I had thought we could celebrate the fifth anniversary of the Golden Era. But, you know, so many things happened. It's not because of China.

Mark Burgess from the OMFIF: We seem to have slipped into a bilateral world which I don't think helps with global trade, which we all benefit from. How do we get that balance between multilateral and bilateral back on track?

Liu Xiaoming: China is very committed to multilateralism. This year, as I said, is the 75th anniversary of the founding of the United Nations. Not many people know that China was the first country who put its signature on the UN Charter. China has been committed to the international system with the UN at the core. China has fulfilled its international obligation. China never says China comes first, and China never withdraws from any international treaties. We've signed about five hundred international treaties, and joined one hundred international organizations. We also support the WHO in playing a leading role in global response to COVID-19. And we have increased our donations to the WHO. We disagree with the United States' withdrawal from the WHO. We also support the WTO as the body superintending international trade, even though that system is not perfect. To date you cannot find a replacement.

Martine Doyon from Goldman Sachs: The question I have for you is what are the prospects and the practical steps for cooperation between China and Europe on climate change?

Liu Xiaoming: China is very committed to the Paris Agreement on climate change. This year was supposed to be the year of environmental cooperation for China and the UK. As you know, China was due to host the COP15 and UK is the host for the COP26. But because of the pandemic, we postponed these two conferences. China is working very closely with the UK online now. I just had a conversation with UK's COP26 Regional Ambassador Sir Laurie Bristow, and we want to work together to make it a new highlight, not just for China-UK relations. I think China and the UK can provide leadership on climate change, and we both want to work together to make the two conferences a great success.

Ika Hartmann from the British Chamber of Commerce in Germany: Because the EU has introduced new instruments to screen Chinese investments and enforced antitrust measures to create critical conditions for closer cooperation, it seems to me that now we've been talking in two different ways. How can you connect the two things? The EU wants to trade with China, the EU wants to keep you as strong partner. And obviously China wants to do the same, but your level of taste is just investment from Europe in China, and what we request from China in Europe is different. We don't match each other's thoughts and accountability.

Liu Xiaoming: I can say there are enormous opportunities for trade and investment collaboration with China. But the important thing is how the two sides see each other. Will they see each other as opportunities, as partners, or will they see each other as a systemic rival or a potentially hostile state? Now, look at Huawei, and the way the UK treats Huawei. It is really not about a private company. The big picture is about China. How you look at Huawei really symbolizes how you look at and treat China. You know, during the debate, we should listen to people from across the spectrum. But the decision on Huawei was made in face of pressure from these "China hawks" and "China bashers". You know, they all regard China as a hostile or a potentially hostile country. They don't trust China, so they don't trust a Chinese company. We do not want to see this economic relationship politicized. But on the other side, who has politicised our economic relations, joined the United States to sanction a Chinese company and taken China as a threat and a hostile country? How can you conduct normal business when the other side treats you as a potentially hostile country?

David Marsh: Are you saying China is generally blameless for the fact that we don't trust you? Or are you saying that there could have been things that China could have done better in order to produce more trust? You see the great difficulty from the other side for not trusting you, what could you do?

Liu Xiaoming: We have to analyze the matter case by case. Huawei has done everything they can. You know, you don't trust Huawei. You said Huawei had security problems. Then Huawei set up its own centre to analyze the security risk. And the center is managed by British people, not people from Huawei. It was British technicians who assessed the risks. Then they came to the conclusion that they believe the risk was manageable and controllable. So that's why the UK government made their decision earlier this year. Even though they gave Huawei a 35% market cap, they still think the risk is manageable. Huawei is also trying to improve their technology so as to strengthen security. And when we say security risk, it is not necessarily from a country. It may be from a group or an organization. So they want to make the UK 5G network infrastructure more secure and more resilient. They've done their best. I do not see that Huawei has anything we should complain about.

Reza Moghadam from Morgan Stanley: I have two very quick questions. First, Ambassador, you mentioned the support for the WTO both in Europe and China. But of course there is an impasse there at the moment. So my question to you is: What's China's view on WTO reform? Second, you mentioned at the outset that the very large volume of trade between China and the EU. Of course, a lot of that is in goods, but what is missing in that relationship is services. I wonder if the Ambassador has any thoughts on how to increase the volume of services trade between the EU and China. Thank you very much.

Liu Xiaoming: On the WTO, China is forthcoming in terms of engaging with the WTO, but still we have some disagreements with the European countries on how China should be treated. We still believe China is a developing country. It took China 15 years to return to the GATT and to be able to join the WTO through negotiations. It hasn't been easy. Still China has fulfilled, three years ahead of schedule, the commitment made when it joined the WTO. China is still ready to make further progress on that.

On services trade, Europe, including the UK, has its strengths and advantages. I think that's why I said, there's complementarity between China and Europe in the economy. We would like to have more European service businesses in China. If you have been following closely, China's New Foreign Investment Law came into effect at the beginning of this year. There are a lot of new policies regarding the service sector. China's service sector will be opened up wider, and many restrictions on the service sector have been lifted. More foreign banks and insurance companies are able to have more business opportunities in China. The cap has been brought down and the list of negativity has been shortened. We have also lifted the restrictions on the Qualified Foreign Institutional Investor (QFII) and the RMB Qualified Foreign Institutional Investor (RQFII).

Joel Kibazo from the African Development Bank: My question to you is that Africa is going to experience the deepest recession in 25 years. Will China, which holds a third of Africa's total external debt, be prepared to help as we go forward into what is really an unprecedented crisis?

Liu Xiaoming: Yes. China sees Africa as a good brother and good partner. I've been posted twice to Africa. I have a very strong feeling for African countries. We attach great importance to our relations with African countries. During the 73rd World Health Assembly in May, President Xi Jinping announced that China will work with the other G20 members on implementing the Debt Service Suspension Initiative for Poorest Countries. At a recent China-Africa summit on COVID-19 response, China again announced that it will exempt the interest-free debt due by the end of 2020 for African countries within the framework of the Forum on China-Africa Cooperation. In addition, China has sent many medical teams to help them fight COVID-19. We have provided them with PPEs and other most needed supplies. We have also shared experience with them. Even at the Chinese Embassy here, I worked with a British think tank to do that.

David Marsh: In terms of the writing off of debts, is it possible that China would join the Paris Club, in order to give a more formal way of rescheduling or writing off debts to the poorest countries? Is that something that China could do?

Liu Xiaoming: China has joined many multilateral arrangements on debt reduction and exemption. I think we've done more on the bilateral basis between African countries and China. We think that is more effective and more direct.

John Nugee from the OMFIF: I want to understand more on the observed change of China's international policy, its approach to international relations. What stood out for me in the last 30 years is that patience has been the watchword for China. Now we observe a change. Why has China decided to adopt a more urgent approach to many issues facing the world?

Liu Xiaoming: I would say China has not changed. You know, China is a peace loving country and peace is in the DNA of the Chinese nation. China strives very hard for world peace and stability. China benefits from a peaceful environment for the past 40 years since we opened up and implemented reform. Why should we rock the boat and why should we change course? We believe that China will continue to benefit from this peaceful environment. But I think it is the other side that has changed tremendously. China has to make a response to that. Take China-US relationship for example. We want to have a good relationship with the US. We have no reason to have a bad relationship. But it is the United States, who imposes sanctions and demonizes China. Look at this pandemic. Their President, their Secretary of State, keep on using the expression "China virus". Who has changed? I think people have to be objective with regard to change.

On Taiwan, the United States has tried to play this "Taiwan card". They increase their arms sales to Taiwan. They want to give international recognition to Taiwan. They rock the boat and we have to make response.

On Hong Kong, 23 years after the handover, "One Country, Two Systems" has been a great success. But last year, you know, there was turbulence. There was a movement for "Hong Kong independence", "self determination". They even waved the Union Jack and US flags, calling for the United States to land in Hong Kong to liberate Hong Kong. We have a reason to be worried about that and take necessary and firm measures to safeguard "One Country, Two Systems".

Sherard Cowper-Coles from HSBC: Very good to see you, Ambassador. I wanted to ask you about the disparity in understanding between Europe and China. China seems to know a lot about Europe. But there is a great gap in understanding in the UK and across Europe more generally of China and China's history, and the Chinese Communist Party. So I want to ask you, what more should we be doing to try and increase knowledge of China in Europe, particularly among those who make policy or form opinions, because there's a big deficit in understanding?

Liu Xiaoming: Thank you for sharing your question. I assume next time when I prepare my speech, I would put in a fifth deficit, namely, the understanding deficit. I quite agree with you that there's a big gap in understanding between China and Europe, mostly Western countries. So each time when some Western politicians criticize China, they always say China is widely criticized. I would say they only represent a small number of Western countries and they are not the world. Taking the National Security Law for example, more than 70 countries have shown support for this Law. And how many countries have stood against China? It's just one third of the number of countries that supported China. So I think the effective way is to engage actively with each other. I think we should not decouple from each other. That is a very bad idea. I think we need more coupling. We encourage China and Europe to nurture across-the-board engagement among the young people, the students. More Chinese students intend to study here in this country. I hope the UK will continue to be open and welcome Chinese students with open arms.

Kern Andrew from Nomura: Thank you very much, Ambassador, for your speech. I wanted to ask you about the question of interfering in the internal affairs of other nations. I understand very well the Chinese perspective and view on this and respect it. However, is it a realistic view to take in a globalised world where what happens in one country affects another? Taking for example environmental issues which you mentioned, and where China and Britain need to work together because of the upcoming conferences. What happens within China, which is a centre of biodiversity, is really very important and Britain has a real interest. China has a great interest in what happens in other countries. And when we interact, we have to speak to each other about what happens in each other's country.

Liu Xiaoming: I think both Chinese and British people are smart, clever enough to discern what are interferences in others' internal affairs, and what are suggestions and advice given with good intention. When you have complaints about environmental issues in China, we know that you want to improve China's environmental system, you want to make China's environment better. This is certainly welcomed. We can certainly identify what is advice given with a good intention and what is interference aimed at changing China's political and social system, and imposing upon China Western ideas and a Western model. As I said, we have no interest in exporting our models, but we are also strongly against foreign countries, no matter who they are, interfering in our internal affairs.

Michael Maclay from Montrose Associates: Ambassador, regarding the Huawei decision and the current bitterness and absence of trust you describe, maybe there are some specific things that China could do that would help to rebuild trust. Firstly, for example, when the WHO team comes to China, will they be given access to the Wuhan laboratory? Secondly, might China explicitly acknowledge the principle of freedom of navigation in the South and East China Sea? And thirdly, would it still help to use the expression of "peaceful unification"?

Liu Xiaoming: On the WHO, China has been very transparent and responsible. From the very beginning, China was the first country to report a case and the first country to share the genetic sequence. We have nothing to hide and I think it is other countries that are trying to stigmatize China. WTO experts are in China right now and China is working with them. I believe the two sides will share a productive and effective cooperation. We support the WHO in playing a leading role but we have to remember two things. Firstly, research into the origin of the virus should be based on science, not on politics. Secondly, all countries should be subject to review, not only China.

On freedom of navigation, China is a country which is fully committed to the freedom of navigation. 60% of China's oil supply comes through the South China Sea. We have every reason to want to ensure peace, stability in this region and we are working very hard with the neighbouring countries, working on the DOC and the COC. And the situation would be very peaceful, were it not for some foreign naval vessels that come here from time to time to threaten China, to infringe upon China's sovereignty.

On Taiwan, China is committed to peaceful reunification. There is no change to this principled position. I suggest you read my article on this question recently carried by *China Daily* newspaper. I wish to reaffirm that Taiwan is an inalienable part of Chinese territory. China has consistently adhered to the policy of peaceful reunification. By making no commitment to giving up the use of force, the Chinese Government is targeting external interference, and a handful of separatists who advocate "Taiwan independence" and their separatist activities. This is not aimed at our compatriots in Taiwan. China must be reunified and will be reunified. This will not be stopped by anyone or any force.

Meghnad Desai from the OMFIF: China's economy has recovered quickly following the pandemic. Does China have any plan to strengthen the status of the RMB as a possible reserve currency in the near future?

Liu Xiaoming: China is very committed to internationalization of the RMB. In the past decade, we have made many efforts in order to facilitate trade and investment. More and more countries take the RMB as not only a currency for conducting trade or investment, but also use it as a reserve currency. So I'm very pleased to see that London is now playing a leading role in the internationalization of the RMB. London now is the second largest offshore

RMB clearing center, and the largest offshore RMB trading center. Hong Kong is the largest offshore RMB clearing centre, and the second largest offshore RMB trading center. I think the two cities have enormous opportunities for cooperation.

Pablo Riquelme Turrent from the BBVA: Thank you, Ambassador. I would like to hear your opinion about the future relationship with Latin America, and especially with Mexico, being so close to the United States and having this partnership with the United States and Canada. I wonder if it's going to change going forward? Is it a friendly relationship? How do you see it develop?

Liu Xiaoming: We would like to strengthen our relationship with Latin American countries. There's a mechanism between China and Latin American countries, a summit held from time to time. The relationship between China and Mexico is very strong. We are not concerned about Mexico's good relations with the United States. But we hope that the United States will not interrupt China's good relations with the Latin American countries.

John Orchard from the OMFIF: Thank you very much, Ambassador, for talking to us today. You talked at the beginning about China-Europe relations. As the UK has left the European Union, does it remain part of your Europe strategy, or is it practically part of your American strategy or something else?

Liu Xiaoming: It's up to the UK. I always argue with my British colleagues: We are not asking you to take sides between China and the United States; I'm just asking you to take the right side of the argument. That's my first point.

The second point is, I would argue that Britain can only be Great Britain when the UK has an independent foreign policy, rather than to be viewed in China or the rest of the world as just a junior partner of the United States. Look at what happened to Huawei. I do not need to elaborate the obvious. Even yesterday, President Trump said he personally pinpointed Huawei and he made great success. And look at what their Ambassador is tweeting and look at what their Secretary of State is saying after the decision was made by the UK Government. So everybody understands what the reason is behind the UK decision. When the UK wants to build a global Britain, to still exert a global influence, they really have to think deeply about what kind of a role they are going to play, and what kind of a position they're going to take. We want to have good relations with the EU and with the UK. There's no doubt about that.

David Marsh: Ambassador, I'd like to thank you for being so frank and open with us. I do hope this won't be the last time that we have this very good conversation.

Liu Xiaoming: Thank you.

Rainbow Appears after the Storm

——A Keynote Speech and Q&A at the Energy Intelligence Forum

On 13rd October 2020, I attended the Energy Intelligence Forum where he delivered a keynote speech entitled "Address Climate Change and Advance Energy Transition to Make Our Planet a Better Home for All" and answered questions raised by the moderator of the event.

The following is the transcript of the speech and Q&A.

Liu Xiaoming: It is a real delight to join you at the Energy Intelligence Forum.

Taking up the theme of "The Big Energy Reset: COVID, Climate, Consequences", today's Forum could not be more timely. Let me take this opportunity to share with you my views on the theme of the forum. I will focus on three questions:

• How do we assess the current situation in energy and climate change?

• What will China do?

• How can we strengthen cooperation to address climate change and promote energy transition?

COVID-19 has been the most challenging pandemic in the past century. It has dealt a severe blow to many trades and industries. Against this backdrop, what is the situation like with regard to climate change and energy transition? In my opinion, there are three major trends:

First, the connection between climate change and energy transition is increasingly close.

Addressing climate change and promoting energy transition matter a great deal to the planet Earth upon which mankind relies on for survival. In other words, how these issues are addressed holds the key to our future.

Today, we are faced with many climate change challenges, from frequent extreme weather events to the rising sea level, from the deterioration of the eco-environment and the inadequate response from developing countries to the withdrawal of a particular country from the Paris Agreement. All these challenges can be traced back to the energy industry.

Second, COVID-19 is accelerating the energy transition.

COVID-19 has pressed the "pause" button on the world economy and on energy demand, prompting countries of the world to reflect on the direction and routes of the energy transition.

The most urgent task of the day is enhancing global cooperation on fighting COVID-19, restoring the economic and social order and injecting fresh vitality. Pursuing green economic recovery has become the consensus of the international community in the post-pandemic world. The structure of the energy industry will become more diversified and this will put further pressure on energy companies to seek development through transition.

Third, COVID-19 has highlighted the need for harmonious coexistence between man and nature.

The pandemic sounded the alarm. Mankind must stop ignoring the repeated warnings from nature, stop taking without giving back, stop development at the expense of conservation, and stop utilization without rehabilitation.

Man and nature share a common future. So it is in conservation that we must explore opportunities for development. Only by following the trend of green and low-carbon development can we find the driving force to "restart" the energy industry.

Last month, at a high-level UN meeting in commemoration of the 75th anniversary of the founding of that organization, President Xi Jinping announced that China will:

• scale up its nationally determined contribution,

• adopt even more forceful policies and measures,

• and strive to peak carbon dioxide emissions before 2030 and achieve carbon neutrality before 2060.

This attests to the audacity of China in taking up responsibilities in line with the requirements of sustainable domestic development and the goal of building a community with a shared future for mankind.

It is a major policy announcement on climate change.

It is also a display of China's strong resolve to play an active part in global governance on climate change, to take the lead in global green development and to promote global energy transition.

China will make a greater contribution to advancing global governance on climate change.

With a population of 1.4 billion, China is the world's largest developing country. It is faced with outstanding issues of imbalance and inadequacy in its development.

However, as a responsible global player, China always honors its promises on tackling climate change.

China has implemented the Paris Agreement and achieved remarkable outcomes in energy conservation and emissions reduction.

- From 2005 to 2018, China reduced its carbon intensity by 45.8%, cutting CO_2 emissions by 5.26 billion tons.
- In 2019, China's energy consumption per unit GDP was down by 2.6% from the level of the previous year and by 25.6% from the level of 2012.

Committed as it is to multilateralism, China has been playing an active part in global governance on climate change.

- China has implemented the South-South Cooperation Initiative on Climate Change under the framework of the Belt and Road. Starting from 2012, China has spent $72 million on South-South cooperation in the field of climate change every year.
- China has also worked on pooling international efforts for cooperation on climate change via platforms such as the BRI International Green Development Coalition.

China will make a greater contribution to promoting green development in the world.

China advocates a new development concept, namely one that is innovative, coordinated, green, open and shared development. We are committed to the belief that "clear water and green mountains are mountains of gold and silver". We are seizing the historic opportunities of the new round of scientific and technological revolution and industrial transformation, and playing an active and leading role in the "green economic recovery" in the post-pandemic world.

China's 14th Five Year Plan will map out routes towards building a green, circular and low-carbon economy. This includes:

- a coordinated approach to epidemic response and economic and social development,

• a new path of high-quality development which gives priority to ecological conservation and is led by green technologies,

• an improved system of investment and financing for tackling climate change,

• and promotion of green production and green way of life.

In pursuing post-pandemic economic recovery, China will:

• foster and strengthen energy conservation, environmental protection and clean production industries,

• increase the industrial and domestic use of electronic, digital and smart technologies,

• promote transformation in multiple areas, including energy and transportation,

• and continue to be a global leader in green and sustainable growth.

China will make greater contribution to promoting global energy transition.

China has been committed to improving the quality and efficiency of energy supply, accelerating innovation in energy technology, and advancing market-based reform in the area of energy.

In the past decade, China has become the world's largest investor in renewable energy. We have:

• built the largest network of clean coal power generation,

• made important breakthroughs in deepwater drilling and shale gas exploration and development,

• encouraged the thriving application of new energy, including nuclear, wind and solar energy,

• and fostered "internet plus" and smart energy and other new business models.

China has also taken an active part in international energy cooperation.

• China is opening its energy sector wider to the world and keeps expanding cooperation with other countries in oil, gas and nuclear energy.

• China is implementing the Global Energy Internet, playing an active part in the development of energy routes along the Belt and Road, and participating in global cooperation on energy technology.

• China has established 58 bilateral mechanisms and participated in 33 multilateral mechanisms for cooperation.

In a word, China has played its part and contributed its solution to global development and cooperation in energy transition.

Ladies and Gentlemen:

The history of mankind is a history of difficulties overcome and challenges tackled. Going forward, China will continue to address climate change and promote energy transition. This will not only contribute to sustainable growth in the world. It will also create more opportunities for cooperation with other countries, including the UK.

First, opportunities for global governance on climate change and environment.

Next year will be an important one for global governance on climate change.

In his speech at the UN Summit on Biodiversity last month, President Xi Jinping said that at the COP15 to be held in Kunming next year, China and the other participating parties would discuss and draw up plans together for protecting global biodiversity, and turn Earth into a beautiful homeland for all creatures to live in harmony.

Next year the UK will host the COP26 in Glasgow.

These two conferences will create opportunities for the energy and industrial communities of the world to enhance cooperation and foster greater synergy in areas such as clean energy and green finance. By combining their complementary strengths, the participating parties will be able to deliver concrete outcomes.

Second, there are opportunities for greater openness and cooperation in the energy sector.

China is committed to building an open world economy. Its current "dual circulation" model emphasizes domestic demand and encourages mutual complementarities between domestic and international demand. In this new development model, open cooperation in energy is an integral part.

China remains the world's most important and vigorous market for energy consumption and import. China will continue to be open to investment from all over the world. In November, China will host the third International Import Expo, the CIIE, where we hope to see energy businesses from all countries, including the UK.

The Hinkley Point C nuclear power station is a flagship project of China-UK-France cooperation. Upon completion, it will meet 7% of the UK's total demand for electricity and help to eliminate 9 million tons of CO_2 emissions every year. It points to further opportunities for China and the UK to deepen cooperation in the civil application of nuclear energy.

Third, there are opportunities in energy transition and innovation.

As the new round of scientific and technological revolution and industrial transformation unfolds, China is making vigorous efforts to promote innovation in green technology, and the energy and financial services.

Scientific innovation drives the high-quality development of the energy industry, and new energy technologies will lead to the upgrading of the entire sector.

The development of new technologies and new business models in China, such as the smart grid, electric vehicles, large-capacity power storage and smart energy, will create enormous opportunities for energy businesses from all countries.

Fourth, there are opportunities for building a green Belt and Road.

The Belt and Road Initiative, or the BRI, has become the world's largest platform for international cooperation. The colour green is the salient background of the BRI development roadmap.

China and the UK have jointly issued the Green Investment Principles for the Belt and Road.

Via the BRI platform, energy companies can expand bipartisan, tripartite and multi-party cooperation in the areas of environmental protection, energy conservation, emissions reduction, infrastructure development, green finance and FinTech.

Through such cooperation, energy transition will be better integrated into the global efforts in the fields of ecological conservation, environment protection and sustainable development.

Ladies and Gentlemen:

A Western saying goes, "Every cloud has a silver lining." A similar Chinese saying goes, "Rainbow appears after the storm."

In the "darkest hour" of the raging pandemic, mankind has displayed strength through solidarity, courage, determination and love.

China stands ready to work with the international community to shore up confidence and tide over the hard times. Together we can address climate change and advance energy transition to make our planet a better home for all.

In conclusion, I wish the Energy Intelligence Forum great success!

Thank you!

Now I would like to take your questions.

Moderator: What does 2060 carbon neutrality mean for energy demand in China? Where does this leave fossil fuels—oil, gas, and coal—and renewables?

Liu Xiaoming: China will scale up its nationally determined contributions, adopt even more forceful policies and measures, strive to reach a peak in CO_2 emissions before 2030, and achieve carbon neutrality before 2060. Achieving carbon neutrality by 2060 is a very forceful and positive target. It has been widely recognized by the international community. The energy and economic transition and the reduction of CO_2 and greenhouse gas emissions in China are occurring much faster and with greater intensity than in the developed countries.

As to fossil fuels, China's coal consumption accounted for 57.7% of its total energy consumption in 2019, dropping to a record low. Natural gas has taken a larger share of 7.8% in the energy mix. However, China is still at a stage of rapid economic development, and many industries and regions continue to rely on fossil fuels. The 2060 carbon neutrality target is sending a very clear signal, undoubtedly pushing for transition and upgrading in sectors like energy, transportation, manufacturing, construction and agriculture. China will further develop and improve the carbon emission trading market to allow market-based incentives to do the job of promoting CO_2 emission reduction and corporate technological innovation and channeling investment toward low-carbon, green industries.

As to renewables, the proportion of non-fossil fuels in China's total energy consumption increased to 15.3% in 2019. New industries attendant upon the development of new energy are booming. By the end of 2019, the number of "new energy" vehicles (NEVs) in China reached 3.81 million, accounting for roughly one-half of the global total. Focusing on the 2060 carbon neutrality target, China will continue to promote clean and low-carbon components in its energy structure, increase the proportion of renewables in total energy consumption, and vigorously promote the application of new energy sources including wind, solar, and nuclear energy.

Moderator: How do you view China's remarkable economic recovery after the coronavirus outbreak and its strong energy demand growth?

Liu Xiaoming: While coordinating epidemic prevention and control efforts,

China has been taking measures to restart the economy in an orderly manner and to continue deepening the reform and opening up. The Chinese economy has shown remarkable resilience and huge potential. The momentum for recovery is strong. GDP increased by 3.2% in the second quarter of 2020, bringing the economic contraction to an end. China became the world's first major economy to resume growth.

China's energy industry has made important contribution to the victory over COVID-19 by ensuring supply throughout. In the first half of the year, China's total energy consumption fell by 0.2% compared with the same period last year, which came down significantly from the 2.9% decline in the first quarter. Demand for coal, oil and natural gas rebounded. The construction of energy infrastructure, including electricity facilities and oil and gas pipelines, resumed. The proportion of electricity generated by clean energy has increased, accounting for 27.6% of the total in the first half of the year and rising by 0.1% over the same period last year.

China supports the concept of green recovery. Tackling the challenges and risks of climate change is a long-term, ongoing endeavour that can only be made in the process of green recovery. In his recent speech at the United Nations Summit on Biodiversity, President Xi Jinping said that:

"Globally, the coronavirus has wreaked havoc on every aspect of economic and social development. We need to have our eyes fixed on the long run, have determination and stay the course for green, inclusive and sustainable development."

"Recognizing that 'our solutions lie in Nature', we could strive to find development opportunities while preserving Nature, and achieve win-win in both ecological conservation and high-quality economic development."

Pandemic control has become the "new normal". China will take into account both short-term tasks and long-term goals, and coordinate economic and social development with addressing climate change. Under the guidance of the new development concept, namely "innovative, coordinated, green, open and shared development", China will continue to take vigorous measures to implement the national climate change strategy, to enhance energy conservation and efficiency, to promote the development of green industries and strengthen the weak links in environmental infrastructure as quickly as possible.

Moderator: Why has China stepped up its goals on emission reduction?

Liu Xiaoming: China attaches great importance to advancing ecological civilization. We take our obligations under environment-related treaties seriously, including those on climate change and biodiversity. China has made great achievements in the fields of energy saving and emission reduction. The goal of carbon neutrality is a major policy announcement concerning climate and the environment. It is based on the inherent requirements of domestic sustainable development in China and the responsibility of building a community with a shared future for mankind. It demonstrates China's three "firm determinations":

The first determination is to tackle climate change and firmly adopt the path of green and low-carbon development. The goal of carbon neutrality points to a clear path for China's mid-to-long-term climate action. China will take green, low-carbon and sustainable development as the guideline for its current economic recovery and future high-quality development. China will never waver in its strategic determination to strengthen response to climate change and advance ecological conservation.

The second determination is to firmly support multilateralism. Currently, the global multilateral climate process still faces challenges from unilateralism. COVID-19 has posed new challenges to the countries of the world in their response to climate change. By stepping up its goals on emission reduction, China is injecting positive impetus into multilateralism and boosting international confidence in tackling climate change. This is another vivid manifestation of China's commitment to building a community with a shared future for mankind.

The third determination is to resolutely support the implementation of the Paris Agreement and to strongly promote global climate governance. The submission of updated NDCs in 2020 is an important juncture for the implementation of the Paris Agreement. China's announcement is in line with the global trend of strengthening climate action. It reflects China's firm support for implementing the Paris Agreement, promoting global climate governance and working with all parties to build a clean and beautiful world.

Moderator: After President Xi's speech on carbon neutrality, can we expect the BRI to become greener with the latest commitments? Where does China see growth for its overseas partnerships?

Liu Xiaoming: The BRI is not only a road to economic prosperity but also a road to green development. As President Xi Jinping pointed out in his speech at the United Nations Summit on Biodiversity,

"A sound ecosystem is essential for the prosperity of civilization. We need to take up our lofty responsibility for the entire human civilization, and we need to respect nature, follow its laws and protect it. We need to find a way to ensure harmonious coexistence between man and Nature, a way to balance and coordinate economic development and ecological protection."

China has always adhered to the green concept in BRI development, focusing on its integration with the UN 2030 Agenda for Sustainable Development, promoting green and low-carbon infrastructure and operation management, emphasizing ecological conservation in investment and trade, and strengthening cooperation in the fields of ecological environment governance, biodiversity protection and climate change. In line with the carbon neutrality and other emission reduction targets, we could promote a greener BRI cooperation in three aspects:

The first is to establish a green mechanism. In 2019, China jointly initiated the BRI International Green Development Coalition with more than 140 partners in 42 countries. China will promote the development of conservation industries such as modern recycling agriculture and industries based on bioenergy, energy conservation, environmental protection, information technology and new energy industries with a view to setting up a BRI green project pool. The Chinese government has also established Belt and Road Environmental Technology and Transfer Centre to promote the joint R&D and application of advanced eco-friendly technologies.

The second is to strengthen ecological conservation. Biodiversity impacts upon human well-being and is an important foundation for human survival and development. In designing and constructing BRI projects, Chinese enterprises fully considered biodiversity and conservation needs as well as economic development. For example, when Chinese companies built Karachi-Lahore Highway in Pakistan, they planted nearly 300,000 trees and more than 5 million square meters of grassland along the road. Along with new road infrastructure, they also contributed to the local environment.

The third is to enhance cooperation in green finance. More than 30 large financial institutions around the world have signed the "Green Investment Principles for the Belt and Road", which includes a full understanding of the environmental, social and governance (ESG) risks; full disclosure of environmental information; making full use of green financial tools; adopting green supply chain management, etc.

China will adhere to the concept of open, green and sustainable development, and work with BRI partners to build a green "silk road".

We have implemented the Belt and Road South-South Cooperation Initiative on Climate Change. Since 2012, the annual expenditure for South-South climate cooperation has reached 72 million U.S. dollars.

We have actively carried out third-party market cooperation with developed countries including the United Kingdom on building a green Belt and Road.

We will pool more efforts in international cooperation on climate change via platforms such as Belt and Road International Alliance for Green Development.

Chapter 7

Interview with TASS

Addressing Both Symptoms and Causes of the Korean Peninsula Issue

——An Interview with TASS Russian New's Agency

(17th April 2023, TASS Headquarters)

The following news release was distributed by TASS.

According to the Special Representative of the Chinese Government on Korean Peninsula Affairs Liu Xiaoming, "the United States has publicly declared its readiness to shape the strategic environment around China".

The United States is de facto engaged in nuclear proliferation in the Asian region, including its unlawful transfer of nuclear submarines to Australia, The Special Representative of the Chinese Government on Korean Peninsula Affairs Liu Xiaoming has told TASS in an interview.

"As far as Australia is concerned, the United States and the United Kingdom are transferring submarines to Australia. In essence, this constitutes a serious risk of nuclear proliferation and poses a serious threat to peace and stability in this region. In fact this shows that the US is the biggest troublemaker for regional peace and security," he said.

According to the Chinese official, "the United States has publicly declared its readiness to shape the strategic environment around China."

"They have put forward the Indo-Pacific strategy under the pretext of promoting freedom and openness, but in reality this is just an attempt to pull together small groups and exclusive blocs to contain China's development," Liu Xiaoming said.

"In North-East Asia, the United States, South Korea and Japan continue to hold large-scale military exercises that stir tensions on the Korean Peninsula. And in Southeast Asia, the United States is also conducting joint military exercises with the Philippines, with the participation of 12,000 US servicemen. The United States repeatedly stokes tension in the South China Sea as well," he added.

Moreover, Liu Xiaoming continued, "the Americans are attempting to use Taiwan for containing China by playing the Taiwan card, resulting in tensions in the Taiwan Strait."

At the same time, China is "firmly committed to the path of peaceful development and a defensive national defence policy, and, through its concrete actions, promotes world peace, common development and the building of a community with a shared future for mankind."

"On the one hand, we need to promote development on the basis of extensive discussion, joint contribution and shared benefits," he said. "But, on the other hand, we also need an army for peace that defends the fruits of our independent development."

"In a nutshell, we need to strengthen national defence and create a world-class military, to defend the sovereignty, territorial integrity and the hard-won development achievements of our country," Liu Xiaoming said. "This is also necessary for the security of our region and the entire world."

Washington fanning Ukraine crisis, while Beijing proposes peace plan—Chinese envoy

"The Chinese side always takes a prudent and responsible approach to the export of military products, Special Representative of the Chinese Government on Korean Peninsula Affairs," Liu Xiaoming said.

The United States has been fanning the conflict in Ukraine, while China has come up with a peace plan, a senior Chinese diplomat said in an interview with TASS.

"The Chinese side always takes a prudent and responsible approach to the export of military products. Unlike the United States and other Western nations, who have been adding fuel to the fire in the Ukrainian crisis, we put forward a peace plan to resolve it," said Liu Xiaoming, the Special Representative of the Chinese Government on Korean Peninsula Affairs.

In late February, the Chinese Foreign Ministry published a position paper on a political settlement of the crisis in Ukraine. The twelve-point document includes calls for a ceasefire, respect for the legitimate interests of all countries in the field of security, settlement of the humanitarian crisis in Ukraine, the exchange of prisoners of war between Moscow and Kiev, as well as the cancellation of unilateral sanctions imposed without a corresponding decision of the UN Security Council.

In the published document, China described dialogue and negotiations as the sole way of resolving the crisis in Ukraine and called on all parties to support Moscow and Kiev in "working in the same direction", urging a resumption of direct dialogue as soon as possible. The international community should create conditions and platforms for the resumption of talks, the document emphasized.

China cannot pledge to abstain from using force against separatists on Taiwan, says envoy

"We strive to achieve peaceful reunification, but we reserve the right to take all necessary measures to protect our country's sovereignty and territorial integrity," the Special Representative of the Chinese Government on Korean Peninsula Affairs Liu Xiaoming stressed.

"China reserves the right to take all necessary measures to protect its sovereignty and territorial integrity, and makes no promises to abstain from using force against separatists on Taiwan," Liu Xiaoming, the Special Representative of the Chinese Government on Korean Peninsula Affairs said in an interview with TASS.

"One country, means one China, and one country is the precondition of 'One Country, Two Systems' and the foundation upon which everything else, rests. We strive to achieve peaceful reunification under 'One Country, Two Systems', but we reserve the right to take all necessary measures to protect our country's sovereignty and territorial integrity. In particular, we have never promised not to use force. Had we made such a promise, peaceful reunification would have become absolutely impossible," he pointed out.

"However, this position of ours is not directed against our Taiwan compatriots; it is a tiny number of 'Taiwan independence' separatists and other external forces seeking to divide our country that it is against," the Chinese special envoy explained.

When asked about the likelihood of a military conflict around Taiwan breaking out this year, Liu noted that, in his view, "it's better to stress to all countries around the world about the importance of upholding the one-China principle."

"The One-China principle is the anchor for stability and peace in the Taiwan Strait. As long as the principle is observed, peace and stability will be ensured in the Taiwan Strait, as well as peaceful development on both shores. Otherwise, the Taiwan Strait would plunge into instability. We can also see that it was the visit made by (former US House Speaker Nancy) Pelosi to Taiwan and the visit by the head of the Taiwan authorities to the US that gave rise to tension," the Chinese envoy emphasized.

China not supplying weapons to Russia, Ukraine—special envoy

Liu Xiaoming also noted that the US had no right to issue orders to Beijing on its relations with Russia.

"China has never supplied weapons to Russia or Ukraine, but Beijing does not countenance blackmail and will not bow to orders issued by the US," Liu Xiaoming, the Special Representative of the Chinese Government on Korean Peninsula Affairs said in an interview with TASS.

"I would like to reiterate that China is neither the instigator of nor a party to the Ukrainian crisis and it has never supplied weapons to either of the parties to the Ukrainian conflict," he pointed out.

The envoy also noted that the US had no right to issue orders to Beijing. "We won't accept any kind of lecturing or blackmail from the United States," Liu added.

Chinese envoy points finger at negative US role in stoking escalation on Korean Peninsula

Liu Xiaoming criticized the United States for not having paid due attention to the DPRK's security concerns.

"Beijing is extremely concerned about the escalation of tensions on the Korean Peninsula, with the United States playing a negative role by holding joint drills with ROK," Liu Xiaoming, Beijing's Special Representative on Korean Peninsula Affairs said in an interview with TASS.

"My trip to European countries and Russia comes against the backdrop of the latest changes on the Korean Peninsula. On the one hand, we often hear Westerners—both Europeans and Americans—complain that since last year the DPRK has conducted a number of missile launches, while on the other hand, we can see that the ROK and the Americans held the largest drills over the past five years on the peninsula," the senior Chinese diplomat lamented. "The escalation of tensions on the Korean Peninsula is ongoing, and this makes us very concerned," he added.

Liu also criticized the United States for not having paid due attention to the DPRK's security concerns.

"First of all, I shall try to give my European and Russian counterparts a clear understanding of how China views the situation. The US always blames the DPRK for causing tensions, but there is another reason that is worth noting.

We see the reason as stemming from the US conducting such major military exercises. Second, a very important cause of instability on the Korean Peninsula, and of the Korean Peninsula becoming an issue, is that the United States has not paid due attention to the DPRK's concerns in the field of security and has imposed economic sanctions," the Chinese envoy said. "They continue to increase pressure and contain the DPRK's development; they exert political pressure and have imposed economic sanctions," he added.

According to Liu, the goal of his tour is to share the Chinese assessment of the situation on the Korean Peninsula with his counterparts and to find a recipe for promoting a political settlement jointly with his European and Russian counterparts.

The senior Chinese diplomat said Moscow was the last stop on his 24-day foreign itinerary during which he said he had already visited Switzerland, Great Britain, Brussels, Germany and France.

Liu urged efforts to ease tensions on the Korean Peninsula. "Amid the lack of a peace mechanism, the escalation of tensions is ongoing, which threatens peace and stability on the Korean Peninsula," he concluded.

Chinese envoy does not see sovereign future for Taiwan

"From time immemorial, Taiwan has been an integral part of China; it has never been a country and it will never become one," Liu Xiaoming emphasized.

"Taiwan is an inseparable part of China and will never become a country," Liu Xiaoming, Beijing's Special Representative on Korean Peninsula Affairs, said in an interview with TASS.

Forces seeking independence for Taiwan have lately colluded with external forces, the senior Chinese diplomat explained. "They have conducted a number of activities that threaten stability in the Taiwan Strait and violate the One-China principle," he said, referring to the visit of then—US House Speaker Nancy Pelosi to Taiwan as well as the visit by head of Taiwan authorities Tsai Ing-wen to the United States.

"From time immemorial, Taiwan has been an integral part of China; it has never been a country and it will never become one," the envoy emphasized.

Liu reiterated that the peaceful reunification of the two shores of the Taiwan Strait was "the common aspiration of the Chinese people and an important component of the nation's rejuvenation". "We will display maximum sincerity and exert utmost efforts in pursuing peaceful reunification," he assured the TASS reporter.

He also said that Chinese compatriots on Taiwan would hopefully join together to contribute to what he said would be the great rejuvenation of the Chinese nation.

"You know that Mr. Deng Xiaoping formulated that policy with the specific aim of resolving the Taiwan question, and over time we resolved the issues of Hong Kong and Macao, and the 'One Country, Two Systems' principle proved its efficiency precisely in Hong Kong and Macao, and therefore we have confidence that this policy will be a success in Taiwan, too," Liu concluded.

Army developing amid challenges to defence of sovereignty—China's special representative

Liu Xiaoming stressed that China was following a path of peaceful development and pursuing a defence policy based on defending the nation and has always made great contributions to defending global peace, promoting international development and protecting world order.

"The development of the Chinese army in the context of new challenges is aimed precisely at protecting the country's sovereignty and security interests, but, however developed China may become, Beijing will never seek hegemony or expansion, Beijing's special envoy for Korean Peninsula affairs," Liu Xiaoming, told TASS in an interview when asked for comment on Chinese President Xi Jinping's recent instructions to the Chinese People's Liberation Army (PLA) to step up training for real combat operations.

"China's work on its defence posture and efforts to strengthen the Chinese army pursue exclusively defensive aims to protect China's peaceful environment and to allow our country to make new achievements in economic development and improve the well-being of our people. In other words, any growth in China's military strength is growth in the force for global peace," he said, adding that the Chinese army was actively involved in UN peacekeeping missions in escorting ships in the Gulf of Aden and in other humanitarian operations.

"We are exerting great efforts to provide more public goods for the world in the sphere of security," Liu added.

"At present, the world faces multiple challenges. Under these circumstances, we need to pay attention to the fact that China has not achieved reunification of the country thus far. The development of the Chinese army is aimed precisely at protecting our sovereignty, territorial integrity, national security and development interests. Let me stress once again: No matter how developed China may become, we will never pursue hegemony or expansion. We will continue to make our contribution to building a world of lasting peace, universal security, common prosperity, openness, inclusivity, and a clean and beautiful environment," he stressed.

Liu noted that the Chinese president recently "visited the Chinese army's Southern Theater Command and, in his speech there, pointed to the importance of implementing the Communist Party of China's thinking on strengthening the military in the new era, adhering to the military strategy of the new era, intensifying the military's training for real combat operations, accelerating the reform and upgrade of the Chinese army, and resolutely fulfilling the tasks set by the Party and the people".

Liu stressed that China follows a path of peaceful development and pursues a defence policy that is defensive in nature, and had always made great contributions to defending global peace, promoting international development and protecting the world order. He stressed the Chinese people's commitment to peace.

"In the 70-plus years since the establishment of the People's Republic of China, we never provoked a single war or took an inch of other people's land," Liu said.

Beijing sees military operation with regard to Taiwan as legitimate opion—China's envoy

When asked if Beijing considers a special military operation against Taiwan possible, Liu Xiaoming insisted that the Chinese government reserves the right to take all necessary measures to ensure the territorial integrity and sovereignty of the country.

"The question of Taiwan is not a diplomatic issue and is of no concern to outside powers, while all necessary measures are legitimate options for Beijing," China's Special Representative for Korean Peninsula Affairs, Liu Xiaoming, told TASS in an interview.

"You asked about the possibility of resolving this issue by diplomatic means, so I would like to emphasize that the Taiwan question is an internal affair of China. This is not a diplomatic issue. But if you mean a peaceful way when you say 'diplomatic method', then I think that 'One Country, Two Systems' is exactly the plan to resolve this question in a peaceful way," he said.

When asked if Beijing considers a special military operation against Taiwan possible, Liu Xiaoming said that the Chinese government reserves the right to take all necessary measures to ensure the territorial integrity and sovereignty of the country.

"This is not directed against our compatriots in Taiwan, it is directed against a tiny number of 'Taiwan independence' separatists and other external forces, because their actions violate the Chinese constitution and contravene the Anti-Secession Law. So we will counter these actions in accordance with the law. We will take all necessary measures to protect the sovereignty and territorial integrity of our country. This is our sacred right," he said.

The diplomat also noted that, among all world powers, China is the only country that has not yet achieved its reunification, so its reunification is the common aspiration of the entire Chinese people, as well as the clear stipulation of the Chinese constitution.

"Peaceful reunification under 'One Country, Two Systems' is a basic policy that is in the interests of the entire Chinese nation, including our Taiwan compatriots. This is a plan of peace, democracy, goodwill and mutual benefit, as well as the most realistic, most tolerant project for resolving the issue of the differing political systems on the two shores of the Taiwan Strait," he added.

Chinese diplomat says Beijing immediately notified Washington about the balloon

Liu Xiaoming emphasized that Beijing had called on Washington "to be rational, cool-headed and professional" in order to jointly settle this situation, but that the US ignored basic facts and fired a missile to down the balloon.

A senior Chinese diplomat lambasted the recent incident with a Chinese balloon above the United States as a farce on the part of Washington, saying that Beijing notified the Americans as soon as the balloon entered their airspace.

Commenting on the incident in an interview with TASS, Liu Xiaoming, Beijing's Special Representative on Korean Peninsula Affairs said that this civilian airship was used purely for meteorological purposes and that it posed no threat to either the US population or other facilities on US soil. The balloon was brought into the US airspace by westerlies as it deviated from its designated course, Liu maintained. He insisted that the incident had been caused by "force majeure events".

"The incident with the Chinese balloon is, in fact a farce directed by the United States. The Chinese side took a very responsible approach, and it promptly passed the relevant information to the US side and the international community," he said.

Liu emphasized that Beijing had called on Washington "to be rational, cool-headed and professional" in order to jointly settle this situation, but that the US ignored the basic facts and fired a missile to down the balloon.

"The hysteria bewildered us completely. That was 100% an abuse of military power and a gross violation of relevant international conventions and international practice. This is no proof of US greatness, but quite the opposite. We have already expressed strong protest to the US side and urged them to show sincerity, change their mistaken policies, and squarely recognize and rectify the damage caused by that incident to bilateral relations," he maintained.

The senior Chinese diplomat warned that Beijing would not sit by and wait if the United States inflated the situation. "It is the United States who is to blame for all the consequences," he added.

Special envoy highlights China's determination to defend national dignity from US actions

According to Liu Xiaoming, China has always believed that "healthy, stable relations between China and the US benefit not only the people of the two countries but also world peace and prosperity".

Beijing is determined to vigorously defend its sovereignty and national dignity from the actions of the United States, Liu Xiaoming, Beijing's Special Representative for Korean Peninsula Affairs said in an interview with TASS.

"President Xi Jinping outlined the main principles for building relations with the US, which include mutual respect, peaceful co-existence and win-win cooperation. We are willing to build good relations with the US based on these principles," the Chinese special envoy noted. "However, should our sovereignty, national dignity and territorial integrity be violated, we will firmly defend our sovereignty, security and development interests," he added.

"Unfortunately, the US views China as its primary rival and the biggest geopolitical challenge," he went on to say, "Their perception and definition of China are seriously mistaken. They chose an erroneous strategy towards China, which is summed up in three words: invest, align and compete."

According to Liu, China has always believed that "healthy, stable relations between China and the US benefit not only the people of the two countries but also world peace and prosperity".

"President Xi Jinping pointed out that whether China and the US can manage their relations well bears on the future of the world. Getting the relationship right is not optional, but something we must do and must do well," the Chinese special envoy concluded.

有問必答

劉曉明

目錄

序言

我於二〇一〇年二月至二〇二一年一月擔任中國駐英國大使。這十一年，國際形勢和中英關係發生了許多變化。每逢大事，國際輿論都希望了解中國的立場和主張。我頻頻出現在英國各大電台和電視台，第一時間發出中國的聲音。英國是西方輿論高地，也是國際輿論中心之一。這裏雲集了眾多國際媒體，其中不乏西方大牌媒體。遇到突發事件，各國媒體都提出採訪中國大使。作為駐英大使，我總是首選英國媒體，但也不能忽視其他國家媒體。解決的辦法就是在使館舉行記者會，邀請中外記者參加。對於這樣的記者會，各國記者都踴躍參加，可謂「座無虛席」。他們不僅裝備精良，有「長槍短炮」，還準備各種刁鑽問題。英國廣播公司（BBC）多次對記者會進行現場直播，各大主流媒體也廣泛、充分報道。

使英十一年，我共舉行了十多場記者會，涉及中英關係、香港問題、南海問題、新冠肺炎疫情。二〇一九年六月，香港「修例風波」引發的暴亂愈演愈烈。激進暴力犯罪活動嚴重踐踏香港法治和社會秩序，嚴重挑戰「一國兩制」原則底線。香港反對派和暴力極端勢力，大肆鼓吹「港獨」，公然宣揚「光復香港」，企圖把香港從祖國分離出去。西方媒體，包括英國媒體，不僅沒有公正客觀報道，反而混淆是非、顛倒黑白、誤導公眾。針對這種情況，我多次發表演講，接受媒體採訪，並在各主流大報發表文章。後來，英國報紙拒絕刊登我的涉港文章，稱它們只能登支持所謂「民運分子」（即反中亂港分子）的文章。

我就把主要精力投向廣播電視媒體和記者會，僅二〇一九年六月至二〇二〇年七月一年多一點時間，我就香港問題七次接受英國各大電視台現場直播採訪，先後舉行四場中外記者會，BBC對記者會進行現場直播。我利用這些電視採訪和記者會，澄清事實，批駁謬論，揭穿謊言，為「一國兩制」正名，為香港國安法助陣，讓世界聽到中國聲音，看到香港真相。

我把上電視接受現場直播採訪，比作高難度、高強度、高烈度的「大考」，把記者會比作「中考」。因為記者會是我的主場，主題、時間、節奏比電視採訪易於掌控。但另一方面，它也有難度。一是問題多，涉及中國內政和外交方方面面；二是問題刁鑽、敏感，記者們放開問，無禁區、無限制；三是時間長，一般是一至兩個小時；四是現場直播，包括在社交媒體〔推特（現已更名為「X」）、臉書〕上直播記者會全程實況，這一點與上電視直播採訪大同小異。在外國記者看來，中國大使應當能回答任何關於中國的問題。這是他們的期待，也是我給自己提出的要求，即「有問必答」。對每一次記者會，我都進行認真的準備，與使館有關處室負責人，即我的「軍師」們集思廣益，設想各種刁鑽問題。上場後，我認真對待每一個記者的提問，從不用「無可奉告」搪塞。對挑釁者，據理批駁，不予糾纏；對誤解者，耐心傾聽，不扣帽子，認真詳細解答，重在用事實說話，努力消除誤解，增進了解。

本書收錄我使英期間八場記者會實錄和十場演講座談後回答聽眾提問。另外，還收錄了我作為中國政府朝鮮半島事務特別代表二〇二三年四月訪問歐洲期間接受俄羅斯塔斯社副總編的專訪和中央廣播電視總台《魯健訪談．對話劉曉明》訪談實錄，讀者朋友可以從中看到我退休不退崗，仍在為講好中國故事、傳播好中國聲音積極努力。

劉曉明

二〇二四年元旦

第一章

中英關係

本章收錄了我兩場記者會和兩次演講後回答聽眾提問。第一場記者會是二〇一五年一月十二日。在中國海軍第十八批護航編隊開始對英國進行友好訪問之際，我在編隊旗艦「長白山艦」上舉行中外記者會，二十多家中外媒體的三十多名記者參加。

第二場記者會是二〇二〇年七月三十日。由於英方一再違反國際法與國際關係的基本準則和中英關係的基本原則，中英關係遭遇一系列困難，面臨嚴峻形勢。我在記者會上闡述了中方對中英關係的原則立場，並回答記者提問。近三十家中外媒體的三十餘名記者參加。英國議會議員、工商界人士、專家學者出席。韓國、老撾駐英大使，歐盟、俄羅斯、吉爾吉斯斯坦、墨西哥、阿根廷、緬甸、巴西、沙特等國駐英外交官參加。駐英使館通過我的社交媒體賬號對記者會進行全程直播。中國國際電視台、路透社、美聯社等對記者會進行了直播報道。BBC、天空新聞台等媒體在各自電視台和網站進行了廣泛報道。

兩次演講答問，一次是二〇一五年十一月十三日，我在英國劍橋大學發表題為《為中英關係「黃金時代」增光添彩》的演講之後，回答師生們的提問。一次是二〇二〇年十一月十七日，我出席中國英國商會、四十八家集團俱樂部、英中貿協、英中協會聯合舉辦的中共十九屆五中全會精神宣介會，發表題為《把握新機遇，注入新信心，開啟新征程》的主旨演講並回答聽眾提問。四十八家集團俱樂部主席佩里、英中貿協主席古沛勤爵士、英中協會主任葛珍珠，以及英國滙豐銀行、桑坦德銀行、巴克萊銀行、德勤會計師事務所、普華永道會計師事務所、奧雅納、大成律師事務所、致同事務所、農業園藝發展協會、劍橋國際教育中心等英國公司、機構和部分中國在英企業代表二百三十多人出席。

和平之師，友誼之師

——關於中國海軍第十八批護航編隊訪英中外記者會

（二〇一五年一月十二日，中國海軍長白山艦）

中國中央電視台：我們了解到，中國護航編隊與英國皇家海軍在反海盜領域有著良好交流。此次中國艦艇編隊來到英國皇家海軍的母港樸次茅斯訪問，具有什麼重要意義？

劉曉明：中國護航編隊此次訪英將開展包括反海盜等在內的一系列交流與合作，內容豐富，目的多重，意義重大。

首先，訪問充分顯示了中英全面戰略夥伴關係的豐富內涵。中英全面戰略夥伴關係涵蓋政治、經濟、金融、文化、教育、科技等眾多領域，軍事交流也是其中重要組成部分。加強軍事交往有助於增進雙方戰略互信。這是中國艦艇編隊第三次訪英，正值二〇一五年伊始，是新一年中英兩國和兩軍關係的良好開端。

其次，此訪將為英國各界了解中國、了解中國軍隊和中國國防政策提供良機。英國公眾通過此訪可以看到，在中國經濟實力上升、經濟迅速發展的同時，中國軍隊也在國際舞台上發揮積極作用。中國已是世界第二大經濟體，每年對世界經濟增長貢獻率達三分之一左右。除經濟領域外，中國在政治和安全領域也為世界做出重要貢獻。在維護世界和平方面，中國軍隊是和平之師，積極參與亞丁灣和索馬里海域護航國際行動，在聯合國安理會五個常任理事國中是提供維

和人員最多的國家。我希望英國公眾在艦艇開放日登艦參觀，近距離地了解和認識中國軍隊。

BBC：中國艦隊到訪的樸次茅斯港是英國皇家海軍的象徵，在這裏停泊的納爾遜將軍的旗艦——「勝利號」曾為英國帶來一個多世紀的海上霸權。當前中國的一些鄰國對中國海軍力量增長及其對地區形勢的影響感到擔憂。中國海軍如何做到既作為一支和平力量增進各國間戰略互信，又作為一支具有國際水平的藍水海軍保護中國利益？兩者間如何實現平衡？

劉曉明：要認識這一問題，最重要的是要了解中國的國家戰略和國防政策。中國堅持走和平發展道路，是維護世界和平的重要力量。中國不僅為了自身發展爭取世界和平，也通過自身的和平發展為世界和平與繁榮做出貢獻。中國海軍的發展服務於這一宗旨。一些人擔心中國的軍力發展，是由於他們不了解中國的和平發展理念和防禦性國防政策。中國是一個愛好和平的國家，歷史上從未對外掠奪殖民地、對外侵略，反而是中國在近代遭到列強入侵和凌辱。現在，除參加聯合國維和行動外，中國未向國外派駐一兵一卒。中國是聯合國安理會五個常任理事國中提供維和人員最多的國家，截至二〇一四年九月已派出維和人員二點七萬人。隨著中國的發展強大，中國將會為世界的和平與穩定做出更大貢獻。中國海軍艦隊此次訪英也是加強中英戰略互信的重要舉措，揭開了新一年中英兩軍高層往來的序幕。英國第一海務大臣在此訪之後也將訪華，訪問期間雙方將就兩國軍事戰略、海軍發展等議題廣泛交換意見。對中國海軍走向深藍，沒什麼可擔心的。正是在藍水，中國海軍執行亞丁灣和索馬里海域護航任務。二〇〇八年以來，中國海軍圓滿完成近六千艘中外船舶護航任務，承擔了保護過往船舶及海上通道安全、維護海上航行自由和打擊海盜的國際責任。

BBC：當英國民眾看到在英國軍港停靠的這些中國軍艦時，你想向英國民眾傳遞什麼信息？目前，中國海軍已是世界第二，有些人擔心中國海軍力量的發展，

中方如何消除其疑慮？

劉曉明：我要告訴英國民眾，中國海軍是和平之師、友誼之師，他們訪問英國旨在促進中英友好關係，增進了解和友誼。

我不同意你對中國海軍的定位。中國經濟總量居世界第二，但中國海軍並非世界第二。中國海軍船隻數量可觀，但質量上與世界海軍強國還有距離。中國還是世界海軍大國中最晚擁有航母的，甚至晚於印度、泰國等國。

中國幅員遼闊，擁有十四個陸上鄰國、八個海上鄰國，擁有三點二萬多公里的大陸和島嶼海岸線，中國海軍承擔著保衛本國海疆的職責，同時也願與其他國家海軍共同維護世界和平與地區穩定，保障國際航行安全。外界大可不必對中國海軍的發展感到擔心。

《星島日報》：中國海軍除參加反海盜等國際行動外，如遇到中國與周邊鄰國發生爭執、摩擦等情況，將發揮什麼作用？如何平衡中國軍事實力發展與防止爭端糾紛？

劉曉明：剛才我在回答 BBC 記者提問時已就這一問題闡述了中方的立場。關於中國與部分鄰國的海洋爭端，我們一貫主張通過和平方式加以解決，但如果我們的利益受到侵犯，我們必須要做出反應。老祖宗留下的土地我們一寸不能丟，不是我們的，我們一寸也不要。中國軍隊的首要職責是捍衛國家主權和領土完整，維護國家安全和發展利益，包括海洋權益。同時，中國海軍與其他國家海軍積極開展合作，共同維護地區安全；參與護航國際合作，維護國際航運通道安全，為維護和促進世界和平貢獻自己的力量。

對中國海軍的發展和「走向藍海」，不能僅看中國有多少軍艦和多少飛機，而首先要看中國和平發展戰略和防禦性國防政策。中國堅持走和平發展道路已寫入憲法，中國不稱霸，不僅今天不稱霸，將來永遠也不稱霸。我們不會陷入西方大國歷史上的「修昔底德陷阱」，不會走其「國強必霸」的老路。我們要走出一條和平發展的道路，這條道路一定會取得成功。

在這方面，需要國際媒體的理解，希望貴報和其他媒體多做全面、客觀的報道，避免在一些西方媒體影響下跟風炒作「中國威脅論」。

中國國際廣播電台：二〇一四年是中英建立代辦級外交關係六十週年和建立全面戰略夥伴關係十週年，能否請您介紹一下近年中英兩軍關係發展情況？

劉曉明：近年來，中英兩軍關係保持良好發展勢頭，兩軍高層交往頻繁，兩軍關係更加深入。一是兩軍保持副防長級防務磋商機制，不斷增進互信，擴大共識。二是兩軍專業技術領域和人員培訓等方面的交流逐步深入，英方專家、學者赴華交流，中方每年向英軍院校派遣軍事留學生。三是兩軍在反恐、反海盜、救災等領域開展了良好交流與合作。四是艦艇互訪，今年中國艦艇來訪為中英軍事交往開了好頭，雙方還將有一系列高級別互訪。兩軍各層級、各領域的交流合作，將推動兩軍關係不斷深入發展。

《中國日報》：中國艦艇編隊在亞丁灣已成功完成護航任務。請問中國海軍今後是否會更多參與國際海上行動，承擔更多責任和義務？

劉曉明：近年來，中國海軍積極參與國際海上行動，派遣海軍護航編隊赴亞丁灣、索馬里海域執行護航任務是其中之一。中國海軍積極參與國際人道主義救援任務，如參與馬航 MH370 航班搜尋工作，赴菲律賓、印尼等國參加人道主義救援行動，等等。今後，中國海軍將繼續積極參加反恐、反海盜和國際人道主義救援等行動。

《樸次茅斯日報》：你剛才講到，這是中國海軍編隊第三次訪問英國，與前兩次相比，有何不同之處？

劉曉明：中國海軍艦隊此前曾分別於二〇〇一年和二〇〇七年兩度訪英。此訪離上一次訪問時隔七年多，國際形勢、中英關係、中國及中國海軍本身都發生了許多變化。二〇〇七年中國只有兩艘艦船來訪，而此

次來訪的三艘艦艇都是中國最新型艦艇，裝備精良，顯示了中國海軍的風采。在過去七年中，中英全面戰略夥伴關係深入發展，合作領域不斷拓寬，雙邊交往的「量」和「質」均大幅提升。相信這次中國海軍護航編隊來訪必將有力促進中英兩國和兩軍關係向前發展。

《英國僑報》：請介紹一下為迎接此次中國海軍艦隊訪英，中國駐英大使館和當地華人華僑做了哪些工作？

劉曉明：中國駐英使館將中國海軍護航編隊來訪列為中英兩國、兩軍間的一件大事，高度重視，全面動員，積極與英國海軍和英國政府有關部門協調，全力做好接待工作。比如，我們會同英國軍方，根據天氣變化，提前調整軍艦進港時間，保證了護航編隊順利開啟訪問。

在英華人華僑、中資企業和留學生接待海軍艦隊熱情高漲，十分踴躍。今天到場歡迎的只是全英六十多萬華人華僑和十三萬留學生的一小部分。對全英華人華僑、中資企業和留學生來講，祖國艦艇編隊的到訪是一件喜事、盛事。

《歐洲時報》：近來，法國發生恐怖襲擊事件，英國的恐怖威脅也在上升。請問中國海軍在反恐領域可發揮什麼作用？

劉曉明：中國政府強烈譴責在法國發生的恐怖事件，我們反對任何形式的恐怖主義。事件發生後，習近平主席即致電奧朗德總統，對襲擊行為予以強烈譴責，向不幸遇難者表示深切哀悼，向傷員和遇難者家屬表示誠摯慰問。在國際反恐問題上，我們的立場是明確的、一貫的，我們主張通過國際合作加強國際反恐。中國海軍在國際反恐方面發揮了自己應有的作用，他們與有關國家海軍舉行聯合反恐演習，開展人員培訓、情報等領域的交流與合作，都是發揮積極作用的具體體現。

感謝各位出席今天的記者會。

互相學習，取長補短，相得益彰

——回答英國劍橋大學師生提問

（二〇一五年十一月十三日，英國劍橋大學）

二〇一五年十一月十三日，我在英國劍橋大學發表題為《為中英關係「黃金時代」增光添彩》的主題演講後，回答了師生們的提問，實錄如下：

劍橋學生：雖然中英關係已進入「黃金時代」，但在英國仍然有不少關於中國的負面看法。有人認為中國崛起是威脅，有人覺得中國經濟增速放緩帶來嚴峻挑戰。作為中國大使，你會對這些人說些什麼？你怎樣把這些人對中國的疑慮減到最小？

劉曉明：作為中國大使，我盡可能多地接觸英國社會各界人士，向他們講中國故事，講中英關係的重要性，促進中英交流與合作。不知你是否關注了習近平主席對英國的國事訪問。訪問前，我分別接受了BBC、英國電視四台、天空新聞台、獨立電視台的採訪，實現了四大電視媒體全覆蓋。我努力回答他們的各種問題，比如中國為什麼要投資英國核電站，再比如中國的人權狀況、網絡安全，等等。人們對中國有誤解是可以理解的，因為英國媒體對中國的報道存在偏見，時常為追求轟動效應而炒作負面消息。如果你們比較英國媒體如何報道中國和中國媒體如何報道英國，就會發現強烈的對比。

此外，我還在《泰晤士報》《金融時報》《每日電訊報》上發表文章，多渠道傳遞中國的聲音。同時，我也主動上門與英國媒體座談，因為我知道，儘管我不停地接受電視採訪，但每期節目也就五至十分鐘，

英國公眾主要還是通過英國記者的大量涉華報道來了解中國。因此我在國事訪問之前主動登門走訪 BBC 總部，與 BBC 新聞總監和資深編輯以及負責王室活動、國際事務、外交事務報道的記者共三十餘人進行了兩小時的座談，可以說，把媒體工作「做到家」，受到編輯和記者們的普遍歡迎。我還邀請了《金融時報》《每日電訊報》的總編和記者到使館做客，向他們介紹國事訪問的意義並回答他們的問題。今天我來到劍橋演講並回答你們的問題也是我這方面工作的一部分。

劍橋學生：你演講中提到中英在反恐領域的合作，能否就此更詳細介紹一下？

劉曉明：恐怖主義是全人類的共同敵人，這是個全球性問題，需要國際合作應對解決。中英均為聯合國安理會常任理事國，承擔著維護世界和平與穩定的重任，兩國政府之間就安全和反恐問題保持著密切溝通，包括共享信息。中英均堅定支持聯合國有關反恐問題的重要決議。

劍橋學生：中國國家主席習近平和台灣「總統」馬英九不久前進行了歷史性會晤，這對不久將舉行的台灣選舉以及兩岸關係會帶來什麼影響？中國是否支持民族自決政策？

劉曉明：首先，我要糾正你關於馬英九頭銜的錯誤說法。我們從不承認台灣有什麼「總統」，因為台灣不是一個國家，而是中國的一部分。中國只有一個國家元首，那就是習近平主席。由於兩岸政治分歧尚未徹底解決，此次會面採取了務實的做法，以兩岸領導人的名義舉行，雙方彼此均稱「先生」。這是一次歷史性的會晤，其重大意義人們還需要時間去深刻理解領會。

我們當然關注台灣的選情，但我們更關注海峽兩岸的和平與穩定。要保持海峽兩岸的和平與穩定，必須堅持一個中國的原則，這就是我們所說的「九二共識」。「習馬會」中，雙方對「九二共識」進行了

再確認，其核心就是堅持一個中國原則，反對「台獨」。堅持「九二共識」是兩岸建立政治互信、實現良性互動的前提和基礎。放棄或背離「九二共識」，兩岸關係就會重新回到動盪不定的老路上去。雖然兩岸迄未統一，但中國的主權和領土完整從未分裂。台灣目前與祖國分離的狀態是暫時的，是有歷史原因的。一八九四年，日本通過甲午戰爭非法吞併了台灣。一九四三年的《開羅宣言》明確要求日本將所有非法竊取的中國島嶼，包括台灣和釣魚島都歸還給中國。我擔任中國駐埃及大使時，曾專門訪問過中、美、英三國首腦簽署《開羅宣言》的地點——米納豪斯飯店。雖然由於種種原因，台灣還沒有回到祖國的懷抱，但這不能改變一個基本事實：台灣過去、現在和將來都是中國的一部分。

我相信，海峽兩岸的中國人有足夠的智慧和耐心和平解決這一問題，實現祖國統一。我們已經等待了六十多年。「習馬會」表明，我們的耐心贏得了回報。我完全有信心，越來越多的人，特別是越來越多的台灣同胞認識到，堅持「九二共識」，推動兩岸關係和平發展，維護台海和平穩定，實現互利共贏，實現中華振興和民族復興，是符合海峽兩岸民眾的根本利益的，「台獨」是沒有出路的。

劍橋學生：你認為英國媒體對華報道失之偏頗，那麼英國可以向中國學習哪些東西？

劉曉明：中英兩國可以相互學習借鑒之處很多。中英均有悠久的歷史文化，兩國既有共同點也有區別。第一，中國是愛好和平的國家，沒有侵略其他國家的傳統。從唐朝到明朝長達數個世紀的鼎盛時期，中國的經濟總量曾佔世界的三分之二，比今天的美國還要強大，但從不侵略。明朝航海家鄭和率領兩百多艘船隻組成的龐大船隊遠航，到達印度洋甚至東非肯尼亞等國，只是為了開展貿易和友好交流，沒有佔領他國一寸領土。鄭和下西洋比哥倫布發現美洲還要早，這在西方發展史上是難以想像的。時至今日，對於國際衝突，我們首先想到的仍是通過政治、外交方式解決，而一些西方國家卻傾向於認為武力解決更有效。我們

對和平、非軍事方式的愛好深植於傳統哲學和歷史文化。

第二，我們堅持整體、全面的觀點看待問題。中國有句俗話說，「大河有水小河滿」。我們強調大局觀，更注重社會、國家的總體利益。西方包括英國更注重細節和個人，雙方在這方面可以互鑒。

第三，我們強調計劃性和前瞻性，也很有耐心。我剛才介紹了中國的五年規劃，它始於一九五三年，我們現在正在制訂的是「十三五」規劃，為未來五年中國的經濟社會發展規劃藍圖。而且，中國還有「兩個一百年」奮鬥目標，體現了我們長遠規劃的能力。美國前國務卿基辛格曾說，中國的一個朝代比美國的整個歷史還長。所以說，我們善於思考長遠的問題。

第四，中國人勤勞。英國衛生大臣亨特曾因誇獎中國人勤勞而受到輿論的非議，我在接受電視採訪時也被問及此事。我回答說，中國人的確勤勞，但英國人具有創造力。中英兩國應互相學習，取長補短，相得益彰。

劍橋學生：英國和阿根廷關於馬爾維納斯群島的爭端對中英關係有何影響？英國公投如果選擇脫離歐盟是否會對中英關係帶來不利影響？

劉曉明：馬爾維納斯群島是英國和阿根廷之間的問題，我們希望兩國能通過和平方式解決爭端。

關於英歐關係公投，這需由英國人自己來決定。我們希望同歐盟機構和每個成員國都發展良好關係。英國是歐盟的重要成員，英國領導人多次表示，願意做中國在西方和歐盟最好的夥伴，願意帶頭推動中歐盡快完成雙邊投資協定談判，盡早啟動自貿協定談判。如果英國離開了歐盟，將如何發揮帶頭作用？我們希望英國在歐盟中發揮重要作用，為促進中歐關係發展做出貢獻。

劍橋學生：西方常常批評中國特色的民主不是真正的民主，對此你如何回應？

劉曉明：首先，我們要多講中國民主的故事，我希

望你作為中國學生也多對你周圍的英國老師和同學解釋中國特色的民主是怎麼回事。每個國家的民主都各有特點。英美文化同宗同源，都講英語，但民主形式和法律體系也不盡相同。我們中國特色社會主義的民主制度，是以選舉民主為主要標誌的人民代表大會制度。公民通過廣泛選舉組成各級人民代表大會，人民代表大會通過廣泛的民主選舉組成國家權力機構、行政機構和司法機構。中國的縣、區、鄉、鎮實行直接選舉，縣以上是間接選舉，即縣級人大代表由本縣選民通過普選產生，市級人大代表由各縣人大代表選舉，省級人大代表由各市人大代表選舉，全國人大代表由各省人大代表選舉，國家領導人由全國人大代表選舉。全國人大代表近三千名，每年開會，五年換屆。

如我們所知，英國是實行間接選舉，首相不是由全國人民選舉產生，而是由選區選舉產生議員，最後由獲得多數席位的政黨領袖出任首相。美國則是全國範圍內選總統，與英國模式也不同。你不能根據自己的體制來評判其他國家的體制是否民主。世界上沒有完美的民主，也沒有完美的制度模式，國家之間應該相互學習，相互借鑒。我們與很多國家就治國理政、法治、人權等開展對話交流，就是希望以此增進了解，消除誤解，互學互鑒。

劍橋學生：英國是否充分了解亞投行和「一帶一路」的意義？在英國的中國年輕人在中英關係的「黃金時代」是否面臨更多機遇？

劉曉明：中英兩國領導人都很重視亞投行和「一帶一路」並進行充分溝通與交流，我作為大使也利用各種機會進行宣介，英國各界對亞投行和「一帶一路」的理解正不斷深化。

我們鼓勵中國年輕人回國發展，為祖國建設貢獻聰明才智。每年都有很多省市派團組前來英國招聘人才，大家可以充分利用這類機遇。當然如果你們選擇留在英國發展，也會有用武之地。越來越多的英國企業希望發展對華合作，需要聰明能幹的中國學子助其一臂之力。中英關係「黃金時代」一定會給你們帶來

更多機會，我也衷心希望你們成為中英交流合作的橋樑。

劍橋教授：目前歐盟和俄羅斯之間關係相當緊張。中國即將成為超級大國，如何平衡與歐盟和俄羅斯的關係？

劉曉明：中國和歐盟、中國和俄羅斯都是互利共贏的合作關係。俄羅斯是中國最大的鄰國和全面戰略協作夥伴，兩國政治和經貿合作密切。中歐關係也發展得很好。俄羅斯不構成中歐之間的障礙，我沒有感到這兩者之間存在什麼難以平衡的問題。我不認為中國即將成為超級大國，中國仍然是世界上最大的發展中國家。儘管中國經濟總量位居世界第二，但人均國內生產總值卻比羅馬尼亞、保加利亞還要低，排在世界第八十位之後。我們主要關心的是把自己的事情辦好，將發展作為第一要務。

劍橋教授：你剛才引用狄更斯的名言，說明我們正處在一個「最好的時代」，但他還說過我們處在「最壞的時代」。兩年前中國共產黨擁有的《環球時報》曾說英國是一個持續衰落的老牌歐洲國家，現在只適合旅遊和學習，你現在卻說中英關係進入「黃金時代」。這兩年到底發生了什麼？

劉曉明：《環球時報》是中國的一家媒體，它並不代表中國共產黨和中國政府，就像我們不能說英國媒體的言論代表英國政府一樣。而我作為中國大使，在這裏代表中國政府講話。我始終認為，英國是一個重要國家，是一個具有全球影響力的大國。作為中國大使，我不僅在英國宣講中國故事，也在中國介紹英國，講英國的重要性。《環球時報》作為一家獨立的媒體，會刊登各種不同觀點，下次我會給你找一篇《環球時報》對英國積極評價的文章。

劍橋教授：美國共和黨候選人特朗普對中國批評甚多，如果他當選美國總統，會對中美關係產生什麼影響？

劉曉明：我曾在美國工作多年，經歷過三次大選，比較了解美國的選舉文化。我們關注美國競選人的言論，更關注其當選美國總統之後的行動。這裏，我想借用英國的一句諺語：「在小雞沒有孵出之前，不要急著去數。」

劍橋學生：中英在高附加值製造業方面如何開展合作？

劉曉明：中英之間還有很多合作潛力和機遇，高附加值製造業也是其中之一，大型客機製造可以說是很有潛力的領域。英國羅爾斯·羅伊斯是世界上兩大大型發動機製造商之一，正在拓展與中國企業的合作。飛機製造十分複雜，涉及上千家企業，能大幅帶動就業和經濟發展。近年來英國意識到經濟過於依賴金融服務業的弊端，希望重振製造業，中英在這方面合作空間很大。英國汽車製造業位居世界前列，中國是後起之秀。中國上海汽車集團收購了英國 MG 公司，在長橋建立了研發中心，保留了英企業全部三百名科研人員。上汽負責人告訴我，他們從 MG 公司的設計和製造中獲益良多。中國吉利集團收購了倫敦出租車公司，和英國研發人員一起研製環保電動出租車，習主席夫婦在國事訪問期間還在劍橋公爵夫婦陪同下參觀了他們最新研製的樣車，相信不久倫敦街頭行駛的都將是環保節能的新型出租車。此外，中英在綠色能源、電信、機器人、航天、航空等領域也開展了卓有成效的合作。相信隨著「黃金時代」的到來，中英在高端製造業領域的合作將迎來更加廣闊的前景。

中英關係怎麼了？

——關於當前中英關係中外記者會

（二〇二〇年七月三十日，中國駐英國大使館）

劉曉明：大家上午好！歡迎大家出席今天的中外記者會。

今年是中英關係開啟「黃金時代」五週年。年初以來，習近平主席與約翰遜首相兩次通電話，就推進中英關係及兩國共同抗疫達成重要共識。兩國政府各部門認真落實這一重要共識，積極開展多領域合作。中英雙方本應珍惜這一良好勢頭，推動兩國關係向前發展，但令人遺憾和痛心的是，近來，中英關係遭遇一系列困難，面臨嚴峻形勢。

人們在問，中英關係怎麼了？英國媒體也在問，中英關係出現問題原因何在？是中國變了，還是英國變了？今天我就來回答這個問題：中國沒有變，變的是英國。中英關係遭遇困難，責任完全在英方。

第一，中方堅定奉行國際關係基本準則沒有變。互相尊重主權和領土完整、互不干涉內政和平等互利，是《聯合國憲章》確立的國家間關係的基本原則，是國際法與國際關係的基本準則，也是中英關係的基本原則，被寫入兩國建立大使級外交關係的聯合公報。中國從不干涉別國的內政，包括英國的內政，也決不允許別國干涉中國的內政。但是，近期英方卻一再違反這些重要原則：在涉港問題上無端指責香港國安法，改變英國國民（海外）（BNO）政策，暫停與香港的移交逃犯協定，粗暴干涉香港事務和中國內政，嚴重干擾香港穩定與繁榮；在涉疆問題上罔顧事

實、顛倒黑白，在雙邊和多邊渠道對中國治疆政策大肆抹黑攻擊，藉所謂新疆人權問題干涉中國內政，嚴重毒化中英關係氛圍。

第二，中方堅持走和平發展道路沒有變。走和平發展道路，是中國堅定不移的戰略選擇和鄭重承諾。中國沒有侵略擴張的基因，沒有也不會輸出自己的模式。中國發展是為了讓人民過上好日子，而不是要威脅誰、挑戰誰、取代誰。歷史已經並將繼續證明，中國始終是世界和平的建設者、全球發展的貢獻者、國際秩序的維護者，中國的發展壯大只能使世界更和平、更穩定、更繁榮。而英國一些政客，抱守「冷戰思維」，與英內外反華勢力遙相呼應，大肆渲染「中國威脅」，將中國視為「敵對國家」，揚言要與中國全面「脫鈎」，甚至叫囂要對中國發動「新冷戰」。

第三，中方認真履行自身國際義務沒有變。今年是聯合國成立七十五週年，中國是第一個簽署《聯合國憲章》的國家。中國參加了一百多個政府間國際組織，簽署了五百多個多邊條約。中國始終認真履行自身承擔的國際責任和義務，從未「退群」「毀約」，從不謀求本國利益優先。英方妄稱中方出台香港國安法違反《中英聯合聲明》、未履行國際義務，這完全是錯誤的。《聯合聲明》的核心要義是中國恢復對香港行使主權，而香港國安法正充分體現了中國中央政府對香港的全面管治權。中國政府在《聯合聲明》中闡述的對港方針政策是中方的政策宣示，既不是對英方的承諾，更不是所謂國際義務，「不履行國際義務」的帽子扣不到中國頭上。反倒是英方不履行國際義務，違背自身承諾，改變BNO政策，暫停與香港的移交逃犯協定，擾亂香港人心，干擾香港國安法實施，干涉中國內政。

第四，中方致力於發展對英夥伴關係的意願沒有變。二〇一五年習近平主席對英國國事訪問期間，中英發表聯合宣言，決定構建面向二十一世紀全球全面戰略夥伴關係。中國始終將英國看作夥伴，致力於發展健康穩定的中英關係。正如王毅國務委員兼外長前天與拉布外交大臣通話時指出的那樣：「對英國而言，中國始終是機遇而不是威脅，是增量而不是減量，是解決方案而不是挑戰。」然而，英方近來對華

認知和定位發生重大變化，出現嚴重偏差，「禁用華為」就是最突出例證。這不是英國如何對待一家中國企業的問題，而是關係到英國如何看待中國的問題。英國究竟是把中國看作機遇、夥伴，還是威脅、對手？是把中國看作友好國家，還是「敵對」或「潛在敵對國家」？英方領導人多次表示要發展平衡、積極、建設性的中英關係。我們聽其言，觀其行。

當前，世界百年未有之大變局正向縱深發展。新冠肺炎疫情仍在全球肆虐，經濟全球化遭遇嚴重衝擊，世界經濟陷入深度衰退。面對這樣的形勢，我們需要一個什麼樣的中英關係？中英都是聯合國安理會常任理事國和二十國集團等國際組織重要成員國，都是具有全球影響的大國，都肩負著維護世界和平、促進發展的重要使命。一個健康穩定發展的中英關係，不僅符合中英兩國人民的根本利益，也有利於世界的和平與繁榮。我們有一千條理由把中英關係搞好，沒有一條理由把中英關係搞壞。如何搞好中英關係？我認為，做到以下三點至關重要：

一是相互尊重。歷史告訴我們，只要國際法和國際關係基本準則得到遵守，中英關係就向前發展；反之則遭遇挫折，甚至倒退。中國尊重英國主權，從未做任何干涉英國內政的事。英方也應以同樣態度對待中方，尊重中國主權，停止干涉香港事務和中國內政，避免中英關係受到進一步損害。

二是互利共贏。中英經濟互補性強，利益深度融合，雙方從彼此合作中都獲得了巨大收益，不存在誰更依賴誰、誰多佔誰便宜的問題。希望英方不要受個別國家的壓力和脅迫，為中國企業提供開放、公平、非歧視的投資環境，重塑中國企業對英國的信心。在「後脫歐時代」和「後疫情時代」，中英在貿易、金融、科技、教育、醫療衛生領域有廣闊合作空間，在維護多邊主義、促進自由貿易、應對氣候變化等全球性挑戰等方面擁有廣泛共識。英國要打造「全球化英國」，繞不開、離不開中國。與中國「脫鈎」，就是與機遇脫鈎，就是與發展脫鈎，就是與未來脫鈎。

三是求同存異。中英歷史文化、社會制度、發展階段不同，難免存在分歧。七十年前，英國在西方大國中第一個承認新中國。七十年來，中英本著求同存

異的精神，超越意識形態差異，推動中英關係不斷向前發展。七十年後的今天，中英關係更加豐富、更加深入，不是你輸我贏的「對手關係」，更不是非此即彼的「敵對關係」，而是平等相待、互利共贏的夥伴關係。我們應當有足夠的智慧和能力管控和處理好雙方分歧，不讓反華勢力和「冷戰分子」「綁架」中英關係。

我常說，只有擁有獨立自主的外交政策，「不列顛」才是名副其實的「大不列顛」。無論是一九五〇年英國在西方大國中首個承認中華人民共和國，一九五四年與中國建立代辦級外交關係，還是英國選擇加入亞投行、與中國構建面向二十一世紀全球全面戰略夥伴關係，英國在關鍵歷史節點，都頂住外部壓力，做出了正確的戰略抉擇。現在，中英關係再次處於關鍵歷史節點。我希望，英國政治家和各界有識之士，認清國際大勢，排除各種干擾，把握時代潮流，做出符合中英兩國人民根本利益的戰略抉擇。

下面，我願回答大家的提問。

BBC：劉大使，如你所說，最近幾週，英中關係由於香港、華為、新疆問題明顯惡化。在這個過程中，上週我們看到，你以及好幾位中國政府代表均威脅稱，英方將承擔嚴重後果、中方將採取反制措施或反擊行動。但到目前為止，我們還不清楚到底是什麼樣的反制措施。你能否具體介紹一下？這些措施是秘而不宣的，還是雷聲大，雨點小？

劉曉明：首先我要澄清，我們從未威脅任何人。那些認為我的話是威脅的人是在斷章取義。正如我所說，中國希望成為英國的朋友和夥伴。但如果不想和中國做夥伴、做朋友，把中國視為「敵對國家」，就將付出代價。什麼代價？很簡單，你將失去把中國視為機遇和朋友所能得到的好處，這也是把中國當作「敵對國家」帶來的必然後果。

關於反制措施，我相信你已經看到，英方宣佈將改變英國國民（海外）護照（BNO）政策後，中方也做出回應，宣佈考慮不再承認 BNO 護照為合法旅行證件。這完全是因為英方行動違背了其在一九八四

年備忘錄中的承諾。當時英方明確承諾不給予 BNO 護照持有者在英居留權，在此基礎上中方承認 BNO 護照為合法旅行證件。現在英方違約在先，中方必須做出回應。

此外，英方還無限期暫停與香港的移交逃犯協定，損害了英國與香港司法合作的基礎。中方做出回應，宣佈香港暫停與英國的移交逃犯協定和刑事司法互助協定，這是因為雙方司法合作的基礎遭到破壞。

天空新聞台：關於香港，近幾天，根據新的國家安全法，一些人因為在網上發表評論被拘捕。今天，還有些「民主運動人士」被取消參加選舉資格。這些情況是否印證了英國關於國家安全法破壞香港自由的擔憂？關於新疆，你是否願意澄清幾週前接受 BBC 採訪時所看到的視頻？據歐洲安全部門消息稱，那些戴著手銬腳鐐、被剃光鬚髮、身著囚服的人是維吾爾族人。他們為什麼被押送？為什麼受到如此待遇？

劉曉明：香港國家安全法是為了堵住維護國家安全的法律漏洞。香港回歸二十三年來，一直沒有維護國家安全的法律。我們也看到去年香港遭遇的情況。一些人空談「一國兩制」，我們卻看到「一國」受到侵蝕，陷入危險之中。中國中央政府和全國人大及時通過並實施香港國安法，堵住漏洞，根本不存在所謂破壞言論自由的問題。

國家安全法明確規定，基本人權將得到充分尊重。該法只針對極少數妄圖破壞國家安全的罪犯，明確列出四類犯罪行為。如果你沒有這幾類犯罪行為，就不會有任何問題，依然享有言論自由、遊行自由、示威自由。香港的資本主義制度不會改變，獨立的司法體系包括終審權不會改變。國家安全法將確保「一國兩制」行穩致遠，也因此得到香港民眾的廣泛支持。有三百萬香港市民簽名支持國安法，因為他們都希望香港能有一個安寧、繁榮、穩定的環境。關於你提到的涉疆問題，我一會兒再回答。

中國國際電視台：劉大使早上好。你剛才提到中國將不承認 BNO 作為有效旅行證件。從實踐上看，這對

香港居民來英意味著什麼？現在中英兩國相互間的信任和善意已大幅減少，你認為應該如何重建？

劉曉明：中國沒有做任何損害中英互信的事。我說過，我們將英國視為夥伴和朋友，想要推進中英關係「黃金時代」。今年是中英關係「黃金時代」五週年，雙方本應進行慶祝。但遺憾的是，英方卻無端指責香港國家安全法，干擾該法實施，干涉香港事務，損害中英互信。

我在開場白中已經闡明，中英關係的出路在於堅持三個原則：相互尊重、互不干涉內政、平等相待。我們承認存在分歧，但雙方應在互相尊重的基礎上處理分歧。中國無意改變英國，英國也不應該試圖改變中國。我們的合作基礎和共同利益遠大於分歧。中英都是具有全球影響的大國，我們肩負著維護世界和平、促進全球發展的重要使命，我們之間有廣泛的共同議程。

關於你提到的具體問題，由於英方違背了其關於BNO的承諾，我們不得不採取措施，不承認此護照為有效旅行證件。

路透社：謝謝大使。我想問一個比較宏觀的問題。美國總統特朗普似乎已將中國作為二十一世紀最大的地緣政治敵人。你認為中國和西方是否已在進行「新冷戰」？有人說，中國近年來更加強硬，引起美國不安，你如何評價？謝謝。

劉曉明：我認為你已經回答了你自己的問題。中國並沒有變得更強硬，而是太平洋對面的國家想對中國挑起「新冷戰」，我們不得不做出反應。我們不希望打「冷戰」，我們不希望打任何戰爭。當美國對中國掀起「貿易戰」的時候，我們就說「貿易戰」沒有贏家。我們主張接觸，雙方達成了第一階段貿易協議。現在我們仍願與美方進行接觸。但是，美國國內情況大家都看到了，新冠肺炎疫情形勢不斷惡化，美國想把中國當作「替罪羊」，把自己的問題都歸咎於中國。

大家知道，今年是美國大選年。我在美國常駐兩次，五次近距離觀察美國大選。人們說，在大選年美

國政客為了贏得選票口不擇言。我覺得今年他們不僅口不擇言，而且不擇手段，包括將中國作為敵人。他們認為需要對中國發動「冷戰」，但中國對此不感興趣。我們一直向美方表示，中國不是美國的敵人，中國是美國的朋友和夥伴；美國的敵人是病毒。我希望美國政客能將精力放在抗疫和拯救生命上，而不是專注於指責中國。

中國中央電視台：大使上午好！我的問題是，英國工商業聯合會總幹事近日在《金融時報》撰文稱，中英合作使英方獲益巨大，英國無法承受單方面與中國減少往來的代價。但正如你剛才所說，一些英國政客對此持完全相反的看法。你對此怎麼看？如果允許，我還想再問一個問題。你近期接受英國媒體採訪時曾看過相關視頻和圖片，你也曾多次闡明中方在新疆問題上的政策立場。但西方媒體在這個問題上還是不斷指責中國。你對此有何評論？

劉曉明：我在開場白中講過，中英關係是互利共贏的夥伴關係。我非常贊同英國工商業聯合會總幹事的觀點。有人說中國從雙邊關係中獲益更多，我認為這有違事實。

我可以用一系列數字來說明：一九九九年至二〇二〇年，英國對華出口增長約二十倍；自我擔任中國駐英大使以來，中英雙邊貿易額翻了一番；在過去十年，中國對英投資增長約二十倍。這兩個「二十倍」很能說明問題。

中英經貿關係為英國創造了大量就業。此外，中國遊客每年赴英旅遊，也為英國帶來一點一萬個就業崗位。英國還是接收中國留學生最多的歐洲國家，這些學生在英求學獲益匪淺，同時他們也為英國發展做出了貢獻。劍橋大學研究表明，中國赴英留學人員在英各種開支，僅在二〇一八年就給英國創造一點七萬個就業崗位，更不要說華為公司為英國電信產業發展做出的巨大貢獻。中國企業還參與中、英、法三方共同建設的英國核電項目，我認為這一項目符合英國自身利益，能幫助英國實現二〇五〇年「零排放」的目標。但在那些「冷戰鬥士」眼中，這個項目卻是下一

個攻擊目標。我希望這些英國政客能客觀看待中英關係，認識到它是一個互利共贏的關係。

關於新疆問題，現在有太多的謬論和謊言，可謂「世紀謊言」。不僅如此，一些西方國家利用新疆問題大肆抹黑、攻擊中國，干涉中國內政。很遺憾，英國也難辭其咎。因此，我願藉今天的機會揭穿謊言、澄清事實，向大家介紹一個真實的新疆。

第一，所謂新疆問題根本不是什麼人權、民族、宗教問題，而是反暴恐、反分裂、去極端化問題。二十世紀九十年代以來，特別是「九一一」事件之後，「三股勢力」在中國新疆地區製造了數千起暴恐案件，造成大量無辜群眾生命和財產損失。其中，震驚世界的新疆「七五」事件（二〇〇九年）造成一百九十七人死亡，一千七百多人受傷。面對嚴峻形勢，新疆維吾爾自治區政府依法打擊暴恐活動，同時重視源頭治理，積極推進去極端化工作。這些措施十分有成效，確保新疆三年多未發生一起恐襲事件，最大限度保障了各族人民的生命權、健康權、發展權等基本權利，得到新疆各族人民廣泛支持和衷心擁護。

這些措施也為全球反恐事業做出積極貢獻，得到國際社會積極評價。二〇一八年底以來，聯合國官員、外國駐華使節、有關國家常駐日內瓦代表、媒體記者和宗教團體等七十多批團組、九十多個國家的一千多人赴疆參訪，他們紛紛稱讚新疆反恐、去極端化做法符合聯合國打擊恐怖主義、維護基本人權的宗旨和原則，值得充分肯定和學習借鑒。二〇一九年十月，六十多個國家代表在第七十四屆聯大三委會議期間發言稱讚新疆人權進步。今年七月，四十六個國家代表在人權理事會第四十四屆會議上做共同發言，支持中方在涉疆問題上的立場和舉措。

為幫助大家認清恐怖主義、分裂主義、極端主義在新疆造成的危害以及開展反恐、反分裂、去極端化活動的必要性和重要性，我們現在播放一段視頻。

（播放視頻）

第二，新疆「教培中心」根本不是什麼「集中營」或「再教育營」，而是預防性反恐和去極端化的有益嘗試和積極探索。這一舉措旨在根除極端主義、防止暴力恐怖活動升級，符合《聯合國全球反恐戰略》等

一系列反恐決議的原則和精神，本質上這與英國設立的轉化和脫離項目（DDP）、美國推行的「社區矯正」和法國成立的去極端化中心沒有什麼區別。受極端主義思想影響以及有輕微違法犯罪行為的人員參加教培中心培訓，通過學習國家通用語言文字、法律知識，進行職業技能教育培訓，去除極端化思想，掌握勞動技能，不僅使這些學員結業後重返社會，做守法公民，而且自食其力，有了穩定的工作和收入，生活水平明顯提高。

教培中心嚴格貫徹落實中國憲法和法律關於尊重和保障人權的基本原則，充分保障學員的人格尊嚴不受侵犯，嚴禁以任何方式對學員進行人格侮辱和虐待；充分保障學員人身自由，實行寄宿制管理，學員可以回家，有事可以請假；充分保障學員使用本民族語言文字的權利，各項規章制度、課程表、食譜等均同時使用國家通用語言文字和少數民族語言文字；充分尊重和保護不同民族學員的風俗習慣，為少數民族學員免費提供各種清真飲食；充分尊重和保護學員宗教信仰自由，信教學員回家時可自主決定是否參與合法宗教活動。

現在我們播放一段教培中心學員的視頻，聽聽他們講述教培中心的真實情況。（播放視頻）

第三，在新疆問題上，不能讓謊言與誣衊橫行，不能讓傲慢與偏見充斥頭腦，而要用事實與真相說話，用客觀與理性評判。下面，我願用事實揭穿西方媒體「廣為流傳」的四大謊言：

一是謊稱「新疆近百萬維吾爾族人被拘押」。事實上，這是兩個反華機構或人員炮製的謠言。幕後黑手之一是美國政府支持的「中國人權捍衛者網絡」（Chinese Human Rights Defenders，CHRD），它僅僅通過對八名維吾爾族人的採訪和粗略估算，就得出「新疆地區兩千多萬人口中，百分之十的人被拘押在『再教育營』的荒謬結論」。幕後黑手之二是受美國政府資助的極右翼原教旨主義基督徒鄭國恩，他在《中亞調查》雜誌上發文稱，「據估計，新疆在押人員總數超過一百萬」。據美國獨立新聞網站「灰色地帶」披露，鄭國恩得出這一數字，依據的是總部位於土耳其的一家維吾爾流亡媒體組織——Istiqlal

TV的一篇報道，而Istiqlal TV根本不是一家新聞組織，而是推進分裂主義、極端主義的組織。鄭國恩本人則自認「受上帝的引領」，肩負著反對中國的「使命」。

最近，我在接受BBC《安德魯·馬爾訪談》節目採訪時，馬爾先生播放了一段經所謂西方情報機關和澳大利亞專家確認的視頻，以此說明大批維吾爾族人被拘押。現在讓我們來看看這段視頻的真相到底是什麼。

事實上，這是新疆喀什看守所（Kashi Detention House）集中轉運服刑犯人的場景，根本不存在所謂大批拘押維吾爾族人的問題。中方打擊犯罪從不與任何民族、宗教掛鈎。司法機關押送服刑人員屬於正常司法活動，不容歪曲和抹黑。

二是謊稱「新疆強拆清真寺」。事實是，目前新疆共有清真寺二點四四萬座，平均每五百三十位穆斯林就擁有一座清真寺，比例高於一些伊斯蘭國家，也高於英格蘭地區人均擁有教堂數量。被誣稱「拆除」的葉城縣加米清真寺、和田艾提尕爾清真寺等根本未被拆除，而是被修繕後重新使用，編造謊言的人用清真寺危房的圖片來支撐其謊言，但不會展示清真寺修葺一新的照片。現在，讓我們用修葺一新的清真寺的照片來揭穿謊言。（展示照片）

三是謊稱「新疆強制絕育」。事實是，新疆維吾爾自治區是中國五個少數民族自治區之一，是一個多民族聚居區，擁有十三個世居民族，兩千五百萬各族人民和睦共處。中國政府始終一視同仁地保護包括少數民族在內的各族人民合法權益，人口政策長期以來對包括維吾爾族在內的少數民族更為優待。一九七八年至二〇一八年，新疆地區維吾爾族人口從五百五十五萬增長到一千一百六十八萬，整整翻了一番。

關於網上那些宣稱維吾爾族人「受迫害」的視頻，新疆方面已經多次揭穿了這些人的身份，他們有的是從事反華分裂活動的「東突」分子，有的是美西方反華勢力培植的「演員」。他們的說法根本站不住腳。他們中有些人在疆內的親友已經直接站出來闢謠，駁斥了他們的謊言。

我在接受BBC《安德魯．馬爾訪談》節目採訪時，馬爾先生播放了一段「訴苦者」的視頻，真實情況是：這個女性名叫早木熱．達吾提（Zumrat Dawut），謊稱「被強制絕育」。但她的姐姐和哥哥去年十一月公開揭穿其謊言，她從來沒有進過教培中心；她生第三個孩子時被查出患有子宮肌瘤，因此做了手術，根本沒有「被強制絕育」。讓我們看一下她姐姐和哥哥接受採訪的視頻。（播放視頻）

四是謊稱「新疆存在大規模強迫勞動」。事實上，這是另一黑手憑空捏造出來的。長期接受美國政府和軍火商資助的「澳大利亞戰略政策研究所」（ASPI）今年三月炮製所謂《出售維吾爾族人》報告，將南疆貧困民眾前往內地務工就業、脫貧增收的自發性行為，歪曲為「強迫勞動」。此後，「美國國會—行政部門中國委員會」將這一謬論作為「依據」，炮製《全球供應鏈，強迫勞動和新疆維吾爾自治區》報告，進行大肆誣衊和誹謗。現在讓我們放一段視頻揭穿他們的謊言。（播放視頻）

我們中國人常說，不到新疆，不知道中國之大；不到新疆，不知道中國之美。當前，新疆經濟持續發展，社會和諧穩定，民生不斷改善，文化空前繁榮。新疆各族人民安居樂業，和睦相處，享受著充分的生存權、發展權，宗教信仰自由依法得到保障，正常宗教活動受到法律保護，新疆處於歷史最好發展時期。任何謠言都不能抹殺新疆人權事業發展進步的事實，任何圖謀都不能干擾新疆發展繁榮的進程。希望大家不要聽信反華分子的謠言，不要受反華政客的蠱惑。我們敦促英國政府全面客觀看待新疆發展成就，停止在新疆問題上發表不負責任的言論，停止利用新疆問題干涉中國內政。我們也希望英國媒體摒棄傲慢與偏見，客觀、公正地報道新疆，讓英國民眾了解一個真實的新疆。

獨立電視台：請問劉大使，中國是否允許聯合國人權高專署派團，在不受中國共產黨干擾的情況下，獨立訪問新疆，到剛才視頻裏展示的那些地方，親眼看看發生了什麼？

劉曉明：自二〇一八年以來，已經有幾十個國家和國際組織的一千多名外交官、記者和代表訪問了新疆。我們歡迎人權高專署訪問新疆。

我們反對的是別有用心的所謂「獨立調查」，這實際是企圖藉新疆問題干涉中國內政。新疆的大門是敞開的，每年迎接成千上萬的遊客來新疆旅遊、參觀。我們歡迎所有善意、客觀、不持偏見的人士訪問新疆。

美聯社：劉大使，你曾經在美國長期工作過，請問從特朗普政府的一系列言論和威脅來看，你是否認為中美關係已經「沒有回頭路」可走？

劉曉明：我希望不是這樣。中國仍然相信不衝突、不對抗、互相尊重、合作共贏的中美關係符合兩國利益。中國無意破壞中美關係，中方將繼續努力與美方保持接觸。

但我也在很多場合說過，探戈需要兩個人跳，一個巴掌拍不響。我認為，支持中美關係的民意基礎仍然十分廣泛。一九七二年尼克松總統訪華以來，中美雙方始終致力於建立基於共同利益的中美關係。這種共同利益基礎仍在，中美關係在美國民眾中的民意基礎仍在。當美國國務卿發表反對中國共產黨的「新冷戰」宣言後，我們看到很多美國人站出來批評這種論調，他們對美國政府將中美關係引入歧途憂心忡忡。

所以，我不認為中美關係已經「沒有回頭路」，將中美兩國聯繫在一起的根本利益仍在，很多美國有識之士仍在努力維護中美關係的基本盤。我希望人們最終能回歸理性。

新華社：華為一直聲稱自己是一家獨立的私人控股公司，與中國政府沒有隸屬關係，那為什麼中國政府不遺餘力地維護華為？如果中英關係持續惡化，兩國會否像當年的中日關係一樣，陷入「政冷經熱」的局面？

劉曉明：關於華為，我剛剛在《南華早報》發表了一篇文章。我不是為自己的文章做廣告，而是希望

大家能花些時間讀一下。英國政府決定禁用華為後，我努力向英國主流媒體投書，因為這個問題對英國很重要。英國公眾需要了解問題的全貌。但不幸的是，英國主流報紙都表示不能刊登我的文章。我已在英國工作十多年，算是領教了什麼是英國標榜的「新聞自由」。他們非常直白地告訴我，只願刊登有利於報紙銷量的文章。因此他們不願刊登我關於香港的文章，不願刊登我關於華為的文章。我不得不讓我的文章「飛越」萬里到香港《南華早報》發表，當然《南華早報》在英國也有不少讀者。我的文章主要觀點是，拒絕華為就是拒絕機遇，就是拒絕增長，就是拒絕未來。

關於華為與中國政府的關係，首先，正如我在開場白中所說，華為問題不是一家中國公司的問題，而是關乎英國如何對待中國的問題：是將中國視為機遇，還是威脅？是把中國作為夥伴，還是競爭對手？這是一個必須做出選擇的根本問題。

其次，任何政府都應維護本國企業的合法權益。這一點不僅中國政府如此，英國政府也一樣。我在英工作十年間，清楚記得英國領導人和政要是如何為英國企業說項的。我記得英國首相在接待中國領導人訪問時，不忘推銷帝亞吉歐項目，堅持訪問期間能夠簽署有關項目。我記得英國財政大臣努力向中方推銷羅爾斯·羅伊斯公司的發動機，堅稱羅爾斯·羅伊斯公司生產的發動機比包括美國通用電氣在內的其他任何國家的產品都好。我還記得英國商業大臣為了推銷英國鋼鐵公司專程訪華，最終促成中國敬業集團收購英鋼，並同意在未來十年投資十二億英鎊實現英鋼轉型升級。

我認為，一國政府維護本國企業權益無可厚非。一些「冷戰鬥士」藉中國政府努力維護本國企業權益來證明華為與中國政府關係密切，並以此作為攻擊華為的理由，這是非常荒謬的。中國政府對每一家中國企業都一視同仁。我們希望華為在英國取得成功，實現雙贏。所以，在英方宣佈禁用華為那天，我說，這一天對華為是黑暗的一天，對中英關係也是黑暗的一天，對英國則更是黑暗的一天，因為英國將錯失成為5G領軍者的機會。

關於中英關係會否「政冷經熱」，我認為政治和經濟密切相關，很難完全分開。我們需要一個良好的氛圍和條件才能進行合作。我說英方關於華為的決定對中英關係是黑暗的一天，是因為這一決定破壞了中英互信，損害了英國信譽。在英國宣佈「禁用華為」後，我與在英中資企業舉行了座談，中資企業都表達了他們的擔憂和關切，因為這不僅涉及安全風險，也包括投資風險。我們無意將經貿問題政治化，但是信任和信譽在國與國關係中至關重要。

謝謝大家。

構建「雙循環」新發展格局

——回答中英工商界關於十九屆五中全會精神提問

二〇二〇年十一月十七日，我在中國英國商會、四十八家集團俱樂部、英中貿協、英中協會聯合舉辦的中共十九屆五中全會精神在線宣介會上發表題為《把握新機遇，注入新信心，開啟新征程》的主旨演講並回答提問。答問全文如下：

英國四十八家集團俱樂部主席斯蒂芬·佩里： 感謝劉大使的精彩演講，演講清晰而全面地闡述了十九屆五中全會的內容。我對中國區域發展規劃很感興趣。中國將建設四個主要城市群，每個區域的人口可能超過一億。請問英國如何與這些區域開展合作，向其提供英國的服務和商品？

劉曉明： 中國是一個幅員遼闊的國家，不同省、市和地區的發展情況不盡相同，發展不平衡不充分問題仍然突出。對此，中國政府因地制宜，積極促進區域協調發展。

第一，中國西部發展落後於東部，二十多年前中國政府開始實施西部大開發戰略。我擔任駐埃及大使後，曾到中國西部省份甘肅省掛職，擔任了兩年省長助理，對此有切身體會。二十多年來，西部大開發戰略取得顯著成績，西部地區發展面貌煥然一新。如果各位有機會到甘肅省省會蘭州看一看，一定會留下非常深刻的印象。第二，中國的中部地區相對發達，但仍落後於東部沿海地區。中部地區有很強的自身優勢，既不同於西部，也不同於東部。為此，我們實施了中部崛起戰略，旨在挖掘中部六省的發展潛力。第三，東部大部分地區位於沿海地帶，擁有上海、廣

州和深圳等許多發達城市，我們鼓勵東部地區率先發展、加快推進現代化。第四，我們實施東北振興戰略。東北地區過去和現在都是中國的重要工業基地。早在二十世紀五十年代，東北地區就匯聚了一大批工業項目，為中國現代化建設做出了巨大貢獻。除了工業外，這一地區在農業上也非常重要。東北土地肥沃，是中國最優質的大米和小麥等作物產地。我們通過統籌區域發展，更好促進發達地區和欠發達地區、東中西部和東北地區共同發展。

關於城市群建設，我們也制訂和實施了發展規劃。我們正深入推進京津冀協同發展、長三角一體化和粵港澳大灣區建設，這些地區都各有優勢。英國也制定了「英格蘭北方經濟中心」「中部引擎」等區域發展戰略。我認為，中英在區域發展合作方面潛力巨大。我們要挖掘雙方地區優勢和機遇，加強區域發展戰略對接，努力實現合作共贏、共同發展。

英中貿協主席古沛勤爵士：英中貿易協會見證了中國經濟的快速發展。很高興看到今年前八個月英國對中國出口額增長近百分之十，表現十分搶眼。中國在英留學生數量穩定，中國對英投資前景廣闊。根據英中貿協調查，英中貿易為英國本地貢獻了超過十萬個就業崗位。我們十分歡迎中國擴大對外開放。開放不僅對中國十分重要，也能為英國帶來繁榮。我們企業界對「雙循環」非常關注，希望劉大使再談談對「雙循環」的看法以及英國企業如何能從中獲益。

劉曉明：構建「雙循環」的新發展格局是中國積極應對國際國內形勢變化做出的戰略抉擇，不是權宜之計，而是長期戰略。第一，當前經濟全球化遭遇逆流，單邊主義、保護主義上升，新冠肺炎疫情帶來廣泛而深遠的影響，傳統國際經濟循環明顯弱化。在這種情況下，中國強化國內經濟大循環，有利於增強經濟發展的韌性，也有利於帶動國際經濟循環。第二，中國國內大循環的動能明顯增強。中國作為世界第二大經濟體，和其他大國經濟一樣，國內供給和國內需求對於中國經濟循環日益起到主要支撐作用。第三，新發展格局強調的絕不是封閉的國內循環，而是開放

的國際國內「雙循環」。中國將在充分發揮超大規模市場優勢的同時，深入參與國際循環，擴大外資企業的市場准入，打造市場化、法治化、國際化營商環境，依託國內強大市場，成為吸引全球優質要素資源的強大引力場，成為外商投資興業的沃土。

在「雙循環」格局下，中國將在更高水平上擴大對外開放，努力使國際國內市場相互促進，充分利用兩個市場優勢實現共贏。這對英國企業而言意味著更大機遇。我衷心希望英國工商界能夠充分抓住「雙循環」機遇，增強信心，進一步擴大中英經貿等領域合作。

英中協會主任葛珍珠：感謝劉大使介紹「十四五」規劃和二〇三五年遠景目標。我來自英中協會，與中國很多機構都有密切合作。請問劉大使如何看待未來中國的法治建設？中國將如何推進相關領域改革？

劉曉明：「十四五」規劃和二〇三五年遠景目標不局限於經濟領域，而是中國的全面發展戰略。「十四五」規劃明確了未來五年中國經濟社會發展的主要目標，可以概括為「六個新」：一是經濟發展取得新成效；二是改革開放邁出新步伐；三是社會文明程度得到新提高；四是生態文明建設實現新進步；五是民生福祉達到新水平；六是國家治理效能得到新提升。其中提高社會文明程度和提升國家治理效能，都與社會主義法治建設密切相關。十九屆五中全會通過的這些建議明確了指導原則和方向。明年「兩會」期間，中國政府將進一步制定和通過具體的政策、框架和舉措。建議你密切關注明年「兩會」。總之，中國將加快建設社會主義法治國家，全面推進依法治國，不斷完善中國特色社會主義法律體系。

英國中國商會會長方文建：中國和有關國家剛剛簽署了《區域全面經濟夥伴關係協定》（RCEP）。該協議獲批生效後，中國會否更重視與該協議簽署國的合作？這是否會影響未來中英經貿投資合作？你如何看待中英商談自貿協定前景？這與RCEP有何關係？

劉曉明：RCEP是中國與有關國家共同努力達成的重大成就，是自由貿易和多邊主義的勝利，不僅將有力推動亞太地區發展，也為促進世界經濟增長提供新動力。這並不意味著未來中國只關注亞太地區。正如我在演講中所說，中國積極發展全球夥伴關係，英國和歐洲都是中國的重要合作夥伴。習近平主席在第三屆中國國際進口博覽會開幕式上指出，中國願同更多國家商簽高標準自由貿易協定。我們對與英國達成高標準自貿協定持積極開放態度。英國工商界對此完全不必擔心。我擔任駐英大使十多年來，中國對英直接投資增長約二十倍，這在中英關係史上從未有過。英國對包括中國企業在內的外資企業仍具有吸引力。

當然，毋庸諱言，中國企業對英國也有關切。首先，是脫歐帶來的不確定性。目前仍不清楚英國最終會「有協議脫歐」還是「無協議脫歐」，我們密切關注英歐談判進展。其次，英國有些勢力企圖推翻英國主流社會形成的共識，即中國是英國的合作夥伴，中國的發展是英國的機遇。他們把中國視作威脅，甚至是「敵對國家」。現在英國議會正在審議《國家安全和外國投資法案》。英政府高官告訴我有關法案並不針對具體國家。我們希望英國能繼續為中國企業提供公平、公正、透明和非歧視的營商環境。如能做到這一點，我相信未來仍會有更多的中資企業來英投資興業。

英國中國商會會長方文建（代表與會人員提問）：近日，（針對中國全國人大常委會關於香港特區立法會議員資格決定）英國外交發展部多次「指責」中國違反國際義務和《中英聯合聲明》。有報道稱英方可能因此「制裁」中國官員。針對英國政府和議會的有關言行，中方將做何反應？

劉曉明：近日有媒體炒作，我因涉港問題被英國外交發展部常務次官「召見」。實際上，我在會見中向他清楚闡明中方嚴正立場，即中方堅決反對英方干涉香港事務和中國內政。英方總是藉口《中英聯合聲明》指責中國「沒有履行國際義務」。今年是聯合國成立七十五週年，可能有些人不知道，中國是七十五年

前第一個簽署《聯合國憲章》的國家。中國一直遵守《聯合國憲章》，始終履行應盡的國際義務；中國加入了幾乎所有政府間國際組織，簽署了五百多項國際公約。沒有任何證據證明中國違反了國際義務。恰恰相反，是英方違反了國際義務。《聯合國憲章》確立的基本原則，首先就是國家主權平等、互相尊重、互不干涉內政。英國干涉香港事務和中國內政，就是違反國際義務的行為。中國全國人大常委會關於香港特區立法會議員資格的決定合理、合法、合憲，符合中國憲法和香港基本法。

我在許多場合談到過，中英關係面臨的一大問題是，互相尊重主權和領土完整、互不干涉內政的國際關係基本準則遭到破壞。這就是當前中英關係遭遇困難的根本原因。今年是英國承認新中國七十週年。七十年前，英國成為第一個承認中華人民共和國的西方大國。七十年來，中英關係取得巨大發展，但也經歷起伏。事實證明，只要恪守國際法和國際關係基本準則，中英關係就能向前發展；反之則遭遇挫折，甚至倒退。中方仍然重視中英關係，一個良好的中英關係不僅有利於兩國人民，也有利於世界和平與穩定。中英都是具有全球影響力的國家，都是聯合國安理會常任理事國和二十國集團重要成員。在雙邊領域和全球事務上，我們有很多共同議程。因此，我們有一千條理由發展好中英關係，而沒有一條理由把中英關係搞壞。但是，「探戈需要兩個人跳」，希望英方珍惜來之不易的中英關係，與中方相向而行，共同推動兩國關係早日重歸正軌。

我常說，經貿合作是中英關係的基石。我常鼓勵在英中資企業在雙邊關係中發揮「穩定劑」和「推進器」作用。但是，政治互信與經濟合作密不可分，如果政治互信受損，整體雙邊關係就會受到影響。有互信才能做好生意。希望中英兩國企業共同努力，克服當前困難，為兩國關係發展貢獻正能量。

英國議會跨黨派「一帶一路」與中巴經濟走廊小組顧問阿夫塔布：「一帶一路」已經將中國和外國市場聯繫在一起，現在中國提出了國內國際「雙循環」，請問「一帶一路」與「雙循環」是什麼關係？

劉曉明：「雙循環」是在新形勢下中國推動構建的新發展格局。「一帶一路」已成為規模最大的國際合作平台。「雙循環」與共建「一帶一路」之間有著密切的關係。「一帶一路」是構建「雙循環」的重要渠道。「絲綢之路經濟帶」聯通了中國與中亞、歐洲等地區國家，「二十一世紀海上絲綢之路」將中國與東南亞等地區國家聯繫起來，「雙循環」也為共建「一帶一路」提供了更大動力。我認為，未來「雙循環」與「一帶一路」將相互促進、相得益彰，會讓「一帶一路」更加高效、更富有成果。

第二章

香港問題

本章收錄了我就香港問題舉行的四場中外記者會。第一場是二〇一九年七月三日，我就香港發生暴力衝擊立法會事件舉行中外記者會。我指出，極端激進分子以極為暴力的方式衝擊香港立法會大樓，踐踏了香港法治，破壞了香港社會秩序，損害了香港的根本利益，是對「一國兩制」底線的公然挑戰。在這樣一個大是大非的問題上，英國政府選擇站在錯誤一邊。英方不僅發表不當言論，干預香港事務，而且為暴力違法分子撐腰打氣。更有甚者，英方試圖干擾香港法治，阻撓特區政府將肇事者繩之以法。我強調，香港是中國的特別行政區，不是英國殖民統治下的香港。香港事務純屬中國內政，任何國家、組織和個人都無權干預。我們對英方粗暴干涉香港事務和中國內政表示強烈不滿和堅決反對。

第二場記者會是二〇一九年八月十五日。自前次記者會後，香港暴力事件不斷升級，社會波及面越來越廣，嚴重挑戰香港法治和社會秩序，嚴重威脅香港市民生命財產安全，嚴重破壞香港繁榮穩定，嚴重觸碰「一國兩制」原則底線，致使香港面臨回歸以來最嚴峻的局面。我在記者會上指出，中國中央政府絕不會放任少數人以暴力行徑把香港拖向危險的深淵，絕不允許任何人破壞香港的法治與良好發展局面，絕不允許任何人以任何藉口破壞「一國兩制」。如果香港局勢進一步惡化，出現香港特區政府不能控制的動亂，中國中央政府絕不會坐視不管。按照《基本法》規定，中國中央政府有足夠多的辦法、足夠強大的力量迅速平息可能出現的各種動亂。

我在準備第三場記者會的時候，外交部宣佈習近平主席將於二〇一九年十一月十四日赴巴西出席金磚國家領導人第十一次會晤。我預感到習主席將在出訪期間就香港問題發表重要講話，便把記者會的時間安排在習主席出席金磚會晤之後。果不出我所料，習主席在出席會議期間就香港局勢表明中國政府嚴正立場。習主席用「三個嚴重」給香港局勢定性，指出香港持續發生的激進暴力犯罪行為，嚴重踐踏法治和社會秩序，嚴重破壞香港繁榮穩定，嚴重挑戰「一國兩制」原則底線。用「三個堅定支持」表明中央人民政府對特區政府的支持，強調中央人民政府將繼續堅定支持行政長官帶領香港特別行政區政府依法施政，堅定支持香港警方嚴正執法，堅

定支持香港司法機構依法懲治暴力犯罪分子。用「三個堅定不移」表明中國政府的決心，強調中國政府維護國家主權、安全、發展利益的決心堅定不移，貫徹「一國兩制」方針的決心堅定不移，反對任何外部勢力干涉香港事務的決心堅定不移。

四天後，我在倫敦舉行第三次涉港中外記者會，在第一時間通過西方主流媒體平台向世界解讀習主席的重要講話，指出習主席的講話字字鏗鏘，句句千鈞，是中國中央政府對香港當前局勢和未來出路發出的最權威的聲音。

英國各大電視台和主流報刊對這次記者會進行廣泛、滾動報道，大幅引用我轉述的習主席的重要講話，突出報道「中國要求西方停止干涉香港事務」，「中國有決心有能力平息香港動亂」，對西方反華勢力和反中亂港分子產生有效震懾。

第四場記者會是二〇二〇年七月六日，我就《中華人民共和國香港特別行政區維護國家安全法》舉行中外記者會。我有針對性地批駁了英國媒體對香港國安法的誤讀、誤解甚至歪曲，指出香港國安法的實施，為「一國兩制」行穩致遠提供了強大支撐，為香港居民的權利和自由提供了堅實保障，堪稱「一國兩制」實踐進程中的重要里程碑，具有重大現實意義和深遠歷史意義。

四場記者會，中外主流媒體悉數出席、踴躍提問，包括英國廣播公司（BBC）、BBC廣播四台、天空新聞台、英國電視四台、獨立電視台、《金融時報》、《每日電訊報》、《泰晤士報》、《衛報》、《經濟學家》、路透社，新華社、《人民日報》、中國中央電視台、中國國際電視台等中國媒體，以及美聯社、彭博社、美國全國廣播公司、美國哥倫比亞廣播公司、法新社、今日俄羅斯電視台、加拿大廣播公司、鳳凰衛視資訊台、《南華早報》、《歐洲時報》、《英中時報》、《僑報》等三十三家媒體近五十名記者出席。BBC、天空新聞台、中國國際電視台對記者會進行了現場直播。

「一國兩制」底線不容挑戰

——關於香港發生暴力衝擊立法會事件中外記者會

（二〇一九年七月三日，中國駐英國大使館）

劉曉明：七月一日，是香港各界人士紀念香港回歸祖國和香港特別行政區成立的喜慶日子。但在這一天，卻發生了一些極端激進分子以極為暴力的方式衝擊香港立法會大樓、肆意損壞立法會設施的事件。他們的行為早已突破了言論自由和和平示威的界限，踐踏了香港法治，破壞了香港社會秩序，損害了香港的根本利益，是對「一國兩制」底線的公然挑戰，我們對此予以強烈譴責。特區政府將依法追究暴力犯罪者的刑事責任，中央政府堅決支持香港特區政府對這起嚴重違法事件追究到底，依法處置；支持特區政府盡快恢復社會正常秩序，保障市民人身和財產安全，維護香港的繁榮穩定。

在這樣一個大是大非的問題上，英國政府選擇站在錯誤一邊。英方不僅發表不當言論，干預香港事務，而且為暴力違法分子撐腰打氣。更有甚者，英方試圖干擾香港法治，阻撓特區政府將肇事者繩之以法。中方已就此向英方多次提出嚴正交涉。在此我想再次強調，香港是中國的特別行政區，不是英國殖民統治下的香港。香港事務純屬中國內政，任何國家、組織和個人都無權干預。我們對英方粗暴干涉香港事務和中國內政表示強烈不滿和堅決反對。

中方維護國家主權、安全和發展利益的決心堅定不移，維護香港繁榮穩定的決心堅定不移，堅決反對外部勢力干預的態度堅定不移。我們要求英方深刻反

省錯誤言行的後果，立即停止以任何方式干預香港事務和中國內政。

多國媒體，特別是英國媒體對此次事件作了大量報道，但坦率地講，一些報道存在嚴重偏見，有些甚至是惡意中傷。我接到了不少媒體的採訪要求，今天舉行這場中外記者會，就是為了使更多媒體聽到中方的聲音，了解中方的立場，以正視聽。現在我願回答各位記者提問。

BBC：第一個問題，此時此刻此地你能否保證，中國將遵守其簽署的、直到二〇四七年都有效的國際條約《中英聯合聲明》的承諾？第二個問題，中國中央政府接下來會怎麼做？會不會以七月一日事件為藉口對未來和平示威進行鎮壓？

劉曉明：你認為中國會「鎮壓和平示威」的想法依據是什麼？首先，你對中方立場的理解完全是錯誤的。中國政府奉行「一國兩制」的決心堅定不移。我要指出的是，「一國兩制」是中國政府向全世界做出的莊嚴承諾，並不是對英國政府的承諾。根據《基本法》，香港一九九七年回歸，其基本制度保持五十年不變。《中英聯合聲明》已經完成了其歷史使命，成為歷史文件。根據這個文件，英國政府向中國交還香港，中國恢復對香港行使主權，自一九八四年至一九九七年的過渡期內，英國政府負責香港的行政管理。隨著香港回歸祖國的懷抱，《中英聯合聲明》中沒有任何條款允許英國對香港行使任何權利。我建議你仔細閱讀一下《中英聯合聲明》。

BBC：《中英聯合聲明》第十二條寫明，中華人民共和國對香港的方針政策五十年不變。這不僅指《基本法》，還應包括《中英聯合聲明》。

劉曉明：我們說的五十年不變，指的就是「一國兩制」，不是《中英聯合聲明》，希望你注意文字的嚴謹性。《中英聯合聲明》沒有任何條款給予英方插手香港事務的權利，也沒有賦予英國所謂「監督」「一國兩制」實施情況的權利。

中央政府堅決支持香港特區有關機構依法將暴力犯罪者繩之以法，根本不是你所說的對香港遊行示威進行所謂「鎮壓」。衝擊立法會是一起嚴重的暴力事件，我們對香港特區政府依法妥善處置事件有信心。

獨立電視台：中方稱英國政府干涉香港事務，是否要求英國政府就有關言論道歉？

劉曉明：中方已多次向英方提出嚴正交涉，要求英方停止干涉香港事務，避免進一步損害中英關係。

路透社：今天，英國保守黨領袖候選人約翰遜對路透社記者表示，香港目前的局勢令人擔憂，懷疑「一國兩制」是否仍在發揮作用。你對他的表態有何評論？鑒於約翰遜和亨特均有可能當選下任首相，你是否認為英中關係的未來將走下坡路？

劉曉明：無論誰當選英國首相，我們都希望他能遵守中英兩國政府達成的共識，即相互尊重主權和領土完整，互不干涉內政，這是中英關係的基石。如新任首相違背了上述原則，中英關係肯定將出現問題。

英國電視四台：你認為逃犯引渡條例什麼時候能通過？

劉曉明：香港特區政府已宣佈暫停修例，林鄭月娥行政長官已明確表示，本屆立法會對修例不設時間表。修例需要大量工作和時間，本屆立法會明年七月任期屆滿，已無時間處理修例問題。我們對香港特區政府的決定表示理解和尊重，並且完全支持。

英國電視四台：你認為修例是就此終止還是會重新啟動？

劉曉明：這應由香港特區政府決定。我相信香港特區政府將同民眾進行充分溝通，讓民眾理解修例符合港人的利益，香港應該堵塞法律漏洞，不應繼續成為「避罪天堂」，而應成為「正義天堂」。我希望特區政

府能夠成功地同民眾溝通並達成共識。

天空新聞台：你將衝擊立法會的人稱為極端激進分子，你認為他們的行為是恐怖主義嗎？你希望英國政府不再干涉香港事務，以免給英中關係帶來進一步損害。英國政府的舉動是不是已經損害了英中關係？關於衝擊立法會大樓事件有一種「陰謀論」，對此你怎麼看？

劉曉明：首先，衝擊立法會的是什麼人，不歸我來定義，最終將由香港法庭來確定他們是不是違法犯罪分子。他們公然破壞立法會設施，這是一種公然違法行為，應該為他們的行為負責。我認為中英關係在某種程度上已經因英方干涉香港事務受到損害。如我所言，中英關係的基石是相互尊重、互不干涉內政。如果英方繼續干涉，無疑會繼續損害兩國關係。我希望英國政府反思其在香港問題上的言行，認識到干涉中國內部事務的嚴重後果，避免給兩國關係造成進一步損害。

天空新聞台：有傳言說衝擊立法會大樓的行動是一些混在示威人群中的親中分子挑唆的，你對此怎麼看？

劉曉明：首先，謠言不值一評。其次，根據香港警察部門負責人的介紹，衝擊立法會大樓的人目的在於擾亂香港社會秩序，他們是極端分子，違反了香港的法律。

中國國際電視台：外交大臣亨特表示英國支持香港人民爭取自由，我們都知道，香港在英國統治時期，沒有任何形式的民主，包括選舉權，你認為英國為什麼現在如此關注香港的民主？

劉曉明：我認為亨特外交大臣談自由是大錯特錯了，這不是所謂自由問題，而是違反了香港的法律問題。這樣一個高級別官員對違法者表示支持，我感到非常失望。我們都記得二十二年前在英國殖民統治下的香港是什麼樣子，當時沒有任何形式的自由和民主，歷屆港督均由英國政府指派，老百姓沒有選舉權，司法

不獨立，沒有終審權，終審權屬於英國樞密院司法委員會。我們都應該看到，與英國殖民統治下的香港相比，現在港人擁有更多民主和自由權利，他們通過選舉委員會選舉自己的行政長官，參政熱情高漲。二〇一五年，中國全國人大同意香港實行普選，一人一票選舉他們的行政長官，但遺憾的是該提案沒有在香港立法會通過。香港人民還享有高度自治權，自己決定自己的事務，除了立法權、獨立司法權外，還擁有終審權，香港真的是今非昔比。一些英國政客對香港的自由和法治說三道四，但當香港法治被破壞時，他們不僅不譴責違法者，卻反過來支持和同情他們，這樣的表現令人難以置信。

鳳凰衛視資訊台：你對英國未來的首相在香港問題上的立場怎麼看？約翰遜今天就香港問題發表了一些評論，會不會影響未來中英合作？

劉曉明：如我之前所說，中國希望英國政府履行承諾，恪守兩國建交時達成的基本原則，即互不干涉內政。中英之間在攜手努力、共同維護香港繁榮穩定方面有共同利益。一九八四年之前，香港是中英關係發展的障礙，自從我們達成《中英聯合聲明》，尤其是香港回歸以後，香港不僅不再是中英關係發展的障礙，而且成為中英關係的橋樑和積極因素。香港應在中英之間繼續發揮積極作用，而不是重新變成障礙。

《中國日報》：有人認為西方媒體在報道香港事件時充滿偏見，請問你如何看待西方媒體在此次事件中扮演的角色？

劉曉明：我們都看了英國媒體近期的相關報道，很不平衡。這些報道只關注遊行示威，甚至對暴力極端分子表示同情。我前段時間接受BBC和天空新聞台採訪時，給他們講述了事件的另一面，我稱之為「沉默的大多數」的群體被英國媒體完全忽視了。八十萬香港人聯署支持香港特區政府修例；特區政府發出四千五百份民意調查問卷，廣泛徵求意見，收到的回覆中有三千份支持修例，只有一千五百份反對。這些

信息在英國媒體上沒有任何報道。因此，英國媒體的報道嚴重失衡。我希望英國媒體能本著對大眾負責的態度，平衡客觀報道事實真相。七月一日後，英國媒體不間斷採訪支持抗議的人，而忽視了強烈反對暴力的意見。香港立法會不少議員對暴力抗議表示堅決反對，並對上述損害香港利益的行徑表示強烈不滿，但是在英國，我們看不到任何這方面的報道。

英國電視四台：在《中英聯合聲明》這份國際條約中，包括保護香港居民的人身、言論、新聞、集會、結社、旅遊、通信、罷工、宗教信仰自由等規定，你能否肯定地說這些權利和自由得到了充分的保障？

劉曉明：我可以向你保證，這些權利得到了百分之百的保障，如果對比香港今昔，就可以看到這些權利得到很好保障。

英國電視四台：那麼黃之鋒被捕和香港民族黨被取締事如何解釋？

劉曉明：在一個法治社會，違反法律者理應依法受到懲罰。言論自由並不代表想做什麼就做什麼，違法者必將付出代價。香港是法治社會，你提到這些個案時，應該仔細研究一下他們違反了哪些法律。

路透社：目前英國兩位競選首相的候選人均表示可能對華為5G設備實施更嚴格的審查，你如何看待未來英國首相對華為的政策？

劉曉明：我認為現在談未來英國首相對華為政策還為時過早，你的說法只是一種猜測。當然，我們需要為應對各種可能的情況做好準備。我必須告訴大家，華為在英國投資不僅是出於企業自身利益，更是為了實現雙贏，華為為英國電信產業發展做出了巨大貢獻。英國如果禁止華為，將失去很多機遇。同時，華為很好地履行了企業的社會責任，他們在英國當地雇用了一萬多名員工，在英投資超過二十億英鎊，建立了聯合研究中心，華為相信與英國同行合作有利於促進企業自身發展，有利於促進英國經濟和科技發展。更重

要的是，華為是開放透明的，他們斥資建立監督自己的網絡安全分析監測中心，聘請清一色英國團隊，檢查自己的產品。華為沒有所謂「後門」。在發展 5G 網絡方面沒有比華為更好的合作夥伴。我經常提醒英國的朋友們，要珍惜華為帶來的機遇，失去華為就意味著失去許多良機，將對外界，不僅對華為，而且對中國企業，甚至對全世界，發出非常負面和消極的信號。

新華社：關於中美經貿磋商，一些人認為，二十國集團（G20）大阪峰會期間中美元首會晤的成果有限，達成共識也只是暫時的，今後中美貿易爭端將難免再次升級。你怎麼看待中美經貿磋商前景？

劉曉明：習近平主席與特朗普總統在 G20 大阪峰會期間的會晤非常重要，人們會因為這次重要會晤而記住大阪峰會。首先，習主席為中美兩國關係發展指明了方向。習主席總結了中美建交四十年來的經驗啟示，指出中美合則兩利、鬥則俱傷，合作比摩擦好，對話比對抗好。特朗普總統對此表示贊同。習主席為中美兩國關係指明了根本發展方向，將對中美關係的長遠發展產生重要影響。其次，雙方宣佈將在平等和相互尊重基礎上重啟經貿磋商，美方同意不再向中國商品徵收新的關稅。這些重要共識向國際社會和全球市場發出非常積極的信號。我們希望雙方磋商團隊繼續努力，切實遵循雙方元首最新共識精神。我對中美關係的未來發展和中美經貿磋商的前景持樂觀態度。

中國中央電視台：我注意到，有些英方政府官員還在就香港問題表達關切甚至妄加評論。一九九七年香港回歸，至今已經二十二年了，他們憑什麼還在對中國內政指手畫腳？昨晚英國電視四台採訪中，一些人表示希望亨特外交大臣就香港問題表達更多關切。你對此有何評論？

劉曉明：外交大臣亨特關於香港的有關言論是完全錯誤的。英方在香港問題上應擺正自己的位置。在某些人眼中，香港仍被視為昔日英國殖民統治下的地

方。但現實是，香港已回歸祖國，是中國的一個特別行政區，不是英國領土的一部分。很顯然，英國一些政客仍沉浸在昔日英國殖民者的幻象之中。我希望英方停止插手香港事務，尊重香港「一國兩制」取得的建設成就。只要他們端正位置，客觀公正地處理涉港事務，中英兩國在香港問題上的合作就簡單得多。香港事務與英國無關，他們應當把香港作為中國的一部分來看待，我們願意與他們對話。根據中英之間的協議，英國與香港保持經濟、貿易、文化關係沒有問題，我希望香港能繼續成為中英之間的橋樑，為中英關係發揮積極正面作用。

《每日電訊報》：你提到英國政府應該反思他們的言行可能引發的後果，到底是什麼後果呢？中國正在考慮採取某種報復行動嗎？暫緩修例是否意味著承認上街示威遊行的人是有道理的，承認修例舉措破壞了英中雙方協議？

劉曉明：英方的言行已經產生了後果，這就是破壞了兩國的互信和友好關係。中方已多次向英方提出交涉。中國副總理胡春華剛剛結束對英國的訪問，與英國財政大臣共同主持了第十次中英經濟財金對話，訪問成果很豐碩，雙方開通了「滬倫通」，我本人代表中國政府簽署了一項對英國牛肉出口解禁的協議，這意味著不久之後英國的安格斯牛肉和威爾士黑牛肉將被端上中國民眾的餐桌。維持良好的雙邊關係需要互信，需要遵守基本準則，英國政要發表的不當言論傷害了雙邊關係。我希望英方珍視來之不易的中英關係，與中國一道努力，共同促進兩國和兩國人民的利益。修例是合理和必要的，有其正常合法程序，可能過程中有需要改進的地方。香港特區政府已經認識到這一點，他們需要與民眾進行更多溝通，但這不意味著他們的思路錯了，也不能說修例是壞事。我希望特區政府與民眾進行更多、更積極的溝通和對話，聽取他們的意見，完善相關程序。

獨立電視台：習主席堅信應該維護香港的秩序和國家的團結，如果事態惡化，作為終極手段，中國軍隊會

介入嗎？

劉曉明： 中國在香港駐軍的任務是國防。根據《基本法》，中央政府負責管理香港特區有關的外交事務和防務，中國人民解放軍駐香港部隊的任務就是保衛香港，抵禦外敵。就像我之前所說，我們對香港特區政府完全有信心，相信他們會依法處理。香港警察部隊很專業，我們對他們也很有信心。

獨立電視台： 如果他們不能很好地處理呢？

劉曉明： 我們相信他們能妥善處置。

天空新聞台： 你提到英國媒體在報道香港時沒有採取平衡的態度，但是中國媒體對抗議示威的報道就全面平衡嗎？在中國政府看來，英國政府的表態令人十分憤怒，但在英國有人批評英國政府表態太軟弱，太克制。英國政府並未對暴力行為表示同情和支持，只是對和平抗議者表示同情和支持。中方認為這樣有何不妥？

劉曉明： 中、英媒體對香港事件的報道有很大不同。中國媒體肩負社會責任，服務人民利益，他們向本國民眾還原了香港事件的事實真相，而不是幫助散佈謠言和負面情緒，替反華勢力搖旗吶喊。英國媒體需要反思應如何履行社會責任、恪守新聞職業道德。要真正服務於英國人民的利益，就不應進行不負責任的報道。現在，有三十多萬英國公民生活在香港，英國肯定希望看到香港保持繁榮與穩定，但香港近期的抗議活動與此背道而馳。你們不妨深入思考這些活動的後果，那些不法分子一旦得手、大行其道，必將嚴重損害香港法治，難道這符合英國的利益嗎？符合在港生活的英國公民的利益嗎？答案顯然是否定的。我希望英國媒體能做有利於香港繁榮穩定和符合英國國家利益的報道。

BBC： 你剛才所談似乎對香港街頭抗議的人與衝擊立法會大樓的人不加區分，你是刻意這麼做的嗎？

劉曉明：我當然有區分。我此前接受 BBC、天空新聞台採訪時曾談到，香港抗議活動起初是和平的，但後來演變為暴力行徑，甚至有人用不明液體、有毒粉末襲擊警察。當不法分子衝擊立法會大樓時，一些不法分子試圖持械傷人，警方暫時後撤，避免造成人員受傷。真正對此不加區分的是英國一些政客，從最初的和平示威到後來的暴力事件，他們一概支持，還稱讚不法分子所謂「勇氣」；他們甚至敦促香港特區政府不要以暴力事件為「藉口」實施「鎮壓」，試圖阻撓香港特區政府正當執法。中國中央政府都已表示應由香港特區政府和警方依法處置。香港特區政府有權將暴力違法分子繩之以法，英國政府應尊重香港司法獨立。我希望一些英國政客停止對香港特區政府正當執法、處置有關事件說三道四，停止發表錯誤言論，不要採取「雙重標準」。

《中國日報》：有人說 G20 已不像二十年前應對國際金融危機時那麼有力了，你如何看待 G20 的未來？

劉曉明：習近平主席在 G20 峰會上發表十分重要的聲明，為世界如何應對單邊主義和保護主義指明了方向，提出我們要堅持改革創新，為高質量發展提供更多動力，同時堅持完善全球治理，改革國際金融體系，受到國際社會的廣泛歡迎。此次峰會是成功的，對外發出了積極的信號。二〇〇八年國際金融危機發生後，G20 確立了其作為國際經濟合作主要論壇的定位，推動國際社會加強宏觀經濟政策協調。習主席堅持發展視角，推動 G20 將發展置於宏觀經濟政策協調的優先位置，為 G20 的未來發展做出重要貢獻。毫無疑問，上述成果向國際社會傳遞了積極信號，我們相信 G20 的前景一定是光明的。

謝謝大家！

中央政府有足夠多的辦法平息動亂

——關於香港街頭暴力激進活動中外記者會

（二〇一九年八月十五日，中國駐英國大使館）

劉曉明：七月三日，我在使館舉辦了一次中外記者會，介紹香港「修例」問題及中方立場。此後一個多月以來，香港反對派和一些激進勢力繼續藉口「反修例」進行各種街頭激進抗爭活動，暴力化程度不斷升級，社會波及面越來越廣，完全超出自由集會與和平抗議範疇，嚴重挑戰香港法治和社會秩序，嚴重威脅香港市民生命財產安全，嚴重破壞香港繁榮穩定，嚴重觸碰「一國兩制」原則底線，致使香港面臨回歸以來最嚴峻的局面。

一些極端激進分子在香港興風作浪，打著所謂民主的幌子，掩蓋其反法治、反社會、反「一國兩制」的真實面目和險惡用心，是兼具欺騙性與破壞性的「新極端主義」。他們打砸立法會，衝擊中聯辦，暴力襲擊警員，在香港機場非法集結致使機場全面停止運營，已經構成嚴重暴力犯罪，開始出現恐怖主義的苗頭。中國中央政府絕不會放任少數人以暴力行徑把香港拖向危險的深淵，絕不允許任何人破壞香港的法治與良好發展局面，絕不允許任何人以任何藉口破壞「一國兩制」。如果香港局勢進一步惡化，出現香港特區政府不能控制的動亂，中國中央政府絕不會坐視不管。按照《基本法》規定，中國中央政府有足夠多的辦法、足夠強大的力量迅速平息可能出現的各種動亂。

當前，香港處於關鍵時刻。如何結束香港亂局？

這是所有關心香港前途的人都在思考的問題，也是英國各大媒體頭版頭條和「封面文章」之問。我們的回答堅定而明確：我們希望香港事態平穩有序結束，同時我們做了最壞準備。如何實現香港事態平穩有序結束？我認為，以下四點至關重要：

第一，堅決支持香港特區政府止暴制亂、恢復秩序。希望廣大香港市民，特別是一些不明真相的年輕人，認清當前香港局勢，珍惜香港回歸後來之不易的良好發展局面，顧全大局，團結一致，堅定不移挺特首、挺政府，守護香港的法治與正義，維護祖國統一和香港繁榮穩定。希望香港各界人士不要被激進勢力所利用和裹挾，要向一切暴力行徑大聲說「不」，要向一切踐踏法治的行徑堅決說「不」，堅定支持特區政府依法施政，堅定支持香港警方嚴正執法。

第二，堅決依法嚴懲暴力犯罪分子。有法必依、違法必究是任何一個法治社會的基本要求。暴力就是暴力，違法就是違法，這不會因為暴力違法分子打著什麼幌子就發生變化。只要是違法行為，無論怎麼粉飾，都要受到法律的制裁；只要參與暴力犯罪活動，無論是誰，都要追究其法律責任。試問，英國會允許極端激進分子衝擊議會、破壞議會設施而逍遙法外嗎？英國會允許極端激進分子用致命武器襲擊警察、燒毀警署而不受懲罰嗎？英國會允許暴徒打著所謂民主的幌子佔領機場、堵塞交通、破壞社會秩序、威脅民眾生命財產安全嗎？這些行為在英國難道不構成違法犯罪嗎？姑息違法，就是褻瀆正義；縱容暴力，就是踐踏法治。任何一個法治國家，任何一個負責任的政府，都不會對上述暴力行徑坐視不管。中國中央政府堅定支持特區政府和香港警方嚴正執法、果斷執法，盡快將違法分子繩之以法、嚴懲不貸，依法維護香港法治環境和社會秩序。

第三，外部勢力停止干預香港事務。有諸多證據顯示，香港局勢惡化到今天的地步，與外部勢力介入和煽風點火是分不開的。一些西方國家政客和機構明裏暗裏為暴力激進分子提供各種支持，為他們撐腰打氣，甚至干擾香港司法獨立，阻礙香港警方將暴力犯罪分子繩之以法。我想重申，香港是中國的香港，香港事務絕不容外國插手。我們奉勸那些外國勢力，尊

重中國主權和安全，立即停止以任何方式干預香港事務和中國內政，立即停止縱容暴力犯罪，不要誤判形勢，在錯誤的路上越走越遠，否則必將搬起石頭砸自己的腳。

第四，媒體承擔起應有的社會責任。香港事態發生以來，西方媒體扮演了十分不光彩的角色，不僅沒有公正客觀報道，反而混淆是非、顛倒黑白、誤導公眾：連篇累牘地渲染所謂「和平示威權利」，卻對極端暴力分子破壞社會秩序、襲警傷人的違法犯罪行為熟視無睹，對支持特區政府、守護香港法治正義聲音更是鮮有見報；將破壞香港法治、為非作歹的暴徒美化為「支持民主的人士」，卻將特區政府和警隊維護香港法治、保護市民生命財產安全的正當合法舉措惡意誣衊為「鎮壓」。正是這些媒體的「選擇性失聲」和「歪曲性報道」，使錯誤輿論大行其道，誤導了許多不明真相的民眾特別是香港年輕人。可以說，西方媒體對香港今天的局面負有不可推卸的責任！我真誠地希望西方媒體反思自己行為的社會影響，承擔起應有的社會責任，公正客觀地報道香港局勢，不要再為極端暴力分子說項，不要再給香港亂局火上澆油，為平穩、有序結束香港亂局營造良好的輿論環境。為了幫助各位理解我說的第四點，我們製作了一個短片，讓大家看一看在西方媒體看不到的畫面，聽一聽在西方媒體聽不到的聲音。（播放短片）

「治則興，亂則衰。」這句中國古訓對今天的香港再適用不過。目前，有三十多萬英國公民在香港工作和生活，三百多家英國公司在香港投資興業。香港保持繁榮穩定，不僅符合中國的利益，也符合包括英國在內的各國共同利益。我衷心希望，英國各界有識之士認清大局，多做有利於香港繁榮穩定的事，抵制和反對任何干涉香港事務、破壞香港法治的言行。我堅信，在中國中央政府的大力支持下，在香港特區政府和林鄭月娥行政長官的帶領下，香港社會一定能夠盡快止暴制亂，盡早恢復正常秩序，使香港這顆東方明珠重放光彩。

下面，我願回答大家提問。

彭博社：我注意到視頻裏一位香港官員表示香港警察

從未打出真正槍彈。社交媒體上傳播的視頻顯示，中國軍隊正在香港之外進行反恐演習，如果軍隊派往香港，是否將被授權使用真槍實彈？

劉曉明：我想這樣回答你的問題。香港的形勢十分嚴峻，但我們對特區政府和行政長官處理與平息局勢、恢復秩序有充分信任和信心。正如我在開場白中所說，如果香港局勢進一步惡化、出現特區政府不能控制的動亂，中國中央政府絕不會坐視不管。中國政府有足夠多的辦法和足夠強大的力量迅速平息動亂。

CNN：特朗普總統已表示希望與習近平主席討論香港問題。中方是否已正式回應其提議？如習主席同意與其見面，將有助於緩解香港當前形勢嗎？

劉曉明：我不認為特朗普總統已正式提出要與習近平主席會面，他應該是在推特發文提到香港形勢。我們可以討論香港問題，但最重要的是，香港事務是中國內政，中方堅決反對任何外部干涉，包括一些外國組織為極端暴力行為提供資金支持，一些美國議員提出所謂關於香港的法案，違背國際關係準則。我特別要強調的是，中方堅決反對任何外國政府官員給特區政府打電話施壓，公開支持暴力分子。

路透社：你剛才提到一些抗議示威活動開始出現恐怖主義的苗頭，你能否解釋構成恐怖主義行為的紅線和轉折點是什麼？依照中國法律，這是否將成為中方向香港派軍隊的合法依據？

劉曉明：剛才視頻所顯示的以及我們最近看到的在香港發生的殘暴惡劣行為，特別是香港機場事件，被不少媒體稱為恐怖主義行為。暴徒攻擊警察、損毀設施，甚至襲擊記者，你們的同行、一位中國記者就受到圍攻。對此，中國記者協會表示強烈譴責。這些都是恐怖主義的苗頭，我稱其為「新極端主義」。如任其發展，將演變為恐怖主義。我們相信特區政府和香港警方現在能掌控局面。如局勢進一步惡化，特區政府難以控制，中央政府絕對不會坐視不管。

今日俄羅斯電視台：根據美國媒體報道，美國國家民主基金會（NED）為部分香港抗議示威者提供了資金支持。中方是否掌握美國在背後策劃香港抗議示威活動的證據？

劉曉明：你已經部分回答了這個問題。我們相信這些極端暴力活動都有幕後「黑手」，一些外國勢力和組織為其提供資金和其他支持，甚至有外國官員會見「港獨」分子。他們出於不可告人的政治目的，就是要把香港變成中國的麻煩，阻止中國發展繁榮。因此，為了使香港亂局盡快平息，外部勢力應立即停止干預香港事務，停止你剛才提到的那些行為。

《泰晤士報》：英國議會下院外交委員會主席圖根哈特表示，英國應考慮給予香港居民英國國籍，中方對此如何評論？

劉曉明：我認為，英國的某些政客，雖然身體已經進入二十一世紀，但腦袋卻還停留在殖民時代。他們依然將香港當作大英帝國或英國的一部分。他們應該改變思維模式，擺正自己的位置，認識到香港是中國的一部分，而不是英國的一部分。

獨立電視台：你剛才說，中國已經做好最壞的打算，你能澄清一下這究竟意味著什麼？有人看到軍隊和武警在深圳集結，這是否意味著採用軍事手段的可能性上升？

劉曉明：我剛才在開場白中已經回答了你的問題。採取果斷措施是必要的。我已經說了，如果局勢進一步惡化，變得無法平息、不能控制，中國中央政府不會坐視不管。中央政府有足夠多的手段、足夠強大的力量平息事態。如果你認真聽我的講話，就能找到答案。

獨立電視台：能不能詳細解釋一下「平息」（quell）一詞的含義是什麼？

劉曉明：平息就是終止目前的事態。

天空電視台：你剛才說北京有力量在必要的情況下平息香港的事態，能否說明在何種情況下會派軍隊赴香港？他們將如何應對普通民眾的抗議？在上次記者會上，你說英中關係因為英外交大臣的言論受到損害。這次記者會，我們有了新首相。英中關係是改善了，恢復正常了，還是繼續受到損害？你有什麼話要對英國首相說？

劉曉明：關於第一個問題，我想我已經回答了。首先，當前我們仍然相信香港特區政府有能力處理好香港事務，特首是很有能力的領導人，贏得了廣泛尊敬和支持。當前，他們對事態處理得當，值得信任。我們有信心、有決心，也有能力迅速平息事態。關於第二個問題，中方當然希望中英關係能夠進一步發展，良好的關係符合中英雙方共同利益。媒體上關於英國政局評論很多，我倒是不希望你們那麼快再換首相，否則下次記者會可能又要把新首相拿出來說事了。（眾人笑）約翰遜首相是我任駐英大使以來打交道的第四位首相，我們對推進雙邊關係抱有期待，希望雙方沿著習近平主席訪英時開啟的中英關係「黃金時代」大方向繼續前進。但良好的雙邊關係必須建立在相互尊重主權和領土完整、互不干涉內政的基礎上，這是我們在建交聯合公報中就已明確的原則。只要堅持這些原則，雙邊關係就能順利發展，反之就會遇到困難。希望英國新政府在香港問題上堅持原則、妥善處理，即香港是中國的領土，香港關乎中國主權，香港事務是中國的內政。

《衛報》：你說的「不能控制」是什麼意思？如何確定事態處於不能控制的狀態？

劉曉明：「不能控制」就是失去控制，這個意思很清楚，大概不需要查《牛津大辭典》。我們希望事態處於香港特區政府和特首管控之下。我們相信當前局勢仍是可控的。

BBC廣播四台：第一個問題，你是否承認大多數抗議者並不是「暴力分子」「極端分子」，而是普通市民？他們有律師，有公務員，他們對中國政府感到很失望，要求享有更多言論自由，支持普選。你能否解釋中國政府為何反對普選？第二個問題，中國是否仍然遵守《中英聯合聲明》？

劉曉明：埃文，距離上次接受你採訪已經很長時間了，很高興再次見到你。你第一個問題是關於示威者。我們當然會區分普通示威者和極端暴力犯罪分子。一小撮極端暴力分子不能代表大多數遊行示威者，許多參加示威的人是被蒙蔽的，一些香港和西方媒體誤導了民眾。每個社會都有自己的問題。香港回歸祖國以來，取得巨大發展成就，「一國兩制」取得巨大成功，但仍有許多需要改進的地方，比如年輕人的發展問題。香港經濟存在一些問題，過於倚重金融服務業和房地產業，年輕人上升通道有限，他們有抱怨，我們都理解。中央政府和特區政府非常重視這些問題，正採取切實措施予以解決。粵港澳大灣區建設將給年輕人帶來更多發展機會。如果把香港和一河之隔的深圳做一個比較，就會發現很大差別。深圳在三十年間從一個小漁村發展成為一個充滿生機和活力的大都市，成為年輕人創業之地，擁有諸如華為、騰訊、大疆等眾多高新科技公司。在香港卻沒有一家像這樣的世界一流科技企業。特區政府正在想辦法解決這些問題。我們應注重發展問題，但抗議示威不是解決問題之道，社會混亂只會讓年輕人蒙受更多損失。我們關注年輕人的發展，會將受蒙蔽而走上歧途的年輕人與少數極端暴力犯罪分子區分開來。

關於《中英聯合聲明》，一些人經常把「一國兩制」和《中英聯合聲明》混為一談。《中英聯合聲明》已經完成了歷史使命，即將香港歸還中國以及在一九八四年至一九九七年十三年間確保香港在回歸前平穩過渡。《中英聯合聲明》提到「一國兩制」，但「一國兩制」是中國政府的政策宣示，寫入《基本法》。因此，我們說中方堅定遵守《基本法》和「一國兩制」五十年不變，而不是遵守《中英聯合聲明》五十年不變。

關於普選，中央政府支持香港實行普選，這是香港政制改革的終極目標。但改革必須有序推進，必須符合香港的實際情況，依法循序漸進地推進。二〇一五年，如果不是反對派的抵制，香港立法會就已經通過關於普選的立法了，結果實行普選的進程被迫推遲。西方普通民眾對此了解甚少。

BBC：第一個問題，你提到中國內部事務不容外國干涉，如果英國政府要求就香港面臨的危機進行對話，是外國干涉嗎？關於「修例」，除了擱置還有其他解決辦法嗎？中方是否準備撤銷「修例」？第二個問題，你提到中國將不惜一切代價平息抗議活動……

劉曉明：不是抗議，是動亂。

BBC：如果派出軍隊，是否意味著「一國兩制」、香港高度自治遭到破壞？會對香港經濟造成巨大傷害嗎？

劉曉明：你實際上是提了三個問題，我從最後一個問題開始回答。我說過，我們有足夠多的辦法和足夠強大的力量結束香港事態。我們這樣做才是真正在捍衛「一國兩制」。一些極端勢力要求「香港獨立」，他們企圖利用香港向內地滲透，破壞內地的社會主義制度，這是在破壞「一國兩制」。我們應該知道，「一國」的意思是香港是中國的一部分，中國對香港擁有主權。「一國」是「兩制」的前提，沒有「一國」，「兩制」就無從談起，二者是有機統一的整體，不能只強調一個，削弱另一個。中國要做的正是為了維護「一國兩制」。

關於英國外交大臣打電話干涉香港內部事務，這不是一般的打電話討論問題，而是用打電話向特區政府施壓。英方說對警察使用暴力表示關切，譴責雙方的暴力，這種「各打五十大板」的做法是混淆是非。指責正確的，就是支持錯誤的。這裏的關鍵是電話談話內容是不是干涉內政。英國政要經常訪問香港，我們對此不持異議。但如果英方言論是在干預香港司法獨立，比如之前一些政客要求香港特區政府「不能懲

罰暴力違法者」，這就是干擾破壞香港的司法獨立，是完全不能接受的。

我們已經對英國政客的言論表達了關切。英方要改變思維方式，要有大局觀，香港保持穩定和繁榮不僅有利於香港和中國內地，也符合英國的利益。

關於「修例」問題，「修例」已經暫緩，下一步將由香港特區政府來決定，林鄭特首已承諾要與社會各界進行更多溝通和討論。我在上次記者會上說過，這是一個好條例，完善香港的法律制度，符合香港的利益，將香港變為「正義天堂」而非「避罪天堂」。特區政府需要時間解釋「修例」符合香港利益，從而說服香港公眾，爭取公眾理解。

BBC：剛才的短片包含一名記者在香港機場被抗議者圍攻的畫面。另外一個人也在機場受到抗議者圍攻，但他是來自深圳的便衣警察。請問目前有多少內地警務人員在香港活動？

劉曉明：我了解的情況是，昨天一個深圳居民在機場為他的朋友送行，遭到了暴亂分子的圍攻。另一個遭圍攻的是中國內地記者，有人聲稱他是個警察，把他綁起來，但其實他是個有名、有姓、有註冊的記者。

中國國際電視台：我的第一個問題是，隨著抗議者的暴力行為升級，香港警方的應對措施也不可避免地升級。近日來，香港警隊遭遇襲擊，如果放在其他地方，同樣的襲警行為會受到嚴厲處理。為什麼媒體，特別是西方媒體仍然嚴厲批評香港警隊？第二個問題，昨天英國企業得到警告，要評估香港目前存在的投資風險，而且有二十八個國家已經針對香港發出了不同程度的旅行警告，這是否意味著香港經濟面臨一個轉折點？

劉曉明：關於香港警察的履職表現，我認為你說得很對，他們展現了極大的克制，超過很多其他國家的警察。他們非常專業，贏得包括美國、加拿大、法國等許多國家同行的欽佩。短片中看到的情況，如果發生在西方國家，警方處理時會使用更多強制手段，但香

港警隊保持了克制。這讓我想起不久前的六月，英國環保組織申請在希思羅機場抗議，警方警告其如果這麼做將面臨終身監禁，敦促其三思而行。我們也都知道英國警方是如何處理倫敦騷亂的，使用了何等強制手段。

香港經濟的確受到衝擊，香港的國際形象和聲譽也受到損害，令人痛心。香港是個非常安全的城市，法治指數很高，根據二〇一八年世界正義工程法治指數排名，香港排名十六，領先美國三位，美國排名十九。這還只是法治指數，在安全指數方面，香港與西方城市相比更是遙遙領先。的確，我們都看到恆生指數下跌百分之九，港元匯率等也下滑了，非常令人痛心。正如我在開場白中所說，我認為香港民眾應當珍惜來之不易的發展成果，我希望並期待香港回歸理性。昨天我也聽到一些來自香港工商界的聲音，他們沉默了一段時間，但現在開始發聲了，他們認識到這樣的動亂將給香港這座城市、給香港的繁榮穩定造成多麼大的損害。

路透社：感謝大使給我第二次提問機會。你剛才回答BBC記者提問時提到，香港特區政府有權決定是否暫緩或撤銷「修例」。可否明確一下，如果林鄭月娥特首及其領導的香港特區政府決定撤銷「修例」，中國中央政府會否同意？

劉曉明：很多人以為「修例」是特區政府按中央政府指令或授意所為，實際情況不是這樣。「修例」完全是由特區政府發起的，林鄭特首本人也在多個場合表示，她從未收到中央政府任何相關「指令」。香港特區政府已決定暫緩「修例」，我們對此表示尊重、理解和支持，希望英國媒體注意我用的這三個詞。我認為中國中央政府將繼續這麼做。

今日俄羅斯電視台：自美國政府將華為公司列入「實體清單」，中美經貿摩擦逐步升級，你認為美方是否會把香港問題作為解決貿易問題的籌碼？如果是這樣，中方將如何應對，是否會在香港問題上做出讓步？

劉曉明：中美經貿磋商仍在繼續，我對此持審慎樂觀態度。中共中央政治局委員、中央外事工作委員會辦公室主任楊潔篪日前訪問紐約，會見了美國國務卿蓬佩奧，就包括貿易問題在內的中美關係交換了意見。中方不會在香港問題上犧牲原則，來換取與美方達成貿易協議。我們從不拿原則做交易。香港問題純屬中國內政，我們堅決反對任何外來干涉，不管這個干涉來自哪個國家。

彭博社：你提到當前亂局將損害香港經濟和營商環境，我認為香港工商界贊同這一點，他們十分擔心街頭示威會削弱香港的國際金融中心地位。但他們中很多人也憂慮中國中央政府會直接干預香港事務，比如派軍隊鎮壓所謂街頭暴力。你認為中央政府出於維護香港繁榮穩定和國際地位的需要，今後是否會創造更多與街頭抗議者接觸和對話的空間？

劉曉明：我要反問你一下，如果面臨兩種形勢，一種是香港局勢失控、持續動盪；一種是中央政府果斷介入、終止動亂，哪一種符合工商界利益？我認為答案顯然是後者。當然，這只是極端情況，並不是現實。我們希望香港事態平穩有序結束。這需要在廣大愛國愛港人士堅定支持下，香港特區政府和香港警方嚴正執法、果斷執法，盡快將違法分子繩之以法、嚴懲不貸，依法維護香港法治環境和社會秩序。這是香港的當務之急。

BBC 廣播四台：感謝大使給我第二次提問的機會。我注意到你在剛才的答問中表示，對香港暴徒與和平抗議者要加以區分。你可否在此對香港市民明確一點：如果結束暴力，大家仍可繼續進行和平抗議，不會遭受中國中央政府的干預，即中央干預只針對嚴重損害中國利益的暴力行徑？

劉曉明：你不妨回憶一下我剛才的開場講話，如果香港局勢進一步惡化，出現香港特區政府不能控制的動亂，中國中央政府絕不會坐視不管。按照《基本法》規定，中國中央政府有足夠多的辦法、足夠強大的力

量迅速平息可能出現的各種動亂。目前香港局勢是可控的，仍在香港特區政府有效管控下，不存在你談的假設情況。

BBC廣播四台：如果和平示威一旦失控呢？

劉曉明：這反映出你對有關問題缺乏了解，低估了香港特區政府和警方的能力。他們有準備、有能力妥善應對和平抗議示威。當然，前提是示威必須是和平的、非暴力的。

CNN：感謝大使也給我第二次提問的機會。你剛才反覆提及中國中央政府仍對香港局勢保持耐心，並強調你們有足夠的辦法和力量迅速平息事態。那麼你認為下週的這個時候，香港特區政府能否使事態出現根本改觀？或者你再舉行一次記者會，繼續回應外界關切？

劉曉明：我在此重申，我們堅信在中國中央政府的大力支持下，在香港特區政府和林鄭月娥行政長官的帶領下，香港社會一定能夠盡快止暴制亂，盡早恢復正常秩序。這樣，我也就不需要再次舉行記者會了。

謝謝大家！

香港的出路在哪裏？

——關於香港局勢中外記者會

（二〇一九年十一月十八日，中國駐英國大使館）

劉曉明：大家上午好！歡迎大家出席今天的中外記者會。

這是自香港事態發生以來，我第三次在使館舉辦記者會。五個多月來，「修例風波」演變為持續不斷的暴力活動，特別是近期大規模違法暴力行徑全面升級，已經把香港推到了極為危險的境地。所有真正關心香港的人都在思考：香港到底怎麼了？應當如何看待當前香港亂局？香港的出路在哪裏？

四天前，習近平主席在巴西出席金磚國家領導人第十一次會晤時，就當前香港局勢表明中國政府嚴正立場。習主席指出，香港持續發生的激進暴力犯罪行為，嚴重踐踏法治和社會秩序，嚴重破壞香港繁榮穩定，嚴重挑戰「一國兩制」原則底線。止暴制亂、恢復秩序是香港當前最緊迫的任務。我們將繼續堅定支持行政長官帶領香港特別行政區政府依法施政，堅定支持香港警方嚴正執法，堅定支持香港司法機構依法懲治暴力犯罪分子。中國政府維護國家主權、安全、發展利益的決心堅定不移，貫徹「一國兩制」方針的決心堅定不移，反對任何外部勢力干涉香港事務的決心堅定不移。

習主席的重要講話字字鏗鏘，句句千鈞，是中國中央政府對香港當前局勢和未來出路發出的最權威的聲音。

第一，習主席講話深刻指出了激進暴力犯罪活動

的實質與嚴重危害。當前香港局勢發展的本質絕不是一些西方政客和西方媒體所標榜的所謂「民主自由」問題，而是極端暴力違法分子破壞香港法治和社會秩序，妄圖搞亂香港、破壞「一國兩制」的問題，這是赤裸裸的激進暴力犯罪活動。

激進暴力犯罪活動嚴重踐踏香港法治和社會秩序。五個多月來，暴徒們自稱和平示威，卻瘋狂打砸縱火，有預謀地襲警、刺殺香港立法會議員，將多所大學變成罪惡基地，圍攻襲擊內地學生；自稱與弱者同行，卻無差別殘害普通市民，甚至向一名反對他們破壞活動的市民身上澆淋易燃液體並點火焚燒；自稱捍衛民主自由，卻限制和剝奪他人的人身與言論自由。這種光天化日之下殺人放火、慘無人道的暴力行徑是對法律底線、道德底線、人類文明底線的嚴重踐踏！我們對此絕不能容忍！反中亂港分子還將黑手伸到境外，伸向英國：他們面戴「黑口罩」，到中國駐英國大使館門前尋釁，污損使館正門及兩側牆壁，塗寫「港獨」標語；他們圍攻來英出席活動的香港特區政府律政司司長並將她推倒致傷。我們對這些暴力行徑表示最強烈的憤慨和最嚴厲的譴責！

激進暴力犯罪活動嚴重破壞香港繁榮穩定。自由開放的經濟活力、包容多元的文化魅力、專業高效的社會管理、法治安全的社會環境曾是香港閃亮的國際名片。但是今天，暴力極端分子在香港製造「黑色恐怖」，市民的生命財產安全受到嚴重傷害；香港經濟連續兩個季度環比下跌，第三季度本地生產總值滑至負百分之二點九的負值，已經步入技術性衰退，香港特區政府經濟顧問辦公室近日下調二〇一九年香港經濟增長預測至負百分之一點三；相關國際評級下降，香港國際形象、營商環境受到嚴重衝擊。如今出現在媒體上的香港，是持續不斷的暴力活動，是混亂不安的社會秩序。香港回歸二十二年來取得的發展成就與大好局面正在受到侵蝕，「東方之珠」正在變成「東方之殤」，「香港」正滑向「亂港」的深淵，前景不堪設想。

激進暴力犯罪活動嚴重挑戰「一國兩制」原則底線。香港反對派和暴力極端勢力，大肆鼓吹「港獨」，公然宣揚「光復香港」。這徹底暴露出其所謂

社會訴求背後真正的險惡政治用意，那就是衝著摧毀「一國兩制」中「一國」這個根本來的，企圖搞亂香港、癱瘓特區政府，進而奪取香港的管治權，把香港從祖國分離出去。「一國兩制」是一個完整的概念。「一國」是「兩制」的前提和基礎。沒有「一國」，就沒有「兩制」。我們絕不能容忍任何破壞「一國兩制」的暴力犯罪活動！

第二，習主席講話為解決香港亂局指明了出路，即止暴制亂、恢復秩序是當前香港最緊迫的任務。有法必依、違法必究是任何一個法治社會的基本要求。極端暴力活動是任何社會都絕不能容忍、絕不會姑息的。只有依法制止和懲治暴力活動，恢復法治和社會秩序，才能維護香港廣大民眾的福祉，才能守護香港美好的明天，才能穩固「一國兩制」的根基。我們堅決支持特區政府、香港警方和司法機關堅守法治原則，採取有力行動，遏制打擊各種暴力違法行為和恐怖主義行徑，將違法犯罪分子盡快繩之以法、嚴懲不貸，依法維護香港法治環境和社會秩序，還香港以穩定，還民眾以安寧。

第三，習主席講話彰顯了中國政府維護國家主權安全發展利益、貫徹「一國兩制」方針的堅定決心。不久前舉行的中共十九屆四中全會明確指出，「一國兩制」是中國共產黨領導人民實現祖國和平統一的一項重要制度。中國政府將全面準確貫徹「一國兩制」、「港人治港」、高度自治的方針。貫徹「一國兩制」方針，要始終堅持「三條底線」不容觸碰，即絕對不能允許任何危害國家主權安全、絕對不能允許挑戰中央權力和《基本法》權威、絕對不能允許利用香港對內地進行滲透破壞的活動。中國政府將健全依照憲法和《基本法》對香港實行全面管治權的制度，完善香港融入國家發展大局、同內地優勢互補、協同發展機制，著力解決影響社會穩定和長遠發展的深層次矛盾和問題。

第四，習主席講話顯示了中國政府反對任何外部勢力干涉香港事務的堅定決心。近期香港事態不斷升級，外部勢力的姑息縱容和推波助瀾難辭其咎。一些西方國家政客和西方媒體罔顧事實、顛倒黑白，把激進暴力犯罪分子稱為所謂「和平示威者」和「民主抗

議者」，卻對恪盡職守、維護香港法治、保護市民生命財產安全的香港警方百般指責。一些西方國家政客赤裸裸地為激進暴力違法分子撐腰打氣。美國國會眾議院通過所謂《香港人權和民主法案》，粗暴干涉香港事務和中國內政。英國政府和議會下院外委會出台涉華報告對香港問題說三道四。更有甚者，個別英國政客還要為鼓吹「港獨」、鼓動極端暴力活動的「急先鋒」授獎。如果有人還懷疑外部勢力插手香港事務，這些事實難道還不夠嗎?!我們要正告那些外部勢力，中國政府反對任何外部勢力干涉香港事務的決心堅定不移！我們要奉勸那些外部勢力，立即停止以任何方式干預香港事務和中國內政，立即停止縱容香港暴力犯罪，否則必將搬起石頭砸自己的腳！

為了幫助各位更好地了解當前香港激進暴力犯罪事實，我們這次又製作了一個短片，讓大家看一看那些被西方政客和媒體稱為「和平示威者」和「民主抗議者」的真實面目，看一看今天的香港究竟面臨什麼樣的危險局面。(播放視頻)

事實無法掩蓋，真相擊破謊言。這是我對這個短片的評價，希望大家看後也有同感。我曾多次向英國各界人士表示，香港保持繁榮穩定、維護「一國兩制」，不僅符合中國的利益，也符合包括英國在內的各國共同利益。英國在香港有三十多萬公民、七百多家企業。香港亂下去對英國有百害而無一利。我衷心希望，英國各界有識之士認清形勢，看清大局，支持香港特區政府止暴制亂、恢復秩序、維護法治，抵制和反對任何干涉香港事務的言行，多做有利於香港繁榮穩定的事情，使香港亂局早日結束，使「東方之珠」重現光彩。

下面，我願回答大家提問。

BBC：此前我給貴使館寫過郵件，詢問關於新疆「集中營」的情況，你能否告知真相？

劉曉明：你的問題超出了今天記者會的主題，但我可以做出回答。首先我必須澄清，新疆沒有你所說的「集中營」。新疆設立了職業技能教育培訓中心，目的是預防恐怖主義。

BBC：最近我看到一些中國政府發給「集中營」的命令，內容包括改變相關人員的行為，進行普通話培訓，這是給他們洗腦。

劉曉明：這完全是假消息。新疆是中國一個自治區，是一個風光美麗、和平繁榮的地方。但是從二十世紀九十年代到二〇一六年不是這樣的，新疆發生了幾千起恐怖事件，數千名無辜群眾遇害，當地民眾強烈要求政府採取應對措施。設立教培中心後，新疆三年來沒有發生一起恐怖事件，恢復了昔日的美麗、和平與繁榮。我倒是想問問，如果英國某個地方也集中發生恐怖事件、民眾深受其害，英國政府會怎麼做？

中方採取的預防性措施根本不是什麼宗教清洗。新疆民眾享有充分的宗教自由。希望你有機會去新疆走一走、看一看，體會一下當地民眾享有的宗教自由和幸福生活。新疆有二點八萬個宗教場所、三萬名宗教教職人員，平均每五百三十個穆斯林就擁有一座清真寺，比例超過許多伊斯蘭國家，也比英國基督教徒擁有教堂的比例高很多。所以說，新疆根本不存在所謂宗教清洗的問題，當地民眾享有充分宗教自由。

設立教培中心是為了更好地幫助那些曾參與恐怖活動、極端主義活動但情節相對輕微的年輕人改邪歸正，開展語言培訓可幫助這些人成為合法公民和合格的勞動者。當地民眾可以使用自己民族的語言，但為了改善生活水平、更好地與其他地區民眾交流，需要掌握更多的語言技能和職業技能。缺乏法律知識也容易使他們成為恐怖主義的受害者。學習好語言有助於幫助他們更好地學習職業技能和法律知識，實現自食其力，這才是教培的目的。最重要的是，這一舉措是成功的，新疆變得更加安全。去年，赴疆旅遊人數增長40%，國內生產總值（GDP）增長超過百分之六。

BBC：但據我掌握的文件，大量被關進「集中營」的人既沒有接受審判，也沒有被起訴，至少會在裏面待一年。

劉曉明：你所說的那些文件都是編造的虛假信息。中方已就新疆反恐去極端化鬥爭、職業技能教育培訓工

作等發佈了七本白皮書，記者會後我們向你提供這些官方文件，希望你認真閱讀，不要聽信假消息。

英國電視四台：我曾與一些「集中營」裏的人交流過。如果主要是針對年輕人的話，為什麼還有許多老年人和婦女被關進「集中營」？關於香港，中方要將香港「融入」內地，變成「一國一制」嗎？

劉曉明：教培中心的學員涉恐情節輕微，無須予以法律懲戒。政府希望給他們機會改正，離開教培中心後不會再發生犯罪行為。這才是設立教培中心的目的，事實證明這一舉措十分成功。教培中心裏大多數是年輕人，當然也有一些年齡較大的人，年齡不是問題，主要取決於他們的行為是否對社會構成威脅。

中國共產黨十九屆四中全會已再次重申將繼續堅持「一國兩制」，習近平主席在慶祝中華人民共和國成立七十週年大會等多個場合予以重申。「融入」的意思是祖國要給香港提供更多發展機遇，如推進粵港澳大灣區建設。這些機遇可以幫助香港實現更好的發展，解決存在的一些深層次問題，如收入差距、年輕人就業等。我們會繼續堅持「一國兩制」的成功實踐，但目前這一政策受到暴力極端分子的破壞。正如我剛才所說，「一國兩制」是一個完整的概念，不能割裂。「一國」的含義是香港已經回歸，是中國的一部分，我們不允許任何外部勢力干涉香港事務。「一國」是「兩制」的前提和基礎，「一國」受到損害，「兩制」也無從談起。

《南華早報》：大使先生，剛才你在講話中敦促國際社會支持香港特區政府止暴制亂。但實際情況是香港特區政府的舉措效果有限，暴力活動還在升級。我想問的是，中國政府是否將考慮部署軍隊平息局勢？

劉曉明：據我所知，包括特首在內，香港特區政府已採取多種措施與民眾進行溝通，聽取意見建議，舉行各類活動逾百場。我們需要給他們機會和時間。開展對話需要和平的環境，但當前暴力活動猖獗，顯然無助於特區政府與民眾開展實質性、有成效的對話，我

們需要創造有利的條件。駐港部隊肩負著維護國家主權、安全、領土完整和香港安全的重任。此前記者會上我已多次說過，我們信任香港特區政府和林鄭月娥特首。不久前，習主席會見林鄭特首時高度肯定特首及特區政府管治團隊的工作，表達了充分信任。特區政府正在努力控制局勢，但如果事態失控，中央政府不會坐視不管，我們擁有足夠多的辦法和足夠強大的力量平息動亂。

《南華早報》：第二個問題，香港立法會前主席、民建聯前主席曾鈺成是香港最親內地的人士之一，幾天前他在接受採訪時表示，支持赦免輕微犯罪的暴力分子並對警察開展獨立調查。你對此有何評論？

劉曉明：這個問題應該由香港特區政府回答，我不對具體的司法問題做出評論。

天空新聞台：第一個問題，關於解放軍是否會介入，你重複了上次記者會的表態，怎麼理解「無法控制」？事態已經延續了五個月，仍未改善。放手香港特區政府處理事態的政策是否失敗了？下一步是向抗議者做實質性的妥協還是中央政府會派軍隊干預？第二個問題是關於新疆。《紐約時報》週末公佈了數百份文件並進行相關報道，你對此有何評論？

劉曉明：關於第一個問題，我認為香港特區政府對當前事態仍在進行有效處理，在這種形勢下，我要求外部勢力停止干涉，停止煽動暴力，停止火上澆油，尊重特區政府，讓特區政府依法施政。關於第二個問題，我的回答是，根本不存在這樣的文件，有關報道純屬編造，一派胡言、用心險惡。這不是《紐約時報》第一次揑造假新聞了，不值一駁。

《每日電訊報》：你提到外部勢力煽風點火、「港獨」等，你還提到英國政府，特別是英國議會下院外委會，你數次提到外部勢力煽動暴力，你是否指責英國政府煽動暴力和支持「港獨」？

劉曉明：當英方發表不負責任的涉港言論時，我們向英方表明了立場。英國政府批評香港警察，批評香港特區政府處置事態，就是對中國內政的干涉。英方某些言論表面上看起來平衡，但實質是在偏袒暴徒。我們讚賞英方反對「港獨」的立場。英國高級官員已數次表示，「港獨」不是選項。我希望英方對「港獨」進行更強烈的譴責，也希望英方遵守承諾，言行一致，採取實際行動反對「港獨」。

獨立電視台：在過去二十四小時，我們看到香港形勢急劇惡化，是否鎮壓已迫在眉睫？

劉曉明：不存在所謂「鎮壓」。我認為香港警察在履行他們的職責。一些人指責香港警察，但在我看來，他們是最專業的警察，保持了極大的克制。比如說，如果在英國的校園裏發生類似的事件，在英國議會及周邊地區出現類似的事態，你可以想像一下英國警察會怎樣應對。香港警察努力避免傷亡，他們不想傷害被極端分子洗腦的學生，如果不是這個原因，事情恐怕不會是現在的樣子了。

《衛報》：第一個問題關於香港局勢，你認為下週的香港區議會選舉會照常舉行嗎？第二個問題，為什麼中國政府反對英國給予在香港的英國國民（海外）護照（BNO）持有者以英國公民身份、允許他們獲得居英權並在英工作？

劉曉明：根據中國國籍法，所有香港中國同胞，不論是否持有「英國屬土公民護照」或「英國國民（海外）護照」（BNO），都是中國公民，中國不承認雙重國籍。關於二〇一九年香港特別行政區區議會選舉，我們當然希望選舉正常進行，但這將由香港特區政府來決定。我們希望香港局勢能迅速穩定，港人能不受滋擾地去投票點投票，選舉地方議員。這是我們的期望。

BBC：你播放的短片讓我們看到一個令人震驚、充斥暴力行為的香港，我們在英國電視以及社交媒體上也

看到過類似的畫面，但你的視頻裏沒有香港警方針對這些暴行使用武力執法的畫面。

劉曉明：你是指警方應對暴力而採取的執法措施嗎？

BBC：我說的不僅是警方，也包括一些不明身份的人員，比如「白衣人」，他們今年夏天襲擊地鐵站的行人。換句話說，雙方都有暴力行為。我只是想知道，你是否承認雙方都實施了暴力？在某種意義上說，示威者的暴力是「以暴力還擊暴力」。我的第二個問題是，二〇〇八年，北京舉辦奧運會時，多數香港人認為自己是中國人，他們表現出了很高的自豪感，後來比例大幅下降，現在很少人承認自己是中國人，越來越多的人認為自己是香港人。你是否擔心中國會失去七百萬港人的信任？

劉曉明：首先，我們反對任何形式的暴力。其次，你應該弄清這些暴力背後的原因，如果不知道暴力的起因，就無法應對。香港的暴力起源於極端分子的行徑，他們應該受到法律的嚴懲。毫無疑問，其他違法犯罪者也應被繩之以法。法治是一個城市的基礎。關於香港居民身份認同，我不認為失去了一代人，這些暴力分子並不能代表香港年青一代。一些青年學生不明真相，我們有責任與他們交流，幫助他們了解祖國，了解香港回歸後的發展進步。我們應該幫助他們把今天的香港和二十二年前的香港做比較。回歸前的香港沒有自由、沒有民主、沒有權利，港督都是英國政府任命的。但現在香港能夠定期選舉特首。我們的制度並不完美，就像我說過的，世界上最大的空間就是不斷改進的空間。但我們是開放的，我們堅定不移地努力工作，為的就是使香港更美麗、更安全、更民主。

如果沒有新的提問，今天的記者會到此結束，感謝大家出席。

「法者，治之端也」
——關於香港維護國家安全法中外記者會
（二〇二〇年七月六日，中國駐英國大使館）

劉曉明：大家上午好！歡迎大家出席今天的中外記者會。

六月三十日，在香港回歸二十三週年之際，中國全國人大常委會通過《中華人民共和國香港特別行政區維護國家安全法》，並將該法列入香港基本法附件三，由香港特別行政區在當地公佈實施。香港國安法的實施，為「一國兩制」行穩致遠提供了強大支撐，為香港居民的權利和自由提供了堅實保障，堪稱「一國兩制」實踐進程中的重要里程碑，具有重大現實意義和深遠歷史意義。

香港國安法通過後，英國媒體做了大量報道和評論。但坦率地講，其中充斥著誤讀、誤解甚至歪曲。

今天，我舉行中外記者會，就是希望幫助英國各界全面、客觀、準確地認識和理解香港國安法。針對英國媒體的報道和評論，我想著重回答五個問題：

第一，為什麼要出台香港國安法？維護國家安全是香港繁榮穩定的基礎和前提。基本法第二十三條，授權香港特區就維護國家安全自行立法。但二十三年來，由於反中亂港勢力勾連阻撓，相關立法遲遲未能完成，導致香港在維護國家安全方面法律制度空白，執行機制缺失，長期處於「不設防」狀態。去年六月香港「修例風波」發生以來，反中亂港勢力公然鼓吹「港獨」「自決」，打砸搶燒，暴力襲警，衝擊香港立法會，叫囂「武裝建國」，嚴重踐踏香港法治，嚴重

破壞社會穩定，重創香港經濟，嚴重危害國家安全。香港民眾痛心疾首，迫切希望香港轉危為安、變亂為治、絕境重生。在此形勢下，國安法從國家層面立法建立健全香港維護國家安全的法律制度和執行機制，得人心、順民意，勢在必行、刻不容緩。

第二，香港國安法是否違反「一國兩制」？該法不僅完全符合「一國兩制」方針，並將保障「一國兩制」行穩致遠。香港國安法開宗明義指出，堅定不移並全面準確貫徹「一國兩制」、「港人治港」、高度自治方針。「一國兩制」是一個完整概念，「一國」是「兩制」的前提，「兩制」從屬和派生於「一國」。只有「一國」安全，「兩制」才有保障。何為「一國」，它既體現在中國對香港恢復行使主權，也體現在中央政府對香港擁有全面管治權。維護國家安全歷來是各國中央事權。中國中央政府通過《基本法》第二十三條授權香港特區維護國家安全的部分立法權，並不改變國家安全立法是中央事權的屬性，也不影響中央政府繼續建構維護國家安全的法律制度和執行機制。香港出現了挑戰和破壞「一國兩制」的活動，香港國安法正是為了捍衛「一國」權威，最終是為了堅持和完善「一國兩制」，而不是要改變「一國兩制」。

第三，香港國安法是否破壞香港高度自治和香港居民權利自由？該法充分體現了中央全面管治權和香港特區高度自治權的統一，不改變香港實行的資本主義制度，不改變香港高度自治和特區法律制度，不影響特區行政管理權、立法權、獨立的司法權和終審權。該法明確規定，香港特區維護國家安全應當尊重和保障人權，依法保護香港特區居民根據《基本法》和《公民權利和政治權利國際公約》《經濟、社會及文化權利國際公約》適用於香港的有關規定享有的言論、新聞、出版、結社、集會、遊行、示威等權利和自由。該法規管的是分裂國家、顛覆國家政權、組織實施恐怖活動、勾結外國或者境外勢力危害國家安全四類罪行，懲治的是極少數犯罪分子，保護的是絕大多數民眾。正因為如此，短短八天，近三百萬香港民眾簽名支持國安法，充分體現出求穩定、保安全的主流民意。

第四，香港國安法是否違反中方國際義務？今年是聯合國成立七十五週年，中國是第一個簽署《聯合

國憲章》的國家，參加了一百多個政府間國際組織，簽署了五百多個多邊條約。中國始終致力於維護國際法和國際關係基本準則，認真履行自身承擔的國際責任和義務。中國從未「退群」「毀約」，從不謀求本國利益優先。「不履行國際義務」的帽子扣不到中國頭上。英方將《中英聯合聲明》與「一國兩制」混為一談，指責中方未履行國際義務，這完全是錯誤的。「一國兩制」的版權屬於鄧小平先生，中國政府治理香港的法律依據是中國憲法和香港《基本法》，絕非《中英聯合聲明》。中國政府關於「一國兩制」的方針政策，已充分體現在《基本法》中，並得到全面貫徹。因此，根本不存在所謂香港國安法違反中方國際義務問題。

第五，究竟誰在違反國際義務、踐踏國際關係準則？主權平等、不干涉內政是國際法和國際關係的基本準則。中國從不干涉別國內政，包括英國內政，也希望英方不要干涉中國內政。英方應當十分清楚，香港已經不是英國殖民統治下的香港，香港早已回歸中國，是中國的一部分。英國對回歸後的香港無主權、無治權、無監督權。然而，英國政府仍不停地發表所謂《香港問題半年報告》，對香港事務說三道四，現在又對香港國安法指手畫腳，甚至聲稱將改變對香港「英國國民（海外）護照」（BNO）持有者的安排。這是對中國內政的粗暴干涉，是對國際關係基本準則的公然踐踏，中方對此表示強烈不滿和堅決反對，並已就此向英方提出嚴正交涉。我想強調指出的是，香港是中國的香港，香港事務是中國內政，任何外國無權干涉。香港國安法的一項重要任務就是防範、制止和懲治勾結外國或境外勢力危害香港國家安全的行為。任何人都不要低估中國捍衛國家主權、安全發展利益的堅定決心，任何干擾和阻撓香港國安法實施的企圖都必將遭到十四億中國人民的堅決反對，都注定失敗！

「法者，治之端也。」香港國安法是香港恢復秩序、由亂到治的治本之策。我們堅信，在中國中央政府的堅強領導下，在包括廣大香港同胞在內的全體中國人民的共同努力下，在香港國安法的有力保障下，香港一定會更加安全、更加美好、更加繁榮！

謝謝！下面，我願回答各位的提問。

中國國際電視台：英方稱，將為持有英國國民（海外）護照（BNO）的香港居民提供更多居留權限，中方表示將保留採取相應措施的權利。你能否談一談中國是否將就此採取具體措施以及何時宣佈？英國首相約翰遜表示，自己是喜愛中國的，但香港國安法明顯嚴重違反《中英聯合聲明》。你認為如何避免英中關係進一步惡化？

劉曉明：我在開場白裏已經回答了你的問題。關於BNO以及中方要採取的具體舉措，你應該先問英國政府下一步要幹什麼。我剛才講過，中英之間以及任何國家之間的關係必須建立在國際法和國際關係基本準則之上。國際法的基本原則是主權平等，互不干涉內政。這一原則已被寫入《聯合國憲章》，並在四十多年前被納入中英建立大使級外交關係的聯合公報，是中英關係的基本準則。

七十年前，英國政府宣佈承認中華人民共和國。七十年來，中英關係雖有起伏，但總體保持發展。實踐證明，只要上述基本準則得到遵守，中英關係就向前發展，甚至是跨越式發展；反之，兩國關係就遭遇挫折，甚至出現倒退。

BBC：香港國安法第三十八條規定，該法還適用於非香港居民和身處香港以外的人。根據國際法的通行做法，域外法權一般只適用於最嚴重的犯罪，國安法該條規定將如何與國際法保持一致？在香港的記者、活動分子以及其他相關人士將如何在繼續堅持言論和新聞自由的同時，確保自己免於被起訴？

劉曉明：你提到的第三十八條是國際通行做法。即便根據英國法律，犯了罪和侵犯了英國國家利益的人都應被追究責任。如果他們的行為威脅英國國家安全，無論行為是發生在英國國內，還是國外，都應被追責。香港國家安全法在香港維護國家安全，沒有超出國際通行做法。

你提到記者的工作。香港國安法規定得很明確，列出了危害國家安全的四種犯罪行為。記者們只要遵守法律，就沒什麼可擔心的，就可以正常開展工作。

國安法還規定，香港居民和在香港生活工作的所有人的人權都將得到充分尊重和保障，這些權利包括新聞自由和言論自由。因此，只要你守法，就無須擔心。

天空新聞台：英國政府正在研究是否在 5G 網絡系統中使用華為，有傳言稱他們會推翻此前的決定，禁止在英國的 5G 網絡中使用華為。這將對英中關係產生怎樣的影響？你提到中國不干涉英國的內政，但有人不這麼認為，他們認為中國正採取顛覆性措施，試圖影響英國政商學界，以擴大中國的影響、推進中國的利益。對此你如何回應？

劉曉明：我反對任何關於中國干涉英國內政的說法。我出使英國已超過十年，從未遇到過英國政府或機構指責中國政府干涉英國內政的情況。如果你有證據，請拿出來。但請不要製造有關中國的假消息並進行無端指責。

正如我在開場白中所說，中國一貫、全面遵守國際法和國際關係基本準則。我已就華為問題多次表態、撰文和發表演講。一言以蔽之，華為是中英合作雙贏的範例。我認為，英國使用華為，不是為了中國，而是基於英國自身的利益。英國政府已經制訂雄心勃勃的計劃，要在二〇二五年實現 5G 全覆蓋。華為可以為此做出貢獻。但如果英國願意高價購買質量不如華為的產品，這是英國自己的決定。我們要爭取最好的結果，同時也要做最壞的準備。

華為在一百七十個國家開展業務，沒有一個國家能證明華為安裝了後門。華為很透明，他們建立了完全由外國人、而非華為人員運營的安全評估中心，這證明他們很有信心。除了華為，世界上還有哪家公司建立了由東道國運營、專門檢測公司自己產品的中心？沒有。華為沒什麼好怕的，用不用華為是你們自己的決定。英語有句成語：「當一扇門關上時，另一扇門會打開。」我們中國也有一句俗語：「西方不亮東方亮。」近來，我聽到不少有關華為的噪聲，但我們不怕。我對在英中資企業說，你們應該保持信心。一旦你有拳頭產品，你就不應該擔心沒有市場。世界足夠大，足以讓華為發展。我相信，華為能帶來雙

贏，不僅有利於華為，也有利於英國。我們已盡己所能講述華為的故事，但最終決定要由英國政府來做。我們不能替英國政府做決定。確實有很多猜測，我們已為可能的結果做好準備。我相信，華為不僅能生存下來，而且會日益發展壯大。越是面臨來自所謂超級大國及其盟友的壓力，華為就越變得強大。我對此堅信不疑。

彭博社：還是關於華為的問題，英國政府即將做出的決定，很明顯出於安全關切，而非你所說的商業考慮。眾所周知，美國對華為也存在嚴重安全關切，而你說中方不認為存在安全問題，也不擔心英方會在政治層面做出相關決定。

劉曉明：最終決定要由英方來做。關於安全問題，我認為華為已經盡其所能，回應各方關切。談到安全問題，要看是出於政治角度還是技術角度。安全有很多種，例如在通信方面，我們的技術是否足夠安全可靠，能夠保護我們免受來自某些國家或黑客或公司的攻擊。不要片面談安全問題。華為為解決安全問題和關切採取了所有必要措施，不斷改進他們的技術。英國情報機構的分析報告也顯示，華為的安全風險是可控的，華為的技術總體上是安全的，這也是為什麼英國政府雖然設定了百分之三十五的市場份額上限，仍然決定允許華為參與5G。現在是否要決定放棄華為，這取決於英方自己。正如我所說，世界很大，足夠讓華為發展。目前華為已在一百七十個國家運營，一個國家放棄華為，還有一百六十九個國家。我一直鼓勵華為人，要向前看。首先你要努力向英國政府、商界和人民證明，你擁有最先進的技術和最具競爭力的價格，堅持不斷改進，解決大家的關切，做行業的領軍者。但如果他們不選擇你，那是他們的決定，你們還要繼續發展。華為歷經種種阻礙仍不斷進步，我對他們充滿信心。

你提到安全問題，我也正想談談這一點。一些英國政客一提到華為，就炒作中英關係。他們中的一些人將中國視為威脅，甚至是敵對國家，這是完全錯誤的，這與兩國領導人達成的共識不符。很多人談及中

英關係「黃金時代」，但他們對到底什麼是「黃金時代」毫無概念。事實上，「黃金時代」是英國領導人首先提出的，我們認為這符合兩國的共同利益，就同意將其作為中英關係的定位。如果英方放棄「黃金時代」、將中國視為敵人，這就大錯特錯了，也不符合英方自身利益。美國戰略家布熱津斯基曾說，如果你把中國當作敵人，那麼中國就可能真的成為敵人。中國希望成為英國的朋友、夥伴，但如果你們把中國當作敵人，就要承擔由此產生的後果。

《泰晤士報》：中方會採取措施阻止擁有英國國民（海外）護照（BNO）的香港人接受英方的安排來英居留嗎？

劉曉明：最近我們聽到很多關於英方改變 BNO 立場的說法。一九八四年，中英雙方通過交換備忘錄達成一致，英方明確承諾不會給予持有 BNO 護照的香港中國公民在英居留權。但英方執意單方面改變這一立場，中方視之為違反國際法和國際關係準則，將保留做出進一步反應的權利。首先，中方堅決譴責英方此舉，因為它違背了英方自身承諾；其次，中方認為這是對中國內政的干涉，是針對香港維護國家安全法的政治操弄；最後，中方將視英方具體實際行動，決定將採取何種反制措施。

《經濟學家》：能否請你介紹一下英方在香港問題上的相關立場將帶來什麼樣的後果？例如，在華經營的英國企業和英中貿易是否會面臨這些後果？將涉及哪些行業？英國銀行和服務消費行業的英國公司在華經營是否會面臨風險？

劉曉明：正如我在開場白中所說，國家間的關係應建立在一些基本原則之上，包括相互尊重主權和領土完整、互不干涉內政、尊重彼此核心利益和重大關切等。上述原則也得到中英兩國領導人的認可。疫情期間，習近平主席和約翰遜首相兩次通電話，重申了有關基本原則。但是，一旦這些原則被違背，必將帶來相應後果，雙方的互信將受損，信心將遭到削弱。至

於具體在哪些領域帶來哪些後果，我們還要看。中方切實希望英方從維護中英雙方根本利益出發，停止錯誤做法。我們要好好把握中英關係根本利益的大局。

新華社：最近一項調查發現，英國超越美國，成為中國學生「首選留學目的地」。若中英關係因政治分歧而進一步惡化，中國對學生來英留學的態度和政策會改變嗎？

劉曉明：包括留學生交流合作在內的中英正常關係將會繼續發展。我看到了有關報道，由於美國的一些原因，轉到英國學習的中國學生正在增多。我們歡迎並鼓勵更多中國學生到英國留學。駐英國使館教育處一直非常忙碌，向中國學生提供信息，回答他們的各類諮詢，幫助他們與英國的大學建立聯繫。目前，我還未看到對中英教育合作的負面影響。目前，中國有二十多萬留學生在英學習。疫情期間，我給英國一百五十四所有中國留學生的大學校長寫信，除了要求他們照顧好中國留學生，我也重申中方致力於發展同英國各大學的合作關係。

路透社：當前，英國一些人正重新審視對華為政策。英國政府表示將提出關於外國收購和兼併法案，外界認為這是針對中國公司的。你之前提到英中關係「黃金時代」。在中方看來，英中關係「黃金時代」是否已經終結？如果沒有終結，英方怎麼做才能推動「黃金時代」向前發展？

劉曉明：中英關係「黃金時代」最早是由英方提出，隨後中英雙方均予以認可。我希望「黃金時代」沒有終結。但是，是否終結並非取決於中方。在中英合作抗擊新冠肺炎疫情期間，英國領導人表示致力於推動兩國關係「黃金時代」。我常說，「一個巴掌拍不響」，國家間的關係需要雙方去呵護。因此，我衷心希望中英關係能夠健康穩定發展，造福兩國人民。這需要中英雙方共同努力。中方視英國為夥伴，我們希望與英國發展良好關係。我們從來不會用「潛在的敵對國家」這樣的說法來形容英國，不論是中國領導

人，還是政府官員從來未用過這種說法。因此，我真誠提醒英國領導人和政府官員，希望他們談到中英關係的性質時，務必謹言慎行。

《衛報》：大使先生，你說香港國安法得到香港社會廣泛歡迎，近三百萬香港民眾簽名支持國安法。但在去年的香港區議會選舉中，我們看到「泛民」成績不俗。你能否保證，今年秋天香港立法會選舉也能如往年一樣保護參選和競選的自由？

劉曉明：對於去年以來香港發生的事情，我們有不同解讀。你們認為那是支持民主。我們認為那是暴亂、違法行為，甚至是恐怖主義行徑。如果有人衝擊英國議會，相信你不會稱之為支持民主。過去幾週，英國街頭舉行了大量遊行示威活動，但我沒見哪家英國媒體說這是支持民主，你們把一些遊行示威人員稱作違法分子和暴亂分子。那麼，為什麼提到香港時，你們的評判標準就變了呢？這是赤裸裸的雙重標準！今年九月香港立法會選舉將依法舉行。關於香港國安法，我想強調，該法會依法實施。香港國安法充分體現了中央全面管治權和香港特區高度自治權的統一，不改變香港實行的資本主義制度，不改變香港高度自治和特區司法制度，不影響特區行政管理權、立法權、獨立的司法權和終審權。香港居民的權利自由將得到良好保障。只要不觸犯香港國安法，一切都不會改變。你應該對香港抱有信心。

《每日電訊報》：劉大使早上好！如果英國繼續推行其給予香港英國國民（海外）護照（BNO）持有者來英計劃，中方將採取哪些報復舉措？你能告知英方具體安排嗎？另一個問題，英國通信管理局（Ofcom）今天或將嚴厲批評中國國際電視台此前播放英國人韓飛龍（Peter Humphrey）被迫認罪的有關視頻，你對此有何評論？

劉曉明：我已回答過關於英國國民（海外）護照（BNO）的問題。我的回答還是一樣，中方已向英方表明立場，我們希望英方重新考慮其立場。至於中方

將如何應對，我們將視英方採取的措施而定。

關於中國國際電視台的問題，中國國際電視台已批駁了韓飛龍的指控，韓的指控毫無事實根據。我認為中國國際電視台已經非常清楚地表明了立場。

美國全國廣播公司：非常感謝大使先生。你剛才講，新的香港國安法與已執行幾十年的「一國兩制」政策不衝突。但「一國兩制」在很大程度上保障了香港的政治和言論自由。今天早上有報道稱，香港公共圖書館下架了部分香港活動人士撰寫的書籍，一些活動人士被拘留，你們稱其為暴徒和恐怖分子。我的問題是，香港國安法的頒佈是否意味著香港幾十年來享有的言論自由的終結？

劉曉明：完全不是。香港民眾的言論和新聞自由將得到充分保障。你提到一些書在香港公共圖書館下架，這完全取決於書的內容。如果一本書的目的是煽動分裂和顛覆，按照香港國安法就可能被視為犯罪，建議你仔細閱讀香港國安法。英國有很多涉及國家安全的法律，如果有人發表支持恐怖主義和仇恨的言論，將被視為犯罪行為。為什麼英國可以有這樣的法律，而中國卻不能有自己的國家安全法來懲罰煽動分裂國家、顛覆國家政權、危害國家安全的人？為保護國家安全而制定法律是各國的普遍做法。至於香港言論自由和新聞自由，我認為，香港國安法將保障絕大多數香港人的新聞、遊行、示威等權利和自由。但任何人都不能做破壞國家安全的事情，不能從事香港國安法規管的四類犯罪行為。權利和自由都是有邊界的。儘管《公民權利和政治權利國際公約》保護言論自由等權利，但這些權利也是受限制的。公約明確規定，行使這些權利不能破壞國家安全和公共秩序。我建議你仔細閱讀有關公民權利的國際公約。因此，只要香港民眾遵守國安法、不觸碰國安法底線，他們將享受充分的自由，完全不用擔心權利和自由問題。英美部分媒體危言聳聽，妖魔化香港國安法的行徑是完全錯誤的。他們並未仔細閱讀香港國安法。該法詳細規定了四種犯罪行為，只要不觸碰法律底線，在憲法、基本法和有關國際公約所規定的範圍內行使權利，就不會

有任何問題。

《金融時報》：很多在中國內地和香港經營的英國企業對香港國安法表示擔心，如果企業拒絕香港警察查看或使用其數據和系統將會有什麼後果？

劉曉明：香港警方將依法執行香港國安法。香港國安法寫得很明確，包括香港警察、國安相關工作人員在內的執法人員，都要遵守香港法律，執法部門將依法行事。

今日俄羅斯電視台：約翰遜政府正打算給幾百萬香港人居英權，幫助他們逃離中國法律管轄。為什麼英國認為香港是前殖民地，可以給予居英權，卻不肯給其他前殖民地人民同樣的權利呢？例如伊拉克遭受了非法戰爭，成千上萬人逃離了伊拉克。

劉曉明：首先，一些英國政客抱守很強的殖民心態。他們不願意相信香港已經不是英國殖民統治下的香港，無視香港已經在二十三年前就回歸中國的事實。正因為如此，他們總是「好事」，仍把香港看成是英國的一部分，對香港事務指手畫腳、大肆干涉。但他們徹底錯了，香港早已是中國的一部分。其次，他們沒有意識到香港的穩定和繁榮不僅符合中國的利益，也符合英國的利益。英國有三十多萬公民在港生活，有七百多家企業在港經營。香港有近三百萬人署名支持香港國安法，其中就包括滙豐、太古、怡和、渣打等英國企業。但他們卻遭到了一些英國政客的批評。這些政客又錯了，因為沒有和平的環境，英國公民和企業根本無法正常生活和經營。去年的「修例風波」已經說明了這一點，在「黑色恐怖」籠罩下，人們甚至都不敢上街，因此民眾呼籲盡快止暴制亂。在這一背景下，香港國安法的誕生將幫助香港恢復穩定和繁榮。

英國電視四台：謝謝劉大使。我能否回到關於華為的問題？如果英國把華為排除在其5G建設之外，會面臨什麼樣的後果？你認為這是敵對行為嗎？

劉曉明：可能面臨多種後果。第一，這會損害英國

標榜的開放、宜商、自由、透明的形象。中國的工商界人士認為，英國的營商環境良好，適合在這裏做生意。這也是為什麼過去五年中國對英投資超過此前三十年投資總和的原因。但是一旦英國將華為剔除，就會發出非常錯誤的信號。這會損害英國堅持自由貿易的形象。第二，這會損害英國獨立自主的國家形象。這意味著英國屈從外國壓力，不能堅持獨立自主的外交政策。我經常說，只有擁有獨立自主的外交政策，「不列顛」才能成為「大不列顛」。如果沒有獨立自主的外交政策，隨他國起舞，大不列顛之「大」又該如何體現呢？第三，我認為這也會向在英中國企業發出非常負面的信號。他們都在看英國如何對待華為。禁止華為將不僅向其他中國企業，也將向其他外國企業釋放負面信號。第四，這關係到基本的信任問題。國與國關係必須建立在相互尊重、相互信任的基礎上。中國有句俗話叫「朝令夕改」。如果你變來變去，別人怎麼信任你？因此，這關係到信任問題。我希望英國政府做出不僅有利於中英合作，而且符合其自身利益的決定。

《中國日報》：謝謝大使。有人認為，香港國安法也將有助於保護英國投資及其在香港的合法權益。大使先生，你對此有何看法？

劉曉明：確實是這樣。我想我在此前的講話和問答中已經回答了你的問題。做生意需要穩定與和平的環境。這就是為什麼香港國安法會受到歡迎，它不僅受到非常關注自身安全的普通民眾的歡迎，也受到包括英國企業和許多其他國家企業在內的工商界的歡迎。近期美國商會有一份報告稱，美國商會對香港有信心。這是因為香港國安法可以為各國工商界保障良好的營商環境。因此，我希望包括英國媒體在內的英國公眾能夠客觀、正確和準確地看待香港國安法，不要試圖妖魔化這部法律。國安法將為香港的安全與繁榮提供保障和保護。正如我在開場白中所說，在香港國安法的有力保障下，香港將成為一個更加安全、更加美好、更加繁榮的地方。

謝謝大家出席今天的中外記者會。

第三章 南海問題

二〇一六年五月二十日，我在倫敦國際戰略研究所就南海問題發表題為《中國是維護南海和平穩定的中堅力量》的主旨演講，並就如何看待美軍機對中國抵近偵察活動、美亞太再平衡戰略對地區局勢影響、中美在亞太地區如何管控分歧、中國對南海仲裁案裁決結果的立場等回答了現場聽眾提問。英國政界、工商界，英美學術界以及俄羅斯、美國、法國、巴西、澳大利亞、印尼、新加坡、文萊、日本、加拿大、波蘭、以色列、土耳其、塞浦路斯等國駐英使節和外交官一百多人出席。路透社、BBC、《泰晤士報》、《每日電訊報》、《經濟學家》、天空新聞台、獨立電視台等英國主流媒體，中國中央電視台、《人民日報》、新華社等駐英央媒及主要華文媒體對演講進行報道。

倫敦國際戰略研究所是國際著名智庫，成立於一九五八年十一月，主要從事國際戰略、國防安全和防務政策研究，每年出版《全球軍力平衡報告》《戰略研究》等重要刊物。許多國家的政要及戰略界知名人士曾在該所發表演講。該所每年與新加坡、巴林政府分別合作舉辦「香格里拉對話會」和「麥納麥對話會」，在國際問題研究領域具有重要影響。

七月十九日，我在駐英使館就南海仲裁庭裁決結果舉行中外記者會，闡述中國政府對南海仲裁庭裁決結果的嚴正立場。指出裁決結果是無效的，沒有拘束力，中國不接受、不承認任何基於該仲裁裁決的主張和行動。中國堅定致力於維護南海和平穩定，致力於同直接有關的當事國在尊重歷史事實的基礎上，根據國際法，通過談判協商和平解決有關爭議。二十三家中外媒體近四十名記者出席。

七月二十五日，我在英國皇家國際問題研究所（簡稱「皇研所」）就南海問題發表題為《浮雲難遮望眼，正道總是滄桑》的主旨演講，闡述中方對南海仲裁案的立場和中國在南海問題上的政策主張。英國政界、工商界、學術界、外交界及中外主流媒體三百多人出席。演講後，我回答了聽眾關於美國大選對中美關係的影響、南海仲裁案的性質、南海斷續線的法律地位、「南海各方行為準則」談

判、中國島礁建設、南海資源開發、仲裁案對中國與鄰國關係的影響、中日釣魚島爭端、中國外交走向等提問。

皇研所成立於一九二〇年，是英國規模最大、歷史最悠久的國際問題研究機構之一，擁有高水平的研究隊伍，主要從事國際戰略、國際關係和外交政策研究，在英國和世界國際關係學界享有較高聲譽，會員超過三千人。皇研所與英國政府、企業、媒體和學術界聯繫密切，對英國外交政策具有一定影響。該所主要刊物有《國際事務》《今日世界》等。

中國是維護南海和平穩定的中堅力量

——在倫敦國際戰略研究所發表演講並回答提問

（二〇一六年五月二十日，倫敦國際戰略研究所）

二〇一六年五月二十日，我在倫敦國際戰略研究所發表題為《中國是維護南海和平穩定的中堅力量》的主旨演講並回答聽眾的提問。演講和答問實錄如下：

劉曉明：很高興時隔三年之後再次應邀來到倫敦國際戰略研究所。三年前，我應齊普曼所長的邀請在這裏就「新時期的中國外交」發表過一次演講。今天，我要講的主題還是中國外交，不過這次集中談一個問題，這就是南海問題。

南海問題的熱度最近幾個月來不斷升溫，很多人在關注南海問題，很多媒體也在炒作南海問題，但對於南海問題的真實情況人們卻往往不甚清楚，有時甚至存在誤解。因此我特意選倫敦國際戰略研究所這樣一個研究國際政治和安全問題的知名智庫，來闡述中國對南海問題的立場和政策，並回答大家的提問。希望通過今天的交流，讓各位對南海問題能有一個比較全面和準確的了解。

首先我還是要從中國與南海的歷史淵源說起。我們要想客觀、公正、理性地看待南海問題，就要追本溯源，從源頭上弄清事情的本來面貌。

南海諸島自古以來就是中國領土，之所以強調「自古以來」，是因為南海諸島屬於中國這一歷史事實源遠流長，可以用四個「最早」來概括：

一是最早發現：一些國家宣稱南海島礁是「無主地」，企圖以所謂「先佔原則」據為己有。事實上，

早在公元前二世紀的漢代，中國就已經有了大規模、頻繁的遠洋航海及漁業捕撈活動，南海自古就是中國重要的海上航路，當時的中國人頻繁航行於南海地區，最早發現了南海諸島。著名南海問題學者馬文·塞繆爾斯在二十世紀八十年代的著作《南海爭端》中明確提出：「是南海和南海上的島礁幫助中國人在地理上形成了對世界秩序的認識。」

二是最早命名：現在西方人多用 SPRATLY 群島稱呼中國的南沙群島，這緣於一八四三年英國船長 Richard Spratly 所謂「發現」並「命名」了南沙群島。而事實是，兩千多年前，中國人就已經開始認識南海，並在各種歷史文獻中將這片海域稱為「漲海」，把海中的島、礁、灘、沙稱為「崎頭」。後來歷朝歷代均出現了專指西沙、南沙群島及其具體島嶼的古地名。明清時期形成的航海指南《更路簿》，更是詳細記載了包括南沙群島在內的南海諸島數十處地名，不少沿用至今並被各國航海家廣泛承認和採用。

三是最早實施行政管轄：自一千二百多年前的唐代開始，中國歷代政府就不斷通過行政設治、水師巡視、資源開發管理等方式對南海諸島進行有效管轄。到公元十世紀的宋代，地方誌明確記載南海諸島屬瓊州也就是現在的中國海南省管轄。公元一二七九年，元代著名天文學家郭守敬曾到南海開展測量活動並建立天文觀測據點。明清兩代也均將南海納入水師巡防範圍。

四是最早開發利用：中國人民長期以來一直在南海諸島及海域從事捕撈、種植和其他生產活動，許多島礁上都曾留下中國漁民生產生活的遺跡。英國海軍部測繪局一八六八年編制的《中國海指南》一書中就明確記錄了南沙群島僅有中國人生產、生活的事實。

以上四個「最早」均有充分史實作為支撐，這說明中國在歷史上早已將南海諸島併入中國版圖並持續和平有效行使管轄。事實上，直到二十世紀七十年代之前，南海諸島屬於中國是國際社會普遍認知。舉兩個典型的例子：一八八三年，德國曾派軍艦到西沙、南沙群島附近進行測量，清朝廣東地方政府以主權為依據提出抗議，德國被迫停止測量活動並撤走；一九五八年，中國政府發表關於領海的聲明，並宣佈

聲明中的規定適用於包括西沙、南沙等南海諸島在內的所有中國領土，時任越南政府總理范文同就此專門照會時任中國國務院總理周恩來，明確承認西沙和南沙群島屬於中國。類似這樣的例子還有很多。

既然南海諸島屬於中國是無可爭辯的歷史事實，那麼南海爭端又是怎樣產生的？

從二十世紀七十年代開始，一些南海周邊國家由於覬覦南海的豐富自然資源，開始對中國南沙島礁提出領土要求。越南、菲律賓等國先後派兵非法侵佔了南沙部分島礁，南海問題就此產生。迄今為止，越南共侵佔二十九個島礁，菲律賓共侵佔八個島礁，馬來西亞共侵佔五個島礁。

進入八十年代以來，《聯合國海洋法公約》經過九年的談判於一九八二年簽署。隨著現代海洋法制度的發展，各國又逐步提出了專屬經濟區和大陸架等海洋權益主張，這些主張覆蓋的範圍有部分重疊，從而又產生了海域劃界的問題，這就使得問題進一步複雜化。

由此可見，南海爭端的根源：一是一些國家非法侵佔中國南沙群島部分島礁而產生的領土爭議；二是一些國家提出的海洋管轄權主張重疊而產生的海域劃界爭議。這兩方面原因相互交織，使南海問題異常複雜。但無論從哪方面原因看，中國都不是挑起事端的一方，恰恰相反，中國是南海爭端的受害方。

那麼，中國對南海問題的立場和政策是什麼？

面對一些國家的侵權挑釁行為，中國始終保持克制和忍讓，以建設性態度負責任地處理南海爭端。事實上，如果不是中方長期保持克制態度，南海地區的局勢早已不是今天的樣子。中方在南海問題上的態度和立場，主要體現在五個「堅持」上：

一是堅持維護南海的和平穩定。中國是地區和平穩定的堅定捍衛者和維護者，始終奉行「與鄰為善、以鄰為伴」的周邊外交政策。這既是因為中國人民血液中流淌著的愛好和平的基因，也是中國自身利益和發展的現實需要。三十年來，中國在和平穩定的環境中實現了人類歷史上從未有過的高速度、大規模工業化。中國的發展得益於和平穩定的國際和周邊環境，中國當然不希望南海生亂，也決不允許南海生亂。

二是堅持當事國通過友好談判協商和平解決爭議。世界上領土問題的最終解決，無論經過哪些機制和過程，最後都要由當事方通過平等談判達成協議，才能獲得根本、長久的解決。談判協商最能體現國家主權平等原則，最能體現當事方的意願，是最行之有效的解決爭端方式。新中國成立以來，中國與十四個陸地鄰國中的十二個簽訂了邊界條約，劃定和勘定的邊界長度達兩萬餘公里。這些鄰國中絕大多數都是中小國家，從來沒有哪一國說過中國在談判中以大欺小，以強凌弱。這些都是中國與當事國通過直接談判協商解決問題的範例，解決南海問題同樣也不例外。實踐證明，有關各方只有通過談判協商，才能不斷增進互信、管控危機、縮小分歧、促進合作。處理南海問題，必須堅持談判協商這一現實有效途徑。

三是堅持通過規則機制管控分歧。中國和東盟國家二〇〇二年簽署《南海各方行為宣言》，二〇一三年啟動「南海行為準則」磋商。「準則」磋商啟動以來，已經取得了積極進展。中國與東盟國家還積極推動建立「海上緊急事態外交熱線」和「海上聯合搜救熱線」。各方同意積極探討制定「海上風險管控預防性措施」，從而在「準則」最終達成前有效管控海上局勢，防止不測事件發生。事實證明，地區國家間通過規則機制管控分歧的努力是有效的。

四是堅持維護南海航行和飛越自由。中國作為南海最大的沿岸國，每年有大量的能源和海上貨物貿易運輸經過南海，沒有哪個國家比中國更關心南海地區的航行和飛越自由。近一段時間，航行自由成了熱門話題，一些人大談所謂保護航行自由，彷彿在該地區的航行安全遇到什麼問題。但事實是，每年有十萬多艘船隻經過南海地區，從未聽說有哪艘船隻抱怨過航行自由受到過任何影響。如果南海存在威脅海上航行的風險，通常會導致航運保費瞬間上漲。但是這樣的情況並沒有發生。據今年初英國路透社報道，沒有跡象顯示南海地區商業航運受到了任何影響。報道還稱，英國知名保險機構「勞合社聯合戰爭險委員會」（Lloyd's Joint War Committee）並未將南海列入高風險地區，保險公司也不會向通過該地區的船隻多收保費。常識告訴我們，商人特別是保險商們對風險的

嗅覺是最靈敏的，連他們都沒有察覺出南海航行自由受到了威脅，我不知道一些人所聲稱要「保護」的是什麼樣的航行自由？

近來，個別國家打著「行使航行和飛越自由」的旗號，不斷在南海炫耀武力，派遣軍用艦機抵近中國南沙群島有關島礁鄰近海空域進行挑釁，製造緊張局勢，威脅中國主權和安全。就在十天前，美國「勞倫斯號」驅逐艦未經中國政府許可，非法進入中國南沙群島有關島礁鄰近海域。這些行為所要維護的恐怕不是航行自由，而是憑藉力量優勢行使海上霸權的「橫行自由」，這才是南海地區和平穩定以及真正航行自由的最大威脅。我要奉勸這些國家，如果它們真的關心航行和飛越自由，就應遵守國際法，尊重沿岸國主權、安全和相關權益。

看美國的行為，要看其對待國際法的態度。如果美國認真致力於國際海洋法，那麼早就應該簽署包括中國在內的廣大國際社會均已簽署的《聯合國海洋法公約》。尊重國際法，和平談判解決爭端，對於維護南海和平穩定至關重要。藉航行自由之名，行軍事挑釁和威脅之實，是極其危險的行為，它直接擾亂地區的和平穩定。

五是堅持通過合作實現互利共贏。中國一貫致力於發展與周邊各國的友好合作關係，主動提出了「擱置爭議，共同開發」，這為解決南海爭議提供了有益思路，也充分考慮到各方的實際利益。根據這一思路，中國與有關各方相繼開展了一系列合作。例如：中、菲、越三國石油公司於二〇〇五年簽署《在南海協議區三方聯合海洋地震工作協議》，推動共同開發南海地區的油氣資源；二〇一一年，中國宣佈設立總額三十億元人民幣的中國—東盟海上合作基金，支持海上務實合作項目；近兩年，中國又提出以東盟國家為樞紐建設「二十一世紀海上絲綢之路」戰略構想，進一步深化海上務實合作。這些倡議和措施充分展示了中方開展合作的努力和誠意，受到周邊國家的普遍歡迎。

從上述五個「堅持」可以看出，中國是在真心實意地尋找南海問題的解決辦法，從而促進南海地區的和平穩定和周邊國家的共同發展。

剛才我向大家介紹了中國與南海的淵源以及中國對南海問題的基本政策，現在我想就當前幾個南海熱點問題談一些看法。

第一個問題是菲律賓仲裁案。菲律賓單方面提起南海仲裁一事最近鬧得沸沸揚揚。我想首先說一說接受菲律賓仲裁請求的仲裁庭。一些媒體報道對該仲裁庭的性質缺乏清晰的認識。其中最關鍵的一點在於，該仲裁庭只是一個非常設的仲裁機構，與真正意義上的「法庭」有著本質區別。此外，就仲裁機制而言，只有當爭議雙方自願達成一致，仲裁程序才能啟動。但中國自始至終都已明確表達了不參與、不接受的立場。

一些媒體和政客伺機炒作，稱中國必須接受仲裁，否則就是「不遵守國際法」，就是「破壞基於規則的國際體系」，這種說法是完全錯誤的。中國拒絕接受和參與仲裁，是在行使國際法賦予的合法權利。與此相反，菲律賓方面的做法則是在挑戰國際社會的法律和道德底線，既不合情，也不合理，更不合法。

說它不合情，是因為菲律賓破壞了它對中國和其他東盟國家做出的莊嚴承諾。中菲兩國早在一系列雙邊文件中就通過雙邊談判解決爭端達成協議。包括菲律賓在內的東盟各國和中國所共同簽訂的《南海各方行為宣言》中也明確規定，要通過當事國和平談判解決爭議。菲律賓在二〇一一年還與中國發表共同聲明，承諾堅持通過談判協商解決問題，一年後就突然變卦，在事先未告知中方，更未徵得中方同意的情況下單方面提起仲裁。國際關係中有一條成文的規則：「約定必須遵守」，這是每個國家自立於國際社會所必須嚴守的道德底線。中國有一個成語：「出爾反爾」，用來形容菲律賓的所作所為再合適不過。

說它不合理，是因為菲律賓拿到仲裁庭上要求裁決的島礁都是我前面所說中國自古以來的固有領土。這就好比鄰居搶走了你家的東西，然後就堂而皇之地要求法院把東西判給他。敢問世間哪有這樣的道理？英國個別政客總是在強調「基於規則的國際秩序」，請問如果每個國家都如此行事，何談規則？何談國際秩序？

說它不合法，原因更明顯。一則，《聯合國海洋

法公約》明文規定：締約國享有自主選擇爭端解決方式的權利。菲律賓未經中國同意單方面強行仲裁，侵犯了中國的這一合法權利。二則，《公約》規定：締約國如果已協議自行選擇和平方法解決爭端，則只有在這種方法未得到解決以及爭端各方之間的協議並不排除其他程序的情況下，才適用第三方爭端解決程序。而中方對雙邊談判的態度在任何時候都是開放的，中菲之間還遠未窮盡雙邊手段。三則，《公約》還規定，如果締約國之間對本公約的解釋或適用發生爭端，應迅速就以談判或其他和平方法解決爭端一事交換意見。而菲律賓從未就此與中國進行過任何協商。中菲兩國同為《公約》締約國，但菲律賓單方面提起仲裁的做法明顯違背了上述《公約》規定，是明目張膽的違法行為。

與菲律賓的所作所為相比，中國才是在真正踐行和維護國際法。菲方所提十五項仲裁訴求涉及領土主權和海洋劃界，主權問題不屬於《公約》的調整範圍；至於海洋劃界問題，中國早在二〇〇六年就依據《公約》第二九八條有關規定做出排除性聲明，將有關海洋劃界等爭端排除在《公約》強制爭端解決機制之外。中方的行為是在行使《公約》賦予的合法權利，完全符合國際法規定。

我還要指出的是，做出了類似排除性聲明的除了中國之外還有三十多個國家，其中也包括英國。這些聲明構成了《公約》不可分割的組成部分，這些國家合理合法的關切和訴求也應該得到重視。如果南海仲裁案形成了慣例，那就意味著只要有人願意，上述任何一個國家都可能在毫不知情的情況下被拉入仲裁。這將對各國主權、國際秩序和國際法的尊嚴和權威造成嚴重打擊。媒體稱仲裁案的結果即將公佈，但中方對仲裁堅持不參與、不接受、不承認、不執行，並不是因為擔心所謂不利結果，而是為了堅守國際法治的底線。

讓我們擔憂的是，對上面所列舉的有關仲裁案的種種不合情、不合理、不合法之處，仲裁庭心知肚明，卻仍然堅持按照菲律賓的要求強推仲裁程序，這不能不讓人質疑其公正性、合法性，對其背後的政治目的提高警惕。仲裁案實質上是一起披著法律外衣的

政治鬧劇，無論其結果如何，中方都不會接受。

儘管不接受仲裁，但中國與菲律賓之間直接談判解決問題的大門依然是敞開的。兩國畢竟是近鄰，兩國人民之間也有傳統友誼。我們注意到菲律賓近期舉行了大選，希望新一屆菲政府能與中方共同努力，妥善處理分歧，使南海局勢重回以《公約》和國際法為主導的正常軌道。

第二個問題是中國的島礁建設。近年來，中國在南沙群島幾個島礁上開展了建設活動。中方的建設除了為改善駐島人員的生產生活條件之外，主要目的是為各類民事需求服務，以便向本國、本地區乃至國際社會提供必要和急需的公共產品。中方在島礁建設中安排了很多公益設施，包括大型綜合燈塔、海上安全通信設施、海上應急救撈設施、綜合性醫療設施等，從而更好地履行中國在海上搜救、防災減災、海洋科研、氣象觀察、生態環境保護、航行安全、漁業生產服務等方面承擔的國際責任和義務。同時，中國也根據所處的安全環境，在自己的島礁上部署了必要的防禦設施，這是在行使國際法賦予主權國家的自保權。據英國路透社報道，一些東南亞船東認為，中國在南海的活動有利於海域的安全，中國在南海島嶼部署援救力量，會縮短營救時間，增加營救機會。剛才我提到，南海地區的航行安全與自由對國際貿易意義重大，我想任何秉持公正立場的人都能看到，中國在南海的島礁建設，將使這條國際經濟大動脈更加安全。

有人說，中國的島礁建設太大，規模太快。我想說，規模和速度從來不是評判對錯的標準。中方建設活動的規模、速度與其在南海承擔的國際責任和義務相匹配。中國不能因為自己塊頭大，就自縛手腳，不做正確的事。

也有人說，中國的島礁建設是改變現狀。我想問，所謂「現狀」是什麼？中國的島礁建設完全是在自己領土上進行的，根本不存在所謂「改變現狀」的問題。我還想問，當一些國家非法侵佔中國島礁，並在這些非法侵佔的島礁上大興土木的時候，那些大喊不要改變現狀的人跑到哪裏去了？

第三個問題是所謂南海「軍事化」。近來，外界關於南海「軍事化」問題的炒作不絕於耳，其中美國

的聲音叫得最兇。事實上，只要認真觀察一下事實，就能看出到底是誰在南海搞「軍事化」。美國將一半以上的軍力部署在本來和平穩定的亞太地區，拉幫結派，不斷開展針對性極強的軍事演習，頻繁派遣軍用艦機到中國島礁鄰近海空域炫耀武力。正是美國的這些挑釁和敵對行動，加劇了南海緊張局勢，同時也助長了菲律賓等國家在非法侵佔的島礁上大肆部署軍事設施。由此可見，美國才是南海「軍事化」的最大推手。我們希望美方作為負責任的大國，在南海這一複雜敏感問題上謹言慎行，與中方相向而行。因此，要解決南海「軍事化」問題，美國首先要停止損害中國主權和安全的危險挑釁行動，其次要停止惡意炒作和渲染南海「軍事化」問題，再次要嚴格遵守國際法，最後要以實際行動做一些有利於南海地區和平穩定的事。

女士們、先生們，南海問題儘管複雜敏感，但在中國和周邊國家的共同努力下，南海地區局勢一直保持穩定。隨著中國國力的增強，我們將會為維護南海地區的安定與繁榮做出更大貢獻。正如習近平主席所說，中國將通過和平、發展、合作、共贏的方式推進海洋強國建設。中國的成就得益於和平發展道路，我們絕不會捨棄這一寶貴財富。展望未來，我們有信心也有能力通過友好談判協商解決爭議，通過合作共同維護好南海的和平穩定，我們願與各國共同攜手，把南海真正建設成「和平之海、友誼之海、合作之海」。

謝謝！下面我願回答大家的提問。

畢馬威會計師事務所：我想請你再澄清一點，你剛才提到美國軍艦經過中國島礁臨近區域是非法的。但根據《聯合國海洋法公約》規定的「無害通過權」條款，外國船舶享有無害通過他國領海的權利。

劉曉明：我認為美國軍艦抵近中國有關島礁臨近海域的做法是在濫用「無害通過權」。美方沒有尊重中國的主權，沒有事先通知中方，也未尋求獲得中方的許可。因此美方的做法是違反國際法和國際慣例的。

倫敦政治經濟學院：非常感謝你的演講。你剛才在

演講中提到中美之間存在一定的緊張關係。在我看來，中國與菲律賓、中國與越南之間的緊張關係都是可控的，但中美關係並非如此。從國際體系演變角度看，美國作為現行國際體系的守成力量一直試圖維持現狀，不少美國官員和研究報告則認為中國將取代美國。你如何看中美管理這種「權力轉移」過程？雙方能否確保這一轉移過程是和平與穩定的？

劉曉明：正如我在演講開始時所說，在南海問題上，中國並不是麻煩製造者，而是受害者。相信我已對此進行了清楚解釋。在美國實施所謂亞太再平衡戰略之前，整個南海地區局勢是穩定的。中國與包括菲律賓、越南在內的周邊鄰國進行雙邊談判，我們與東盟國家也在穩步落實《南海各方行為宣言》，有效管控分歧。南海爭議已經存在三十多年，但整個地區保持了穩定局面。然而，自從美國在二〇〇九年實施亞太再平衡戰略以來，南海形勢出現變化。一些地區國家受到了慫恿，認為有美國為其撐腰打氣。例如，菲律賓改變了對南海問題的立場，頒佈了所謂「領海基線法案」，越南也改變立場。菲方甚至拒絕與中方談判，並單方面提出涉南海仲裁案。解決主權爭議的方法有很多，根據《聯合國海洋法公約》，國際仲裁只是輔助途徑。解決主權爭議問題的最主要途徑是當事國進行和平協商談判。菲方捨本逐末，拒絕與中國和平協商談判，單方面挑起所謂國際仲裁，就是因為有美國為其撐腰。

關於中美關係，中方歷來致力於建設良好的中美關係。這是毋庸置疑的。我的外交生涯中有一半多的時間參與對美關係，兩次在中國駐美使館工作，深知中美關係的重要性。中方認為，如果中美關係出現問題，亞太地區將難以實現穩定與繁榮。我們一貫主張積極發展中美關係，推動雙方密切合作。目前中美副外長級安全對話正在華盛頓舉行。中美之間有很多對話與溝通渠道，但重要的是，美方應從根本上改變那種認為中國有朝一日要取代美國成為全球領導者的思維定式。這並不是中國追求的目標。我們追求的是實現中華民族偉大復興的中國夢。作為一個擁有十三億多人口的大國，我們對前進道路上的挑戰有清醒認

識。我出使埃及之後，曾在中國西部的省份之一甘肅省擔任省長助理，我知道中國的一些貧窮地區有多窮，我也深刻體會到中國發展任務之艱巨、挑戰之巨大。中國不願意看到中美交惡，對當超級大國不感興趣。英國曾當過超級大國，當超級大國是有代價的。而我們中國現在的首要任務是實現自身的發展、提高本國人民的生活水平。

倫敦國際戰略研究所：昨天美國五角大樓對外表示，中國派遣兩架戰機對美EP-3偵察機進行了「不安全」攔截。我想請問你，這也屬於美方的敵對行為嗎？

劉曉明：我認為，美方行為十分危險。美國打著「航行自由」的旗號，挑戰中國對南海諸島的主權，這種做法十分危險。我們都知道，海洋那麼寬闊，足夠軍用艦機自由通行，但美方卻偏偏選擇對中國抵近偵察，企圖挑戰中國的國防能力，這種行為十分危險。至於你提到的具體事件，中國外交部發言人已對此闡明了立場。中國有充足的理由維護國家主權，中國軍機有權查明美國軍機想幹什麼，但我們始終保持安全距離，有關操作符合專業和安全標準。中方努力避免發生意外，特別是避免發生衝突。但如果美方一意孤行，將會陷入危險境地。

BBC：兩個問題。劉大使，你在演講中批評仲裁庭，我也曾聽到中方官員表示中方不會接受仲裁結果。你剛才的意思是不是也是這樣，即不管結果如何，中方都不會接受仲裁判決？

另外一個相關的問題是，你好像將仲裁庭判決和主權問題聯繫到了一起。據我所知，仲裁內容是南沙海域部分島礁的地位問題，和主權並無關係。你一直說，中國數百年來在南海海域開發利用，那麼仲裁庭的判決一定會對中方有利，為什麼中方仍拒絕接受仲裁案和仲裁庭判決？

劉曉明：讓我來告訴你為什麼。仲裁庭從一開始就是非法的，一個非法的仲裁庭怎麼能判出好的結果?!中方對仲裁庭不承擔任何義務。我們始終認為，仲裁案

本身即違反了《聯合國海洋法公約》和國際法。

BBC：中方不承擔哪些義務？

劉曉明：中方對仲裁案不承擔任何義務。我可以明確地告訴你，不論仲裁結果如何，都不會影響中方對南海島礁的主權，仲裁案判決結果對中方不具任何約束力。關於仲裁內容，我說過，這就好比鄰居搶走了你家的東西，然後堂而皇之地拿到法官面前，要求法官進行判決。不管判決對象是物品所有權，還是物品性質，只要法官受理，都與所有權密不可分。菲律賓曾向仲裁庭提出了十五項仲裁申請，其中八項遭到了拒絕，原因就是這些仲裁申請明顯違背了《公約》，仲裁庭不希望捲入其中。雖然菲律賓變換手法，對仲裁案進行包裝，給它披上合法的外衣，但這不能改變問題的實質。仲裁案始終與主權問題和海洋劃界問題密切相關，超出了仲裁庭的管轄範圍，違反了《公約》的規定。仲裁庭的設立本身即違反了《公約》規定，是不合法、不合理的。中國堅持不接受仲裁的立場恰恰是為了遵守國際法，恰恰是為了維護國際法的權威。

倫敦政治經濟學院：你如何看待美國對南海地區經濟影響。安全方面，美國國防部部長卡特等人在南海問題上不斷提高調門，步步緊逼。但在經濟方面，美國雖達成了跨太平洋夥伴關係協定，但美國能否在大選前後簽署該協定還是個未知數。中國同東南亞開展了卓有成效的合作，經濟領域尤其如此，你認為美國總統大選結果是否會影響中國同東南亞的經濟合作態勢？

劉曉明：我們一直密切關注美國總統大選情況。當然，沒有人能夠預測大選結果。不論美國人民選擇了誰，不論白宮橢圓形辦公室的新主人是誰，我們都願意並準備與之打交道。與競選期間的言論相比，我們更注重其上台後的所作所為。我希望，美國新一屆政府能以中美關係大局為重。中方願與美方新領導人一道，共同推動中美關係發展。

因克斯特主任（主持人）：劉大使，非常感謝。我們已經超時了，今天的活動只能到此為止。請允許我分享一點體會。近來，倫敦國際戰略研究所的人普遍有一種感受，就是中國的國際戰略影響越來越大，研究所很大一部分精力放在研究中國上。我們還發現，研究所的系列研究報告三分之一以中國為題。所有這些都十分說明問題。最後，讓我們再一次以熱烈的掌聲感謝劉大使內容詳細、全面的演講。

中國不接受、不承認南海仲裁庭裁決結果

——關於南海仲裁庭裁決結果的中外記者會

（二〇一六年七月十九日，中國駐英國大使館）

劉曉明：各位記者，大家上午好。

歡迎出席中國駐英國大使館舉辦的中外記者會。今天的記者會只有一個主題，就是解讀中國對所謂南海仲裁庭裁決結果的政策立場。

七月十二日，菲律賓南海仲裁庭公佈了所謂裁決結果，中國政府第一時間重申了不接受、不承認的嚴正立場。中國國家主席習近平強調，南海諸島自古以來就是中國領土。中國在南海的領土主權和海洋權益在任何情況下不受所謂菲律賓南海仲裁案裁決的影響。中國不接受任何基於該仲裁裁決的主張和行動。中國堅定致力於維護南海和平穩定，致力於同直接有關的當事國在尊重歷史事實的基礎上，根據國際法，通過談判協商和平解決有關爭議。

為進一步宣示中國的政策主張，中國政府發表了《中華人民共和國政府關於在南海的領土主權和海洋權益的聲明》，中國外交部發表了《中華人民共和國外交部關於應菲律賓共和國請求建立的南海仲裁案仲裁庭所作裁決的聲明》，中國國務院新聞辦發表了《中國堅持通過談判解決中國與菲律賓在南海的有關爭議》的白皮書。國務委員楊潔篪接受專訪，外交部部長王毅發表談話，外交部副部長劉振民介紹情況，對聲明和白皮書進行深入解讀。上述聲明和白皮書全面、清晰、權威地闡述了中國的政策主張。在此，我願向各位做簡要介紹。

《中華人民共和國政府關於在南海的領土主權和海洋權益的聲明》重點是重申中國在南海的領土主權和海洋權益，強調中國最早發現、命名和開發利用南海諸島及相關海域，最早並持續、和平、有效地對南海諸島及相關海域行使主權和管轄，明確指出中國在南海的領土主權和海洋權益包括中國對南海諸島擁有主權；中國南海諸島擁有內水、領海、毗連區、專屬經濟區和大陸架；中國在南海擁有歷史性權利。強調中國一向堅決反對一些國家對中國南沙群島部分島礁的非法侵佔及在中國相關管轄海域的侵權行為。同時指出中國願繼續與直接有關當事國通過談判協商和平解決爭議，共同維護南海和平穩定，維護南海國際航運通道的安全和暢通。

《中華人民共和國外交部關於應菲律賓共和國請求建立的南海仲裁案仲裁庭所作裁決的聲明》重點指出菲律賓提起仲裁事項超出《聯合國海洋法公約》管轄範圍，侵犯中國作為《公約》締約國享有的自主選擇爭端解決程序和方式的權利，違反中菲兩國以及中國與東盟國家通過談判解決南海有關爭議的協議與承諾，揭露仲裁庭擴權、越權、濫用仲裁程序的本質，強調該裁決是無效的，沒有拘束力，中國不接受、不承認。

《中國堅持通過談判解決中國與菲律賓在南海的有關爭議》的白皮書，全面闡述中國對南海諸島主權的歷史形成過程以及中國維護在南海的領土主權和海洋權益的努力，展現中菲南海爭議來龍去脈，溯本清源，以正視聽。同時重申中方堅持通過談判協商解決爭議，強調只有談判取得的成果才更容易獲得當事國人民的理解和支持，才能夠得到有效實施，才具有持久生命力。正如楊潔篪國務委員在接受媒體專訪時指出的，只要中菲都堅持《南海各方行為宣言》的原則和精神，通過對話協商妥善處理分歧，堅持互利友好合作，就一定能為兩國關係開闢美好未來。

為了便於各位記者全面深入了解中方主張，我們準備了中方聲明、白皮書、專訪和談話的中英文版本，歡迎大家會後領取。

下面我願意回答各位的提問。

《中國日報》：我們注意到，習近平主席表示中國致力於通過直接談判解決有關爭議，但他同時表示，中國在南海的領土主權和海洋權益在任何情況下不受所謂菲律賓南海仲裁案裁決的影響。請問，中國願在哪些領域開展談判？

劉曉明：習主席闡述的是中國一貫的政策立場。在南海問題上，中方的立場是明確的、一貫的。我們對包括南沙群島在內的南海諸島擁有主權，同時我們也注意到存在爭議，因此我們主張將爭議擱置起來，著手共同開發。中方有十二個字：「主權在我，擱置爭議，共同開發。」中國不會就主權問題進行談判，但我們意識到爭議的存在，始終堅持通過談判協商和平解決爭議。

新華社：我的問題是關於英國外交部前副法律顧問霍默斯雷發表的一份法律研究報告。他在報告中指出，仲裁庭的觀點「不能令人信服」，仲裁庭的裁決「將撼動國際關係的整體穩定」，因為該裁決允許菲律賓放棄其在正式法律文件，如《南海各方行為宣言》中的立場。你能談談對霍默斯雷觀點的看法嗎？你認為他的觀點正確嗎？

劉曉明：我同意這個觀點。中方堅決反對仲裁庭的裁決，該裁決開了一個「惡例」。有人認為裁決書是廢紙一張，也有人認為應當束之高閣。我是學國際法的，我看這份判決只能作為國際法教學的反面教材，作為「惡例」收錄到歷史書裏。這份裁決在多個方面違反了國際法。首先，它違反了《公約》的宗旨。《公約》旨在維護國際海洋和國家間關係的和平與穩定。但仲裁庭不但背離《公約》的宗旨，還加劇了國家間的緊張關係。仲裁庭不僅否定了談判解決的外交渠道，而且否定了《南海各方行為宣言》的法律地位，而《南海各方行為宣言》是中國和東盟十國達成的一份莊嚴的官方文件。因此這份裁決根本不能達到和平解決爭議的目的。相反，它給相關國家間的緊張關係火上澆油，給地區形勢火上澆油。正如我在開場白中所說，中方不承認、不接受裁決，裁決沒有拘束

力。沒有一個國家會把這份裁決當真，任何國家都不應在所謂裁決的基礎上提出新的主張。裁決是非法的，沒有任何法律地位。如果有人在裁決基礎上提出新的主張，這將導致新的違法行為，將進一步損害地區和平與穩定。

普羅派樂衛視：我來自普羅派樂衛視。你認為，菲律賓新一屆政府是否暗示中菲關係將轉圜？

劉曉明：我們當然期望如此。杜特爾特總統就職後，我們聽到了一些積極的表態，比如他希望中菲雙邊關係保持友好，希望中菲能通過雙邊談判解決有關爭議等。事實上，這也是我們多年來一直努力的方向。因此中方從一開始就強烈反對這個強加的仲裁。我們認為仲裁無助於問題的解決，只有談判才是解決問題的唯一出路。我們願意同菲律賓新一屆政府開展合作，也期待菲律賓新政府能夠採取進一步的行動。中國有句老話叫作「聽其言，觀其行」。我們希望通過對話協商妥善處理分歧，使兩國關係回到正確的軌道上。中菲兩國作為隔海相望的近鄰，有著上千年友好交往歷史，我們深信這些爭議不應影響兩國保持友好關係，也希望杜特爾特總統領導的新一屆政府為中菲關係帶來新的氣象。

《金融時報》：我希望能請你解釋一個關於仲裁庭的問題。據我所知，中方反對該仲裁庭主要有兩項理由：第一，仲裁應由當事國雙方同意後才能提出；第二，仲裁庭對菲律賓提出的仲裁事項沒有管轄權。但是《公約》有兩項條款似乎與中方上述立場相悖。一是《公約》第二八六條指出，事關《公約》的解釋或適用問題可由任意爭端一方提出仲裁，無須雙方共同提出。二是《公約》第二八八條指出，仲裁庭自己有權決定是否有管轄權。請問中方對此有何看法？

劉曉明：關於《聯合國海洋法公約》第二八八條和二八六條，中方有不同解讀。中方反對仲裁庭的理由不僅限於你提到的兩項。我希望你能認真研讀《中華人民共和國政府關於在南海的領土主權和海洋權益的

聲明》《中華人民共和國外交部關於應菲律賓共和國請求建立的南海仲裁案仲裁庭所作裁決的聲明》《中國堅持通過談判解決中國與菲律賓在南海的有關爭議》白皮書。我認為菲律賓南海仲裁案至少從八個方面違反了國際法。

第一，它違反了《聯合國海洋法公約》對領土主權爭端沒有管轄權的規定。儘管南海仲裁案被菲律賓精心包裝成一個關於解釋公約的技術性案件，但其實質是關於領土主權爭端。從仲裁庭的裁決過程和結果看，任何人都能得出結論，此案事關中國在南海領土主權。

第二，它違反了中國做出的排除性聲明。中國早已聲明將有關海洋劃界、歷史性海灣和歷史性權利、軍事和執法等活動排除出《公約》強制爭端解決程序，其他三十多個國家也做出了類似聲明。這些排除性聲明被視為是《公約》不可分割的一部分，而仲裁庭裁決顯然與海洋劃界有關。這一裁決證明仲裁庭肆意擴權，侵犯了中國根據排除性聲明所享有的合法權益。《公約》締約國之所以做出排除性聲明，是因為預見到各國有可能就海洋劃界問題產生爭端。如果此類聲明被拒絕，將會構成不良先例，造成嚴重後果。今天是中國，試問明天會是哪個國家？

第三，它違背了中國與菲律賓達成的雙邊協議。菲律賓已與中國就如何通過外交談判解決爭端達成了一系列協議，包括雙邊簽署的文件、宣言和協議。

第四，它違背了中國與東盟國家簽署的《南海各方行為宣言》。該宣言是國際法的一部分，各方承諾通過友好磋商和談判，維護南海地區和平穩定。宣言的作用十分重要，一直為中國和東盟國家所尊重並遵守。

第五，仲裁旨在否定中國對南海有關島礁的主權，否定中國包括斷續線在內的歷史性權利，挑戰了《聯合國憲章》關於維護國家主權、獨立和領土完整的基本準則，因此嚴重違反了國際法。

第六，仲裁庭曲解《公約》第二八六條，非法受理菲律賓單方提出的仲裁案，卻否定了中國作為《公約》締約國自主選擇爭端解決方式的權利。

第七，仲裁庭對《公約》斷章取義，破壞了《公

約》的完整性和嚴肅性，樹立了「壞典型」。

第八，仲裁背離了《公約》促進爭端和平解決的初衷。相反，它加劇了地區局勢緊張。

回到你剛才所提的兩個條款。仲裁庭雖然可以自行對管轄權做出解釋，但並不意味著它可以不顧事實亂做解釋。南海仲裁案仲裁庭只看到《公約》賦予的權利，卻看不到應當履行的義務，包括對《公約》管轄權的尊重，對中國就海洋劃界所做排除性聲明的尊重，對中國主張通過雙邊外交談判解決爭議的立場及為之做出努力的尊重，對中國與東盟十國達成的《南海各方行為宣言》的尊重，等等。所以，在管轄權問題上，仲裁庭沒有絕對權力，更沒有不履行《公約》規定義務的權力。

《人民日報》：我有兩個問題。第一個問題是，仲裁案對中菲關係有何影響？今後中菲關係將如何發展？第二個問題是，就我們所知，過去許多個世紀，甚至在過去數十年，南海是非常和平、安寧的海域。但如今南海局勢越來越複雜，成為越來越受關注的熱點。你認為其原因是什麼？

劉曉明：首先，仲裁結果不會對中國在南海的領土主權和海洋權益產生任何影響，也沒有任何拘束力，它是非法的，不能作為未來談判的基礎。如果菲律賓同意我們的意見，我想我們可以很快恢復雙邊談判。如果菲律賓將裁決作為談判的基礎，那是行不通的。

我希望地區國家站在中國的一邊。已經有一些國家表示支持中國的立場，一些國家對裁決所產生的後果表示擔憂。怎樣做最符合中國和東盟國家的利益？怎樣做最有利於該地區的和平與穩定？我希望中國和東盟國家能夠達成共識。我們注意到菲律賓新政府的一些積極表態，但還不清楚他們就裁決結果持什麼立場。可以明確的是，我們不會執行這個裁決。希望有關方面不要藉所謂仲裁結果採取進一步的非法行動，使本已緊張的局勢進一步升級。那是我們所不想看到的。

關於第二個問題，在二十世紀七十年代前，沒有人對中國南海主權提出挑戰。斷續線受到普遍承認，

美國、英國、法國、蘇聯和許多其他國家印製的官方地圖都標明了斷續線。隨著七十年代南海發現了石油和天然氣，一些地區國家趁機非法侵佔南海島礁。我們就這些非法侵佔問題向有關國家提出了強烈抗議。但不幸的是，當時中國正在進行「文化大革命」，因為內亂，中國無暇顧及維護對這些島嶼的主權。

最近幾年南海發生的事和美國所謂的亞太再平衡戰略有關。儘管我們和菲律賓、越南、馬來西亞等一些鄰國之間存在一些問題，但我們之間仍然保持著雙邊溝通的渠道。中國和越南完成了北部灣海上劃界。我們與包括菲律賓在內的地區國家簽署三方聯合海洋地震工作協議。但美國所謂的亞太再平衡戰略提出後，這些項目中斷了。有美國撐腰，這些國家更大膽地向中國提出挑戰。現在美國不再滿足於幕後操縱，而是跳到台前，派出戰艦和飛機到中國南沙群島有關島礁鄰近海空域抵近偵察，挑戰中國的主權。這些行為造成了局勢緊張。我們希望南海消除緊張局勢，希望和美國在內的有關國家一道努力，使南海成為和平之海、合作之海、友誼之海。這是中國國家領導人一再強調和重申的，是中國對該地區和平與穩定的承諾。

中國國際廣播電台：海牙仲裁庭是《公約》框架下設的法律機構。中國宣稱「不接受」「不承認」該仲裁庭裁決，你做何解釋？中國「不接受」「不承認」仲裁庭裁決，究竟意味著什麼？是否意味著中國將不會就此做出任何反應？

劉曉明：首先，我要糾正一下這個仲裁庭的性質。該仲裁庭不是國際法院的一部分，與聯合國沒有關係，甚至也與常設仲裁法院（PCA）關係不大。該仲裁庭是應菲律賓政府請求為本次仲裁案臨時組建的，據我所知，它與常設仲裁法院唯一的關係，就是使用了後者的場地，並且借用了其秘書處的一些人員，僅此而已。它的法律基礎十分薄弱。

我願進一步介紹一下這個仲裁庭的組成。這個仲裁庭由五名仲裁員組成，除了菲律賓自己指定的仲裁員外，其他四名仲裁員都是由國際海洋法法庭時任庭

長、日本籍法官柳井俊二指定的，此人曾任日本駐美國大使。我對其政治動機非常懷疑。他是日本首相安倍晉三的政策顧問，在協助安倍修改和平憲法、解禁集體自衛權、挑戰「二戰」後國際秩序等方面起了很大作用。我認為本次仲裁案為他再次挑戰戰後國際秩序提供了新的機會。

中國擁有南海諸島主權的歷史可追溯至兩千多年前。日本在「二戰」期間曾非法侵佔中國南海諸島。「二戰」結束後，日本根據《開羅宣言》和《波茨坦公告》的規定，將其歸還中國。如果任由該仲裁庭否定《南海各方行為宣言》，這將鼓勵其他南海國家爭相效仿，並引發一系列類似事件。或許終有一天，他們會宣佈《開羅宣言》和《波茨坦公告》也沒有法律依據。我不知道屆時事態將如何演變。

根據《開羅宣言》，日本必須歸還所竊取的所有中國領土和島嶼，其中包括南海諸島。事實上，當年中國政府的軍隊正是乘坐美國軍艦收復了南海諸島。仲裁庭此次試圖將中國南沙群島太平島定性為「岩礁」而不是「島」，暴露出其提起仲裁的目的是企圖否定中國對南沙群島的主權及相關海洋權益，這是違反國際法的、完全不能接受的，受到了台灣海峽兩岸中國同胞的一致強烈譴責。

中國不參與南海仲裁，是因為從第一天起，我們就堅信這是一場政治鬧劇。只要你對仲裁庭的組成及其仲裁背後的政治動機有所了解，就會立即判斷出其結果會是什麼。我們清楚這場鬧劇不會有任何結果，自然也沒有興趣參與其中。仲裁庭的裁決沒有法律拘束力，中國決不會接受該仲裁裁決，並且希望其他國家不會執行所謂的裁決。你怎麼能指望如此毫無公信力、不具合法性的仲裁庭，能做出有公信力的裁決？如果該裁決得到執行，勢將對地區形勢造成進一步破壞。

《每日電訊報》：許多不是南海爭端當事方的人士指出，中國是在有選擇性地遵守國際法。中國聲稱將和平崛起，中國既然能遵守其他領域的國際法，是否在南海問題上也應遵守國際法？有觀點認為是美國鼓勵菲律賓提出南海仲裁案，你如何看待美國在南海爭端

中扮演的角色？

劉曉明：我不同意你關於中國有選擇性地遵守國際法的看法。中方立場有堅實的法律基礎。正如我剛才談到，南海仲裁庭在八個方面違反了國際法。而中國完全遵守《公約》規定。中國堅定遵守雙邊達成的協議，包括中菲之間曾達成的協議。中國同樣致力於遵守與東盟國家達成的《南海各方行為宣言》。中國嚴格遵守國際法，依照國際法行事。國際法的基礎之一是《聯合國憲章》，中國作為聯合國安理會常任理事國，肩負維護憲章的重要責任。這是毫無疑問的。

關於美國，我認為應給美國在南海問題上的所作所為畫上一個「大問號」。首先，美國迄未批准《公約》，不斷違反《公約》的條款，但卻自詡為所謂的《公約》「守護者」。如果美國真的如此熱愛《公約》，為什麼不立即批准《公約》？這是因為美國擔心《公約》可能會妨礙他們所謂「航行和飛越自由」。美國要的是完全不受國際法限制為所欲為的權利。其次，南海仲裁案完全是政治操縱的產物。這是美國戰略的一部分。一方面，美國不斷派軍艦和軍機抵近中國領土；另一方面，美國希望利用針對中國的南海仲裁案，藉此在外交上侮辱中國，損害中國的國際形象，並為挑戰中國主權尋找法律基礎。但美國的上述圖謀是注定會失敗的，因為其所作所為從一開始就沒有法律基礎，而南海仲裁案已完全演變成為一場政治鬧劇。迄今為止，我們沒有聽到多少國家支持仲裁庭的裁決，與此相反，已有七十多個國家、二百九十個政黨和組織表達了支持中國通過外交談判解決爭端的立場。我們希望仲裁案結束後，常識和理性終將佔據上風，相關沿岸國能夠重返談判桌，接受中國提出的「擱置爭議，共同開發」倡議，進行認真嚴肅的外交談判。這樣做符合有關各方的共同利益。中國希望美方能切實尊重中方的關切和權利。美國在亞太地區有利益，但是不能為維護自身利益而損害他國的正當合法權益。中國和鄰國在南海地區是命運共同體。中國最不希望看到南海地區動盪。南海是重要的國際航運通道，中國將繼續確保該地區的和平穩定，並維護航行及飛越自由。

《歐洲時報》：有人認為南海爭端是中國歷史性權利與美國基於規則的國際秩序觀之間的衝突。你如何看待這個問題？你認為爭端是否將長期化？你提到談判是解決爭端的唯一途徑。中方是否已經開始這方面的準備？

劉曉明：首先回答你的第一個問題，我們談歷史性權利，這是中方在長期歷史過程中形成的。有人稱，中方已經拋棄了「韜光養晦」的戰略，不再單純關注經濟發展，正在謀求更多權利。這種看法是不正確的。我們捍衛的是中方自古以來擁有的領土主權。斷續線是一九四八年中國政府正式公佈的，並且得到國際社會的承認，不是創設新的權利。直到南海地區發現了資源才引發一些國家競相侵佔中國的島礁。中國過去沒有，現在和將來也不會尋求屬於自己的領土主權以外的東西。正如我在接受路透社採訪中指出的，別人的領土，我們一寸都不要。我們對別人的領土不感興趣，也不羨慕，但我們珍視、捍衛自己的領土。中國曾經失去太多領土，當時中國積貧積弱，遭受外強入侵，被迫接受割地賠款等不平等條約。所以，捍衛國家主權權益是中國與生俱來的基因決定的。我們希望國際社會能尊重中國擁有的歷史性權利。

二十世紀七十年代以前，美國是承認中方歷史性權利的，許多歷史、法律和國際法文件均對此予以確認。但是，現在情況變了。他們有新的盟友，新的利益。我曾在《世界郵報》撰文談到，「超級大國歷來是來了又走，走了又來」。應當知道，鄰國比超級大國更重要。鄰國無法選擇，必須相處。

中國無意挑戰美國的地位，但也不能接受不平等的國際秩序。中國尊重現有國際秩序，中國也是這一秩序的受益者。中國多次重申願與國際社會合作，共同維護戰後國際秩序。我們無意改變現有秩序，無意「重起爐灶」。但今天世界發生了很大變化，需要與時俱進，需要改革過時的國際秩序，特別是要適應發展中國家的需求。中國也是發展中國家的一員。

習近平主席指出，寬廣的太平洋有足夠空間容納中美兩個大國。我們希望中美攜手合作，而不是走向對抗。我們希望美國認識到中國無意挑戰其地位。我

們承認，美國雖然不是域內國家，但在地區擁有經濟和安全利益。我們尊重美國的利益，也希望美國尊重中國的利益。中美兩個太平洋大國可以攜手合作，共同維護地區和平與穩定。

謝謝各位出席今天的記者會。我們下次再見。

浮雲難遮望眼，正道總是滄桑

——在英國皇家國際問題研究所發表主旨演講並回答提問

（二〇一六年七月二十五日，英國皇家國際問題研究所）

劉曉明：很高興再次來到皇家國際問題研究所。這是我擔任中國駐英國大使以來第五次到訪皇研所。

聽說近來皇研所最熱的議題是「英國脫歐」，我沒想到今天會有這麼多人來聽我的演講，這說明南海問題確實很重要，我通過皇研所這個講壇介紹中國對南海問題的政策主張也確實很必要。

關於南海問題，最近最突出的事件就是菲律賓南海仲裁案。所謂仲裁庭裁決結果一出台，中方在第一時間發佈了《中華人民共和國政府關於在南海的領土主權和海洋權益的聲明》《中華人民共和國外交部關於應菲律賓共和國請求建立的南海仲裁案仲裁庭所作裁決的聲明》以及《中國堅持通過談判解決中國與菲律賓在南海的有關爭議》的白皮書，中國領導人和多位政府高官也分別發表談話、接受採訪，重申中國在南海的領土主權和海洋權益，揭露仲裁庭擴權、越權、濫用仲裁程序的本質，闡明中方對非法裁決結果不接受、不承認的嚴正立場。

今天，我願向大家面對面地進一步闡述為什麼中方堅持認為仲裁庭的裁決結果是非法的、無效的。我們認為：

第一，仲裁庭對有關事項沒有管轄權。菲律賓前政府單方面提起仲裁的有關事項，其背後的本質和真正目的都指向領土主權和海洋劃界問題，領土主權問題不在《聯合國海洋法公約》的調整範圍內，海洋劃

界問題也早已被中國根據《公約》第二九八條規定而作的排除性聲明所排除。因此仲裁庭首先是在自身無權管轄的領域隨意擴權、濫權，又何談此後會程序公正和實體公正？

第二，仲裁程序與《公約》規定相違背。在《公約》設計的爭端解決機制中，締約國通過雙邊渠道解決爭議應予以優先適用，只有窮盡雙邊渠道仍未得到解決時才適用第三方解決機制。中菲之間早已選擇通過談判協商解決爭端，兩國也根本沒有就菲律賓所提的仲裁事項進行過雙邊溝通，仲裁庭何以認定雙邊渠道已經用盡？在訴諸仲裁所需的所有條件都不成熟的情況下，仲裁庭卻強行推進審理。這種做法不合常理，很不正常，違反《公約》的一般實踐，在程序上本身就是違法。大家知道，程序正義是實體正義的前提和基礎。

第三，仲裁結果背離了《公約》合理解決爭端的基本宗旨。《公約》誕生的初衷是公正地解決問題、化解矛盾，仲裁庭的做法卻與此背道而馳，帶有明顯傾向性和政治目的：對菲律賓的非法主張照單全收，對中國的合理關切則一概拒絕。為了給菲律賓違反雙邊談判解決爭議的承諾開脫，仲裁庭不惜貶低《南海各方行為宣言》和中菲之間的一系列雙邊文件。為了最大程度否定中國的合法權利，仲裁庭竟把太平島硬稱為「礁」。

這讓我想起一個中國成語：「指鹿為馬。」這個成語講的是兩千多年前中國秦朝一位丞相專橫跋扈、越權濫權的故事，沒想到在二十一世紀的今天，這一幕又在菲律賓仲裁案仲裁庭上演。明明是鹿，為什麼硬要說是馬呢？明明是島，為什麼硬要說是礁呢？時代不同，但手法如出一轍，動機都是不可告人。仲裁庭這種毫無顧忌的偏袒不是在解決問題，而是在製造問題；不是在化解矛盾，而是在挑起矛盾。因此本案不具實體正義。

基於以上管轄權、程序和實體三大違法事實，所謂仲裁案自始至終就是一場非法的政治鬧劇。難怪一些知名法學家認為這一仲裁「必將會被視為毒樹之果，無法得到認可和支持」。如果有些人非要拿仲裁結果當作什麼「寶貝」，我奉勸他們，這就是一劑花

高價買來的「精神幻藥」，開始會讓他們亢奮一陣，後面會讓他們飽受折磨。

中方堅決反對仲裁案及其結果，同時將堅定既定政策，不會讓仲裁案成為南海局勢走向的所謂「分水嶺」，更不會讓仲裁案來干擾當前南海地區總體和平穩定的局面。

第一，仲裁結果對中國在南海的領土主權和海洋權益沒有任何影響。國際法的基本規則是「非法行為不產生合法效力」，因此非法的裁決結果對包括中國在內的南海問題各當事方而言只是一紙空文。中國不會接受任何未經中方同意的第三方解決方式，也不會接受任何強加於中國的解決方案。

第二，仲裁結果對中國以談判協商和平解決南海問題的既定方針沒有任何影響。正如我不久前在一篇文章中的標題：「中國無意統治南海」，中國一貫致力於與直接當事國在尊重歷史事實的基礎上，依據國際法通過談判協商和平解決有關南海爭議，主張有關各方在解決爭議的過程中均應保持克制，不採取使爭議擴大化、複雜化的行動，倡導有關各方在爭議最終解決前基於諒解和合作精神做出臨時性、過渡性的安排。中國也一直主張「擱置爭議，共同開發」，這一點沒有改變，以後也不會變。

仲裁案沒有改變中國與菲律賓談判解決爭議、改善雙邊關係的願望。雖然菲律賓前政府執意單方面提起仲裁，給中菲關係造成損害，但中菲畢竟是隔海相望的近鄰，我們仍希望菲新政府從中菲共同利益和兩國關係大局出發，回到對話協商解決問題的軌道。仲裁結果也沒有改變中國和東盟之間的合作勢頭。今年是中國與東盟建立對話關係二十五週年。雙方將於九月舉行紀念峰會，並以此為契機全面規劃未來合作戰略，更加緊密地團結在一起，造福雙方人民。在南海問題上，中國願與東盟國家保持坦誠友好的溝通，按照「雙軌思路」，全面、有效落實《南海各方行為宣言》，穩妥推進「南海行為準則」磋商進程，共同維護南海的和平穩定。就在今天，中國和東盟外長發表聯合聲明，重申《南海各方行為宣言》是具有里程碑意義的文件，各方再次承諾由直接有關主權國家通過友好磋商和談判，以和平方式解決領土和管轄權爭

議，同時鼓勵其他國家尊重《南海各方行為宣言》所包含的原則。

第三，仲裁結果對中國走和平發展道路的方針沒有任何影響。中國始終是國際法和國際秩序的維護者、建設者、貢獻者。中國在南海的主權和權益本身就是「二戰」後確定的國際秩序的一部分，中國的有關主張也從未超出該秩序所涵蓋的範圍。中國堅持對仲裁說「不」，就是為了捍衛戰後國際秩序，就是為了防止《聯合國海洋法公約》被政治綁架，就是為了維護包括《公約》在內的國際法的權威性和完整性。自新中國成立以來我們已通過協商談判與十四個陸地鄰國中的十二個簽訂了邊界條約，並與越南完成了北部灣海上劃界。這些都是中國遵守國際法，捍衛國際秩序，維護地區和平安寧的生動體現。

南海是世界重要航道，是包括中國在內眾多國家利益聚焦的地方。中國理解國際社會對南海問題的關注，也從來不排斥域外國家在南海地區的合法權益，一直致力於維護該地區的航行自由。但我們反對個別國家以「航行和飛越自由」「維護地區和平」之名，行「炮艦政策」之實，藉仲裁案渲染甚至製造南海緊張局勢。南海不應成為域外大國「秀肌肉」的競技場。威脅、恐嚇動搖不了中國人民維護國家領土主權和海洋權益的決心。

浮雲難遮望眼，正道總是滄桑。

南海問題既是歷史遺留問題，也是現實利益問題，同時被一些國家摻雜了地緣政治因素，解決這個問題需要時間、耐心和當事方之間的相互諒解與尊重。只有當事國在尊重歷史事實的基礎上，根據國際法通過平等談判協商和平解決有關爭議，才能根本、長久地解決問題。南海應成為「和平之海、友誼之海、合作之海」，這是中國致力於實現的目標，也需要周邊各國與中國一道做出努力！

謝謝。下面我願回答大家的提問。

聽眾：美國未批准《聯合國海洋法公約》，但在南海問題上有重要影響。美國將舉行總統選舉，克林頓或特朗普當選總統將對中美關係和南海問題帶來什麼樣的機遇或挑戰？

劉曉明：現在做預測還為時尚早，但我們需要做好與他們兩人之一打交道的準備。希拉里·克林頓曾擔任美國國務卿，多次訪華。我們對特朗普了解不多，一些西方媒體報道稱中國可能對特朗普擔任總統感到擔憂，但我並沒有那種擔心。我曾從事對美工作，經歷過多次總統選舉，對美國選舉政治有一定了解。我們要聽其言，更要觀其行，關注他們當選後會做什麼。我認為，不管誰擔任美國總統，都要從美國的國家利益出發，重視中美關係，對這一點我是有信心的。中美關係涉及方方面面，雙方可能有一些分歧，關係可能有一些起伏，但我相信中美之間的共同利益遠遠大於分歧。

聽眾：大使閣下，感謝你的演講。你提到中國願意就南海爭議進行談判，我想問中國是否能夠澄清斷續線的含義是什麼？比如，中國是否對斷續線內的一切擁有權利？中國在南海國際水域擁有的海洋權益是否源於斷續線？這將有助於談判進程。我還想問另外一個問題。仲裁庭裁決書提到了中國漁民在南海這個世界上漁業資源最豐富的漁場使用炸藥捕魚。中國將採取什麼措施阻止類似情況發生？

劉曉明：首先，我想指出的是，中國一直主張在尊重歷史事實的基礎上，根據國際法，通過雙邊談判解決與周邊鄰國的爭議，這是中國的一貫政策，現在仍然如此。我們希望周邊鄰國與中國通過外交談判找到雙方都能滿意的解決方案。

關於斷續線，我想說明的是，中國的領土主權、海洋權益、歷史性權利是在長期的歷史過程中形成的，是基於中國對南海諸島最早發現、命名、開發及有效管轄的歷史事實，其中當然也包括中國漁民的捕魚活動。因此，一九四八年中國政府公佈斷續線後，國際社會普遍予以承認，沒有國家提出挑戰。二十世紀七十年代，南海發現了豐富的油氣資源，一些國家爭先恐後地非法侵佔南海中國島礁，共侵佔中國南沙群島的四十二個島礁。其中，越南侵佔了二十九個，菲律賓侵佔了八個，馬來西亞侵佔了五個。中國對這些島礁擁有主權，它們是南沙群島的一部分。如果你

查閱一下歷史記錄，就會發現美國、法國、英國等國官方公開發行的地圖上標註了斷續線，表明它們對中國在這一區域主權的尊重。

關於漁業問題，我們當然要有序地管理南海漁業活動。中國政府反對任何對漁業資源造成破壞的漁業活動，這也是中國與周邊國家討論如何共同維持良好漁業秩序的原因。當我們討論這一問題時，我也想提醒你注意，一些周邊國家的漁民在進行大量非法、破壞性的捕撈活動，因此這需要中國與周邊國家共同努力，尋找解決問題的方法。

聽眾：大使閣下在剛才演講中指出，由於主權問題不屬於《聯合國海洋法公約》調整範圍，仲裁庭裁決結果沒有任何效力。在南海當前的緊張局勢下，需要以國際法和平解決有關爭議。中方將仲裁這一和平解決的方式排除在外。當你談到大國與小國之間的雙邊談判時，這某種程度上是否將重演十九世紀「強權即真理」的邏輯？

劉曉明：所謂沒有任何效力，是指仲裁庭所謂裁決結果對中國的領土主權和海洋權益沒有任何影響。我已清楚表明這一點。如果你認為仲裁會對中國上述權益產生影響，那將是一種誤判。這種事情永遠不會發生。

仲裁只是解決爭端的輔助手段。《公約》規定，締約國通過雙邊渠道解決爭議應予以優先適用，只有窮盡雙邊渠道時才適用仲裁機制。仲裁庭的做法違反了這一規定，因此是非法的，中方不會接受。所以，我不能同意所謂仲裁庭是以國際法和平解決爭議的說法。

中菲之間早已達成通過談判協商解決爭端的協議，但雙方從未舉行此類談判，因為菲方認為自己得到了美國支持，能夠通過仲裁得到利益，對與中方談判不感興趣。仲裁庭違反了《公約》基本程序，儘管如此中方仍堅持通過雙邊談判解決爭議。今天（七月二十五日），中國與包括菲律賓在內的東盟十國外長共同發表了聯合聲明，承諾全面有效完整落實《南海各方行為宣言》，重申由直接當事方通過對話協商和

平解決爭議的立場。但另一方面，菲律賓一些人仍對仲裁抱有幻想，相信所謂裁決會產生效力。我希望菲方盡早從這樣的矛盾心態中走出來，越早越好。仲裁結果對中國在南海的領土主權和海洋權益沒有任何影響，對中國以談判協商和平解決南海問題的既定方針沒有任何影響。我相信，唯一、長久的解決方式是由直接當事國進行面對面的談判，而不是將所謂裁決結果強加給一個主權國家。我相信，英國也希望與其他國家通過談判和平解決爭議，不會在談判開始之前接受一個強制仲裁結果。主權國家有通過談判尋找解決方式的權利，這就是我想表達的意思。

關於你所說的大國小國關係問題，中國體量大一些，但中國始終主張大國小國一律平等。中國與十四個鄰國中的十二個劃定了邊界，其中很多是小國，如尼泊爾、緬甸等。但我們通過和平、友好、平等的方式解決了困難的劃界問題。中國是國際秩序和國際法的維護者，中方仍然希望與菲律賓、越南、馬來西亞等國找到解決爭議的方式，共同維護地區和平穩定。

聽眾：我對中國向南海島礁派駐部隊的做法持不同看法，但對中國應對南海問題的總體方式持積極態度。大使先生，你認為在無人生活的島礁上修建飛機跑道，並安排成批的遊客去參觀，是否比單邊仲裁結果更為加劇地區緊張局勢？

劉曉明：中國對南海有關爭議一直呼籲各方保持克制，但有關國家卻變本加厲，在非法侵佔的中國島礁上修建軍事設施。菲律賓和越南在非法佔據的島礁上修建跑道，西方媒體卻刻意保持沉默，一些西方政客更是視而不見。中國對這些挑釁行徑忍無可忍，不得不採取措施應對。中國的島礁建設是在自己的土地上進行的，這一點我希望你注意。而有關國家背棄了與中國達成的共識，在非法侵佔的島礁上修建軍事設施，並部署導彈、坦克、大炮，中國不得不加以應對。

中國島礁建設並未給地區帶來損害。相反，中國修建的設施將在氣象、海洋研究、環境保護等領域提供更好的服務。修建的燈塔也有助於南海的航運安

全。每年大量船舶經過南海，當地的船東都十分贊同修建燈塔。今年初路透社做了一個調查，結果顯示很多船東都十分感激中國提供的海上公共服務，認為修建燈塔及其他救援設施大大縮短了海上救援時間，並極大改善了海上運輸環境。這都是中國正在努力做的事情。

說到這，我建議你讀一讀今天剛剛發佈的中國與東盟國家外交部部長關於全面有效落實《南海各方行為宣言》的聯合聲明。中國與東盟國家外長一致同意，有關各方保持克制，這體現了中國致力於地區和平與穩定的承諾。我手邊就有這份聲明，我現在就讀其中一段，幫助你增進對地區局勢的理解：

「各方承諾保持自我克制，不採取使爭議複雜化、擴大化和影響和平與穩定的行動，包括不在現無人居住的島、礁、灘、沙或其他自然構造上採取居住的行動，並以建設性的方式處理它們的分歧。」

聽眾：大使先生，你剛才談到了中國利用南海海底資源的有關計劃。外界認為中國有意開發這些資源。你能進一步解釋有關開發計劃並提供一些數據嗎？

劉曉明：正如我提到的，中國在本地區享有合法的海洋權益。目前確有一些中國石油公司在南海進行海上勘探開發。當然，你會看到這些開發活動都在中方主權範圍內。同時，中國也認識到在有些區域存在爭議，願意與有關國家擱置爭議，開展對話並進行共同開發。

事實上，中國與越南已經就海上共同開發達成協議。中國、越南、菲律賓也曾確立三方合作項目。在爭議地區開發自然資源問題上，中國願與有關國家進行討論。

聽眾：我研究中國有很多年了，現在正在研究法律政策問題。我認為大使先生的演講十分精彩。我的問題是，你認為某個未加入《聯合國海洋法公約》的國家，可以通過代理人，以十分隱秘的方式濫用國際法嗎？

劉曉明：這當然不可以。

聽眾：非常感謝大使先生的演講。我認為你已將中國政府的立場闡釋得極其清楚，我們也對仲裁結果毫無法律效力這一事實有了進一步的認識。你已經解釋了中國不接受仲裁結果的原因，闡述了中國在南海的歷史性權利，介紹了中國提供的修建燈塔等公共服務。但為什麼很多中國鄰國，如菲律賓、越南、日本等，均不認可中國上述政策？

劉曉明：當你提到不認可中國政策的鄰國時，你用了「很多」這個詞。我必須糾正你，因為這樣的鄰國並不多。

事實上，中國與周邊國家關係很好。俄羅斯作為最大的鄰國，與中國關係十分友好。我曾常駐過的朝鮮，以及韓國、蒙古、巴基斯坦、印度、哈薩克斯坦、尼泊爾、孟加拉國、越南等也都與中國有非常好的關係。當然，國家間關係有起有伏很正常，共同利益將雙方緊密地聯繫在一起。

的確，有少數鄰國不認可中國的政策，那是因為它們與中國存在海上爭議。譬如日本，兩國在釣魚島問題上存有明顯分歧。根據《開羅宣言》，釣魚島應歸還中國。當年中日關係實現正常化的時候，中方不希望釣魚島問題影響兩國關係正常發展，鄧小平先生提出了擱置爭議，他指出下一代比我們更聰明，一定會找到彼此都能接受的方法。中日建交四十多年來，釣魚島問題沒有大的起伏。但近年來，日本政府對釣魚島實施所謂「國有化」，一些右翼勢力甚至提出通過「購島」進行非法佔領，正是由於日方動搖了中日兩國在釣魚島問題上達成的共識，中方才不得不對日方挑釁行為做出回應。

在南海問題上，中國一直是受害者，但中國始終認為國家不論大小，都應在平等基礎上通過談判尋求解決方案。中越之間已成功解決了部分領土爭議，雙方就北部灣劃界問題達成了協議。中國與其他國家不一定照搬中越解決爭議的模式，但只要有信心和耐心，就一定能夠找到解決方法。

現在南海還面臨地緣政治問題。某個域外大國，

一個比中國強大得多的國家，想利用南海問題為其所謂「再平衡」戰略服務。它展示「肌肉」，顯示存在，反而使問題更加複雜，這是我們不願看到的。

聽眾：大使閣下，沒有國家比中國更強大。你的演講很有說服力，可以說是我聽過的最有說服力的演講。中方對仲裁案很憤怒，我認為中方有理由感到憤怒。但中方應該保持耐心，儘量避免發怒。

我想了解中方在「勢力範圍」問題上的長期政策立場。未來二十至三十年，中國的政策立場會不會因南海仲裁案而改變？你談到戰後國際秩序，你認為太平洋哪些部分屬於這一秩序？哪些部分屬於中國的「勢力範圍」？中、美、俄三方有許多問題需要共同應對，應該加強合作，而不是就南海島礁爭吵。你如何展望中國「勢力範圍」的未來？

劉曉明：恕我直言，我認為你仍在用冷戰思維評判形勢。我在演講中提及的戰後國際秩序，指的是第二次世界大戰後，而不是冷戰期間的秩序，戰後國際秩序的基本原則是由《聯合國憲章》等所確定的。

我不同意你關於「勢力範圍」的看法，中國對建立「勢力範圍」沒有興趣。你認為沒有國家比中國更強大，這明顯不符合事實。儘管中國已成為世界第二大經濟體，中國仍是一個發展中國家，人均 GDP 僅排在全球八十多位，比英國落後，與美國差距更大。人均 GDP 直接關係到人民的生活水平，比經濟總量更重要。

我擔任中國駐埃及大使之後，曾在甘肅省擔任省長助理。你可能連甘肅省的名字都沒聽說過，那是中國最貧困的省份之一。當地生活條件十分艱苦，最基本的飲用水都非常匱乏，許多人依靠水窖蓄存雨水來滿足基本生活需要。我去過甘肅許多這樣的地方，這使我更好地了解國家貧困地區的情況，對我做好外交工作很有幫助。上海、天津、廣州等大城市並非中國的全部，就如同倫敦不能代表英國一樣。如果你訪問英格蘭北部地區或蘇格蘭地區，就會發現它們與倫敦存在不小差距。在發展經濟和改善民生方面，中國仍面臨巨大挑戰。

中國對挑戰美國「領導地位」沒有興趣，也無意構築所謂「勢力範圍」。我們的目標是實現中國現代化，提高人民生活水平，使十三多億中國人生活得更好，生活得更幸福。為什麼我們如此看重南海這些島礁？新中國成立前一百多年，中國屢遭列強欺凌，被迫簽訂了不少不平等條約，大片土地被割讓侵佔。如今中國實現了國家獨立，民族解放，中國人民看重自己的領土主權，別國的土地中國一寸不要，但中國的領土我們寸土不讓。中國人常講，寸土寸金。維護中國的主權和領土完整，已經成為中國人民的基因，中國將採取一切必要措施，捍衛領土主權和海洋權益。

聽眾：我來自日本駐英使館。因為你談及了日本和「尖閣列島」，[一]所以我必須有所回應。首先，你提到了受害者問題。中國成為受害者的經歷是七八十年前的事，現在我們不是在討論受害者，而是在討論法治問題。中國是《聯合國海洋法公約》締約國，《公約》對通過仲裁解決爭端有明確規定，中方理應接受。對於「尖閣列島」問題，中國雖不接受一九五一年簽署的《舊金山對日和約》，但直到一九七一年之前，中方都未對「尖閣列島」歸屬日本提出異議。中國似乎在操縱歷史議題，而且有些過分。

布朗院長（主持人）：你是在演講，還是在提問？

劉曉明：你應該向皇研所申請演講。今天是中國大使在發表演講，你的問題是什麼？

聽眾：我想問中方為什麼不設定完成「南海行為準則」（COC）談判的具體日期？請你明確說明這一日期是什麼時候。

劉曉明：我認為你沒有資格提這個要求，因為日本並非 COC 談判當事國。你要求中方設定結束談判的日

[一]「尖閣列島」是日本對中國釣魚島的稱呼，中國不予承認。

期，這很過分，而且充滿了傲慢。COC談判是中國與東盟國家之間的談判，日本卻急著要定談判結束日期，豈有此理？COC談判非常複雜，涉及中國與東盟十國的共同關切。中方已就積極推進談判做出莊重承諾，也希望盡早達成協議。但中國要與東盟國家平等相待、相互尊重。

關於釣魚島問題，我們可以花一整天時間討論。簡言之，中日兩國政府高層和工作層已經多次討論釣魚島問題。中方從未承認和接受《舊金山對日和約》。釣魚島是中國的一部分，是日本用戰爭手段從中國竊取的。「竊取」這個詞不是我首創的，而是在中、美、英三國領導人共同簽署的《開羅宣言》中明確闡明的，即日本所竊取於中國之領土，全部歸還中國。隨著戰後國際形勢發生變化，特別是冷戰開始後，日本成為美國盟友，美國因此改變了立場，不願將釣魚島歸還中國，事實就是這樣。

聽眾：感謝大使就南海問題所做的強有力的闡述。你認為仲裁庭對領土主權和海洋劃界問題沒有仲裁權，這沒有錯。但仲裁庭反覆重申其裁決不涉及領土主權和海洋劃界問題，為什麼中方反覆指責仲裁庭所作裁決實質是主權問題？

劉曉明：首先，仲裁庭的裁決關係到主權問題，事實非常清楚。這也恰恰是菲律賓前政府提出仲裁的目的所在，其想通過仲裁否定中國對南海諸島的主權。有人說，菲方為此次仲裁花銷高達三千萬美元。有誰會相信花這一大筆錢僅僅是為了裁決一些無人居住島礁的地位問題。我想，菲方還不至於愚蠢和瘋狂到這個地步。事實上，菲律賓想通過仲裁否定中國對有關島礁的主權，這一目的非常明確。任何沒有偏見的人，即便不是專家學者，也能從常識角度認清其真實目的。

其次，你怎麼能將有關島礁的地位屬性與國家主權割裂開呢？仲裁庭表面上未直接就主權問題進行裁決，但實質上其否定中國維護主權和海洋權益的權利。中國將南海諸島視為一個整體，中國擁有無可爭辯的主權。仲裁庭卻要把中國的主權與島礁分割開

來，以便否定中國的領土主權和海洋權益。對這一險惡用心，我們看得非常清楚。

仲裁庭還完全否定中國包括斷續線在內的歷史性權利，這違背了《聯合國海洋法公約》的精神。中方已聲明將涉及海洋劃界、歷史性海灣或所有權等方面的爭端排除出《公約》強制爭端解決程序，包括英國在內的三十多個國家也做出了類似聲明。為什麼《公約》認可排除性聲明？因為《公約》的出發點，是為主權國家處理海洋劃界等方面的爭端創造和平環境，並不是想給主權國家製造麻煩。

布朗院長（主持人）：非常感謝劉大使就中國在南海問題上的政策立場所做的全面詳細的介紹。我們期待今後有機會第六次或第七次邀請你來皇研所發表演講。再次非常感謝！

劉曉明：不客氣。

第四章

新冠肺炎疫情

二〇二〇年新冠肺炎疫情發生不久，以美國為首的西方勢力編造各種謊言和謠言，對中國進行污名化、妖魔化，企圖把病毒源頭的帽子扣在中國頭上。二月六日，我在駐英使館舉行中外記者會，介紹中國防控疫情工作成效，闡明中方政策立場，揭穿謊言，說明真相，激濁揚清。二十七家中外媒體五十餘名記者出席。菲律賓、柬埔寨、加拿大、芬蘭、西班牙、韓國等國駐英使節及外交官也出席了記者會。BBC、天空新聞台、中國國際電視台和今日俄羅斯電視台對記者會進行了現場直播。

四月二十三日，我出席「亞洲之家」網上座談會，發表題為《堅定信心，加強團結，攜手戰勝疫情》的主旨演講，並與「亞洲之家」主席格林勳爵進行對話交流，回答聽眾提問。英國政府「一帶一路」特使范智廉爵士，議會上院議員鮑威爾勳爵，英中貿協名譽主席沙遜勳爵，英國候任駐華大使吳若蘭及英內閣辦、外交部、財政部、國際貿易部、國際發展部、商業能源與產業戰略部等部門官員，二十多個國家駐英使節或外交官，以及英國、美國、歐洲、亞洲等工商、媒體、學術等各界人士近二百五十人出席。BBC和天空新聞台進行了現場直播和轉播。

「亞洲之家」是英國非營利、非政治性機構，旨在增進英各界對亞洲的認識理解，深化與亞洲各國政治、文化、商業、教育等各領域交往聯繫，定期舉辦演講、座談、展覽等活動，其會員多為英知名機構、大型企業及各界精英人士。

說明真相，激濁揚清

——關於抗擊新冠肺炎疫情中外記者會

（二〇二〇年二月六日，中國駐英大使館）

劉曉明：大家上午好！今天，我們舉辦中外記者會，通報中國防控新型冠狀病毒肺炎疫情的最新情況。

疫情發生以來，中國政府果斷採取一系列有力防控舉措，行動之快、力度之大、範圍之廣，舉世罕見。我認為，可以從「三個高度」看中國政府採取的有力措施：

一是高度重視。習近平主席多次做出重要指示，始終把人民群眾生命安全和身體健康放在第一位；兩次召開中共中央政治局常務委員會會議，成立應對疫情工作領導小組，全面部署防疫工作。李克強總理受習主席委託，親赴武漢指導疫情防控工作。中國舉國上下，已形成全面動員、全面部署、全面加強的防控工作局面，全力打贏疫情防控阻擊戰。

在國家層面，政府有關部門各司其職，軍隊積極支援地方，各地區成立黨政主要官員掛帥的領導機制；在診療一線，廣大醫務人員無私奉獻、英勇奮戰，湧現出不勝枚舉的感人故事；在社會基層，廣大民眾眾志成城、團結奮戰，打響了疫情防控的人民戰爭。疫情防控工作有力開展，逐步取得成效。總地看，疫情是可防、可控、可治的。

二是高度負責。疫情發生之後，中國政府採取了最全面、最嚴格的防控舉措，很多舉措遠遠超出《國際衛生條例》要求，這不僅是對中國人民的生命安全和身體健康高度負責，更是對維護世界人民的健康和

全球公共衛生安全做出的最大努力。例如，中國在武漢等地暫時採取集中隔離舉措，全力遏制病毒擴散；來自全國各地超過六千名專業醫務人員馳援武漢和湖北其他地區，口罩、防護服、藥品等醫療用品及肉類、蔬菜、日用品等生活必需品及時陸續運抵；武漢火神山、雷神山兩家專門醫院在短短十天內建成並投入使用，集中收治、救治重症病人。需要指出的是，此次疫情雖然感染人數較多，但中國境內病死率非常低，僅為百分之二點一，遠低於埃博拉（百分之四十點四）、非典（SARS，百分之十）、中東呼吸綜合症（MERS，百分之三十四點四）。美國本流感季已有一千九百萬人感染，至少一萬人死亡，從死亡人數看比新型冠狀病毒感染肺炎疫情更加嚴重。目前中國治癒人數在增加，我們對打贏疫情阻擊戰充滿信心。

與此同時，中國也努力承擔應對疫情的國際責任和義務。世界衛生組織總幹事譚德塞充分肯定中方防控工作，高度讚賞中國抗擊疫情為世界做出的巨大貢獻，認為中國舉措「設立了應對疫情的新標杆」。中方高度重視疫情對其他國家和地區的影響，加強了中國公民海外旅行的管控，呼籲公眾在防止疫情傳播方面積極承擔社會責任，努力減少疫情對其他國家的影響。截至二月三日，中國境外確診病例一百五十三例，佔所有病例不到百分之一，這表明中方為控制疫情傳播、保護中國人民和全世界人民的健康和衛生安全，採取了最有力的舉措，做出了重要貢獻。

三是高度合作。中方始終本著公開、透明、負責任的態度開展疫情防控國際合作。第一，我們第一時間向世衛組織、有關國家及中國港澳台地區通報疫情，分享病毒基因序列，以利於各方及時、有效應對疫情，世衛組織及許多國家對此予以高度評價。我們還在雙邊層面與多國就疫情防控等問題保持密切溝通。第二，我們高度重視在華外國人安全，通過各種渠道向各國駐華機構通報疫情，解決好他們面臨的困難。截至二月六日中午，十九名在華外國公民確診感染新型冠狀病毒肺炎，兩人已治癒出院，十七人正接受隔離治療，病情平穩。近期，包括英國在內的一些國家決定從武漢撤僑，中方給予協助。第三，我們正同國際社會一道，加強科學研究、疫苗研發等合作，

共同維護全球和地區公共衛生安全。

疫情無情人有情。面對突如其來的疫情，很多國家政府官員和各界人士都對中國抗擊疫情表達了同情、信任和支持，多國政府及國際組織向中方捐助疫情防控物資。除了英國政府援助外，英國工商界、華人社團、留學生紛紛通過各種渠道捐資捐物。就在幾天前，中國駐英國使館舉行儀式，接受全英二十多個僑學界社團捐款、捐物，這些幫助讓我們深受感動。我們對這些來自英國各界的愛心和善舉表示衷心感謝！

女士們、先生們，中國政府遏制疫情擴散的決心是堅定的，措施是有力的，我們將繼續把疫情防控作為當前最重要的任務。

一是全力以赴救治患者。生命重於泰山。生命權、健康權是最基本，也是最大人權。中國各地醫療機構正努力提高收治率和治癒率，降低感染率和病死率。

二是著力做好重點地區疫情防控工作。湖北省特別是武漢市仍是疫情防控的重中之重，當地正進一步完善和加強防控，嚴格落實早發現、早報告、早隔離、早治療措施，加強疫情監測，集中救治患者，加大對密切接觸人員醫學觀察力度，全力防止疫情向外擴散。

三是加大疫情國際防控合作和科研攻關力度。中方將繼續同世衛組織、相關國家和地區保持密切合作，共同做好疫情防控工作。近日，中國將《新型冠狀病毒肺炎公眾防護指南》翻譯成多語種，通過社交媒體等多種形式快速傳遞給世界各國，這體現了中國與國際社會合作應對疫情的誠意和負責任大國的擔當。據我所知，中國、英國等國科研人員正加緊論證病毒來源和傳播途徑，密切跟蹤病毒變異情況，實施相關數據和病例資料的開放共享，共同研究防控策略和措施，醫藥和疫苗研發也在有條不紊推進中。

女士們、先生們，目前，英國和國際社會對疫情還存在一些擔憂，一些人擔心疫情對中國經濟乃至世界經濟產生不利影響。我們也注意到，個別國家最近對疫情做出過度反應，一些國家還出現針對中國公民的恐慌甚至侮辱性、歧視性的言行。對此，我想強調

四點：

一是各方應全面看待對中國經濟的影響。從目前情況看，疫情對交通運輸、文化旅遊、酒店餐飲和影視娛樂等服務消費方面的影響較大。我想指出，這種影響在短期內的確存在，但是階段性的、暫時性的，不會改變中國經濟長期向好的基本面。中國經濟極具韌性，中長期看仍具有巨大的發展潛力。我們完全有能力、有信心把疫情對經濟的影響降到最低。世界銀行、國際貨幣基金組織及國際知名經濟學家普遍認為，疫情對中國經濟的衝擊是暫時的，對中國經濟的未來充滿信心。

二是各國政府應客觀理性地評估疫情。世界衛生組織反覆強調，不贊成甚至反對採取旅行和貿易限制措施。近日，英方在雙邊層面亦表示充分肯定中方為抗擊疫情付出的巨大努力和採取的有力措施，並願同中方加強合作，盡可能向中方提供協助。希望包括英國在內的各國政府，理解支持中方努力，尊重世衛組織專業建議，不要過度反應，不要人為製造恐慌，確保國家之間正常合作和往來不受影響。

三是各國媒體應客觀公正報道疫情。我們注意到，近期包括英媒在內的多國媒體對疫情做了大量報道，不少報道積極評價中國抗擊疫情的努力，一些建議客觀中肯，我們對此表示讚賞。但也有一些報道存在偏見，有些甚至惡意中傷、蓄意造謠。謠言和恐慌比病毒更可怕，信心和決心對戰勝疫情至關重要。公共衛生安全問題超越國界，需要各方攜手應對，媒體也應為此肩負起應有的社會責任。

四是各方應共同反對任何侮辱性、歧視性言行。我十分贊同世衛組織總幹事譚德塞所說，「這是一個需要事實而不是恐懼的時刻，是需要科學而不是謠言的時刻，是需要團結而不是羞辱的時刻」。希望各界能夠理性、冷靜地認識這場疫情，並做出科學、恰當的應對，同舟共濟、共迎挑戰。

女士們、先生們，中國人常說「人心齊，泰山移」。我堅信，有中國共產黨的堅強領導，有中國特色社會主義制度的巨大優勢，有中國人民團結一心、眾志成城，有國際社會的大力支持，我們一定能戰勝疫情！

每次記者會，我都會播放一段視頻。今天我也想和大家分享一段暖心的視頻，它講述了中英兩國人民共克時艱、共迎挑戰的感人故事。（播放視頻）

現在，我願回答各位記者提問。

中國國際電視台：能否請你詳細介紹一下中英在研製疫苗方面開展合作的情況？約翰遜首相個人尚未表達對中方抗擊疫情的支持，你對此是否感到不滿？

劉曉明：中英科學家確實正在積極推進相關合作。疫情發生前，中國的研究機構與包括牛津大學、帝國理工學院在內的英國大學建成聯合研究中心等合作平台。目前他們正在爭分奪秒地加緊工作，著手開展藥物研發和疫苗開發，希望在不久的將來能取得實質性成果。中國政府十分支持這項工作，中國駐英國使館正在盡我們所能促進兩國科學家的溝通交流。

中方對英國政府的支持表示感謝。疫情發生以來，兩國政府保持了密切聯繫。英國內閣秘書兼首相國家安全事務顧問塞德維爾和外交大臣拉布分別與中央外事工作委員會辦公室主任楊潔篪、國務委員兼外長王毅通電話。英方高度讚揚中方防控疫情的舉措，並表示願意提供幫助，我們對此表示感謝。因此，並不存在中方對英國政府感到失望和不滿的問題。

BBC：你剛才提到中方對包括英國在內的一些外國政府的過度反應和恐慌感到失望，你能具體談一下是哪些過度反應嗎？你指的是不是英國政府警告在華英國公民盡快離開中國？

劉曉明：中英兩國政府間的溝通渠道是開放的，包括最高層和工作層。我與英國外交部官員保持良好溝通，包括代理常務次官和總司長。我的副手及使館主管官員與英國外交部幾乎每天保持聯繫。中方已明確表達相關立場，中國採取的防控措施是有效的，各方不應恐慌或過度反應，建議英方遵循世界衛生組織的專業意見。英方對此表示贊同，高度肯定中方舉措取得的實效，並表示將採納世衛組織意見。

然而，我也看到，英方並未完全做到言行一致。

相信你們也注意到，世衞組織總幹事已經公開批評英國政府通告提醒英國公民全部離開中國的行為，認為這種「一刀切」的做法無助於解決問題。我們只對疫情集中發生地區實施了隔離，並不是整個中國都是疫區，中國的大部分地區生活正常進行。我多次在公開和私下場合講，中方希望英國政府和公眾客觀冷靜看待中國國內形勢。疫情是全世界面臨的共同威脅，需要國際社會合作應對。我們應該相互支持，而不是削弱他國的努力，這就是我的建議。

英國電視五台：大使先生，你表示你對中國與英國政府的合作和密切聯繫感到滿意，但指責英方過度反應。

劉曉明：我並不是指責，而是希望英方能夠言行一致。

英國電視五台：既然英中雙方保持密切聯繫，那麼當你聽到英國政府向在華英國公民發佈警告時，你是否感到十分驚訝？

劉曉明：我們認為不應有如此的恐慌情緒。英方正式發佈警告前向我們做了通報，中方明確表示，這樣做是不妥的，我們認為疫情是可防、可控、可治的，要求英方客觀、冷靜反應，保障雙方正常往來與合作不受影響。

獨立電視台：你是否擔心英國出現第三例確診病例？如果出現這種情況，是否表明中國並不是像你剛才說的那樣有能力控制疫情？

劉曉明：不能排除英國出現新的病例，因為我們對這個新型病毒並不十分了解，這也是為什麼包括中英在內各國科學家正在密切合作，努力研發治療藥物和疫苗。中方認為疫情可治可防，因為到目前為止，治癒病例是死亡病例的兩倍，中國全國的治癒病例仍在穩定增加。正如習近平主席所說，我們在同時間賽跑，與病魔較量，我們有信心！目前累計已有

一千一百五十多例治癒出院，死亡病例五百六十三例，治癒病例數遠高於死亡病例數。

天空新聞台：有報道稱，疫情發生以後，針對在英中國公民和中國留學生的歧視和仇恨在增加，你怎麼看？

劉曉明：總地看，英國民眾對中國是同情和支持的，比如剛才播放的視頻，來自北愛爾蘭一所小學，師生們表達了他們對中國的支持。我們讚賞英國民眾對中國的支持。的確，有針對中國人歧視和仇恨的個案發生。我們向英國政府和警方表達了關切。我們也向中國公民發佈旅行建議，提醒他們注意此類事件，做好自我保護。我們發佈了英國警方和中國使領館的聯繫方式，出現此類情況，他們要先報警，同時向中國使領館尋求領事保護。我們收到一些有關大學存在校園歧視的報告，中小學也有。

引發歧視現象的原因是多方面的，有的是由於對疫情缺乏了解，有的是媒體不實報道誤導造成的。媒體應該以負責、科學的態度報道疫情，不能加劇公眾的恐慌。當然，根深蒂固的種族歧視也是存在的，在英國和其他國家都有。我們面對的是人類共同的敵人，在疫情面前，所有國家的人們應該團結起來，共同反對歧視和仇恨。我呼籲包括媒體在內的各行各業的人們共同應對挑戰。

彭博社：你剛才提到，與非典、中東呼吸綜合症、美國流感疫情相比，新型冠狀病毒引發的肺炎並不嚴重。

劉曉明：我比較的是死亡病例的數字。

彭博社：現在疫情還處於初期階段，你想向中國和中國以外的人傳遞什麼信息？是否與其他流行病相比，當前形勢並不嚴重？

劉曉明：我想傳遞的信息是，我們不應該恐慌。對傳染病應該高度重視，但我們有信心、有資源、有能力

戰勝疫情。現在，中國舉國上下都已經動員起來應對疫情，治癒病例在增加。昨天，習近平主席又一次主持召開會議，他要求醫務人員全力以赴提高收治率、治癒率，降低死亡率，民眾信心倍增。

我們有中國共產黨的堅強領導，有中國特色社會主義的制度優勢，有全國人民的眾志成城，有國際社會的大力支持，我們一定能夠戰勝疫情。我無法預測拐點，但希望盡快到來。一方面，我們必須依靠自己的力量，中國科學家和研究人員正在努力工作；另一方面，我們也與其他國家，包括英國的科學家開展合作。英國在防治傳染病方面處於領先地位。在疫情發生前，中英兩國科學家就已經開展長期合作，我們有合作基礎。這次英國已經提供了支持。我希望公眾不要恐慌。

英國電視四台：你是否已要求英國外交部重新考慮要求英國公民離開中國的建議？

劉曉明：我們已向英國外交部表示，過度反應無助於應對當前疫情。我們希望英國外交部聽從世界衛生組織的建議，理性應對，不要過度反應。

《衛報》：武漢「封城」已經兩週，一些人可能錢物都將用盡，中國政府會提供援助嗎？「封城」會一直持續下去嗎？有報道說，武漢的醫療系統壓力很大，很多人得不到及時的診斷，你們如何保證所有的病例，至少大部分病例得到收治？

劉曉明：隔離措施不是永久的，但目前看仍是必需的。各級政府正全力以赴採取行動。面對疫情，我們採取的是綜合解決辦法。全國上下已經動員起來，為患者提供治療的一線醫務人員正在緊張工作，物流運輸部門也在日夜奮戰。我想問一問，《衛報》在北京有常駐記者嗎？看來他的工作還不夠努力，沒有抓住報道的關鍵。中國國家衛生健康委員會每天召開新聞發佈會對外公佈疫情最新情況並回答人民群眾關心的問題。我每天都在跟蹤進展，尤其關注在哪些方面能與英方開展合作以共同抗擊疫情。中國交通部、海關

總署、工業和信息化部等部門每天都在公佈物資供應信息。儘管民眾正常的生產生活會受到一定影響，但基本物資供應還是有保障的。

習近平主席和李克強總理指示各級政府要把人民群眾的生命安全和身體健康放在第一位，關心包括受感染者在內的全體民眾，竭盡全力保障生活必需品供應。中方所做努力均需要一定時間，但當前舉措在遏制病毒傳播方面已凸顯成效，得到世界衛生組織的高度評價。

你提到一些人有抱怨，我認為這是可以理解的。疫情發生得十分突然，令人措手不及，但從中央到地方各級政府都充分動員，採取了切實有效的應對策略。假以時日，人們會了解疫情的本質，理解形勢的急迫性，最終得出正確結論。

疫情剛剛發生時，我們的應對資源確實有些捉襟見肘，沒有足夠的醫院和床位。正因如此，我們在十天之內建成兩家醫院，全力收治更多病患。世界上沒有其他任何國家能做到這一點。在基層，廣大民眾都在努力防控疫情，醫務工作者都在盡力救治病患，全國上下都在全力以赴防控疫情。

今日俄羅斯電視台：大使曾經提到病毒對中國經濟發展有影響。這是否由於一些媒體的不公正報道造成的？你所說的這些媒體，包括在座記者，其中是否有人在蓄意詆毀、破壞中國經濟？

劉曉明：我注意到了英國媒體的相關報道，總的來說他們對中國經濟仍保有信心。我舉幾個例子，《每日電訊報》的一篇報道認為中國經濟仍充滿彈性和活力。《金融時報》也做了一些積極報道。我並沒有說英國媒體唱衰中國經濟，我只是用事實說明中國經濟仍具活力。我希望你在報道中國的時候也能採取客觀理性的態度。

《金融時報》：目前有多少被困英國的中國公民向使館方面報告？這些人可能是來旅遊、出差、過農曆新年，或因交通困難無法回家。如果此類人員數量很多，中國政府如何向他們提供有效幫助？是否為他們

提供經濟和住宿等支持？

劉曉明：我們正盡最大努力去幫助他們。一些來自湖北特別是武漢的民眾被困國外，中國政府嘗試包機接他們回家。駐英國使館也在努力與來自湖北特別是武漢的同胞取得聯繫，詢問他們是否需要幫助，是否有意願盡快回家，但遇到實際困難。他們當中許多人或有自己的生意，或有未竟的工作，表示仍需留在國外。使館尊重他們的意見並盡力予以協助。

《泰晤士報》：世界衛生組織發出警告，要求對疫情的反應不應過度，不以政治為目的。在當前中美存在貿易爭端背景下，英國政府緊隨美方公佈旅行限制。你認為是否有一些國家採取了政治手段？你對此有何評論？

劉曉明：我贊同你的觀點。一些別有用心的政客利用當前形勢以達到其政治目的。中方對這些不負責任的言行及時表達了不滿和反對。這種行徑不符合美國利益，更不用說破壞中美合作了。我相信中美雙方會共同致力於落實第一階段經貿協議。正如我在不同場合反覆強調的，協議對中美雙方有利，對世界有利。但是「一個巴掌拍不響」，我們會繼續落實協議，希望美方與中方相向而行。

倫敦廣播電台：據報道，你對約翰遜首相未能就疫情與中國政府直接溝通表示關切，能否談一談看法？第二個問題，你對英國政府建議在華英國人盡量離開中國有何看法？這與世界衛生組織的建議背道而馳，你認為英國政府為何會提出這樣的建議？

劉曉明：我認為，中方與英國首相的溝通渠道是暢通的。約翰遜首相在唐寧街十號舉辦了中國春節招待會，我和夫人受邀參加。我們談得很愉快。我轉達了習近平主席和李克強總理對約翰遜首相的問候。約翰遜當選首相後，首相請我轉達對中國領導人的問候。約翰遜首相的問候，首相李克強總理向他發了賀信。約翰遜首相向我表示，他致力於中英關係「黃金時代」，這是一個堅定的承

諾。我認為，中英兩國政府的溝通渠道是暢通的。關於第二個問題，你應該向英國外交部或外交大臣本人求證，他們為什麼會提出這樣的建議？我的回答是，不要做出過度反應。

《每日電訊報》：我最近剛從北京回來，此前也曾去過武漢，當地處於「封城」狀態。今天你講了當地民眾的總體情況是正常的，但實際上除了正式宣佈隔離的地區外，其他很多城市也封鎖了交通，民眾不能隨意離開，這跟你剛才介紹的情況並不一樣。

劉曉明：全國各地的疫情和湖北及武漢的疫情有區別。中國和其他國家也不一樣。其他國家可能不需要舉國動員。我並不是說中國國內一切如常，但不應將中國所有地方都看作疫區。所以不要做出過度反應，這就是我的建議。

《每日電訊報》：事實是，中國國內民眾反應過度了，他們對正在發生的疫情感到擔心。我曾經在中國採訪過一些人，他們的家人在感染了病毒後短短幾天就去世了，甚至來不及檢測是否感染了新型冠狀病毒，也沒有被納入官方統計數字。中國國家衛健委的統計數字是否可信？

劉曉明：我對你的建議是，要相信中國官方發佈的數字。不信謠，不傳謠，不要製造恐慌。正如我剛才所講，現在需要保持冷靜，不要恐慌。我對《每日電訊報》的建議是，可以關注個案，但更要看大局，否則就看不清中國目前的總體情況。這就是我給你的建議。

《每日電訊報》：我想問中央政府給地方的指示是什麼？因為很多地方並沒有感染病例，也採取了封閉交通、設立體溫檢測點等措施。這些做法是地方政府決定的還是由中央決定的？

劉曉明：總體上，各級政府應承擔起應有責任。各地都已成立了主要黨政領導人掛帥的疫情應對工作機

制。中央的指示很明確，習近平主席兩次主持召開中央政治局常委會會議，這是很少見的。昨天，習主席還召開另一個會議，對疫情防控做出重要指示。建議你們仔細閱讀。地方政府必須聽從中央的指示，地方政府及官員如不能有效履職，將為失職承擔責任。

BBC：有人說此次疫情凸顯了中國「一黨專政」國家的優勢和弱點。一方面，中國在極短時間建起兩所醫院，展示了強大的資源動員能力。但另一方面，中共中央政治局常委會會議也提到疫情爆發之初的一些短板和不足，換句話說，就是缺乏透明、推卸責任、試圖掩蓋事實而不是迅速應對疫情等。你如何看待這種挑戰？上述挑戰對中國政治體制有多大影響？

劉曉明：首先，我要糾正你的說法，中國不是「一黨專政」國家。中國是由中國共產黨領導的國家，我們還有八個民主黨派參政議政。所以建議你了解一下中國政治制度的基本知識。民主黨派積極參政，有不少民主黨派成員是著名科學家，為政府應對疫情出謀劃策。當然，沒有任何一種制度是完美的。你也不能說英國的制度就是完美無缺的，否則你們怎麼花了三年時間才搞定「脫歐」，當然我沒有批評你的意思。任何制度都有不斷改進的空間，所以我常說，世界上最大的空間就是不斷改進的空間。

我高興地看到，你仔細閱讀了中共中央政治局常委會會議的新聞稿。正是認識到了短板和不足，我們才可以在未來做得更好。我們的確面臨挑戰，但我們對挑戰的看法不同，我們認為挑戰能夠敦促我們改進工作、完善制度。我們對自己的制度充滿信心，如果沒有我們今天這樣的制度，難以想像疫情會發展到什麼程度。設想一下，如果類似的事情發生在英國，會是怎麼樣一種境況？

如果沒有其他問題，今天記者會到此結束。謝謝大家出席，我們下次再見。

堅定信心，加強團結，攜手戰勝疫情

——與英國智庫談新冠肺炎疫情

（二〇二〇年四月二十三日，中國駐英國使館／英國「亞洲之家」）

二〇二〇年四月二十三日，我出席「亞洲之家」網上座談會，發表題為《堅定信心，加強團結，攜手戰勝疫情》的主旨演講，並與「亞洲之家」主席格林勳爵進行對話交流，回答聽眾提問。演講和答問實錄如下：

劉曉明：感謝格林勳爵的盛情邀請和剛才的熱情介紹。正如格林勳爵所說，我擔任中國駐英大使十年，曾多次做客「亞洲之家」，但通過連線這種特殊方式與大家交流還是第一次。

當世界邁入二十一世紀第三個十年，新冠肺炎疫情大爆發，給人類帶來前所未有的挑戰，給世界經濟帶來前所未有的衝擊，給國際格局帶來前所未有的影響。這是一場沒有硝煙的戰爭，對每個國家都是一場大考。

今天，我想從三個方面談一談，中國是如何應對這場大考的：一是中國的抗疫鬥爭對全球抗疫意味著什麼；二是疫情背景下的中國經濟將如何為世界經濟注入更大動力；三是為什麼中國認為，「團結合作是國際社會戰勝疫情最有力武器」。

當前，疫情仍在全球擴散蔓延，全球抗疫鬥爭進入關鍵階段。中國是最早向國際社會報告疫情、最早取得疫情防控重要階段性成效的國家，我認為中國抗疫鬥爭對全球抗疫具有三大重要意義。

一是中國抗疫為全球健康安全構築了堅固的「中國防線」。中國本著對人民負責、為世界擔當的精

神，迅速採取最全面、最嚴格、最徹底的防控舉措。全國十四億人民團結一心，眾志成城，打響一場抗擊疫情的人民戰爭。經過艱苦奮戰，承受巨大犧牲，中國成為世界上率先控制住國內疫情的國家之一，境內已連續一個月僅呈現零星散發態勢，本土疫情傳播基本被阻斷。中國用力量、智慧與犧牲為世界築牢了捍衛生命和健康的第一道防線。

二是中國抗疫為全球防疫鬥爭積累了寶貴經驗。堅持以人民為中心，一切為了人民，一切依靠人民，始終是抗疫鬥爭中最鮮明的中國特色；中國迅速構建起從中央到地方、全方位、多層次網格狀的防控體系，發揮「一方有難，八方支援」的精神，共同打贏武漢保衛戰；中國始終堅持向科學要答案、要方案，堅持早發現、早報告、早隔離、早治療的防控要求和集中患者、集中專家、集中資源、集中救治的原則，堅持中西醫結合、中西藥並用；中國高度重視統籌疫情防控和經濟社會發展，統籌國內效應和全球影響，精準有序推進復工復產。不少國家領導人稱讚，中國抗疫經驗值得世界借鑒。

三是中國為全球抗疫提供了巨大支援。中國始終秉持公開、透明、負責任的態度，積極開展抗疫國際合作。中國第一時間通報疫情信息，迅速測出並分享病毒基因序列。中國毫無保留地與各國分享防控診療經驗，開設了向所有國家開放的新冠肺炎疫情防控網上知識中心。中國向世衛組織提供兩千萬美元捐款。今天，中國又宣佈增加三千萬美元捐款，用於新冠肺炎疫情防控，支持發展中國家衛生體系建設等工作。中國向十五個國家派遣十七支醫療專家組，已經或正在向包括英國在內的一百五十多個國家和國際組織提供了口罩、防護服、檢測試劑、呼吸機等急需的醫療物資援助。中國克服自身困難，加大力度向國際市場供應原料藥、防疫物資等產品，從三月一日到四月十日，中國共出口口罩約七十二億隻，防護服五千五百五十七萬件，紅外測溫儀三百五十九萬件，呼吸機兩萬台，護目鏡一千三百萬副。「中國支援」為國際社會戰勝疫情提振了信心，為全球抗疫鬥爭注入源源不斷的正能量。

現在，我想談談各位關心的疫情背景下的中國經

濟。近來國際貨幣基金組織大幅下調今年世界經濟增長預期，警告此次疫情對世界經濟的衝擊可能超過二十世紀大蕭條。疫情對中國經濟社會發展帶來嚴峻的衝擊，第一季度經濟同比下降百分之六點八。面對前所未有的風險、挑戰和不確定性，我們更要堅定信心和勇氣，努力化危為機，推動經濟社會不斷發展。

一是中國經濟長期向好的態勢沒有改變也不會改變。中國經濟基礎雄厚，中國是世界第二大經濟體，二〇一九年國內生產總值達到十四點四萬億美元，是二〇〇八年國際金融危機時四點六萬億美元的三點一倍和二〇〇三年非典時一點六七萬億美元的八點六倍。中國是全世界唯一擁有聯合國產業分類當中全部工業門類的國家。中國經濟發展空間廣闊，有十四億人口、九億勞動力、四億多中等收入群體。中國人均國內生產總值剛超過一萬美元，僅為英國的四分之一、美國的六分之一，中國城市化率僅有百分之六十，未來增長潛力巨大。中國高度重視統籌疫情防控和經濟社會發展，生產生活秩序加快恢復，復工達產正在逐步接近或達到正常水平。目前，全國規模以上工業企業平均開工率達到百分之九十九，三月製造業採購經理人指數（PMI）比上月回升十六點三個百分點。根據 IMF 最新的《世界經濟展望》報告，二〇二一年中國經濟增速將強勁回升至百分之九點二。

二是中國經濟更高質量發展的方向沒有改變也不會改變。中國在疫情防控常態化前提下，堅持新發展理念，堅持以供給側結構性改革為主線，完善要素市場化配置體制機制，堅持以改革開放為動力推動高質量發展。我們以更大的宏觀政策力度對衝疫情影響，加大「六穩」工作力度，保居民就業、保基本民生、保市場主體、保糧食能源安全、保產業鏈供應鏈穩定、保基層運轉，維護經濟發展和社會穩定大局。我們堅定實施擴大內需戰略，積極擴大有效投資，敏銳抓住「宅經濟」「雲辦公」等發展機遇，藉助互聯網、大數據、人工智能等新興技術，推動數字經濟、智能製造、醫療健康等新興產業快速成長，促進傳統產業改造升級，擴大戰略性新興產業投資，積極促進綠色經濟發展，加快經濟高質量發展步伐。

三是中國作為世界經濟「動力源」和「穩定器」

的擔當沒有改變，也不會改變。中國堅定不移擴大對外開放，放寬市場准入，優化營商環境，積極擴大進口，擴大對外投資，保障國際物流暢通，推進共建「一帶一路」高質量發展。中國歷史最悠久的廣交會將於六月中下旬首次在網上舉辦，中國還將於十一月舉辦第三屆中國國際進口博覽會，為各國互利合作提供更大機遇。中國推動加強宏觀經濟政策協調，穩市場、保增長、保民生，確保全球供應鏈開放、穩定、安全。作為「世界工廠」的中國經濟率先重回正軌，將為世界經濟復甦注入強大動力。

最後，我想談談國際社會應如何攜手應對疫情。當下，人們都在爭論，疫情使世界變得更團結了，還是更分裂了？我的回答是：疫情使我們再次深刻感受到，人類是一個休戚與共、命運相連的命運共同體。團結合作是最有力武器，國際社會只有團結合作、共克時艱，才能最終戰勝疫情。

一是加強全球行動，打好全球疫情防控阻擊戰。在不久前舉行的二十國集團領導人特別峰會上，習近平主席提出堅決打好疫情防控全球阻擊戰、有效開展國際聯防聯控、積極支持國際組織發揮作用、加強國際宏觀經濟政策協調四點重要倡議，推動開展藥物和疫苗聯合研發、發起二十國集團抗疫援助倡議、共同維護全球產業鏈供應鏈穩定等一系列務實合作，為各國合作應對疫情指明方向。中國將繼續與各國加強抗疫合作，展現大國胸懷與擔當，為全球抗疫做出應有貢獻。

二是凝聚團結共識，堅定戰勝疫情的信心。病毒沒有國界，疫情不分種族。危機面前，指責與推諉無濟於事，傲慢與狂妄害人害己。刻意將病毒標籤化、抗疫政治化以及對特定國家污名化，更是違背人類道德良知，加劇國際社會分裂，侵蝕國際抗疫合作成果，損害全人類的利益。各國應該堅決摒棄意識形態偏見，把保護和拯救生命放在第一位，切實形成抗擊疫情的最大合力。

三是堅持多邊主義，支持國際組織發揮積極作用。中國堅持多邊主義原則，加強和完善以聯合國為核心的全球治理體系。疫情發生以來，世衛組織秉持客觀科學公正立場，為協調推動國際抗疫合作發揮了

重要作用，得到國際社會普遍讚譽。中國將一如既往支持世衛組織工作，支持世衛組織在全球抗疫合作中發揮領導作用。中國將積極加強與各國「一帶一路」衛生合作，共建「健康絲綢之路」。

四是促進開放合作，維護開放型世界經濟。越是面對困難和挑戰，我們越要堅持以開放促合作、以合作促發展。有人鼓噪搞「人為脫鈎」和「科技封鎖」，這是自我封閉、自我設限、自我倒退。中國將堅定不移擴大改革開放，積極推動各方加強宏觀經濟政策協調，著眼「後疫情時代」，採取一切必要舉措，維護全球產業鏈供應鏈穩定，促進貿易投資自由化便利化，共同建設開放型世界經濟。

女士們、先生們，中英是國際抗疫合作的重要夥伴。習近平主席與約翰遜首相一個多月來兩次通電話，共同傳遞了攜手戰勝疫情的堅定決心。中英正加強防疫信息分享和經驗交流，加強科研攻關合作。中英兩國都堅定支持多邊主義，支持世衛組織在全球抗疫中發揮重要作用，支持加強在二十國集團框架內的抗疫合作，推動完善全球衛生治理。在這個抗擊疫情的重要時刻，中英要展現擔當，守望相助，排除雜音和干擾，為雙方合作增加正能量，為全球公共衛生安全做出新貢獻。我相信，疫情過後，中英關係將更加成熟、強勁，雙方合作將更加廣泛、深入，兩國人民友誼將更加牢固、持久！

中國有一句古語，「積力之所舉則無不勝，眾智之所為則無不成」。中國願與包括英國在內的國際社會一道，堅定必勝信念，加強團結合作，攜手共克時艱，共同戰勝疫情，共創世界美好未來！

下面我願回答各位的提問。

「亞洲之家」主席格林勳爵：歡迎劉大使！非常感謝各位與會者！隨著新冠肺炎疫情在全球蔓延，我們正面臨非同尋常的形勢，更多人呼籲開展建設性的國際合作。我認為，現在的形勢至少是第二次世界大戰以來「前所未有」的，給每一個國家都帶來了各種挑戰。中國第一個受到疫情衝擊，看來也將是第一個擺脫疫情影響的國家。我認為，保持謹慎仍是非常必要的。現在英國仍在與疫情做鬥爭，歐洲也在與疫情做

鬥爭。

當前，我們面臨短期、中期和長期的挑戰，其中一些挑戰源於新冠疫情的深刻影響，另一些則不是。在我看來，短期內，我們面臨如何退出封鎖隔離措施的問題。這一問題在英國乃至整個歐洲引起了廣泛討論，並在美國和東亞一些地區引發諸多焦慮。日本採取了特殊的防疫路徑，但極有可能引發病毒「二次衝擊」。在研製出有效疫苗仍需時日的情況下，不同的抗疫策略會帶來不同的挑戰。疫情對經濟也產生短期挑戰。例如，旅遊業如何能重新成為重要的經濟力量？小型零售企業在多大程度上會因疫情影響而倒閉？

從整個宏觀經濟看，各國紛紛推出龐大的財政和貨幣刺激政策，這些措施會產生什麼樣的中期後果？隨著各國試圖修復財政狀況，這是否意味著新一輪財政緊縮？是否意味著將推高稅收或通脹？無論是經濟正在復甦的中國，還是英國、歐洲國家或者美國，都面臨這樣的問題。當然，由於美元的特殊性，美國的情況可能會有所不同。這些都是疫情帶來的中期挑戰。

同時，在疫情影響之外還存在一些中長期挑戰，國際貿易秩序就是其中之一。在疫情發生前，由於缺乏足夠的上訴法官，世界貿易組織正在喪失有效解決爭端的能力。我注意到，今年三月三十日，歐盟和中國以及其他一些國家達成了「多方臨時上訴仲裁安排」（MPIA）。這是支持世貿組織工作的重要一步。我很關注英國將如何參與這一安排。

劉大使剛才在演講中談到為什麼要支持世衛組織。世衛組織是一個重要的國際組織，而世貿組織同樣是一個重要的國際機構，是當前國際多邊秩序的一部分，我們都應予以關注。對於這兩個國際組織，美國目前採取了「非建設性態度」。我認為，重建對國際多邊秩序的信心，符合各方共同利益。

最後，還有一個繞不開的長期性問題，就是生物多樣性、環境退化、氣候變化。疫情導致經濟活動下降，世界各地城市的污染狀況暫時得到改善，二氧化碳排放減少。但由於持續的人口、城市化和經濟發展等壓力，人類將不得不繼續面對環境、氣候等長期挑

戰。短期內，疫情可能增加應對氣候變化的困難，比如英中雙方均不得不推遲舉辦《聯合國氣候變化框架公約》第二十六次締約方會議（COP26）和《生物多樣性公約》第十五次締約方會議（COP15）。劉大使提到這兩次會議是中英共同的重要議程，我也希望會議只是暫時推遲，我們不能因疫情和眼前的困難而忽視長期挑戰。

我們生活的時代非同尋常。疫情帶來的挑戰是多方面的，國際關係也不可避免地受到影響。對於中美關係這一重大問題，我們歐洲人以期待和祈願的心態關注其發展，認為中美關係只有在建設性基礎上才能向前發展。因此，我們今天的對話可謂恰逢其時。「亞洲之家」一直積極為開展各類對話發揮重要的平台作用，這些對話既包括從微觀經濟到宏觀經濟，也包括貿易秩序等中期問題，以及氣候變化及其對經濟發展影響等長期問題。我就講到這裏。劉大使，不知你是否與我「君子所見略同」？

劉曉明：感謝格林勳爵！對於你談到的很多問題，有不少方面的觀點我都贊同。你談到了疫情對各個國家的挑戰。我認為每個國家的情況各不相同，英國不同於德國、意大利或法國。我們正在密切關注疫情情況。儘管存在差異，但我認為各國在抗擊疫情方面仍存在共同之處。我在演講中談到中英合作，這同樣適用於中國與其他國家的合作。當我們面對這些共同威脅時，各國應該共同合作應對。

第一，我們應該加強互相支持。在醫療物資領域，當中國處於抗疫關鍵階段時，英國政府向中國提供了兩批急需的醫療物資。現在英國正與疫情做鬥爭，我們同樣向英方提供了大力支持。正如英國內閣辦大臣戈夫所說，英方收到中方的防疫醫療物資遠遠超過英方給中方的防疫捐贈。目前，英國急需呼吸機，中國已經將七百五十台呼吸機運到英國，未來還會更多。我們還準備向英國及世界其他國家提供更多其他醫療物資和設備。

第二，我們要開展抗疫經驗分享。中國是最早取得疫情防控重要階段性成效的國家之一。我們願與其他國家分享在疫情防控和診療方面的經驗。我很高興

地看到，中英雙方就此保持密切溝通。英國衛生大臣漢考克昨天與中國衛生健康委主任馬曉偉通了電話，雙方就中英抗疫合作進行了非常富有成果和深入的討論。

第三，我們要加強抗疫國際合作。在演講中，我已經談到這方面內容。剛才，格林勳爵以「英國紳士式」的措辭——「非建設性態度」來形容美國的立場和做法。我們對美國宣佈暫停資助世衛組織的決定深感失望。在當前抗疫關鍵時刻，世衛組織扮演著重要角色，我們需要支持世衛組織在全球抗疫合作中發揮領導作用。我很高興地看到，英國政府決定繼續支持世衛組織，中英雙方在這方面持相同立場。中國已向世衛組織提供兩千萬美元捐款。就在我們今天活動開始前數個小時，中國又宣佈向世衛組織增加三千萬美元現金捐款，用於支持非洲和發展中國家衛生體系建設等工作。中國政府有關部門好像知道今天「亞洲之家」要舉辦這一活動，使我能夠第一時間跟各位分享這個信息。（眾人笑）

第四，我們要加強宏觀經濟政策協調。包括中英在內的國際社會可加強宏觀經濟政策協調，促進世界經濟恢復增長。目前，中國全國規模以上工業企業平均開工率已達到百分之九十九，中國政府還採取了更多支持中小企業的政策。同時，中國致力於支持世界貿易組織，推進貿易自由化和便利化。我們願就此與英方加強合作。

中方同樣高度重視氣候變化問題。令人遺憾的是，中英雙方均不得不推遲 COP15 與 COP26。今年初，我曾講，今年是中英氣候變化合作之年。儘管面臨疫情挑戰，中英兩國仍就此保持密切溝通。會議雖然推遲，但工作仍在推進。我同英國商業、能源與產業戰略部大臣兼 COP26 主席夏爾馬保持密切溝通，積極推動他與新上任的中國生態環境部部長黃潤秋建立工作聯繫，兩國工作組也通過網上保持溝通。

另一個重要問題是，當我們加強抗疫國際合作時，也應共同反對「政治病毒」。正如我在演講中所說，一些政客和一些勢力試圖尋找「替罪羊」，企圖對外「甩鍋」、轉嫁責任。各國政府應集中精力應對疫情，保護本國人民生命安全，而不是相互攻擊和破

壞國際合作。對一些美國政客對中國的指責，我們堅決反對。這種針對中國的抹黑無助於國際社會合作抗疫。

關於中美關係，我們完全有理由建立穩定和良好的關係。近一個時期，習近平主席與特朗普總統多次通話。我們始終認為中美合則兩利、鬥則俱傷。一個穩定和良好的中美關係不僅符合中美兩國利益，也符合世界各國的利益。我們希望在不衝突不對抗、相互尊重、合作共贏的基礎上與美國保持良好關係，但是這需要中美雙方相向而行。當中國領導人和中國的駐外使節、外交官們在全世界大力倡導構建人類命運共同體，支持國際社會增強抗疫必勝信心的時候，一些國家的政客和官員在幹什麼？他們到處散佈假消息和謠言——這毫無助益！我們真誠希望中美加強合作，也希望國際社會加強合作，以實現符合全人類利益的共同目標。

怡和集團董事亞當·凱瑟克： 劉大使，你好！感謝劉大使和格林勳爵，你們剛才的發言令人鼓舞。我相信，我們為抗疫而建立的溝通網絡，在戰勝疫情後同樣能促進世界經濟發展。劉大使在演講中對中國所做努力做了全面介紹，令人欣慰。現在，國際社會都很關注中國全國人民代表大會何時召開。有消息稱，這次大會可能會在今年五月晚些時候召開。你認為這次大會將對外傳遞什麼具體信息？這些信息將如何增強國際社會抗疫信心、推動世界經濟恢復到正常狀態？希望聽聽你的看法。

劉曉明： 你提到的會議很重要。每年的「兩會」是中國政治生活中的一件大事。今年的「兩會」受疫情影響推遲了。今年的「兩會」將不只為今年中國發展制訂規劃，還將制訂未來五年的「十四五」規劃，意義更加深遠。當然，抗擊新冠肺炎疫情將是「兩會」的重要議程。正如我在演講中所說，疫情既帶來挑戰，也為中國進一步發展提供機遇。我認為，「兩會」的代表們將會聚焦中國未來發展的新領域和新增長點。我建議你密切關注今年中國「兩會」。

必和必拓公司國際關係和公共事務副總裁埃瑪．羅伯茨：很高興聽到劉大使全面介紹中國經濟正走出危機。必和必拓與中國客戶保持著非常密切的聯繫。截至目前，我們感到即使在中國疫情高峰期，中國客戶對我們公司產品的需求仍保持穩定，這讓我們能夠繼續向中國提供產品。當然，我認為難免還會有一些關切。例如，近期部分媒體關注中國對外需求在今年下半年會否放緩。同時，西方國家正嘗試退出封鎖隔離措施，實現經濟恢復運轉仍很艱難，中國從西方國家的進口可能下滑。你對中國經濟走出危機和保持快速發展勢頭有何看法？受西方經濟復甦乏力影響，中國經濟面臨的風險會增加，是否還會保持穩定和強勁呢？

劉曉明：我認為，隨著逐步復工達產，中國仍將是世界經濟發展的動力源。目前全國規模以上工業企業平均開工率已達到百分之九十九，中國將繼續扮演「世界工廠」的角色。中國市場規模巨大，將為促進全球經濟恢復增長做出貢獻。此次疫情也為中國經濟加快轉型帶來機會，包括「宅經濟」、數字經濟、人工智能及醫療衛生等領域都具有很大的發展潛力。例如，從三月一日到四月十日，中國出口了約七十一點二億隻口罩、五千五百五十七萬件防護服、二點零一萬台呼吸機和一千三百六十九萬副護目鏡。中國已經成為全球醫療用品的主要供應地，這不僅是中國對全球抗疫的貢獻，也有助於打造未來的產業鏈、供應鏈。

中國致力於構建開放型世界經濟。中國過去四十多年來取得巨大成功，得益於改革開放。我認為，中國未來繼續成功，同樣有賴於堅持改革開放。對中國而言，沒有任何理由關上大門，也沒有任何理由停止改革。因此，中國的改革將繼續推進，對世界開放的大門只會越開越大。第一二七屆廣交會將於今年六月在網上舉辦，第三屆中國國際進口博覽會將於十一月舉辦，這些為中國與世界加強互利合作提供了寶貴機會。我已與英國國際貿易部高級官員和商界領袖進行溝通，邀請他們出席這兩場重要活動。這將為中英兩國共同推動重振世界經濟提供重要機遇。

阿斯利康公司英國政府與國際關係副總監曼：感謝劉大使所做的精彩演講。阿斯利康公司一直高度重視對華合作。疫情發生以來，我們與中國以及世界衛生組織、世界經濟論壇合作，向全球有需要的國家捐贈了九百萬隻口罩。你認為未來深化英中關係有哪些重要機遇？例如，在醫療衛生、生命科學等領域的合作。

劉曉明：正如我剛才所講，中英兩國高層保持密切溝通。習近平主席與約翰遜首相一個多月內兩次通電話，這非常罕見。我擔任中國駐英國大使十年有餘，從未見過兩國領導人在這麼短的時間內進行如此密集的溝通。中央外事工作委員會辦公室主任楊潔篪與英國內閣秘書兼首相國家安全事務顧問塞德維爾、王毅國務委員兼外長與英國外交大臣拉布等兩國高官也保持密切溝通。我在倫敦也與英國有關部門大臣、國務大臣等就中英合作交換意見和建議。未來中英很多領域的合作都充滿機遇。

在疫苗研發和經驗交流方面，目前中英兩國科學家正緊密合作加快研發，帝國理工學院、牛津大學、劍橋大學與中國科研機構密切合作。不久前，中國山東聯合工作組來英國期間，與英國醫療專家進行線上交流，開展密切合作。除醫療物資外，疫苗是我們打贏這場全球疫情防控戰的最終解決方案。習近平主席和約翰遜首相都很支持兩國科學家在這一重要領域開展合作。

在國際領域，中英兩國合作密切。雙方都支持多邊主義，支持世衛組織和世貿組織，格林勳爵對此十分關注。我們把英國視作共建「一帶一路」的「天然合作夥伴」。中英還可共同推動「一帶一路」沿線國家加強衛生合作，共建「健康絲綢之路」。

在氣候變化領域，中英也可加強合作。雙方都是環境保護的全球領軍者。中英今年原計劃分別主辦的 COP15 與 COP26 雖因疫情推遲，但雙方準備工作並沒有停止。疫情過後，兩場會議將再次提上日程，為氣候變化、環境保護領域國際合作設定議程和方向。兩國在這些領域合作面臨巨大機遇。

在貿易領域，中英合作前景廣闊。去年，儘管全球貿易增長放緩，中英雙邊貨物貿易額同比增長超過

百分之七，創歷史新高。目前，英國是中國在歐洲第三大貿易夥伴，中國是英國第三大貨物出口市場。英國是中國在歐洲地區最大投資目的地國，過去五年中國對英投資超過了過去三十年的總和，中資企業在英國非常活躍。前不久，我在線出席了英國中國商會首批援助英方醫療物資捐贈儀式，英國中國商會向英國國民醫療服務體系捐贈了呼吸機、防護服、口罩等醫療物資，這充分體現了在英中資企業的全球視野和社會責任。我們鼓勵中英之間加強這樣的交流互動。

畢馬威會計師事務所金融服務副主席塞耶：我想談談現在了不起的技術。劉大使，你剛才說，每個挑戰中也蘊含著機遇。現在通過技術，我們不僅與英國客戶，也能與中國公司進行更快、更直接的對話。我們現在能更容易、更好地與中國夥伴進行視頻會議。而以前，要與中國夥伴對話，我們必須經過近二十個小時飛行，還得有其他安排。我認為此次疫情挑戰所帶來的一個機遇，就是英中各領域對話將加速。在這方面，我們應如何更好地利用新技術？中國駐英國使館為此能發揮什麼作用？

劉曉明：很高興你成為新技術的獲益者之一。華為公司參與英國5G網絡發展後，在線會議速度一定會更快、質量會更高。約翰遜首相提出雄心勃勃的計劃，要在二〇二五年前在全英實現5G網絡全覆蓋，華為將為此發揮重要作用。我希望，不僅中英兩國領導人保持溝通，兩國工商界人士也要加強對話。除了與「亞洲之家」對話外，我最近還參加了其他在線會議。不久前，我與英國中國商會進行視頻座談，接下來我還將與英國工商業聯合會、英中貿協進行視頻座談。我們能進行即時討論，得益於新技術發展。同時，我們應致力於維護自由貿易，共同營造良好營商環境。英國素以自由和開放經濟著稱，這是英國能成為中國在歐洲最大投資目的地國的重要原因。我曾問中國企業家，你們為什麼要到英國來投資，而不是去其他國家。我不久前參加中國河北敬業集團收購英國鋼鐵公司交割儀式時，問過敬業集團負責人同樣的問題。他們表示，英國非常開放、透明，英國從中央政

府及地方政府領導人，到工商界人士和地方社區，都張開雙臂歡迎中國投資。這是英國成功的秘訣。因此，我希望這一勢頭能繼續保持，這不僅有利於中英合作，也符合英國自身的利益。

BBC 記者蘭德爾： 劉大使，你非常重視國際合作。中國是否支持針對病毒源頭的獨立國際調查？是否會完全向調查者開放所有的相關數據、地點和證據？

劉曉明： 中國對疫情從一開始就採取公開、透明、負責任的態度。我們邀請世衛組織專家來華，他們不僅訪問了武漢，還訪問了其他城市。訪問後他們發佈了一份非常全面翔實的報告，不知道你是否讀過。我聽到關於所謂中國掩蓋和隱藏疫情的猜測和虛假信息，這些都不是事實。一些人抱有先入為主的偏見，每當聽到美國政客指責中國掩蓋事實的時候，都會隨波逐流。但是，當中國外交部發言人講出事實真相的時候，西方媒體卻很少報道，因為他們對中國抱有很深的偏見。這就是問題的癥結。

我建議包括英國媒體在內的西方媒體要秉持平衡、客觀立場。我並非要求你們對中國友好，只是要求你們保持平衡、公正的立場。你們報道美國國務卿對中國的所謂「批評」，實際上他是在對中國污名化。同時，你們更應該報道中國的反駁論點，更應該報道世衛組織對此的評論。那些固守偏見的媒體，只會報道他們想聽的東西，而不會報道故事的另一面。這就是問題之所在。

中國政府對抗疫公開、透明、負責任並且反應迅速。美國抱怨中國在疫情發生後一個月沒有分享信息，也沒有向世衛組織和其他國際組織報告，這不是事實。新冠病毒最早由張繼先醫生於二〇一九年十二月二十七日首次報告，要早於李文亮醫生。李文亮醫生是個英雄，為抗擊疫情而犧牲了。在張繼先醫生向當地衛生部門報告三天後，中國政府採取了非常嚴格和迅速的行動，四天後就通知了世衛組織，七天後與美國分享了疫情信息。所以美國才能採取撤僑等行動。如果你查閱中國抗疫的時間線，你會發現我們所有疫情信息都是公開、透明的。

你談到獨立調查，這應該取決於世衛組織。我們支持世衛組織在全球抗疫合作中發揮重要作用。我們應該遵循國際規則，而非某個國家的規則。個別國家甚至在地方法院「起訴」中國，這完全是荒唐至極。我曾兩次在美國常駐。這已不是第一次某些政客想當「世界警察」了。當今時代已不是「炮艦外交」的時代，也不是中國處於半殖民地半封建社會的時代，而是二十一世紀的第三個十年。但這些政客還生活在過去，無法理解今天的世界，自認為能像過去一樣欺負中國、欺負世界。如果世衛組織不能按其意志行事，他們就停止支持世衛組織，指責世衛組織「以中國為中心」，這完全是錯誤的。因此，我們呼籲加強國際合作，這是贏得抗疫鬥爭的唯一武器和唯一出路，而不應找「替罪羊」，不應玩政治遊戲，不應把病毒政治化，不應傳播「政治病毒」。我們在與病毒這個「無形的敵人」做鬥爭時，必須對「政治病毒」保持警惕。

我想強調的是，中國不是美國的敵人，而是美國的朋友，是美國與病毒做鬥爭的夥伴。如果這些美國政客將中國視為敵人，就是選錯了對象。儘管一些美國政客散佈關於中國的虛假信息，我們仍在美國人民需要時伸出援手。中國已向美國提供超過十八億隻口罩，意味著每個美國人可獲得六隻口罩。

中國國際電視台記者戴維德：劉大使，你提到了中國在疫情之後的一些優先關注領域。具體看，你認為這些優先領域有哪些？

劉曉明：首先，要全面實現復工達產。中國高度重視統籌推進疫情防控和經濟社會發展工作。我們在常態化疫情防控中全面推進復工復產達產，恢復正常經濟社會秩序。我們將以更大的宏觀政策力度對衝疫情影響，加大「六穩」工作力度，保居民就業、保基本民生、保市場主體、保糧食能源安全、保產業鏈供應鏈穩定、保基層運轉，堅定實施擴大內需戰略，積極扶持中小企業，維護經濟發展和社會穩定大局。

其次，要確保疫情不反彈。中國政府始終把人民群眾生命安全和身體健康放在第一位。針對國外輸入

病例帶來的風險上升，中國政府正完善各項措施並切實抓好落實，但還需要與其他國家加強合作來實現防疫目標。我們現在已經開放離開武漢的通道，但在其他領域仍存在一些限制。我們必須確保來之不易的抗疫成果不會發生逆轉，不斷鞏固疫情防控持續向好態勢。

再次，要堅持推動改革開放。我們堅持用改革的辦法解決發展中的問題，完善要素市場配置體制機制，堅定不移擴大對外開放，保障國際物流暢通，繼續為國際社會提供高質量的防疫物資，推動共建「一帶一路」高質量發展。

最後，要進一步加強國際合作。正如我剛才談到的，中國將繼續就重要國際議程與各方保持溝通。例如，在氣候變化領域我與英國商業、能源與產業戰略部大臣夏爾馬及其他高級官員進行交流，保持雙方合作勢頭，共同推進相關工作。我們正與英國國際貿易部就英國「脫歐」後推進中英自貿協定保持密切溝通。因此我們的工作日程是很滿的，許多工作都在網上進行。我們時刻做好準備，確保疫情一旦結束，相關工作就可以盡快重回正軌。

格林勳爵：劉大使，這是一次非常精彩的討論。我感到收穫頗豐。你最後的發言是非常好的總結，充分展示了我們在廣泛領域有機會開展有效合作，我們需要保持這一積極勢頭。在新冠肺炎疫情之後，我們將總結經驗教訓，短期內看，我們還有許多修補宏觀經濟等工作要開展；從長期看，我們在根本性問題上有很多共同點，也有很多合作的機會。因此，我代表「亞洲之家」衷心感謝你抽出寶貴時間與我們一起討論，也期待著更多交流。你提到你出任中國駐英國大使已超過十年，這意味著你非常了解英國。我一直很讚賞你對英國的看法，因為你總是對英國和英中關係有深刻的見解。在這場疫情危機中，我們面臨許多重大機遇。我們永遠不要忽略這一點。

再次感謝劉大使，感謝所有嘉賓出席這場非常有意義的座談會。

劉曉明：不客氣。

第五章

與英國議員對話

二〇二〇年十月十三日，我應邀出席英國議會跨黨派中國小組氣候變化問題在線座談會，發表題為《共建美好地球家園》的主旨演講並回答議員提問。英國議會跨黨派中國小組主席格雷厄姆，議會下院環境監察委員會主席鄧恩，外交發展部 COP26 區域大使布里斯托，議會上、下兩院議員，內閣辦、外交發展部、環境部主管官員，保守黨環保機構、英中貿協、英中協會代表等三十餘人參加。

十月二十八日，我出席英國議會跨黨派國際環保小組「保護自然：通向昆明之路」線上座談會，發表題為《譜寫生態文明新篇章》的主旨演講並回答與會人員提問。英國議會跨黨派國際環保小組主席加德納，聯合國《生物多樣性公約》秘書處執行秘書穆雷瑪，南非環境、森林及漁業部長克里西，加蓬森林、海洋、環境和氣候變化部長懷特，英國外交發展國務大臣戈登·史密斯，全球環境基金首席執行官羅德里格斯以及一些國家的議會議員出席。

共建美好地球家園

——與英國議會跨黨派中國小組談氣候變化問題並回答議員提問

（二〇二〇年十月十三日，中國駐英國使館／英國議會）

劉曉明：很高興再次與英國議會跨黨派中國小組各位議員座談。我們今天座談的主題是中英氣候變化合作。二〇二一年將是氣候變化合作之年，中英將分別主辦《生物多樣性公約》第十五次締約方會議（COP15）和《聯合國氣候變化框架公約》第二十六次締約方會議（COP26），這將是中英關係的大事，也將對全球氣變合作和環境治理產生重要影響。

當前，新冠肺炎疫情在全球蔓延，氣候變化問題持續升溫。我認為，人類社會正面臨與氣候變化緊密相關的五大挑戰：

一是全球變暖挑戰。目前全球平均溫度已比工業化前高出一攝氏度以上，全球海平面上升速度達到每年五毫米。未來，一些地區可能不再適宜居住。

二是生態環境挑戰。人類工業化進程創造了前所未有的物質財富，也產生了嚴重環境污染，生物多樣性面臨嚴峻挑戰。

三是新冠肺炎疫情疊加挑戰。疫情客觀上削弱了各國對應對氣候變化問題的關注。COP15 和 COP26 不得不推遲舉行。

四是應對能力不平衡挑戰。與發達國家相比，發展中國家受到氣候變化衝擊影響更大。國際社會消除南北發展不平衡、凝聚應對氣候變化合力依然任重道遠。

五是毀約退群挑戰。個別國家悍然退出《巴黎協

定》，這種單邊霸凌行徑使全球氣變合作和治理遭受嚴重挫折。

不久前，習近平主席在出席聯合國成立七十五週年高級別活動中宣佈，中國將提高國家自主貢獻力度，採取更加有力的政策和措施，二氧化碳排放力爭於二〇三〇年前達到峰值，努力爭取二〇六〇年前實現碳中和。這是中國基於國內可持續發展內在要求和構建人類命運共同體的責任擔當，彰顯了中國積極應對氣候變化的堅定決心。國際社會對此予以高度評價。約翰遜首相稱，習主席宣佈的目標是一件了不起的事情，是向世界發出的強有力信號。中英是應對氣候變化和環境治理的重要夥伴，雙方合作大有可為。

一是共同做氣變治理的領軍者。中國積極落實應對氣候變化國家戰略，切實履行《巴黎協定》國際義務。二〇〇五年至二〇一九年，中國單位 GDP 碳排放下降百分之四十八點一，非化石能源佔比達百分之十五點三，新能源汽車保有量佔全球一半以上。英國確立了到二〇五〇年實現「淨零排放」的目標。中英可以充分利用主辦 COP15 和 COP26 兩次會議之機，為全球氣變治理發揮重要引領作用。習近平主席和約翰遜首相就兩國加強 COP15 和 COP26 相互協調、相互支持達成重要共識。中國生態環境部部長黃潤秋與夏爾馬大臣，我本人與夏爾馬大臣、布里斯托爵士等保持密切溝通。雙方還在工作層建立了聯合工作組。下一步，雙方要加強溝通協調，調動政府、議會、商界、媒體、學界等各界人士積極性，確保兩次大會辦得精彩、取得成功。

二是共同做綠色發展的推動者。疫情形勢下，中國政府統籌推進疫情防控與經濟社會發展，推廣綠色生產和生活方式，加速完善氣候投融資體系。英國在清潔能源、低碳技術等方面獨具特色。中英應加強在新能源、低碳城市等領域合作，實現生態環境保護和經濟高質量發展雙贏。中國在核能等清潔能源領域技術成熟，運營管理經驗豐富。欣克利角 C 核電站是中、英、法在清潔能源領域合作的重要旗艦項目，建成後可滿足英國百分之七的電力需求，每年可以減排九百萬噸二氧化碳。雙方應共同努力確保該項目順利成功。我們還應鼓勵兩國產業界在可再生能源、綠色

金融、綠色「一帶一路」等領域加強合作，助力兩國綠色復產，帶動全球綠色復甦。

三是共同做綠色創新的開拓者。中英都在積極推動綠色科技、能源、金融創新發展。兩國簽署了《中英清潔能源合作夥伴關係實施工作計劃二〇一九至二〇二〇》，共同制定了「一帶一路」綠色投資原則，綠色合作潛力巨大。吉利、比亞迪等中資企業積極投資英國，成為兩國綠色交通合作的典範。

四是共同做多邊主義的捍衛者。中英雙方應堅定維護多邊主義，按照公平、共同但有區別的責任和各自能力原則，盡最大努力落實國家自主貢獻，共同推動《巴黎協定》全面、平衡、有效實施，幫助發展中國家提升應對氣變能力，深化應對氣變國際合作，完善氣候治理體系，共同引領全球氣變治理方向和進程。

女士們、先生們，應對氣候變化、保護生物多樣性是中英合作的重要領域，也是中英兩國作為具有全球影響的大國應肩負的使命。習近平在聯合國生物多樣性峰會上指出，「我們要站在對人類文明負責的高度，尊重自然、順應自然、保護自然，探索人與自然和諧共生之路，促進經濟發展與生態保護協調統一，共建繁榮、清潔、美麗的世界」。英國議會在英國應對氣候變化進程中發揮著重要作用。我衷心期望各位議員繼續發揮積極作用，支持中英兩國政府、兩國企業開展綠色合作，為辦好 COP15 和 COP26 獻計獻策，為構建人類命運共同體、共建美好地球家園貢獻力量！

謝謝！

現在我願回答各位議員的提問。

議會跨黨派中國小組主席格雷厄姆：在新冠肺炎疫情形勢下，明年 COP15 大會能否如期舉行？

劉曉明：現距大會召開還有七個多月，我們對 COP15 如期舉行充滿信心。目前中國國內民眾已恢復正常生活，經濟復工復產取得重要成果。我們將繼續做好國內疫情防控工作，也會密切關注全球疫情發展。正如習近平主席在聯合國生物多樣性峰會上所

說，歡迎大家明年聚首美麗的春城昆明，共商全球生物多樣性大計，共建萬物和諧的美麗世界。

議會上院議員盧卡斯勳爵：英中在新能源特別是新能源汽車領域如何進一步開展合作？

劉曉明：在新能源領域，中國非常願意與英國開展互利合作。截至二〇一九年底，中國新能源汽車保有量達三百八十一萬輛，佔全球一半以上，增量連續兩年超過一百萬輛，均居全球領先地位。無論是中國比亞迪公司製造的電動大巴，還是吉利公司投資倫敦出租車公司後在英生產的全電動出租車，都為英國減少碳排放做出了貢獻。此外，中國是可再生能源領域最大投資國，積極發展太陽能和風能。我認為，中英在相關領域蘊含巨大合作機遇，合作前景十分廣闊。

議會上院議員盧卡斯勳爵：你如何看待英中在核能領域的合作前景？

劉曉明：中國核能技術成熟，運營管理經驗豐富，中方願繼續與英方加強核能合作。截至二〇一九年底，中國運行核電機組達到四十七台，總裝機容量為四千八百七十五萬千瓦，僅次於美國和法國，位列全球第三。欣克利角C核電站是中、英、法在核能領域重要旗艦項目，將幫助英國實現二〇五〇年「淨零排放」目標。目前這一項目面臨一些雜音。我期待中英雙方排除干擾，繼續共同推進這一重要項目。

議會跨黨派中國小組副主席克利夫頓－布朗爵士：英國已淘汰所有煤炭發電廠。中國煤電發展是否會影響二〇六〇年實現碳中和的目標？中國將在何時淘汰煤電？

劉曉明：中國是世界上最大的發展中國家，經濟社會發展任務十分艱巨，發展不平衡、不充分等挑戰仍然突出。對中國部分省區而言，煤炭仍是主要能源，逐步減少煤電需要一個過程。我曾在中國西部省份甘肅省擔任省長助理，當地經濟發展對煤炭仍有相當依

賴。中國正嚴控煤炭消費總量，在工業領域提升能效環保標準，積極推進鋼鐵、建材、化工等高耗煤行業節能減排改造；在民生領域逐步推行天然氣、電力、潔淨型煤及可再生能源等清潔能源替代民用散煤，取得顯著進展。中國高度重視煤電技術創新，已建成全球最大的清潔煤電供應體系，煤電超低排放機組超八億千瓦，排放標準世界領先，為全球各國煤炭清潔利用做出了示範。著眼二〇六〇年前實現碳中和目標，中國將採取有力政策和措施，進一步推進綠色創新和能源轉型，逐步減少化石能源消費，促進綠色高質量發展。

議會上院議員麥康納爾勳爵：人們很關注「一帶一路」建設問題，中國是否會減少並最終停止對巴基斯坦等沿線國家的煤炭項目投融資？

劉曉明：「一帶一路」不僅是經濟繁榮之路，也是綠色發展之路。中國在「一帶一路」建設實踐中始終秉持綠色發展理念，推動基礎設施綠色低碳化建設和運營管理，在投資貿易中強調生態文明理念，加強生態環境治理、生物多樣性保護和應對氣候變化等領域合作。二〇一九年，中國與四十二個國家的一百四十餘家中外方夥伴一道，共同發起成立了「一帶一路」綠色發展國際聯盟。中國還實施「一帶一路」應對氣候變化南南合作計劃，自二〇一二年起每年氣候南南合作資金支出達七千二百萬美元。中國企業在承建和設計「一帶一路」項目時，充分考慮生態因素，有效保護生物多樣性。例如，中國企業在巴基斯坦承建卡拉公路時，在公路沿線植樹近三十萬棵，植草五百多萬平方米，在建設基礎設施的同時，也為當地環境綠化做出貢獻。中國將堅持開放、綠色、可持續理念，與共建國家一道建設綠色「絲綢之路」，與包括英國在內的發達國家積極開展綠色領域第三方市場合作，為應對氣候變化國際合作匯聚更多力量。

議會上院議員麥康納爾勳爵：英中企業和機構在參與推動 COP15 和 COP26 方面能發揮什麼作用？中方對此有何考慮？

劉曉明：我認為，各國企業和民間組織是促進全球生態環境保護、綠色和諧發展的重要有生力量。中方一貫鼓勵利益相關方參與應對氣候變化和生物多樣性多邊議程。明年 COP15 也將開展平行會議，舉辦大量邊會和展覽，充分鼓勵和推動地方和社會各領域參與大會。中方還將按慣例在 COP26 會場設立「中國角」，為中國地方政府、科研院校、非政府組織等參與氣候多邊進程、建言綠色低碳發展提供平台。今年二月，我會見了倫敦金融城市長拉塞爾，就中英金融界和工商界加強綠色金融、氣候變化合作，積極參與 COP15 和 COP26 等交換意見。中英兩國企業及社會各界可加強交流，發揮各自優勢，共同推動 COP15 和 COP26 兩場大會取得成功，為全球可持續發展做出貢獻。

譜寫生態文明新篇章

——出席英國議會跨黨派國際環保小組座談會

（二〇二〇年十月二十八日，中國駐英國使館／英國議會）

劉曉明：很高興出席英國議會跨黨派國際環保小組「保護自然：通向昆明之路」線上座談會。二〇二一年，中英兩國將分別舉辦《生物多樣性公約》第十五次締約方會議（COP15）和《聯合國氣候變化框架公約》第二十六次締約方會議（COP26）。這既是中英兩國的大事，也是全球環境治理的大事。因此，二〇二一年可謂全球環境治理「大年」。

再過整整兩百天，COP15將在中國「春城」昆明召開。今天，我們在「雲端」共聚一堂，為此次大會「預熱」，具有重要意義。當前，新冠肺炎疫情仍在全球蔓延，給人類經濟社會發展帶來嚴重衝擊。在此背景下，保護生物多樣性更顯突出、更為重要，主要體現在以下三方面：

一是保護生物多樣性是人類社會當務之急。全球物種滅絕速度不斷加快，生物多樣性喪失和生態系統退化對人類生存和發展構成重大風險。

二是保護生物多樣性是建設生態文明的內在要求。生態興則文明興。生物多樣性是人與自然和諧共生的集中體現。加強保護生物多樣性，有利於推動經濟和生態協調發展，形成共建良好生態、共享美好生活的良性循環。

三是保護生物多樣性要求踐行多邊主義。只有發揚多邊主義精神，各盡所能，走合作共贏之路，才能加強生物多樣性保護國際合作，促進可持續發展。

不久前，習近平主席在聯合國生物多樣性峰會上指出，「我們要站在對人類文明負責的高度，尊重自然、順應自然、保護自然，探索人與自然和諧共生之路，促進經濟發展與生態保護協調統一，共建繁榮、清潔、美麗的世界」。明年 COP15 將以「生態文明：共建地球生命共同體」為主題，制定「二〇二〇年後全球生物多樣性框架」，為扭轉全球生物多樣性喪失趨勢邁出歷史性一步，將在全球保護生物多樣性進程中留下濃墨重彩的篇章。中國主辦 COP15 充分體現了三個決心：

第一，推進生態文明建設的決心。中國積極做生態文明的倡導者和踐行者，堅持綠水青山就是金山銀山，堅持良好生態環境是最普惠的民生福祉，堅持共謀全球生態文明建設。中國將「生態文明」寫入憲法，提出創新、協調、綠色、開放、共享的發展理念，將生物多樣性納入經濟社會發展和生態保護修復規劃，努力建設人與自然和諧共生的現代化。這與《生物多樣性公約》確定的保護生物多樣性、持續利用其組成部分、公平合理分享由利用遺傳資源而產生的惠益的三大目標，以及「人與自然和諧共生」的二〇五〇年願景高度契合。COP15 是聯合國首次以「生態文明」為主題召開的全球性會議，將發出共建地球生命共同體的強有力信號，進一步推動全球生態文明建設。

第二，保護生物多樣性的決心。中國採取積極有力政策行動保護生物多樣性，堅持山水林田湖草生命共同體，協同推進生物多樣性治理。我們加快國家生物多樣性保護立法步伐，劃定生態保護紅線，建立國家公園體系，實施生物多樣性保護重大工程，提高社會參與和公眾意識。過去十年，中國森林資源增長面積超過七千萬公頃，居全球首位。中國長時間、大規模治理沙化、荒漠化，有效保護修復濕地，生物遺傳資源收集保藏量位居世界前列。中國百分之九十的陸地生態系統類型和百分之八十五的重點野生動物種群得到有效保護。COP15 將成為中國與各國分享生物多樣性保護實踐和經驗的重要平台，進一步形成保護生物多樣性的全球合力。

第三，參與和引領全球生物多樣性治理的決心。

中國是《生物多樣性公約》重要參與者和推動者，率先簽署和批准公約，嚴格履行公約義務，積極促進與其他國際環境條約協同增效，已提前完成設立自然保護區等相關目標。中國與合作夥伴發起成立「一帶一路」綠色發展國際聯盟，積極加強生物多樣性和生態系統保護。中國還在南南合作框架下積極幫助發展中國家提高環境管理能力。COP15 將制定「二〇二〇年後全球生物多樣性框架」，對未來十年乃至更長時間全球生物多樣性治理做出規劃。中國將在 COP15 大會上與各方共同努力，共同推進二〇二〇年後全球生物多樣性治理進程。

二〇二一年是全球生物多樣性治理的關鍵節點，中英是全球環境治理的重要夥伴，在保護生物多樣性和應對氣候變化領域合作潛力巨大，應該相互支持、相互配合，共同確保 COP15 和 COP26 取得成功。

一是加強戰略引領，全力做好 COP15 和 COP26 對接合作。習近平主席在聯合國成立七十五週年高級別活動中宣佈，中國將提高國家自主貢獻力度，採取更加有力的政策和措施，二氧化碳排放力爭於二〇三〇年前達到峰值，努力爭取二〇六〇年前實現碳中和。習近平主席和約翰遜首相就兩國加強 COP15 和 COP26 相互協調、相互支持達成重要共識。中國生態環境部部長黃潤秋剛才在視頻致辭中強調了中英加強兩場大會合作的重要意義。下一步，我們將兩場大會加強政策和議題對接合作，包括積極推廣「基於自然的解決方案」，作為應對氣候變化和保護生物多樣性的協同解決方案，促進兩次大會相得益彰、協同增效。

二是深化綠色合作，引領全球可持續發展。中國制訂並實施了《中國生物多樣性保護戰略與行動計劃》（二〇一一至二〇三〇年），積極探索生物多樣性保護與綠色發展、改善民生協同推進，倡導低碳、循環、可持續的生產生活方式。英國也發佈了《未來二十五年環境保護計劃》，倡導可持續發展，注重恢復陸地和海洋生物多樣性。中英可加強對話交流，加強務實合作，挖掘綠色合作潛力，深化在應對氣變、保護生物多樣性、低碳經濟、綠色金融、綠色科技、能源轉型等領域的合作，在共建綠色「一帶一路」方

面加強三方合作，推動落實聯合國二〇三〇年可持續發展目標，為全球可持續發展注入新動力。

三是堅持多邊主義，凝聚全球生物多樣性治理合力。中英應堅定維護多邊主義，按照「共同但有區別的責任」原則，堅持公平公正惠益分享，照顧發展中國家資金、技術、能力建設方面關切，推動構建更加公平合理、各盡其責的多邊環境治理體系。中方願與包括英方在內的各方一道，遵循公開、透明、平衡、締約方驅動等原則，推動 COP15 達成兼具雄心和務實平衡的「二〇二〇年後全球生物多樣性框架」，為未來生物多樣性保護繪製一幅宏偉且可實現的藍圖，為全球保護生物多樣性開闢更廣闊的前景。

昆明是中國歷史文化名城，四季如春，風景如畫。習近平主席在聯合國生物多樣性峰會上發出邀請，歡迎大家明年聚首美麗的春城昆明，共商全球生物多樣性保護大計，共建萬物和諧的美麗世界。作為 COP15 東道國和候任主席國，中方將全力做好 COP15 各項籌備工作，努力把 COP15 辦成一屆具有里程碑意義的全球環境治理盛會。我讚賞加德納主席和英國議會跨黨派國際環保小組關心和支持中國舉辦 COP15，也期望更多的英國議員以及支持環境事業的各國人士，共同為辦好 COP15 和 COP26 兩場大會、深化中英和全球環境治理合作建言獻策。讓我們攜起手來，共同譜寫生態文明新篇章，共同構建地球生命共同體！

現在我願回答各位嘉賓的提問。

加拿大前議員斯特斯基：能否請劉大使進一步介紹中國的生態保護紅線制度？

劉曉明：關於中國的生態保護紅線制度，我願介紹三點情況：

第一，生態保護紅線是被提到國家層面的「生命線」。這是中國國土空間規劃和管理的重要制度創新，對維繫生態安全格局、維護生態系統功能、保障經濟社會可持續發展具有重要作用。中國計劃到二〇二〇年底，生態保護紅線劃定面積約佔陸域國土的百分之二十五。

第二，生態保護紅線在國土空間規劃中逐級劃定落實。我們將生態功能極重要和極脆弱區域劃入生態保護紅線，覆蓋以國家公園為主體的各類自然保護地等，通過嚴格管理，減少人為活動對生態環境的擾動。截至二〇一八年底，中國各類自然保護地總數量已達一點一八萬個，自然保護地面積超過一百七十二點八萬平方公里，佔國土陸域面積百分之十八以上，提前實現了COP10通過的到二〇二〇年達到百分之十七的目標。

第三，生態保護紅線內的生態資源得到合理利用。保護紅線是中國保護生物多樣性、調整經濟結構、規劃產業發展、推進新型城鎮化不可逾越的紅線，但並不意味著對所有區域都實行「絕對保護」、不能利用，它既不是「無人區」，也不是發展的「真空區」。中國政府鼓勵各地合理利用生態保護紅線內的優質生態資源，探索實現生態產品價值的機制。把綠水青山轉化為金山銀山，實現生態優勢向經濟優勢的轉化。

此外，中國根據公約精神於二〇一〇年制訂並實施了《中國生物多樣性保護戰略與行動計劃》（二〇一一至二〇三〇年），提出中國未來二十年生物多樣性保護總體目標、戰略任務和優先行動。自二〇一五年起，通過實施生物多樣性保護重大工程，對全國野生動植物資源進行調查觀測，調查記錄超過兩百一十萬條，不斷跟蹤評估《中國生物多樣性保護戰略與行動計劃》（二〇一一至二〇三〇年）執行進展情況。我們願就生態保護紅線制度與各方加強交流，促進各自國家行動計劃的實施。

肯尼亞議會議員切普科沃尼：中國發起的「一帶一路」倡議將如何助力沿線國家實現清潔、綠色、可持續的發展？

劉曉明：「一帶一路」不僅是經濟繁榮之路，也是綠色發展之路。在「一帶一路」建設實踐中，中國始終秉持綠色發展理念，注重與聯合國二〇三〇年可持續發展議程對接，推動基礎設施綠色低碳化建設和運營管理，在投資貿易中強調生態文明理念，加強生態環境治理、生物多樣性保護和應對氣候變化等領域合

作。未來「一帶一路」建設將著重在以下三方面加強綠色合作：

一是建立綠色機制。二〇一九年，「一帶一路」綠色發展國際聯盟成立，下設「生物多樣性和生態系統」等十個專題夥伴關係，目前已有四十多個國家的一五〇餘家中外合作夥伴。中國實施「綠色絲路使者計劃」，與發展中國家共同加強環保能力建設，先後為一百二十多個國家培訓環保官員、專家和技術人員兩千多人次。中國政府還成立「一帶一路」環境技術交流與轉移中心，促進先進生態環保技術的聯合研發和推廣應用。

二是促進綠色發展。中國企業在承建和設計「一帶一路」項目時，在促進當地經濟發展的同時，充分考慮環保因素。例如，中國企業在巴基斯坦承建卡拉奇—拉合爾公路時，在公路沿線植樹近三十萬棵，植草五百多萬平方米，在建設基礎設施的同時，也為當地環境綠化做出貢獻。同樣在巴基斯坦，在建設胡布燃煤電站時，使用了先進的清潔煤電技術，整個項目造價約有百分之十用於污染防控，其排放完全符合標準。

三是加強綠色金融合作。全球已有三十多家大型金融機構簽署了《「一帶一路」綠色投資原則》（GIP）。GIP內容包括充分了解環境、社會和治理風險；充分披露環境信息；充分運用綠色金融工具；採用綠色供應鏈管理；等等。中國鼓勵金融機構支持綠色「一帶一路」建設，二〇一九年中國工商銀行發行了首隻「一帶一路」銀行間常態化合作機制綠色債券，深入推進「一帶一路」綠色金融合作。

中國將堅持開放、綠色、可持續理念，願與包括英國在內的發達國家積極開展綠色領域第三方市場合作；通過「一帶一路」綠色發展國際聯盟等平台，助力共建國家實現綠色、清潔、可持續發展。

南非議會議員弗羅里克：中國如何看待《聯合國海洋法公約》在海洋生態環境保護中的作用？

劉曉明：海洋是地球生態系統中不可或缺的組成部分，保護海洋生物多樣性對中國的可持續發展十分重要。中國作為《聯合國海洋法公約》的簽署國，始

終致力於遵守包括《聯合國海洋法公約》在內的國際法。二〇一九年中國與法國達成的《中法生物多樣性保護和氣候變化北京倡議》，明確呼籲動員所有國家根據《聯合國海洋法公約》制定一項具有法律約束力的國際文書，以養護和可持續利用國家管轄外生物多樣性。目前，中國已批准建立國家級海洋公園超過四十個，建立各級海洋自然／特別保護區（海洋公園）兩百七十餘處，海洋保護區數量和面積不斷擴大，保護對象類型日益豐富。

中國將與各國共同做好海洋生物多樣性保護工作，共同打造海洋生物多樣性保護屏障，為保護好海洋這個生機盎然的藍色世界做出更多貢獻。

英國議會上院議員蘭德爾勳爵：在疫情背景下，如何提高公眾參與保護生物多樣性的意識和積極性？

劉曉明：保護生物多樣性不只是政府的事情，社會各界都應廣泛參與進來。提高公眾參與意識是《中國生物多樣性保護戰略與行動計劃》（二〇一一至二〇三〇年）中的八大戰略任務之一。我們建立生物多樣性保護公眾參與機制，開展多種形式的生物多樣性保護宣傳教育活動，引導公眾積極參與生物多樣性保護，加強學校的生物多樣性科普教育。明年COP15也將開展平行會議，舉辦大量邊會和展覽，充分鼓勵和推動社會各界參與大會。中方還將按慣例在COP26會場設立「中國角」，為中國地方政府、科研院校、非政府組織等參與氣候多邊進程、建言綠色低碳發展提供平台。中方願與英方一道，鼓勵更多企業、民間組織等社會各界參與進來，為COP15和COP26成功舉辦、促進全球保護生物多樣性做出貢獻。

墨西哥議會議員加西亞：如何看待明年COP15和COP26之間的關係？如何才能更廣泛地採用「基於自然的解決方案」？

劉曉明：習近平主席在聯合國生物多樣性峰會上指出，人與自然是命運共同體。無論是保護生物多樣性，還是應對氣候變化，都是全球環境治理的重要方

面。生物多樣性保護可以幫助人類更好地減緩和適應氣候變化，同時減緩和適應氣候變化又能減少生物多樣性受到的威脅，二者是相互協同的。COP15和COP26兩場大會可以在三方面協同增效：

一是共同建設生態文明。氣候變化和生物多樣性都關乎人類生存和發展。我們應以兩場大會為契機，站在對人類文明負責的高度，尊重自然、順應自然、保護自然，探索人與自然和諧共生之路，促進經濟發展與生態保護協調統一。

二是共同促進綠色發展。氣候變化和生物多樣性都與新冠肺炎疫情後經濟復甦密切相關。我們要按照聯合國《二〇三〇年可持續發展議程》所指明的方向，堅持綠色、包容、可持續發展。通過舉辦兩場大會，我們可從保護自然中尋找綠色發展機遇，實現生態環境保護和經濟高質量發展雙贏，培育疫情後經濟復甦活力。

三是共同維護多邊主義。《生物多樣性公約》《聯合國氣候變化框架公約》及《巴黎協定》等國際條約是全球環境治理的法律基礎，也是多邊合作的重要成果，得到各方廣泛支持和參與。我們應以兩場大會為契機，堅定捍衛以聯合國為核心的國際體系，維護國際規則尊嚴和權威，凝聚全球環境治理合力。

中英都重視「基於自然的解決方案」（NBS），這也是英方舉辦COP26的重要領域之一。中英應積極推廣NBS，將其作為應對氣候變化、生物多樣性喪失的協同解決方案，促進協同增效，促進全球綠色、低碳、可持續發展。

中國與新西蘭共同牽頭了二〇一九年聯合國氣候行動峰會的NBS領域工作，在峰會上發佈了《基於自然的氣候解決方案政策主張》等成果文件，組建了「NBS之友小組」後續合作平台。我們還結合實踐，提出了「劃定生態保護紅線，減緩和適應氣候變化」這一NBS行動倡議，為豐富NBS貢獻了中國智慧。

下一步，我們願與英方加強有關NBS的交流與合作，共同推動各方提高對自然價值的認識，推動政府、金融機構、企業和所有其他利益相關方在保護生物多樣性和應對氣候變化的進程中優先考慮NBS，制訂富有雄心的計劃並採取切實行動，讓NBS在支持生態系統保護及應對氣候變化方面發揮更大作用。

第六章

與專家學者和政府官員對話

二〇一九年六月二十四日，我出席英國「亞洲之家」對話會，與「亞洲之家」主席格林勳爵就習近平外交思想、中國內外政策及有關熱點問題進行交流，並回答現場聽眾提問。此次係「亞洲之家」首次舉行該機構主席與駐英使節對話會，英國政、商、學、媒體界代表以及新加坡、巴基斯坦、黎巴嫩、比利時、愛爾蘭、美國、澳大利亞、菲律賓、加拿大等國駐英使節和外交官一百四十餘人出席。

二〇二〇年七月十五日，駐英國使館與英國智庫貨幣金融機構官方論壇、歐洲改革中心聯合舉行「『後疫情時代』中歐關係」在線座談會，我發表了題為《「四個堅持」至關重要》的主旨演講，並回答聽眾提問。英國貨幣金融機構官方論壇主席馬什、顧問委員會主席德賽，歐洲改革中心主任格蘭特，英中貿協主席古沛勤爵士以及兩家智庫會員，來自英國和歐洲、北美、大洋洲、拉美等地區的經濟、金融、學術界人士等共約一百人參加。英國廣播公司（BBC）、天空新聞台、路透社、《每日電訊報》、《金融時報》、《衛報》、《獨立報》、中國國際電視台等中英兩國媒體，以及美聯社、彭博社、美國全國廣播公司、法新社、保加利亞電視台等十四家中外媒體參加。BBC、天空新聞台對座談會進行了現場直播，並在當天重要時段滾動報道。

英國貨幣金融機構官方論壇成立於二〇一〇年，是英國知名經濟金融論壇組織，主要為全球各國央行、外匯儲備管理部門和主權財富基金等提供政策諮詢服務。歐洲改革中心是英國知名智庫，成立於一九九六年，重點研究歐洲社會、政治和經濟問題，並為歐洲各國政府、歐盟機構和商界人士提供政策諮詢服務。

十月十三日，我應邀出席國際能源信息論壇大會，發表題為《風雨過後見彩虹》的主旨演講並回答主持人提問。石油輸出國組織秘書長巴爾金多，沙特王子、能源大臣阿卜杜勒，阿聯酋國務部長蘇爾坦，阿聯酋能源及工業部長馬茲魯伊，尼日利亞石油資源部長西爾瓦，印度石油、天然氣和鋼鐵部長普拉丹，美國前助理國防部長傅立民，美國前眾議員庫辛尼奇，能源信息論壇大會主席穆爾、總裁辛德勒，以及來自英國、歐洲、北美、亞洲等地區的經濟界、學術界、能源界人士共兩千多人參加。

中國是世界和平的建設者

——出席英國「亞洲之家」對話會

（二〇一九年六月二十四日，英國「亞洲之家」）

二〇一九年六月二十四日，我出席英國「亞洲之家」對話會，與「亞洲之家」主席格林勳爵就習近平外交思想、中國內外政策及有關熱點問題展開交流，並回答現場聽眾提問。

格林勳爵：今天，「亞洲之家」很榮幸邀請中國駐英國大使劉曉明這位重量級嘉賓，與大家討論中國這個極其重要的話題。中國過去幾十年的高速發展，使世界經濟重心從西方轉向東方，改變了世界格局。當前，英國處於脫歐的關鍵期，正重塑與世界的關係，重點就是在亞洲拓展夥伴關係。英國如何在中美之間保持平衡是各界非常關注的話題。我們期待聽到劉大使對當今國際形勢以及中國如何與世界互動等重大問題的看法。

劉曉明：很高興再次做客「亞洲之家」，就中英關係和中國外交政策等議題與「亞洲之家」主席格林勳爵及各位會員進行對話。「亞洲之家」每次邀請我出席活動的時機都選得非常好。去年五月，我在這裏就中美經貿問題發表演講，恰逢中美達成協議。此後一年，形勢可謂波譎雲詭、瞬息萬變。今天，中美經貿緊張局勢又曙光初現，習近平主席與特朗普總統即將在二十國集團（G20）峰會期間舉行會晤，廣受關注。

環顧當今世界，我們生活在一個快速變化的時代，世界正處於百年未有之大變局。在這樣的背景下，中國的發展成為國際上的熱議話題，有人認為是

機遇，有人認為是挑戰，也有人認為是威脅。那麼，中國的發展對世界到底意味著什麼？我認為，習近平外交思想是新時代中國對外工作的根本遵循和行動指南，構建人類命運共同體是習近平外交思想的核心理念，中國堅持走和平發展道路，推動構建新型國際關係、構建人類命運共同體；中國堅持開放合作，推動「一帶一路」建設，與世界各國分享中國發展機遇；中國不是要挑戰或取代誰、不會走「國強必霸」的老路，永遠做世界和平的建設者、全球發展的貢獻者、國際秩序的維護者。

當前，單邊主義日益抬頭，保護主義甚囂塵上。在這樣的形勢下，中英作為國際上有重要影響的國家，應當加強合作，發出支持多邊主義、倡導自由貿易、攜手應對氣候變化等全球性挑戰的時代強音，共同為人類社會發展進步做出貢獻。上週，第十次中英經濟財金對話在英成功舉行，取得六十九項豐碩成果。我認為，此次對話傳遞出的一個重要信息就是，中英合作互利共贏，不僅造福兩國，也惠及世界。展望未來，中國願繼續將英國作為推動構建新型國際關係、構建人類命運共同體的夥伴，為創造更加美好的世界貢獻力量。

格林勳爵：我曾多次到訪中國，目睹了中國改革發展取得的巨大成就。但中國未來發展面臨東西部發展不均衡、人口老齡化、水資源緊缺等現實挑戰。你對此怎麼看？中國將如何解決這些問題？

劉曉明：二〇一八年是中國改革開放四十週年。四十多年來，中國經濟體量從世界第十躍升至第二，成功使七億人擺脫貧困，中國人民生活水平大幅提高，人均壽命顯著延長，人們的獲得感、幸福感、安全感不斷提升。但中國仍是一個發展中國家，人均國民生產總值與西方發達國家相距甚遠。觀察中國，應該看到中國的「多面」，既看到北京、上海、深圳這樣可比肩歐洲的國際化大都市，也要看到相對不發達的西部省區。你剛才提到水資源問題，我有切身體會。十多年前，我曾在中國西部省份甘肅省擔任省長助理，那裏不少民眾飲水都很困難，只能淨化雨水供人、畜

飲用。

對於當前中國社會的主要矛盾，中共十九大做出了準確論斷，那就是人民日益增長的美好生活需要和不平衡不充分的發展之間的矛盾。展望未來，我們還有很多工作要做，肩上的擔子很重。中國發展崛起不是要在國際上挑戰誰，而是要解決自身發展面臨的諸多挑戰，不斷改善民生，到二〇二〇年實現貧困人口全面脫貧目標，讓發展更平衡、更充分。

格林勳爵：我對當前全球貿易形勢十分擔憂，美國總統特朗普頻頻採取加徵關稅等單邊主義、保護主義舉措，對世貿組織和全球貿易秩序產生巨大衝擊。你怎樣看待全球貿易形勢？中國將如何應對？

劉曉明：關於貿易問題，我與你有同樣的關切，對單邊主義、保護主義逆流感到擔憂。中國認為，世貿組織仍是多邊貿易體制的核心。當然，這套體制並不完美，需要進行必要改革，使全球貿易更加規範、更加便利、更加開放。我們身處一個彼此利益密不可分的「地球村」，如果所有國家都基於自身利益任性自定貿易規則，或將自身利益凌駕於其他國家之上，追求所謂「本國第一」，這將不可避免地導致「貿易戰」，對全球經濟增長造成負面影響。

因此，中國支持世貿組織發揮應有作用，支持對世貿組織進行必要改革。同時，世貿組織改革要以各方共識為基礎。儘管這將花費更多時間，但各方付出的代價也會小得多。中國反對「贏者通吃」「零和博弈」，認為只有互利合作才能實現共贏發展。

格林勳爵：你提到的「共贏發展」是否指中國提出的構建人類命運共同體？我理解中國提出這一倡議的初衷，但在當前中美博弈的背景下，人類命運共同體能成為現實嗎？

劉曉明：我對此持樂觀態度，因為各國開展互利合作是有基礎的。習近平主席提出構建人類命運共同體的主張，得到了國際社會積極響應，並被寫入了聯合國、G20等文件。

貿易戰沒有贏家，中美兩國都將因此蒙受損失。我曾看到一項調查，稱如貿易戰持續，美國將成最大「輸家」；最近我還注意到，很多美國企業家都對政府加徵關稅表示不滿。中國不想看到「雙輸」局面，希望人們最終回歸「理性」，而不要在付出代價之後才意識到貿易戰的負面影響。

格林勳爵：你剛才提到世界正經歷大變局。我也認為，各方力量對比發生很大變化，特別是發展中國家紛紛崛起。在這樣的形勢下，你認為歐洲將在世界舞台上扮演什麼角色？目前，英國脫歐尚無結果，不少歐洲國家遭受民粹主義衝擊。中國怎樣看待歐洲的作用？

劉曉明：中國主張世界多極化發展，認為這有利於實現世界持久和平與穩定。中國重視歐洲的作用，在戰略上將歐洲視為世界重要一極。同時，在經貿上，歐洲是中國的最大貿易夥伴。中國致力於與歐盟及各歐洲國家發展關係、開展務實合作，不僅與英國、法國、德國、意大利等大國保持良好關係，與中東歐國家的「16+1」合作也有聲有色。今年以來，習近平主席、李克強總理相繼成功訪歐，與歐洲領導人共同重申中歐發展關係的重要意義，足見中國對歐洲的高度重視。

關於脫歐問題，我們正密切關注相關進展，認為這是英歐之間的事情，相信雙方有智慧、有能力妥善處理好有關問題。中方希望英歐能達成雙方都滿意的協議，願推動中歐、中英關係並行發展。

格林勳爵：我注意到，英國國內在處理對華關係上有不同意見；此外，歐方一直對「16+1」合作心存疑慮。你怎麼看這些問題？

劉曉明：我聽到一種觀點，認為英國須在中美之間選邊站隊，因此有人對發展對華關係有不同看法。我想指出的是，英國社會主流意見是將中國發展看作機遇，而非挑戰，更非威脅，大都支持推進中英關係「黃金時代」。

歐方確實對中國與中東歐國家開展「16+1」合作有些誤解。事實上，「16+1」合作取得積極成果對中國與歐盟都有利。中東歐很多國家發展低於歐盟平均水平，面臨阻礙進一步發展的共性問題，因此他們擁有與中國加強合作的強烈意願。中國一直與歐方保持密切溝通交流，希望通過增信釋疑讓大家認識到，中國致力於走出一條與以往不同的大國崛起之路，中國發展將給歐洲和世界帶來更多機遇。

格林勳爵：印度和日本都是亞洲的重要國家，但兩國對華關係都有「微妙」之處。比如印度對「一帶一路」倡議持保留態度，中日之間則存在重大歷史遺留問題。你怎樣看待中印、中日關係？

劉曉明：中國十分重視與印度、日本這兩個重要鄰國的關係。沒有良好的中印關係和中日關係，就不會有亞洲的持久和平、穩定與繁榮。對中印關係而言，一些西方媒體熱衷唱衰中印關係，不斷炒作兩國之間的分歧。然而，中印關係中的共同利益遠大於分歧。兩國同為「金磚國家」，在一系列問題上擁有廣泛共同利益。近年來，習近平主席與莫迪總理在不同場合多次會面，建立起良好的個人友誼和工作關係，也體現出中國領導人對發展中印關係的高度重視。

對中日關係而言，兩國之間確實有「苦澀的過去」。中國人民有理由關注日本政府對待歷史的態度，因為我們不想讓歷史「重演」。中國願與日本改善關係，習近平主席即將赴日本出席二十國集團大阪峰會，我們希望這將為推動中日關係改善發展注入強勁動力。

「亞洲之家」首席執行官勞倫斯：華為問題是當前英國輿論關注的焦點。你怎樣看華為在英國的發展前景？

劉曉明：首先我想指出的是，華為是一家優秀的企業，不僅在5G通信領域領先全球，也為英國經濟社會發展做出了巨大貢獻。上個月，我在回國述職期間到深圳參訪了華為公司，在華為大學與公司高管及員

工進行交流。我發現，華為公司上下都對與英國開展務實合作充滿期待。

過去五年，華為在英國創造七千五百多個就業崗位，採購和投資達到二十億英鎊，未來還計劃投資三十億英鎊。更重要的是，華為非常重視網絡安全問題，在英國主動投資建立網絡安全認證中心，聘用清一色英國團隊實施監管，定期評估風險，不斷改進技術。世界上不存在沒有任何風險的設備，但華為願與英國政、商、學界開展合作，提高設備的安全性和可靠性。事實上，英方評估認為，華為設備的安全風險是「可控的」。

我曾聽到一種說法，稱如禁止使用華為設備，英國5G建設將延遲一至兩年。更令我感到擔憂的是，英國素以開放包容的市場環境著稱，一旦華為被禁，恐將對外釋放極為負面的信號，特別是對中國企業在英投資經營產生極大衝擊，這才是我最不願看到的。英國的國名是「大不列顛」，之所以稱其為「大」，就在於英國的獨立性和自主性。我們希望英國政府自主做出符合自身長遠利益並且有利於中英合作大局的決定，而不是聽命於誰的指令、屈從於誰的壓力。

考文垂大學教授莫里森：幾年前我曾在劉大使演講現場聽到，在全球供應鏈中，中國生產價值一美元的商品只能獲得五美分利潤，因此有很大的增長空間。請問中國如今在全球供應鏈中獲利增長了多少？你怎麼看待這種進步？

劉曉明：如你所知，中國不可能永遠停留在全球供應鏈「低端」。這些年，中國人民辛勤奮鬥，積極發展中高端產業，確實取得了一些進步。然而，中國更重視做大「共同利益的蛋糕」，讓各方都更多獲益，而非僅讓自己「分得更大份的蛋糕」，造成大家爭奪有限的資源，這是中國人開展對外合作的哲學。

作為職業外交官，我曾長期從事對美工作。當前中美經貿關係讓我想起三十多年前我在美國常駐時，一位美國領導人的話，他說，美方重視對華貿易逆差，但解決辦法不是減少中國對美出口，而是增加美國對華出口。我贊同這種主張，希望今天的美國當政

者也能遵從同樣的邏輯。美國對華加徵關稅不僅擾亂全球供應鏈，最終「埋單」的只能是美國企業和普通美國消費者。

英國亞能諮詢公司主席理查德：近期香港問題引發英國社會廣泛關注，劉大使接受英國廣播公司（BBC）採訪時表示，《中英聯合聲明》已「不再有意義」。中國政府是否還在香港堅持「一國兩制」政策？

劉曉明：感謝你看了我的採訪，但你的引述並不準確。《中英聯合聲明》的使命是確保香港政權順利交接。一九九七年香港回歸中國後，《中英聯合聲明》就已完成了歷史使命。我注意到一些英國媒體質疑中國中央政府關於「一國兩制」的承諾。我要強調的是，「一國兩制」不是對英國的承諾，而是中國中央政府對包括香港居民在內的全體中國人民的承諾，這已經充分反映在《基本法》之中。當前，香港特區政府處理「修例」相關工作，恰恰是踐行「一國兩制」的生動體現。一些外國媒體和勢力將香港「修例」說成是破壞「一國兩制」，借用一句英國諺語，這完全是「Bark up the wrong tree」（風馬牛不相及）。英國政府高官近期還發表了一些不負責任的言論，這是在干涉香港事務和中國內政。如果英方真心希望香港保持長期繁榮穩定，就不要干預香港特區政府依法施政。

英中貿協主席沙遜勳爵：劉大使提到上週舉行的英中經濟財金對話取得六十九項重要成果，這將有力促進英中務實合作，讓英國商界倍感振奮。關於世貿組織改革問題，請問最終實現改革的可能性有多大？英中如何就此展開合作？

劉曉明：世貿組織改革是一項複雜的系統工程，主要目的是反映當前世界經濟的新現實，特別是充分考慮發展中國家的主要關切，推動全球貿易自由化和便利化，完善貿易爭端解決機制，推動建設包容和開放的世界經濟。

不久前，中方發佈了《中國關於世貿組織改革的

建議文件》，詳細闡述了「中國方案」，建議大家仔細研讀。中英兩國在世貿組織改革問題上擁有共同利益，我們願與英方共同努力，將世貿組織和多邊貿易體制建設得更加完善。

格林勳爵：感謝劉大使的精彩發言。中國與世界關係問題已成為當今時代最重大的戰略性命題之一，劉大使深入解讀了習近平外交思想的精神實質，生動闡述了中國對外政策的關鍵內容。劉大使是「亞洲之家」的常客，但今天是「亞洲之家」首次邀請駐英使節以對話會形式舉辦活動，我們期待與劉大使的對話繼續下去，為英國各界走近亞洲、認識中國、讀懂中國打造更好的平台。

謝謝大家！

「四個堅持」至關重要

——與英國智庫座談「『後疫情時代』中歐關係」

（二〇二〇年七月十五日，中國駐英國使館／貨幣金融機構官方論壇）

劉曉明：很高興通過視頻連線方式與大家座談。我們今天座談的主題是「『後疫情時代』中歐關係」。

今年是中國和歐盟建交四十五週年。近半個世紀以來，中歐關係日趨全面、成熟和穩定，給雙方人民帶來實實在在的好處，也為世界和平與繁榮做出積極貢獻。不久前，習近平主席會見歐洲理事會主席米歇爾和歐盟委員會主席馮德萊恩，李克強總理同兩位歐盟領導人共同主持第二十二次中國—歐盟領導人會晤，為「後疫情時代」的中歐關係指明方向。

當前，新冠肺炎疫情仍在全球肆虐，深刻改變國際格局和全球治理體系。這場百年未遇的疫情凸顯國際社會面臨四大赤字：

一是健康赤字。疫情已波及兩百一十多個國家和地區，影響七十多億人口，近一千三百萬人感染，五十六萬多人病亡。這場疫情成為「二戰」以來最嚴重的全球公共衛生突發事件，對人類生命安全和健康構成嚴峻挑戰，需要中歐與國際社會攜手應對。

二是發展赤字。疫情導致世界經濟陷入嚴重衰退。經合組織預計，歐洲可能是今年受到經濟衝擊最嚴重的地區。疫情阻礙跨境人員流動、影響各國經貿往來，衝擊全球產業鏈。國際貨幣基金組織和世界銀行分別預測今年全球經濟將萎縮百分之四點九和百分之五點二。如何復甦和提振經濟是各國面臨的共同艱巨任務。

三是和平赤字。在疫情背景下，世界和平和安全面臨嚴峻挑戰。地區衝突和局部戰爭持續不斷，恐怖主義猖獗，人道主義危機嚴重，不少國家民眾特別是兒童飽受戰火摧殘。這些都嚴重威脅著世界和平與穩定。

四是治理赤字。此次疫情暴露出全球公共衛生治理體系的不足和短板，亟須完善提升。疫情下，貿易保護主義、單邊主義和逆全球化抬頭，個別國家將疫情政治化，把病毒標籤化，損害國際團結和抗疫合作，全球治理體系和多邊機制面臨嚴峻考驗。

此次疫情使國際社會深刻認識到，人類是一個休戚與共、緊密相連的命運共同體。「甩鍋」「諉責」解決不了問題，更挽救不了生命，團結合作才是戰勝疫情的唯一正確選擇。中歐作為世界兩大力量、兩大市場、兩大文明，更應攜手合作，共同為全球抗疫、恢復經濟、完善治理、破解赤字貢獻力量。

一是共守人類健康安全。中國高度重視同包括歐洲在內的國際社會開展抗疫合作。不久前，習近平主席在世界衛生大會上呼籲構建人類衛生健康共同體，宣佈今後兩年內中國將提供二十億美元國際援助、中國新冠疫苗研發完成並投入使用後將作為全球公共產品等重要舉措。中方積極參與歐盟發起的應對新冠肺炎疫情國際認捐大會和英國主辦的全球疫苗峰會視頻會議。中歐要繼續加強抗疫經驗交流，深化疫苗和藥物研發合作，加大對公共衛生體系薄弱地區的支持，積極探討開展中歐非三方抗疫合作，築牢守衛人類健康的堅固防線，共同構建人類衛生健康共同體。

二是共護世界和平穩定。中國與歐盟面積佔世界十分之一，人口佔世界四分之一，在聯合國安理會擁有兩個常任理事國席位，在維護世界和平穩定中應當發揮關鍵作用。中歐應加強戰略對話，就重大國際和地區問題加強協調溝通。中歐應繼續支持以和平手段，通過對話協商解決各類熱點問題和地區衝突；堅守國際防擴散體制，維護全球戰略穩定；支持打擊一切形式恐怖主義，標本兼治，遏制極端思潮的蔓延。

三是共促國際發展繁榮。越是面臨疫情挑戰，越是要堅持開放合作。中歐作為兩大經濟體應該發揮世界經濟「雙引擎」作用，共同拉動世界經濟復甦，推

動有序復工復產，維護全球產業鏈供應鏈開放、穩定、安全。雙方應加強宏觀經濟政策協調，維護開放型世界經濟。今年上半年，中歐班列開行數量大幅增長，累計開行五千一百二十二列，同比增長百分之三十六，成為確保中歐貿易暢通的重要通道。中歐還應拓展互聯互通、綠色發展、生態環保、數字經濟、人工智能等新領域的互利合作，保持相互市場開放，爭取年內完成中歐投資協定談判，達成一項全面、平衡、高水平的投資協定。

四是共建全球治理體系。今年是聯合國成立七十五週年。中歐都堅決維護多邊主義，都支持國際關係民主化，都主張維護以聯合國為核心的國際體系、以國際法為基礎的國際秩序、以世貿組織為基石的多邊貿易體制，支持世衛組織在國際抗疫合作中發揮領導作用。中歐在維護全球公共衛生安全，應對氣候變化，發展清潔能源、清潔交通、綠色科技，保護生物多樣性方面有共同利益，在推進世界貿易組織改革、共同維護自由貿易等方面有廣泛共識，完全可以加強溝通協作，進一步維護多邊主義，完善全球治理。

女士們、先生們，中歐建交四十五年來，互利共贏始終是中歐關係的主旋律。面對疫情帶來的新挑戰，中歐關係也面臨一些新問題。一些人對中國的猜忌和疑慮增多，稱中國是「制度性對手」，還有人視中國為「潛在敵對國家」，揚言對華關係不會回到從前。如何看待疫情後的中歐關係，如何維護好中歐關係發展大局是我們面臨的共同課題。我認為，做到「四個堅持」至關重要。

第一，堅持相互尊重，反對干涉內政。相互尊重主權和領土完整、互不干涉內政、平等互利，是《聯合國憲章》確立的基本原則，也是國際關係基本準則。中歐關係四十五年的發展經驗表明，只要這些原則得到遵守，中歐關係就能向前發展，反之就遭受挫折，甚至倒退。中國從不干涉別國內政，也堅決反對別國干涉中國內政。

最近，中國全國人大常委會針對香港在維護國家安全方面存在的巨大風險，審議通過香港國安法，目的是防範、制止和懲治分裂國家、顛覆國家政權、恐

怖活動、勾結外國或者境外勢力危害國家安全四類罪行。香港國安法彌補了香港的國家安全漏洞，針對的是極少數嚴重危害國家安全的行為和活動，不影響香港的高度自治，不改變香港的獨立司法權和終審權，有利於保障香港居民的權利和自由，有利於保護外國投資者在港正當權益。因此，香港國安法受到香港居民普遍歡迎，近三百萬市民簽名支持。國際上，七十多個國家表態支持香港國安法，其中包括一些歐洲國家。然而，一些歐洲政要卻對該法說三道四，干涉香港事務和中國內政。我想強調的是，香港是中國的香港，香港事務是中國內政，任何外國無權干涉。我們希望歐盟方面客觀、理性、公正看待香港國安法，切實遵守國際法和國際關係基本準則，停止插手香港事務和中國內政。

第二，堅持互為夥伴，摒棄「冷戰思維」。中歐已建立全面戰略夥伴關係，積極建設和平、增長、改革、文明四大夥伴關係。中國始終走和平發展道路，致力於與包括歐洲國家在內的世界各國和平相處、互利合作、共同發展，始終把歐洲作為平等的夥伴而不是對手。中歐之間不存在地緣政治矛盾，更沒有根本利益衝突。中歐合作遠大於競爭，共識遠多於分歧。

那些把中國看成是「制度性對手」，甚至是「潛在敵對國家」的人，是找錯了對象，看錯了方向。中國最關心的是提高本國人民福祉，最重視的是實現中華民族復興，最期待的是世界和平穩定。中歐應通過平等對話增進互信，通過互利合作實現共贏，通過建設性溝通妥善處理分歧。中歐關係應是相互成就的正循環，而不是你輸我贏的淘汰賽。

第三，堅持互為機遇，反對「零和博弈」。中國的發展對歐洲是機遇而不是挑戰，更不是威脅。中歐作為世界兩大市場，經濟總量佔全球三分之一，雙方互為第二大貿易夥伴，經濟互補性強。疫情下，「宅經濟」、「雲辦公」、智能製造、生命健康、公共衛生等領域呈現出巨大發展活力和潛力，為中歐合作提供了新機遇、新空間。隨著中國進一步深化改革、擴大開放，中歐合作面臨更加廣闊的前景。我相信，中歐互利合作將不僅給雙方人民帶來更多福祉，而且將為我們這個充滿不確定性的世界提供更多穩定性和可預

期性。

第四，堅持互學互鑒，共促文明進步。中歐作為東西方文化的重要發祥地，都有燦爛和悠久的文化傳統。中歐歷史背景、社會制度、發展階段存在差異，這些差異不應是相互交往的障礙，而應是互學互鑒的動力。中國主張「和而不同」，強調「己所不欲，勿施於人」。中國的發展不照搬外國模式，也從不要求別人複製中國的模式。歐盟也強調「多元一體」，促進平等、包容和多元。中歐應相互尊重、相互欣賞、相互借鑒、相互成就。中歐作為推進人類進步的兩大文明，應共同努力，把世界的多樣性和各國的差異性轉化為發展活力和動力，共同促進人類文明之花競相開放。

女士們、先生們，中國古人講：「萬物並育而不相害，道並行而不相悖。」這不僅是人與人相處之道，也是國與國共處之道。人類社會發展的歷史證明，開放才能進步，包容才能交融，合作才能共贏。讓我們攜起手來，不斷為中歐合作貢獻正能量，共同為中歐關係在疫情後實現更高水平發展開創新未來！

現在，我願回答大家的提問。

貨幣金融機構官方論壇主席馬什（主持人）：有人認為，中國應把歐洲團結到自己這一邊，促使歐洲與美國保持距離。劉大使，你對此有何看法？

劉曉明：外界對中國立場存在不少誤解。中國無意在美歐之間打入楔子，我們知道美歐是盟友。中國願同所有國家做朋友，包括與美國保持良好關係。我曾兩次在美國常駐，四十五年外交生涯有一半時間從事對美工作。我們始終認為，一個良好的中美關係有利於世界和平與穩定，但中美保持良好關係應建立在相互尊重和平等相待基礎上。西方人講，「探戈需要兩個人跳」；中國人常說，「一個巴掌拍不響」。我們希望與美國不衝突不對抗、相互尊重、合作共贏，構建以協調、合作、穩定為基調的中美關係。關於中歐關係，我剛才在演講中已經講過，我們始終把歐洲作為平等的夥伴而不是對手，我們應該視彼此為機遇。中歐互為第二大貿易夥伴，雙方之間有很多共同利益把

我們緊密聯繫在一起。

馬什主席：我再問一個與電信相關的問題，這與英國有關，對歐洲國家也可能有影響。昨天英國政府決定不再與華為合作。英國政府知道過去幾年華為對英國5G建設的貢獻，以及該決定造成的經濟損失，但還是這樣做了。劉大使，你認為英國宣佈的這一決定將對中英合作產生什麼具體影響？

劉曉明：我認為，這個決定損害了兩國之間的互信。眾所周知，相互信任、相互尊重是建立任何關係的基礎，人與人之間的關係如此，兩國之間的關係也是如此。昨天我在推特上說：「英國對華為的決定是令人失望的，是錯誤的。」今天，我要加上一句，這個決定不僅令人失望，「更令人寒心」。華為是一家好公司，他們在英國經營二十年，不僅對英國投資了三十多億英鎊，還為當地解決了二點六萬個就業崗位，創造了大量稅收，為英國電信業和經濟社會發展做出了巨大貢獻。令人寒心的是，華為的貢獻被某些英國政客和媒體歪曲成「傷害」英國。而事實恰恰相反，華為才真正受到傷害，其他中國企業也正密切關注英國如何對待華為。當相互信任遭到破壞時，中資企業將很難在這裏進行更多投資。因此，這個問題不需要政府來回答，我認為工商界都會得出自己的結論。中英之間的信任、兩國政府之間的信任以及中資企業對投資英國的信任，都受到嚴重損害。

馬什主席：英中關係「黃金時代」是將延續下去，還是會某種程度上失去光澤？

劉曉明：「黃金時代」意味著中英雙方要共同付出努力。「黃金時代」是二〇一五年習近平主席對英國國事訪問時，由英國領導人倡議提出的。我們認為「黃金時代」體現了中英關係的發展水平、符合兩國利益，因此贊同這一倡議，與英方共同打造「黃金時代」。今年是中英關係「黃金時代」五週年，本應是值得慶祝的年份。現在中英之間發生了很多事情，但責任不在中方。

貨幣金融機構官方論壇會員博格斯：當前各國似乎更加注重雙邊關係，這無助於多邊貿易和多邊合作。我們應如何在多邊主義與雙邊關係之間重新找回平衡？

劉曉明：中方一貫堅持多邊主義。今年是聯合國成立七十五週年，很多人不知道，中國是第一個在《聯合國憲章》上簽字的國家。中國堅定維護以聯合國為核心的國際體系，認真履行應該承擔的國際義務。中國從來不尋求「本國優先」，也沒有退出任何國際條約。中國已簽署了五百多個多邊條約，參加了一百多個政府間國際組織。中國支持世界衛生組織在全球抗疫合作中發揮領導作用，向世衛組織提供了捐款。與歐洲國家一樣，中國不贊成美國退出世衛組織。中國支持以世界貿易組織為基石的多邊貿易體系，儘管這一體系並不完美，但仍是無法代替的。

高盛公司多永：中歐如何在應對氣候變化等領域加強合作？

劉曉明：中國積極參與、推動並簽署了《巴黎協定》，將繼續認真履行《巴黎協定》。今年本應是中英環境保護合作之年，中英分別計劃舉辦《生物多樣性公約》第十五次締約方會議（COP15）和《聯合國氣候變化框架公約》第二十六次締約方會議（COP26）。受疫情影響，兩個會議都被推遲了，但雙方仍就兩次會議保持密切溝通。最近我與英國外交部COP26區域大使布里斯托爵士進行了很好的會談。我們希望通過雙方共同努力，使兩次會議都取得成功。中英可將氣候變化打造為雙方合作的新亮點，共同在全球氣候變化問題上發揮引領作用。

德國英國商會哈特曼：中歐對雙方貿易投資合作期待不同，中國在增加對歐洲的投資，也希望吸引歐洲國家投資，但歐盟正在出台政策加強對中國投資的審查。你如何看待雙方在投資問題上的不同訴求？

劉曉明：中歐貿易與投資合作機遇巨大。但重要的是，中歐雙方如何看待對方，是將彼此視為夥伴和

機遇，還是視為「系統性競爭對手」或「潛在敵對國家」？英國如何看待華為，實際上不僅是對待一家中國民營企業的問題，而是關乎英國如何看待中國的問題。顯然，英國對華為的決定受到「對華鷹派」和「反華勢力」的壓力。這些人把中國視為「敵對」或「潛在敵對國家」，他們不信任中國，所以不信任中國企業。中方不希望把經濟問題與政治問題混為一談，反對將經濟問題政治化。但現在英國將經濟問題政治化了，加入了美國制裁中國企業的行列。當一個國家把中國視為「潛在敵對國家」的時候，試問，我們怎麼能與其正常做生意？

馬什主席：請問，劉大使講的意思是，外界不信任中國，中國難道沒有任何責任嗎？還是為了贏得更多信任，中國本可以做得更好？面對外界的不信任，中國該怎麼做？

劉曉明：那麼，好，我們就以華為為例談信任問題。有人不信任華為，說其存在安全風險。華為主動斥資建立「網絡安全評估中心」，該中心完全由英國人管理運營，華為沒有派任何人。英方運營團隊評估得出的結論是，華為產品安全風險是可控的。這也是今年初英國政府決定允許華為參與英國 5G 網絡建設的原因，儘管英方為華為設定了百分之三十五的市場份額上限。華為還採取措施不斷改進技術，以增強產品的安全性能，努力確保英國 5G 網絡設施更安全、更具韌性。華為已竭盡所能，我看不到對華為還應有什麼抱怨的地方。

摩根士丹利公司莫戈達姆：我提兩個問題：第一，你提到歐洲和中國都支持 WTO，但目前 WTO 面臨僵局，你如何看待 WTO 改革問題？第二，你剛才提到中國和歐盟之間的貿易規模很大，但其中很大一部分是商品貿易，服務貿易還不夠多。你對如何擴大中歐服務貿易有何看法？

劉曉明：關於 WTO，中國支持以 WTO 為基石的多邊貿易體系，支持對 WTO 進行必要改革。同時，中

歐在有關問題上存在分歧，特別是中國仍然是一個發展中國家，希望歐洲正確看待中國作為發展中國家的定位。中國「復關」和「入世」談判歷時十五年，儘管付出了代價，但我們全面履行入世承諾，矢志不渝融入國際秩序和多邊機制。關於服務貿易，歐洲包括英國在內有自己的優勢，中國有廣闊的市場，中歐經濟互補性很強。我們歡迎更多歐洲企業對華拓展服務貿易合作。今年初，中國《外商投資法》正式實施，中國在開放服務業方面出台了很多新政策，外商投資服務業的許多限制被取消，外商投資負面清單進一步縮短，我們還取消了合格境外機構投資者（QFII）和人民幣合格境外機構投資者（RQFII）投資額度限制，包括歐洲國家在內的外國銀行和保險公司在中國將面臨更大商機。

非洲發展銀行卡巴佐：新冠肺炎疫情將使非洲遭受二十五年來最嚴重的經濟衰退，中國是否願意在非洲面對這場前所未有的危機時提供幫助，包括減免有關債務？

劉曉明：中國始終視非洲為好兄弟、好夥伴、好朋友。我曾兩次常駐非洲，對非洲懷有深厚感情。中國積極支持非洲國家抗擊疫情，克服經濟困難。在今年五月舉行的第七十三屆世界衛生大會上，習近平主席宣佈中國將同二十國集團成員一道落實「暫緩最貧困國家債務償付倡議」。在不久前舉行的中非團結抗疫特別峰會上，中方還宣佈將在中非合作論壇框架下免除有關非洲國家截至二〇二〇年底到期對華無息貸款債務。此外，中國還派出多支醫療隊幫助非洲國家抗擊疫情，分享抗疫經驗，提供個人防護裝備和急需物資。最近我在使館還同英國智庫列格坦研究所共同主辦非洲抗疫視頻座談會，就加強中、英、非三方抗疫合作深入交流。

馬什主席：在減免債務方面，中國是否會加入「巴黎俱樂部」？

劉曉明：中國不是巴黎俱樂部的成員。中國已就債務減免問題加入多個多邊安排。中國在通過雙邊渠道減

免對外債務方面做了更多工作，因為這樣做更有效、更直接。中國開展有關對外合作始終堅持平等、開放、透明，遵循市場規律和通行的國際規則，注重債務和發展的可持續性問題。

貨幣金融機構官方論壇專家努格：我想更多了解中國外交政策和處理國際關係方式的變化。過去三十年，中國外交一直保持耐心，但現在似乎正在失去耐心，是什麼讓中國決定採取更加急迫的方式應對外部問題？

劉曉明：中國外交政策沒有改變。中國是熱愛和平的國家，和平深植在中華民族的基因裏，中國致力於維護世界和平與穩定。改革開放四十多年來，中國發展得益於和平的外部環境，我們堅信中國進一步發展仍然需要和平的國際環境。為什麼要改變這一狀況呢？實際上，不是中國變了，而是有些國家對華政策發生了很大變化，中國必須做出應對。在中美關係上，中方願與美國發展良好關係，不希望兩國關係惡化，但美國卻執意向中方施壓、妖魔化中國。在此次新冠肺炎疫情中，美國政客頻頻污稱「中國病毒」。究竟是誰變了？人們應該有客觀判斷。在台灣問題上，美國大打「台灣牌」，擴大對台軍售，企圖助台灣擴大國際空間。是美國想要改變現狀，中國必須做出回應。在香港問題上，香港回歸二十三年來，「一國兩制」取得巨大成功。但去年香港發生「修例風波」，反中亂港分子鼓吹「港獨」「自決」，公開揮舞英國、美國國旗，甚至邀請美軍登陸香港、「解放香港」。面對這樣嚴峻的形勢，我們有充分理由採取必要果斷措施，堅定維護「一國兩制」。

英中貿協主席古沛勤爵士：中國與歐洲在相互了解上似乎存在巨大鴻溝。中國很了解歐洲，但歐洲包括英國似乎對中國歷史、中國共產黨缺乏基本了解，尤其是歐洲決策者們似乎存在很大的對華「認知赤字」。請問劉大使，我們應該如何增加英國和歐洲的對華認知？

劉曉明：你這個問題提得很好。或許我下次演講時可以再加上第五個赤字，即「認知赤字」。我同意你的看法。中歐之間、中國與西方國家之間確實需要加深了解。一些西方政客指責中國時總是說「中國受到國際社會廣泛批評」。我對此指出，他們僅代表了西方國家的一小部分，更談不上代表整個國際社會。以香港國安法為例，國際上有七十多個國家支持中國，但反對的只有支持中國的國家數量的三分之一。我認為，解決「認知赤字」的有效辦法是加強接觸交流。我們需要更多的相互「掛鈎」而非相互「脫鈎」。我們鼓勵中國和歐洲年輕人多交往、多溝通。現在有更多的中國留學生願意到英國來學習。我希望英國能夠繼續保持開放，張開雙臂歡迎中國留學生來英學習。

野村證券安德魯：我非常尊重中國反對干涉內政的立場。但現實情況是，在一個全球化的世界中，一個國家內部發生的事情會影響到其他國家。比如對環境問題、生物多樣性問題，英中都有共同關切。我們應如何理解不干涉問題？

劉曉明：我認為中國人和英國人都有足夠的智慧來區分什麼是干涉內政，什麼是善意的建議。當外界關注中國環境問題時，我們歡迎有助於中國加強環境保護、改善環境質量的建設性建議。我們當然能夠分清哪些是真心幫助中國的建議，哪些是企圖蓄意改變中國政治和社會制度、把西方意志和模式強加給中國的言行。正如中方多次重申的，我們不照搬外國模式，也不輸出中國模式，但我們堅決反對任何國家干涉中國內政。

蒙特羅斯商務諮詢公司麥克雷：劉大使，你講到英國在華為問題上的決定將會損害雙方互信。或許中國可以採取一些具體措施重建信任，比如中方是否願意讓世衛組織專家調查武漢實驗室？能否明確承認在南海航行自由原則？在台灣問題上中國是否繼續堅持和平統一？

劉曉明：關於抗疫問題，中國一直秉持公開、透明、負責任的態度，開展國際抗疫合作。中國是第一個向

世衛組織報告疫情的國家，是第一個同國際社會分享病毒基因測序的國家。我們沒有任何隱瞞，反而是有的國家藉疫情對中國污名化。現在世衛組織已派遣專家赴華，與中國專家一起就新冠病毒溯源工作進行科學規劃。但我們應該明確兩點：一是病毒溯源工作應該以科學為基礎，而不是政治操弄；二是評估要包括所有國家，而不僅僅是中國。

關於南海航行自由，中方一貫尊重和支持各國依據國際法在南海享有的航行自由。中國百分之六十的石油供應經過南海，我們比任何國家都關心這一地區的和平穩定。我們正同域內國家共同落實《南海各方行為宣言》（DOC），繼續推動「南海行為準則」（COC）磋商。現在南海形勢總體平穩，中方堅決反對個別域外國家派遣軍艦到南海挑戰中國領土主權，破壞地區穩定。

關於台灣問題，中國致力於和平統一，這一原則立場沒有變。我推薦你讀一讀不久前我在《中國日報》發表的有關文章。我們願再次重申，台灣是中國領土不可分割的一部分，中國一貫堅持和平統一政策。中國政府不承諾放棄使用武力，針對的是外部勢力干涉和極少數「台獨」分裂分子及其分裂活動，絕非針對廣大台灣同胞。中國必須統一，也必然統一，這一進程是任何人、任何勢力都無法阻擋的。

貨幣金融機構官方論壇顧問委員會主席德賽：中國經濟已在疫後迅速復甦，中國是否計劃在近期內加強人民幣作為國際儲備貨幣的地位？

劉曉明：中國一直穩步推進人民幣國際化。過去十年，我們在促進人民幣貿易和投資方面做了很多努力。越來越多國家將人民幣作為貿易和投資貨幣，人民幣作為國際儲備貨幣的作用也在增強。我很高興看到倫敦在人民幣國際化進程中發揮了重要作用。倫敦目前是全球最大的人民幣離岸外匯交易中心、第二大人民幣離岸清算中心，香港則是全球最大的人民幣離岸清算中心、第二大人民幣離岸外匯交易中心。這兩個城市在推動人民幣國際化方面可以發揮互補優勢。

西班牙對外銀行里克爾梅：我想聽聽你對中國與拉美國家，特別是與墨西哥關係的看法。墨西哥與美國關係密切，這是否會對中國與墨西哥的關係造成影響？

劉曉明：中國願深化與拉美國家的關係。中國與拉美國家之間建立了中拉論壇等合作機制。中墨關係發展良好，我們不會為墨西哥與美國保持良好關係而感到擔憂，同時我們希望美國不要干擾中國與拉美國家發展友好關係。

貨幣金融機構官方論壇首席執行官奧查德：你剛剛談到了中歐關係。隨著英國脫歐，英國在中國處理對歐關係和對美關係中將處於什麼位置？

劉曉明：這取決於英國採取什麼樣的對華政策。我總是對英國朋友講，第一，我們並不要求英國在中美之間選邊站隊，而是希望英國站在正確的一邊。第二，英國只有擁有獨立的外交政策，「不列顛」才能成為真正的「大不列顛」，才不會被中國和世界看作美國的「跟班」。看看英國如何對待華為，人們自然可以得出結論，無須多言。再看看美國領導人在英國政府做出決定後的表現，人們都會清楚英國為什麼會做出這樣的決定。所以，當英國想要打造「全球化英國」的時候，應該認真思考究竟要扮演一個什麼樣的角色，要在國際舞台佔有一個什麼樣的位置。我們當然希望與英國和歐盟都保持良好關係，這一點毋庸置疑。

馬什主席：感謝劉大使，期待今後有機會與你繼續深入交流。

劉曉明：謝謝，再見。

風雨過後見彩虹

——在國際能源信息論壇大會發表主旨演講並回答提問

（二〇二〇年十月十三日，中國駐英國使館／國際能源信息論壇大會）

劉曉明：很高興出席此次國際能源信息論壇大會。在當前形勢下，召開本屆大會可謂恰逢其時。大會的主題是「能源大重啟：新冠疫情、氣候變化及後續」。圍繞這一主題，我願就全球氣候變化與能源形勢、中國引領全球氣變治理和能源轉型以及如何加強相關領域合作談幾點看法。

新冠肺炎疫情是百年來最嚴重的全球傳染病大流行，給諸多行業都帶來巨大衝擊。在疫情背景下，氣候變化與能源轉型發展面臨什麼樣的形勢？我認為，主要有三個動向：

第一，氣候變化與能源轉型關係越來越密切。應對氣候變化、推動能源轉型發展，關乎人類賴以生存的地球家園，關乎人類的前途命運。極端天氣頻發、海平面上升、生態環境惡化、發展中國家應對能力不足、個別國家退出《巴黎協定》等氣候變化挑戰，都與能源行業息息相關。

第二，疫情倒逼能源轉型加快發展。疫情讓世界經濟和能源需求按下「暫停鍵」，促使各國深入思考能源轉型方向和路徑。加強全球抗疫合作、恢復經濟社會秩序與活力是當務之急。實現疫後經濟綠色復甦成為國際社會共識，未來能源行業結構將日趨多元化，能源轉型發展將面臨更大壓力。

第三，疫情啟示我們要探索人與自然和諧共生之路。疫情告訴我們，人類不能再忽視大自然一次又一

次的警告，不能只講索取不講投入，不能只講發展不講保護，不能只講利用不講修復。人與自然是命運共同體，人類要從保護自然中尋找發展機遇。只有順應全球綠色低碳發展潮流，才能為能源行業「重啟」注入動力。

在不久前舉行的聯合國成立七十五週年高級別活動上，習近平主席宣佈，中國將提高國家自主貢獻力度，採取更加有力的政策和措施，二氧化碳排放力爭於二〇三〇年前達到峰值，努力爭取二〇六〇年前實現碳中和。這是中國基於國內可持續發展內在要求和構建人類命運共同體的責任擔當，是對自身氣候環境政策做出的重大宣示，是向國際社會展示中國積極參與全球氣變治理，引領全球綠色發展，推動全球能源轉型的堅定決心。

中國將繼續為推進全球氣變治理做出更大貢獻。中國擁有十四億多人口，是世界上最大的發展中國家，發展不平衡、不充分問題仍很突出。但中國作為負責任大國，在應對氣候變化上始終「言必信，行必果」。中國全面深入落實氣候變化《巴黎協定》，在節能減排等領域成績斐然。中國二〇一八年單位 GDP 碳排放強度比二〇〇五年累計降低百分之四十五點八，相當於減少二氧化碳排放五十二點六億噸。二〇一九年中國單位 GDP 能耗較上年降低百分之二點六，較二〇一二年累計降低百分之二十五點六。中國始終堅持多邊主義，積極參與全球氣變治理，我們實施「一帶一路」應對氣候變化南南合作計劃，自二〇一二年起每年氣候南南合作資金支出達七千兩百萬美元；通過「一帶一路」綠色發展國際聯盟等平台，為應對氣候變化國際合作匯聚更多力量。

中國將繼續為推動全球綠色發展做出更大貢獻。中國積極倡導創新、協調、綠色、開放、共享的新發展理念，貫徹落實「綠水青山就是金山銀山」重要理念，抓住新一輪科技革命和產業變革的歷史性機遇，積極引領疫後世界經濟「綠色復甦」。中國「十四五」規劃將進一步指明綠色、循環、低碳經濟的發展方向，中國統籌推進疫情防控與經濟社會發展，探索以生態優先、綠色發展為導向的高質量發展新路，加速完善氣候投融資體系，推廣綠色生產方式和生活方

式。在疫後經濟恢復中，中國將培育壯大節能環保產業、清潔生產產業，促進產業和社會電氣化、數字化與智能化，推動能源、交通、工業等多領域轉型，繼續引領全球經濟走綠色和可持續發展之路。

中國將繼續為促進全球能源轉型做出更大貢獻。中國始終堅持提高能源供給質量和效率、加快能源技術創新、推進能源市場化改革。過去十年，中國是全球可再生能源領域的最大投資國。中國已建成全球最大清潔煤電體系，深水鑽探、頁岩氣勘探開發等技術實現重大突破，核能、風能、太陽能等新能源應用蓬勃發展，「互聯網＋」智慧能源等一大批能源新模式加快培育。中國積極參與國際能源合作，持續深化能源領域對外開放，海外油氣、核電合作不斷拓展。中國正推動落實全球能源互聯網，積極開展「一帶一路」能源通道建設，參與全球能源技術合作，建立雙邊合作機制五十八項，參與多邊合作機制三十三項，在全球能源轉型發展與合作中發揮中國作用、貢獻中國方案。

女士們、先生們，人類社會發展史就是一部不斷克服困難、戰勝挑戰的歷史。展望未來，中國將繼續應對氣候變化、促進能源轉型，這不僅將為全球可持續發展貢獻力量，也將給包括英國在內的各國帶來更多合作機遇。

一是共商全球氣變和環境治理的機遇。明年是全球氣變治理進程中的重要年份。不久前，習近平主席在聯合國生物多樣性峰會上發表講話，指出明年在昆明舉辦的《生物多樣性公約》第十五次締約方會議（COP15）上，中國將同各方共商全球生物多樣性保護大計，共建萬物和諧的美麗家園。明年英國將在格拉斯哥舉辦《聯合國氣候變化框架公約》第二十六次締約方會議（COP26）。各國能源界和產業界可以參與兩個大會為契機，在清潔能源、綠色金融等領域加強交流對接，充分發揮互補優勢，打造更多務實合作成果。

二是共享能源開放與合作的機遇。中國致力於建設開放型世界經濟，正推動形成以國內大循環為主體、國內國際雙循環相互促進的新發展格局，能源開放合作是其中的重要領域。中國仍是世界上最重要、

最具活力的能源消費市場和進口市場，歡迎各國企業來華投資興業。今年十一月將舉辦第三屆進口博覽會，期待包括英國在內的各國能源企業踴躍參展。欣克利角C核電項目是中、英、法合作的旗艦項目，建成後可滿足英國百分之七的電力需求，每年可以減排九百萬噸二氧化碳。中英雙方可以此為契機，不斷深化民用核能等領域合作。

三是共促能源轉型與創新的機遇。新一輪科技革命和產業革命方興未艾，中國正積極推動綠色科技、能源、金融創新發展。中國以科技創新驅動能源事業高質量發展，以能源技術創新促進產業升級。智能電網、電動汽車、大規模儲能、智慧用能等新技術新業態層出不窮，將給各國能源企業在華投資興業帶來廣闊商機。

四是共建綠色「一帶一路」的機遇。「一帶一路」已成為規模最大的國際合作平台，綠色是「一帶一路」建設的鮮明底色。中國和英國共同發佈了《「一帶一路」綠色投資原則》。能源企業可通過「一帶一路」平台，在環保產業、節能減排、基礎設施、綠色金融、金融科技等領域開拓雙方、三方或多方合作的新模式，把能源轉型發展更好融入全球生態環境保護和可持續發展事業之中。

女士們、先生們，西方有句諺語：「Every cloud has a silver lining.」（每朵烏雲都鑲著銀邊。）中國也有一句諺語，「風雨過後見彩虹」。當前人類正面對疫情蔓延的「至暗時刻」，但人類也展現出團結、勇氣、決心、關愛的強大力量。中國願與國際社會一道，堅定信心，共克時艱，共同應對氣候變化挑戰，共同促進能源轉型發展，共同建設美好地球家園！

最後，預祝本屆國際能源信息論壇大會圓滿成功！

現在我願回答主持人的提問。

主持人：中國二〇六〇年碳中和目標對中國石油、天然氣、煤炭等化石能源和可再生能源需求有何影響？

劉曉明：中國將提高國家自主貢獻力度，採取更加有力的政策和措施，二氧化碳排放力爭於二〇三〇年前

達到峰值，努力爭取二〇六〇年前實現碳中和。中國提出二〇六〇年前實現碳中和，是一個非常有力度的積極目標，獲得國際社會廣泛認可。中國能源消費和經濟轉型、二氧化碳和溫室氣體減排的速度和力度，要比發達國家實現轉型的速度和力度大得多。

在化石能源領域，二〇一九年中國煤炭消費量佔能源消費總量的百分之五十七點七，降至歷史新低，天然氣消費比重提升至百分之七點八。中國仍處在經濟快速發展時期，許多行業和地區發展仍然依賴化石燃料。二〇六〇年碳中和目標傳遞了一個非常明確的信號，對於能源、交通、工業、建築、農業無疑都具有很強的轉型含義。中國將進一步發展和完善碳排放權交易市場，利用市場機制促進二氧化碳減排和企業技術創新，引領社會投資向低碳綠色產業傾斜。

在可再生能源領域，二〇一九年中國非化石能源消費比重提升至百分之十五點三。新能源帶來的新產業蓬勃發展。截至二〇一九年底，中國新能源汽車保有量達三百八十一萬輛，約佔全球總數的二分之一。著眼二〇六〇年碳中和目標，中國將繼續加快能源結構向清潔低碳方向轉型，提高可再生能源消費比例，大力發展風能、太陽能、核能等新能源。

主持人：如何看待疫情後中國經濟快速恢復和帶來的強勁能源需求？

劉曉明：中國統籌疫情防控的同時有序推進復工復產，不斷深化改革開放，經濟顯示出強大韌性和潛力，呈現強勁復甦勢頭。中國二〇二〇年第二季度GDP增速止跌回升，增長百分之三點二，成為世界上第一個恢復增長的主要經濟體。

中國能源行業在疫情期間保證供應，為抗疫做出了重要貢獻。今年上半年，中國能源消費總量同比下降百分之零點二，降幅較第一季度百分之二點九明顯收窄，煤炭、石油、天然氣等能源需求恢復增長。電力基建、油氣管道等建設繼續推進。清潔能源發電比重繼續提高，上半年清潔能源發電量佔全部發電量比重百分之二十七點六，比去年增長了零點一個百分點。

中國支持「綠色復甦」理念，主張在綠色復甦進程中持續應對氣候變化的長期挑戰和風險。正如不久前習近平主席在聯合國生物多樣性峰會上的講話中所指出的，新冠肺炎疫情對全球經濟社會發展造成全面衝擊，我們要著眼長遠，保持定力，堅持綠色、包容、可持續發展，培育疫情後經濟高質量復甦活力；要以自然之道，養萬物之生，從保護自然中尋找發展機遇，實現生態環境保護和經濟高質量發展雙贏。

在疫情防控常態化的背景下，中方將兼顧近期任務和長期目標，統籌推進經濟社會發展和應對氣候變化工作。在創新、協調、綠色、開放、共享的新發展理念指導下，繼續實施積極應對氣候變化國家戰略，持續推進國內節能和能效提升，大力推動綠色產業發展，加快補齊環境基礎設施短板。

主持人：中國為什麼提高了減排目標？

劉曉明：中國重視生態文明建設，切實履行氣候變化、生物多樣性等環境相關條約義務，在節能減排等領域取得巨大成就。碳中和目標是中國基於國內可持續發展內在要求和構建人類命運共同體的責任擔當，對自身氣候環境做出的重大宣示，展現了中國的三個「堅定決心」：

一是應對氣候變化、走綠色低碳發展道路的堅定決心。碳中和目標為中國的中長期氣候行動規劃了清晰路徑。中國將以綠色、低碳、可持續作為當前經濟恢復、未來高質量發展的指導思想，加強應對氣候變化、推進生態文明建設的戰略定力絕不動搖。

二是支持多邊主義的堅定決心。當前，全球氣候多邊進程持續受單邊主義衝擊，新冠肺炎疫情更為各國應對氣候變化帶來新挑戰。中國的積極宣示為多邊主義注入正能量，有力提振了國際社會應對氣候變化合作的信心，是中方構建人類命運共同體理念的又一次生動體現。

三是支持《巴黎協定》履約、推進全球氣候治理的堅定決心。二〇二〇年通報更新「國家自主貢獻」是《巴黎協定》步入實施的重要節點。中國的宣示順應全球加強氣候行動潮流，體現了中國堅定支持《巴

黎協定》履約、推進全球氣候治理、與各方共建清潔美麗世界的負責任大國擔當。

主持人：中國將如何結合碳中和目標，推進建設綠色「一帶一路」？「一帶一路」將如何繼續拓展海外夥伴關係？

劉曉明：「一帶一路」不僅是經濟繁榮之路，也是綠色發展之路。正如不久前習近平主席在聯合國生物多樣性峰會上的講話中所指出的，生態興則文明興，我們要站在對人類文明負責的高度，尊重自然、順應自然、保護自然，探索人與自然和諧共生之路，促進經濟發展與生態保護協調統一。

在「一帶一路」建設實踐中，中國始終秉持綠色發展理念，注重與聯合國《二〇三〇年可持續發展議程》對接，推動基礎設施綠色低碳化建設和運營管理，在投資貿易中強調生態文明理念，加強生態環境治理、生物多樣性保護和應對氣候變化等領域合作。結合碳中和等減排目標，未來綠色「一帶一路」可在以下三方面增進合作：

一是建立綠色機制。二〇一九年，中國政府與四十二個國家的一百四十餘家中外方夥伴一道，共同發起成立了「一帶一路」綠色發展國際聯盟。中國將推動發展諸如現代循環農業、生物質能產業、節能環保產業、新興信息產業、新能源產業等生態產業，構建「一帶一路」綠色項目庫。中國政府還成立「一帶一路」環境技術交流與轉移中心，促進先進生態環保技術的聯合研發和推廣應用。

二是加強生態環境保護。生物多樣性關係人類福祉，是人類賴以生存和發展的重要基礎。中國企業在承建和設計「一帶一路」項目時，在促進當地經濟發展的同時，充分考慮生態因素，有效保護生物多樣性。例如，中國企業在巴基斯坦承建卡拉公路時，在公路沿線植樹近三十萬棵，植草五百多萬平方米，在建設基礎設施的同時，也為當地環境綠化做出貢獻。

三是增進綠色金融合作。全球已有三十多家大型金融機構簽署了《「一帶一路」綠色投資原則》，內容包括充分了解環境、社會和治理風險；充分披露環

境信息；充分運用綠色金融工具；採用綠色供應鏈管理；等等。

中國將堅持開放、綠色、可持續理念，與共建國家一道建設綠色「絲綢之路」。我們實施「一帶一路」應對氣候變化南南合作計劃，自二〇一二年起每年氣候南南合作資金支出達七千二百萬美元；與包括英國在內的發達國家積極開展綠色「一帶一路」第三方市場合作；通過「一帶一路」綠色發展國際聯盟等平台，為應對氣候變化國際合作匯聚更多力量。

第七章

俄羅斯塔斯社專訪

二〇二三年三月二十六日至四月十八日，我開展新一輪「穿梭外交」，先後訪問瑞士、英國、比利時（歐盟總部）、德國、法國、俄羅斯。訪問俄羅斯期間，我於四月十七日接受塔斯社副總編尤莉亞·沙里夫林娜的專訪，回答了有關朝鮮半島局勢、中俄關係、中美關係、亞洲地區形勢、中國國防政策、烏克蘭危機、台灣問題等提問。塔斯社用俄文發表專訪實錄全文，並分別用英文和中文發表專訪詳細新聞稿。以下是專訪俄文實錄中譯文詳細新聞稿。

朝鮮半島問題必須標本兼治

——接受俄羅斯塔斯社專訪

（二〇二三年四月十七日，俄羅斯塔斯社總部）

沙里夫林娜：你認為在當前緊張局勢下，朝韓之間是否有可能發生軍事衝突？

劉曉明：很高興在訪問莫斯科期間接受你的專訪。莫斯科是我此次出訪的最後一站。我已經訪問了六個國家，共二十四天。第一站是瑞士，參加了「采爾馬特東北亞安全問題圓桌會議」。在那裏，我會見了瑞士外交部國務秘書。然後我去了英國、布魯塞爾歐盟總部、德國、法國，與政府高官會談。現在來到了莫斯科，這是我的最後一站，也是壓軸之站。

我此訪是在朝鮮半島局勢出現新的緊張背景下進行的。半島局勢再度緊張，事出有因。一方面，我們聽到西方國家——包括歐美國家——抱怨朝鮮自去年以來進行了一系列導彈發射，但另一方面，我們看到韓國和美國進行了五年來最大規模的軍事演習。朝鮮半島緊張局勢持續升級，這是我們關切的問題。我此訪的目的就是與歐洲和俄羅斯同行分享中方對朝鮮半島局勢的看法，共同尋找推動半島問題政治解決的辦法。

首先，需要讓歐洲和俄羅斯同時清楚地了解中方如何看待當前朝鮮半島的局勢。美國總是指責朝鮮製造緊張局勢，但應當看到另一方面。我們從美國進行了最大規模的軍事演習，看到了導致局勢緊張的原因。其次，朝鮮半島局勢不穩定的一個很重要的原

因，也就是半島問題的根源，恰恰是美國沒有對朝鮮的安全關切給予應有的重視。他們不斷施加壓力，遏制朝鮮的發展，軍事上威脅，政治上施壓，經濟上制裁。因此，對朝鮮半島問題必須標本兼治。一方面，我們需要各方保持克制和理智，相向而行，緩和緊張局勢。另一方面，我們必須解決這個問題的根源，即半島和平機制的缺失。

今年是朝鮮半島停戰協議簽署七十週年，但迄今為止，半島仍未建立任何和平機制。由於缺乏和平機制，緊張局勢持續升級，危害半島的和平與穩定。

按照我們的設想，我們需要在兼顧各方關切的情況下，逐步推進半島無核化和建立和平機制。

朝韓是血濃於水的同胞兄弟，是半島真正的主人。中國歷來支持朝韓改善關係、推進和解合作。希望朝韓繼續秉持民族大義，排除外部干擾，通過對話加強理解、增進互信。

沙里夫林娜：你如何看待中美關係的現狀？華盛頓對於北京是競爭對手、敵人還是商業合作夥伴？

劉曉明：我們始終認為，一個健康穩定的中美關係，不僅有利於兩國人民，也有利於全世界的和平與繁榮。中國國家主席習近平指出，中美能否處理好彼此關係，攸關世界前途命運。中美關係不是一道是否搞好的選擇題，而是一道如何搞好的必答題。

不幸的是，美國將中國視為其主要對手和最大的地緣政治挑戰。美國對華認知和定位出現了嚴重偏差，他們制定了投資、結盟、競爭的對華戰略。我們始終按照習近平主席提出的相互尊重、和平共處、合作共贏的原則致力於推動中美關係健康穩定發展。但與此同時，如果我們的國家主權、國家尊嚴和領土完整受到侵犯，我們將堅決捍衛我國主權、安全和發展利益。

沙里夫林娜：北京在軍事層面如何應對和防範華盛頓影響亞洲地區穩定的圖謀？

劉曉明：美國已公開聲稱要「塑造中國的周邊戰略環境」。他們提出所謂「印太戰略」，表面上標榜自由

開放，實際上是在拼湊小集團、小圈子，目的是圍堵中國，遏制中國的發展。在東北亞，美國、韓國和日本持續進行大規模軍事演習，導致朝鮮半島局勢緊張。東南亞也正在舉行美菲聯合軍事演習，有一萬兩千名美軍參加。美國一再違反一個中國原則，「以台制華」，造成台海局勢緊張。他們還不斷在南海製造事端。

美國和英國還向無核武器國家澳大利亞轉讓核潛艇，構成嚴重核擴散風險，使得這個地區的和平與穩定受到嚴重威脅。事實證明，美國是地區和平與穩定的最大麻煩製造者和最大破壞者。

面對複雜多變的地區形勢和不太平的周邊環境，我們需要共商共建共享的發展之犁，同樣需要捍衛自主發展成果的和平之劍。中國堅定不移走和平發展道路，堅定奉行防禦性國防政策，始終以實際行動維護世界和平、促進共同發展，推動構建人類命運共同體。但是，為捍衛主權和領土完整及來之不易的發展成果，我們需要加強國防，需要建設一支世界一流軍隊，這對於區域及全球安全而言十分必要。

沙里夫林娜：中國國家主席習近平此前要求中國人民解放軍加強練兵備戰，上述表態表明了什麼？

劉曉明：非常感謝你關注習近平主席的講話。就在六天前，習近平主席到中國人民解放軍南部戰區海軍視察調研，他強調要貫徹新時代黨的強軍思想，貫徹新時代軍事戰略方針，深化練兵備戰，加快轉型建設，全面提高部隊現代化水平，堅決完成黨和人民賦予的各項任務。

中國堅持走和平發展道路，奉行防禦性的國防政策，始終是世界和平的建設者、全球發展的貢獻者、國際秩序的維護者。翻開歷史，可以看到中國人民是愛好和平的人民。新中國成立七十多年來，中國從未主動挑起過一場戰爭，從未侵佔過別人一寸土地。中國軍力的增長完全是世界和平力量的增長。中國軍隊積極參加聯合國維和、亞丁灣護航、人道主義救援等行動，努力為世界提供更多的公共安全產品。中國和中國軍隊維護世界和平與繁榮的積極貢獻有目共睹，贏得了國際社會廣泛讚譽。

當前，全球局勢面臨多重挑戰，中國軍隊加強練兵備戰，做好軍事鬥爭準備，是確保本國、區域及全球安全的必要保障。中國還沒有實現國家統一，中國發展軍力旨在維護國家主權和領土完整，捍衛國家安全和發展利益。中國無論發展到什麼程度，永遠不稱霸、永遠不搞擴張，將繼續努力為建設持久和平、普遍安全、共同繁榮、開放包容、清潔美麗的美好世界做出應有貢獻。

沙里夫林娜：美國警告對俄武器供應等同踩美「紅線」，中方對上述警告是否擔心？所謂對俄供武當前是否存在？

劉曉明：中國在軍品出口問題上始終秉持慎重和負責任的態度。與美國等西方國家在烏克蘭危機中拱火澆油形成鮮明對照，我們提供的是和平解決方案。我想強調，中國不是烏克蘭危機的製造者，也不是危機的當事方，更沒有向衝突的任何一方提供武器。美國沒有資格對中國發號施令，我們也從不接受美國對中俄關係指手畫腳甚至脅迫施壓。

沙里夫林娜：不久前「中國氣球」出現在美領空，你對此有何評論？它們的用途是什麼？

劉曉明：近期中美關係中所謂的無人飛艇事件，實際上是美國製造的一場政治鬧劇。一艘中國用於氣象和其他科研的民用無人飛艇，受超強西風帶影響，加之自身控制能力有限，偏離了預定軌道進入美國上空。這原本是一起因不可抗力導致的偶發、意外事件，連美國國防部也說對美地面和人員構不成任何威脅。中方本著負責任的態度，第一時間向美方和國際社會介紹了情況，要求美方以理性、冷靜和專業態度與中方一道妥善處理。但美方無視基本事實，悍然出動戰機，用導彈將其擊落。這種行為匪夷所思，近乎歇斯底裏，是百分百的濫用武力，明顯違反慣例和有關國際公約，這不能證明美國的強大，而恰恰說明它的虛弱。

我們就此向美方提出強烈抗議，要求美方拿出誠

意，改弦更張，正視並解決事件給中美關係造成的損害。如果美方一意孤行，我們將奉陪到底。一切後果由美方承擔。

沙里夫林娜：如何評價台灣周邊局勢？能說今年不會發生衝突嗎？

劉曉明：台海局勢緊張的根源在於島內「台獨」勢力與外國勢力勾結，不斷挑戰一個中國原則。

近期，他們進行了一系列破壞一個中國原則、危害台海穩定的活動，包括佩洛西竄訪台灣和蔡英文竄訪美國。

台灣自古以來就是中國不可分割的一部分，從來沒有也永遠不會成為一個國家——這是台灣問題的基本事實。兩岸和平統一是中國人民的共同心願，是實現中華民族偉大復興的重要組成部分。我們願以最大的誠意、盡最大的努力來實現和平統一。鄧小平先生最早提出用「一國兩制」解決台灣問題，隨著時間的推移我們用「一國兩制」解決了香港和澳門回歸問題。實踐證明「一國兩制」在港澳地區是行之有效的。因此，我們有信心這個構想在台灣也會取得成功。

「一國」就是「一個中國」。「一國」是「一國兩制」的前提，是基礎中的基礎。我們努力在「一國兩制」下實現和平統一，同時保留採取一切必要措施維護我國主權和領土完整，包括我們從來沒有承諾不使用武力。如果我們做了這個承諾，和平統一就根本不可能了。

我們這一立場不是針對廣大台灣同胞，而是針對極少數「台獨」分裂分子和企圖分裂我國的外部勢力。

你問，今年台海會不會發生軍事衝突。我認為，與其預測台海會發生什麼，不如向世界各國強調堅持一個中國原則。

一個中國原則是台海穩定與和平的「定海神針」。只要遵守這一原則，台海地區的和平與穩定就有保障，兩岸就能實現和平發展。否則，台海將無寧日。我們已經看到，正是佩洛西竄台和台灣當局領導

人竄美造成了台海局勢的緊張不定。

沙里夫林娜：還有外交手段可以解決這個問題嗎？北京是否認為有可能對台灣發動特別軍事行動？

劉曉明：在世界大國中，中國是唯一尚未實現國家統一的國家，實現祖國統一是全體中國人民的共同願望，也是中國憲法的明確規定。「和平統一、一國兩制」這一基本方針，最符合包括台灣同胞在內的中華民族的整體利益。這是和平的方案、民主的方案、善意的方案、共贏的方案，是解決兩岸制度不同的最現實、最寬容的方案。

你問，是否可以通過外交途徑解決這個問題，我要強調的是，台灣問題是中國的內政，不是外交問題。如果你所說的外交手段是指和平方式，那麼我認為「一國兩制」正是解決這一問題的和平方案。

正如我已經說過的，我們努力實現和平統一的同時，保留採取一切必要措施維護國家主權和領土完整。這不是針對廣大台灣同胞，而是針對極少數「台獨」分子和境外分裂勢力，因為他們的行為違反了中國憲法，違反了中國《反分裂國家法》。我們將依法制止「台獨」分裂活動，捍衛國家主權和領土完整，維護台海地區和平穩定。這是我們神聖的權利。

第八章

魯健訪談・對話劉曉明

《魯健訪談》是中央廣播電視總台高端人物訪談節目，由魯健擔任主持人，節目時長三十分鐘。這是央視唯一以主持人冠名的節目，旨在打造高端訪談品牌，提升國際傳播影響力。據魯健講，自從《魯健訪談》兩年前開播以來，他一直想對我做一個專訪，談談我的外交生涯，包括我的個人經歷和家庭生活。我曾表示，我在任期間只接受關於外交工作的採訪，不接受關於個人和家庭的訪談。我卸任駐英大使後，魯健和他的團隊很快聯繫上我，再次提出採訪要求。這次我答應了。他們對採訪做了大量功課，準備了一大堆問題。採訪那天，我們聊了整整三個小時，可以說天南海北，無所不談。從英國的茶道談到英國的電視採訪，從我應對英國媒體的「三套武器」談到英國的「新聞自由」，從中英關係談到美英關係，從西方的傲慢與偏見談到東方的理智與情感，從「戰狼外交」談到國際話語權，從朝鮮情結談到半島使命，從外交生涯談到外交官的犧牲奉獻，從講好中國故事談到外交工作薪火相傳。最後三個小時採訪編輯成三十分鐘訪談，於二〇二三年五月二十六日在央視四頻道向海內外播出。

《魯健訪談．對話劉曉明》

——接受中央廣播電視總台《魯健訪談》欄目主持人魯健專訪

（二〇二三年五月二十六日，北京）

魯健：您嚐嚐這個茶，這個茶還挺好。您在英國這十一年，平時喝茶多，還是喝咖啡多？

劉曉明：都喝，總體來講，還是喝茶喝得多。英國人對茶是情有獨鍾的，你別看英國不產茶，但是人均喝茶量是全世界第一。英國有一句俗語叫「當鐘敲響四下，一切為茶而停止」，四下就是下午四點，喝茶雷打不動。

魯健：喝茶聊天那個氣氛就非常輕鬆了。我看您在英國期間還接受了一百七十多場採訪，其中將近三十場的電視直播的採訪，就是那種言辭激烈、唇槍舌劍，跟這個喝茶那是完全不一樣。

劉曉明：那肯定不一樣。

魯健：沒茶喝對吧。

劉曉明：給你一杯水喝就不錯了。

魯健：其實有些時候，第一次的嘗試對於每個人來講都不容易。那您第一次在西方媒體接受訪談，是什麼時候？

劉曉明：你是指的第一次接受電視採訪？

魯健：對，電視直播的採訪。

劉曉明：我記得很清楚，是二〇一二年一月二十三日，是我們大年初一，接受傑里米．帕克斯曼——《新聞之夜》主持人的採訪。帕克斯曼號稱是英國最犀利、最刁鑽的主持人。他來請我上這個訪談節目，說沒有什麼別的主題，就想跟劉大使聊聊，劉大使到英國一段時間了。我當時研究了他的背景，知道這家夥不好對付，是個「橫主兒」，但是你也不能迴避，所以我也接受了他的挑戰。

第一次應該說多少有點緊張，但是我覺得，我身後有強大的祖國，我們中國的發展有很多的故事可以講，所以我有足夠的自信和底氣，準備這場採訪。

魯健：第一次上電視直播，即便是用自己的母語去應對，恐怕也會有忐忑不安的感覺，何況您是用英語、用對方的語言來接受採訪。那您會做什麼樣的刻意的準備？

劉曉明：準備是必須的。我經常講，不打無準備之仗。不要說我們中國外交官上英國的電視台，要講英語，就是很多被稱為西方溝通大師的這些人，克林頓、布萊爾。我看過他們的回憶錄，上台之前，都是進行認真彩排，把他們的助手、軍師叫到一塊，設想各種刁鑽的問題。

魯健：您也有軍師嗎？

劉曉明：我的軍師就是我們各個處室的負責人。我們大家在一塊群策群力，我們設想各種問題，各種刁鑽的問題，進行「戰前」的準備。

魯健：他們很善於挖各種各樣的「坑」，那您印象最深的「坑」是哪一次？

劉曉明：我覺得給我留下最深印象的就是第一次上

BBC《新聞之夜》的直播採訪，也是跟傑里米·帕克斯曼過招。第一句上來就是「你是共產黨嗎」，我想他的目的不是驗證我的身份。因為那一段時間，在西方媒體不斷出現「共產黨中國」的說法。傑里米·帕克斯曼一上來就問這個問題。其實我一直在找機會，要為我們共產黨正名，要為中國正名，我就抓住這個機會。我說中國是共產黨領導的國家，但是你不能把中國說成是「共產黨中國」，就像現在英國是保守黨領導的英國，你不能說「保守黨英國」一樣，他馬上認可這個說法。

魯健：對於這些他們慣於用到的套路和策略，您能夠適應嗎？

劉曉明：我覺得跟他們進行博弈，你就應該做一個頭腦冷靜的鬥牛士，而不是被輕易激怒的公牛。我不是把他看作對手，而是看作對話，通過這種對話能夠跟他進行溝通，增進他們對中國的了解。我看重的是他背後的聽眾和讀者，我是跟西方民眾在對話。

我有三套「武器」。現在實際上是已經發展到高科技導彈時代，但是我把它比喻成冷兵器。第一是長矛，就是主動進攻，我必須有成套的東西，宣介我們中國的內外政策。第二，我還要準備盾牌，就是我們說要準備他挖各種「坑」，準備他扔各種手榴彈，抵擋他各種刁鑽問題。第三，我還有匕首，就是說進行反擊，最好的防禦是進攻。

魯健：為什麼一定要去面對這個挑戰呢？其實這種挑戰是有一定的風險的。

劉曉明：對，風險跟收穫總是成正比。電視直播的優勢，第一，時效快，很多突發事件，媒體提出來了要採訪你，你上不上？我們選擇上，就可以在第一時間發出中國聲音，第一時間揭穿謊言，批駁謬論。

第二，我就覺得電視直播就是直觀、生動，受眾廣、影響大。一個最典型的例子就是二〇二〇年四月份，新冠肺炎疫情發生一段時間了，當時西方充斥著謠言，特別是以美國為主的西方勢力散佈各種謠言，

陰謀論啊，「中國病毒」啊，我就接受了《尖銳對話》主持人薩克的採訪。那次談得比較透徹，傳播也廣。首先是BBC（英國廣播公司）現場直播，接著是在英國國內重播兩次，這就三次了，然後在全球播放五次，薩克的製片人告訴我們，說劉大使這次接受採訪，受眾兩百個國家四億觀眾。

魯健： 有沒有遇到過報紙拒絕發表您的文章？

劉曉明： 當然有，被拒絕過。這種情況主要是二〇二〇年以後，特別是香港黑暴事件發生之後，英國由於它的歷史原因，對香港有一種特殊的情結。一些報刊編輯部的總編就明確說，我們只能登對「一國兩制」提出質疑的文章。我說你這個報紙太偏了，你聽不到中國方面的聲音嘛。它可以登很多別的文章，甚至彭定康的文章，但是中國代表的文章它不登。

魯健： 就拒絕給您發聲的平台。

劉曉明： 對，我覺得它這個所謂的新聞自由在這個時候顯得非常蒼白。

魯健： 那您從內心來講有沒有答案？就是為什麼好像英國的媒體、政界有些時候確實很難放下這種傲慢與偏見？

劉曉明： 主要還是它這個「西方中心論」作怪，他們總是俯視發展中國家。他們的國力在逐漸地走下坡路，但卻總是不能擺正自己的心態。

我覺得也是一種缺乏自信，特別是對中國的崛起、對中國的發展不能夠正確地解讀，老覺得中國構成了一種挑戰和威脅。

我在接受採訪的時候，艾斯勒還曾經問過，就是BBC的《新聞之夜》主持人，他引用了英國著名作家吉卜林的一句話，說「東方與西方永遠無法完全理解對方」。他問，「劉大使，您怎麼看」。我就講，我覺得中國對西方的情況了解得更多一些，而西方對中國的了解不夠。他問，那這是什麼原因呢？我

說西方對中國應該少一些傲慢與偏見，多一些理智與情感。

魯健：二〇二二年九月，您作為中國政府代表團的成員參加了英女王的葬禮，那現在卸任駐英大使兩年之後，您現在最關注的英國政壇的變化是什麼？

劉曉明：我最關心的當然還是中英關係了。中英關係這幾年確實出現了比較大的變化，英國原來把中國看作機遇，現在把中國看作挑戰。

魯健：那您覺得到底是什麼樣的原因造成英國對華政策發生這樣的一種非常大的改變？

劉曉明：我覺得這幾年國際上發生了很多事情，中英之間也發生了很多事情，比較大的事件就是香港。過去我們簽署了《中英聯合聲明》，順利解決了香港回歸問題。隨著香港的回歸，香港成為中英關係的積極因素，但是從二〇一九年「修例風波」以後，英國越來越深地插手香港事務。

我們一貫主張發展兩國關係的準則和基礎，是相互尊重，求同存異，互不干涉內政，但是英國干涉了中國內政，這必然會引起中國堅決反對。所以我說由於中英關係的基礎受到了損害，必然會反映到中英關係的各個方面。

魯健：所以，華為5G進入英國市場也是一個例證，英國對華為5G政策也發生了一百八十度的大轉變，那您覺得英國現在對華政策是不是很大程度上也受到美國政策的影響？

劉曉明：對，一方面確實有美國的壓力，美國出於它自己的私利，調動它的盟友，打壓中國的公司，圍堵中國。但是英國自己內部也發生了變化，英國對中國的認知也出現了偏差，越來越不適應中國的發展，把中國的發展看作是挑戰。

魯健：說到英美關係就有一個詞，叫「特殊關係」，

就是這種關係是不是也使得英國在外交上有些時候難免要跟著美國走？

劉曉明：我覺得這個「特殊關係」呢，這是歷史形成的。主要是「二戰」時期，丘吉爾跟羅斯福他們使兩國形成了這種盟國關係，然後兩國一直保持這樣密切的關係。那麼到了今天，這個「特殊關係」到底怎麼樣，我覺得，這個讓英國人自己去講是最有說服力的。

你要問一些英國人，英國人相反覺得受到美國的壓力，英國人自己心裏也是很不舒服的。有的人說，「特殊關係」已經名存實亡了。所以我覺得這種關係，我們不去過多地評論。我更關心的是，英美「特殊關係」不要影響中英關係，我們並不要求英國在中美之間選邊站隊，但是我希望英國能夠站在正確的一邊，站在正義的一邊。

如果你完全都是 yes-man（「好好先生」），都是跟著美國走，「隨美起舞」，在中美發生衝突的時候，你根本不假思索盲目跟隨美國，損害的是你自己的利益。

魯健：我們也看到這些年來一些西方的政客還有西方的媒體，不斷地給中國貼標籤，什麼「霸凌外交」「脅迫外交」「戰狼外交」等等，您覺得這個對於我們外交官來講，做工作是不是會造成很大的困難和挑戰？

劉曉明：他們是想給我們製造困難，給我們貼標籤，但是我覺得最後都是徒勞的。首先，這恰恰說明我們的影響越來越大，中國的外交影響越來越大，所以他們就使用各種污名化、妖魔化的手段，來貶低和削弱我們的影響。其次，我覺得他們過去總認為自己把握著話語權，不能夠接受中國國際話語權在不斷提升，他們對中國義正詞嚴、理直氣壯地捍衛自己主權、安全、發展利益，維護自己的形象跟尊嚴很不適應，所以就給你冠上「戰狼外交」「霸凌外交」。

魯健：包括您本人不是也被貼「戰狼鼻祖」這樣的標

籤和稱號嘛，您本人對這樣的稱號是什麼樣的態度？

劉曉明：我當然是拒絕這種所謂的「戰狼鼻祖」，我對這個不感興趣。我覺得我們外交官上電視也好，去發表演講也好，我強調我是要進行對話，把辯論變成對話，把每一場對話都變成一個講好中國故事的機會。當你面對各種謠言，你必須進行批駁，你只有揭穿謊言，才能夠說明真相。

魯健：我看到前段時間，您是作為中國政府朝鮮半島事務特別代表出訪了歐洲多國。您也曾經擔任過中國駐朝大使，而且您是志願軍的後代，那您跟朝鮮應該有非常深厚的淵源。

劉曉明：我一歲半的時候，曾經隨著我母親去志願軍在檜倉的總部探望我的父親，那麼後來我出任了駐朝大使，現在又做朝鮮半島事務特別代表，我對這片土地充滿了感情，所以我對我現在擔任的工作更有一種強烈的責任感和使命感。

魯健：幾十年的外交生涯，我知道您的足跡遍佈美洲、歐洲、亞洲、非洲，而且外交官好像這些年來應該是和家人聚少離多，這是外交官的一個工作和生活的常態嗎？

劉曉明：這應該說是一個常態，也是外交官為祖國的外交事業做出的犧牲。我們外交官呢，對過去說的「自古忠孝兩難全」是深有體會的。明年我就從事外交工作五十年了，將近三十年時間駐外。在英國常駐期間，我母親病危，我跟她通了話，我說這次我一定要趕回去，但是在我通話後兩個小時，我的姪兒——我弟弟的孩子給我發了一個短信，說奶奶走了，我悲痛欲絕，立刻請假返回國內。我跟母親的遺體告別，這次算是見了一面，但是母親已經走了。

所以我也是要向我們千千萬萬個外交官的親屬和家人表示衷心的感謝，有他們的支持，我們才能渾身充滿力量。

魯健：您二十世紀七十年代投身外交事業，馬上就要

滿五十年了，接下來在外交領域還有哪些能繼續作為的呢？

劉曉明：我去年出了兩本書，《尖銳對話》和《大使講中國故事》。這兩本書提到，要講好中國故事。我覺得這項任務還是任重道遠。我想講好中國故事，不光是領導的事，也不僅僅是外交官的事，而是每一個中國人的事。我覺得每一個中國人在國外，不論你是留學、經商、旅遊，你都是中國形象的代言人，人家從你的身上就看到今天的中國，所以我願意跟廣大民眾、讀者分享我講好中國故事的經驗和體會。

我還需要做的工作，就是為培養年輕外交官盡一份責任，這樣使我們的外交工作薪火相傳，蓬勃發展。

魯健：現在可能也有很多的年輕人奮戰在外交領域，您覺得作為外交官，最核心的本領到底是什麼？比如說是他的語言能力？思辨能力？還是他的勇敢？忠誠？

劉曉明：我覺得外交官最根本的本領就是信念。你看我在採訪的時候多次提到自信、底氣、擔當，都是有堅定的信念。我們新中國外交隊伍是周總理帶出來的，他曾經對外交人員提出十六字方針：「站穩立場，掌握政策，熟悉業務，嚴守紀律。」這十六字方針一直被繼承到今天，形成了中國外交隊伍的優良傳統。

後記

《有問必答》終於殺青。可以說，它是《尖銳對話》的姊妹篇。《尖銳對話》出版後受到廣泛好評，被《人民日報》「金台好書榜」列為「十大好書」，入選《出版業「十四五」時期發展規劃》，多次在京東外交國際關係圖書排行榜名列第一。《有問必答》與《尖銳對話》有相同之處，都是與西方媒體和民眾對話交流，但也有不同之處。《尖銳對話》唇槍舌劍，短兵相接，很難展開討論問題；《有問必答》則有更從容的時間、更大的舞台、更廣闊的空間。

「有問必答」可以說是一種原則，可以說是一種責任，也可以說是一種境界。對記者和聽眾的提問，特別是敏感問題，你可以「有問不答」，也可以「有問少答」。但我堅持「有問必答」，努力化解誤解和偏見。「有問必答」的英文是「Leave No Question Unanswered」，可直譯為「不留下任何沒有回答的問題」。這是我的原則，也是我的責任。每次記者會、每次演講，我都讓記者和聽眾放開提問，直到回答完最後一位舉手的提問者，不留遺憾。這種答問方式不僅體現對提問者的尊重，也可以贏得對方的尊重，拉近演講者與聽眾的距離，增強感染力和親和感，努力達到不僅「聽得到」，而且「聽得懂」，「聽得進」，進而「聽而信」的境界。

雖然我們已經進入信息時代，但讓世界聽到中國聲音仍任重道遠。黨的二十大報告提出，要加強國際傳播能力建設，全面提升國際傳播效能，形成同我國綜合國力和國際地位相匹配的國際話語權。習近平總

書記指出，講好中國故事，傳播好中國聲音，展示真實、立體、全面的中國，是加強我國國際傳播能力建設的重要任務。為此，我們要更加積極主動地講中國故事，不僅能講中國故事，而且會講中國故事，講好中國故事；不僅「有問必答」，而且「有問會答」，「有問妙答」。

在此，我要感謝北京出版集團、聯合出版集團。他們的支持，特別是編輯和出版團隊的高效工作，使本書在較短時間順利出版。我還要感謝我的朋友和同事們，他們一些人參與了本書的核稿和校對，並提出寶貴意見。

劉曉明

二〇二五年春分

2023-05-26

接受中央廣播電視總台《鲁健訪談》欄目主持人鲁健專訪

Giving an Exclusive Interview to Lu Jian, Anchor of China Media Group's 'Conversation with Lu Jian' Program

2020-10-28

與英國議會跨黨派國際環保小組座談

Attending a Discussion with the All-Party Parliamentary International Environmental Group of the UK Parliament

2023-04-17

接受俄羅斯塔斯社副總編輯尤莉亞・沙里夫林娜專訪

Giving an Exclusive Interview to Yulia Sharifullina, Deputy Editor-in-Chief of Russia's TASS News Agency

2020-07-30

在中國駐英國大使館就中英關係舉行線上中外記者會

Holding an On-Line Press Conferenceon China-UK Relationship, at the Chinese Embassy in the UK

2020-10-13

在國際能源信息論壇大會發表主旨演講並回答提問

Delivering a Keynote Speech at the Global Energy Intelligence Forum, followed by Q&A

2020-02-06

在中國駐英國大使館就抗擊新冠肺炎疫情舉行中外記者會

Holding a Press Conference for Chinese and Foreign Media about the Fight against the COVID-19 in China, at the Chinese Embassy in the UK

2019-11-18

在中國駐英國大使館就香港局勢舉行中外記者會

Holding a Press Conference for Chinese and Foreign Media on the Situation in Hong Kong, at the Chinese Embassy in the UK

2019-08-15

在中國駐英國大使館就香港街頭暴力激進活動舉行中外記者會

Holding a Press Conference for Chinese and Foreign Media on the radical violence in Hong Kong Streets, at the Chinese Embassy in the UK

2019-07-03

在中國駐英國大使館就香港發生暴力衝擊立法會事件舉行中外記者會

Holding a Press Conference for Chinese and Foreign Media on the Violent Attack against the Legislative Council Complex of Hong Kong Special Administrative Region, at the Chinese Embassy in the UK

2019-06-24

出席英國“亞洲之家”對話會

Attending the Asia House Dialogue in the UK

2018-09-10

在英國議會就“一帶一路”發表主旨演講並回答議員提問

Delivering a Keynote Address on the Belt and Road Initiative at the UK Parliament, followed by Q&A with Parliamentarians

2017-11-21

在英國議會發表主旨演講，宣介中共十九大精神並回答議員提問

Delivering a Keynote Address on the gist of the 19th CPC National Congress at the UK Parliament, followed by Q&A with Parliamentarians

2017-11-07

對英國工商界宣介中共十九大精神並回答提問

Presentation on the Gist of the 19th CPC National Congress to the UK Business Community, followed by Q&A

2016-07-25

在英國皇家國際問題研究所發表主旨演講：《浮雲難遮望眼，正道總是滄桑》

Delivered a keynote speech entitled 'Let No Fleeting Clouds Block Our Vision' at Chatham House (Royal Institute of International Affairs) in the UK

2016-07-19

在中國駐英國大使館就南海仲裁庭裁決結果舉行中外記者會

Holding a Press Conference for Chinese and Foreign Media on the South China Sea Arbitration Tribunal's Ruling, at the Chinese Embassy in the UK

2016-05-20

在倫敦國際戰略研究所發表演講：《中國是維護南海和平穩定的中堅力量》

Delivering a Speech at the International Institute for Strategic Studies: 'China is a Staunch Force for Peace and Stability in the South China Sea'

2015-11-13

在英國劍橋大學發表演講：《為中英關係“黃金時代”增光添彩》

Delivering a Speech at the University of Cambridge: 'Adding Splendor to the Golden Era of China-UK Relations'

2015-11-13

在英國劍橋大學發表演講後回答師生提問

Answering Questions from Faculty and Students after Delivering a Speech at the University of Cambridge

2015-01-12

看望中國海軍第十八批護航編隊

Visiting the 18th Escort Task Group of the Chinese Navy

2015-01-12

在“長白山艦”甲板上就中國海軍第十八批護航編隊訪問英國舉行中外記者會

Holding a Press Conference for Chinese and Foreign Media regarding the Visit of the 18th Chinese Naval Escort Task Force to the United Kingdom, on the Deck of PLA Navy's 'Changbaishan' Amphibious Landing Ship